KLEMER'S MARRIAGE AND FAMILY RELATIONSHIPS

KLEMER'S MARRIAGE AND FAMILY RELATIONSHIPS

Second edition

Richard H. Klemer

Late, The University of North Carolina at Greensboro

Rebecca M. Smith

The University of North Carolina at Greensboro

Harper & Row, Publishers

New York, Evanston, San Francisco, London

Sponsoring Editor: John A. Woods
Project Editor: Karen A. Judd
Designer: Gayle Jaeger
Production Supervisor: Stefania J. Taflinska

Library of Congress Cataloging in Publication Data
Klemer, Richard H.
    Klemer's marriage and family relationships.
    First ed. published in 1970 under title: Marriage and family
relationships.
    Bibliography: p.
    1. Marriage.   2. Family.   I. Smith, Rebecca M., joint author.
II. Title.   III. Title: Marriage and family relationships.
HQ728.K55   1975   301.42   74-14634
ISBN 0-06-046311-2

CONTENTS

PREFACE TO THE FIRST EDITION

This book has the hopeful intention of offering students of the 1970s a way of studying marriage and family relationships that can have direct pertinence in their own living experiences. To achieve some of this personal significance, the "empathetic approach" is introduced early in this volume and is used extensively. This is a modified case study method that although not wholly unique in its concept, will be a new way of learning for many students. The empathetic approach can be an exciting experience that promises an active partnership for the student in the process of learning and furthering learning.

To assure a more complete understanding of the empathetic approach, the first two chapters contain discussion of its techniques and rationale. It is hoped that each reader will examine these chapters carefully and critically, for much of his ability to deal with the cases that follow will depend both on his familiarity with the basic principles of case analysis and on his self-generated conviction that he can grow toward educational and social fulfillment by his own personal insights and his own perceptive sensitivity, as well as by the absorption of knowledge from a teacher and a textbook.

A few words of explanation about the case reports that follow are appropriate here. Although the "cases" are founded on actual experiences, they are now hypothetical to the extent that all names, places, and occupations, and some circumstances, have been changed. In many instances, behaviors and attitudes from several different interpersonal relationship situations have been rearranged and recombined to form a single new "case." Moreover, although the cases are often reported in a conversational, first-person style, it should not be inferred that these are the words the participants really used. Actual case interviews often are rambling, confused, vague, and hesitant, and short excerpts rarely express the real meaning of the participants. Consequently the first-person style used in this book represents condensed and synthesized recreations of attitudes manifested—sometimes over long periods of time—by the participants.

My list of acknowledgments must begin with the many scholars in the social and behavioral sciences who created the knowledge on which this book is based. I am also indebted to the many students and research repondents who have led me to new insights and understandings of today's marriage and family problems; and to my mother, Dora H. Klemer, one of the pioneer marriage counselors and family life educators, who encouraged my early interest in relationships.

More immediately, I am inestimably grateful for the help and advice of Robert H. Coombs and Rebecca Smith, who reviewed the entire manuscript for this book. Carl M. Cochrane, Barbara James, Herbert Otto, Sarah Shoffner, Mary Stegall, and James Walters supplied guidance for various parts. Evelyn Freeman and David Klein, graduate students while I was at the University of Washington, and Nancy Taylor Coghill, Roswell Cox, Irene Johnson, Polly Lewis, and Charles Snow, recent graduate students here at the University of North Carolina at Greensboro, provided invaluable research and editorial assistance. Trudy Voogd and Firth Fabend also made very important research and editorial contributions, and a large measure of appreciation must be reserved as well for Donna Humphreys, Joan Haynes, Sally Shelton, Ann Smith, and Karen Judd, whose technical skills prepared the manuscript for publication.

Further, I am also especially appreciative for the help of Anthony Mellor and his successor as editor in the College Department at Harper & Row, Mike Mattoon. It was Tony Mellor's early vision and his continuing support that made this book possible.

Finally, I am grateful to my wife, Margaret Grim Klemer, and my daughter, Caralea Klemer, who gave up some of the family life that was ours so that this husband and father could write to other family members about improving family relationships. In a very real way, though, our family has already made back its loss, for now that the job is done, the satisfaction is infinitely more satisfying because it can be shared.

RICHARD H. KLEMER

PREFACE

This revised edition has essentially the same purpose as the first edition—that of teaching college students to understand human behavior through the empathetic approach. After the first edition had been in use for a while, a few very important needs became clear.

The most important need was to teach students how to apply generalizations about human behavior. To assist the teacher and the students, an appendix with a list of generalizations has been added to this edition. Another major need was the acknowledgment of varying family forms. A whole new chapter was added on this topic. A need to present nonmarital sexual relationships in the wide sense was taken care of by substituting one chapter entitled "Male-Female Relationships Among the Singles" for the previous three chapters on premarital sex. Also, since much empathy is needed between generations, a separate chapter was added on intergenerational relations into which the former chapter entitled "The In-Law Problem" was incorporated.

Aside from these obvious changes, the entire book reflects current attitudes and behaviors without negating the traditional bases from which new ideas generate. The cases remain open, as they were in the first edition. To have the cases analyzed limits the input of the students and cuts short their personal meaning and empathy-producing value. However, different questions are asked after some of the cases from those asked in the first edition.

Numerous new cases were added that come from experiences of peers of students using the book, and some new cases reflect experiences from counseling with students and adults. No case is a true story in its entirety. They were all adapted to exemplify the principles in specific chapters.

The teacher is encouraged to organize the course for progression in empathetic ability in this order: expressing own feelings, applying principles of behavior, understanding how own conditioning affects case analysis, empathizing, and predicting. As in any course, one method is not sufficient. Lectures, discussions, and case analyses are not enough. Any method is applicable to this course. Valuable activities, which may vary from year to year, include having the students write cases, analyze plays or films, carry out projects on empathetic listening, and participate in group sessions on interpersonal relationships.

Students in current classes read and criticized the entire book for purposes of revision. Two students, Kathy Bivens and Melba Wooten, edited the draft of the entire revision. Suggestions from students and colleagues from across the United States and from Canada were inestimably appreciated. Typing and editorial assistance were given by Mrs. Elizabeth R. Hunt, whose experience with both families and book editing made the revision easier.

My deepest gratitude goes to my mother-in-law, Mrs. Mattie T. Smith, to my husband, George C. Smith, Jr., and to our son, John R. Smith, all of whom are very empathetic to writers who must meet deadlines. I am most grateful for the opportunity to have studied and worked with Dr. Richard H. Klemer.

In preparing the manuscript for this revision, many teachers of family relationships in colleges and universities who had used the first edition as a text gave me considerable insight and help in making major changes. I am grateful to all of them and especially to Helen Redden and Vera Borsage. After the major revisions were outlined, Al Abbott, Editor-in-Chief of the College Department at Harper & Row, gave me the inspiration and guidance to proceed. Melinda Teel thoroughly edited the manuscript and gave it the clarity of which I am most appreciative. I am indebted to Karen Judd, Managing Editor for the College Department who also edited the first edition, who was responsible for the smooth production of the revision.

REBECCA M. SMITH

KLEMER'S MARRIAGE AND FAMILY RELATIONSHIPS

1

THE EMPATHETIC APPROACH

This is a different kind of textbook about marriage and family relationships. It is based on the empathetic approach to learning.

The empathetic approach assumes that much of your understanding about relationships comes to you in a breakthrough moment of insight when you all at once perceive new meanings and new cause-and-effect associations. The young mother who suddenly recognizes that her little daughter is threatening a doll in exactly the same tone and inflection that the mother has used just minutes before in threatening the child may have an important learning experience in family relationships even though she has gained no new knowledge in the usual textbook sense.

Such dramatic changes in perceptions often take place as a result of your own day-to-day living experiences. They can also take place vicariously through studying the experiences of others. For that reason, a large part of this book will be devoted to case presentations that realistically portray the attitudes, conflicts, and adjustments of present-day marriage partners and their family members. It is intended that you will empathize with (feel with) the family members in the case illustrations to the point where you will get the insights, draw the inferences, and figure out the possible alternatives that could lead to the solutions of the problems presented. Inasmuch as these insights, inferences, and solutions will be in keeping with your own value system and your own personality, they can have immediate meaning in your own living experience. Indeed, often they will have greater meaning for you than other people's generalizations and interpretations might have had.

Just as your understanding of man-woman and parent-child relationships did not begin with the present course you are taking, it will not end when you have completed this book. It has been—and will be—a continuous process throughout your lifetime. Your ongoing progress in understanding the dynamics of human relationships and adjusting to them will have a crucial effect on your success, your happiness, and your emotional health. Perception and skill in interacting with others is a large part of being what psychologist Abraham Maslow has called a "self-actualizing" person —a self-respecting, achieving individual whose manifest adjustment to living makes him pleasant to be with.[1] On the other hand, poor understanding of the dynamics of interpersonal relationships is often a prelude to emotional breakdown. Students of psychopathology since the time of Harry Stack Sullivan have tended to put increasing emphasis upon the individual's interpersonal-relationships ability as a criterion of his emotional health.[2]

[1] Abraham H. Maslow, *Motivation and Personality*, 2nd ed., New York, Harper & Row, 1970.
[2] Harry Stack Sullivan, *Personal Psychopathology: Early Formulations*, New York, Norton, 1972.

The recent Human Potential Movement is an outgrowth of this search for self-actualization.[3] Groups have been initiated all over the United States for the purpose of increasing people's self-awareness and human potential.

It is very important to recognize, though, that no one learns about relationships *entirely* through the dramatic process of insight. You have learned much about personal interaction from your parents' deliberate teaching and from the modifying instruction and correction you got from your teachers, your peers, and your social groups. At least some direct teaching was involved in your "internalizing" all the customs, attitudes, values, and expectations that now strongly affect all your living experiences and all your relationships.

(Because customs, attitudes, values, and expectations are so important, they should be defined and differentiated right here at the book's beginning. Customs, including role behaviors, are the "proper" ways of any cultural group. Attitudes are the beliefs that predispose an individual to think or act one way or another.[4] Values are the enduring criteria that the individual uses to make judgments. Value judgments result from the use of values in making choices. Expectations are the individual's anticipations that people and events will and should behave and occur as he imagines they will. When these anticipations become strongly emotionalized, they become emotional needs.)

Ever since your first elementary-school course in social studies, you have been learning about relationships, including your own, through a study of what psychologists, sociologists, anthropologists, home economists, and other scientists have found from their research data. This "relationships education" may have been a very important factor in your social growth. But more is needed, for, without further study of the psychosocial data that have been accumulated by behavioral scientists, your insights, inferences, and solutions could reflect only your present attitudes and your present knowledge. This is not enough—it can lead you into perpetuating old behavioral habits because you are unaware of new ones.

So, along with the many illustrations and cases that appear on the following pages, there will be a considerable amount of social history, research data, and theoretical interpretation. There will also be some value judg-

[3]Herbert A. Otto, "Man-Woman Relationships in the Society of the Future," *The Futurist,* **7** (April, 1973), 55–61.

[4]As Milton Rokeach suggests, the concept of "attitude" in social psychology has been plagued with ambiguity. Rokeach's own definition is this: "An attitude is a relatively enduring organization of beliefs around an object or situation, predisposing one to respond in some preferential manner." See *Beliefs, Attitudes and Values,* San Francisco, Jossey-Bass, 1968, p. 112.

ments for your critical examination and evaluation. As a matter of fact, this whole book is based on two crucial value judgments.

The first major value judgment is that marriage and family living are continuing "goods" in our changing society. In times past, this judgment might have been so universal and so taken for granted that there would have been no need to make it explicit. But in this era of greater acceptability of varying life-styles, the very continuation of the family as we have known it becomes a subject of controversy. There are now those who propose that both marriage and family living are anachronisms, undesirable vestiges of middle-class conventionality. But we contend that the family in some form will continue.

While an absolutely impartial examination of the pros and cons of the continuance of the family as a social institution may serve the purposes of the social theorist, it does little or nothing for the person who is seeking functionally meaningful help in improving his own relationships ability. Marriage and the family in our time should be (and shall be) critically examined. But to be more than just academically stimulating to a concerned individual, that critical examination must be done with the intent of improving—not just debating—the worth of both marriage and family living *and* that individual's unique relationships within them. Just as the physician does not examine the patient with objective impartiality about whether that patient should live or die, but rather with a transcending value commitment to health improvement, so this book begins with marriage and family living as conceded values and goes on from there.

The second major value judgment is that the empathetic approach offers a uniquely valuable way to study the very personal and very crucial relations between men and women and between parents and children. Reasons why this value judgment may be valid are given throughout this book. If any or all of the cases and concepts that follow improve your sensitivity to the feelings and behaviors of others and so improve your understanding of marriage and family relationships, this book will have achieved its purpose.

THE EMPATHETIC APPROACH

The empathetic approach to the study of marriage and family relationships involves the thoughtful and feelingful examination of people and their problems. Ideally, you should be able to experience vicariously the conflicts, attitudes, and perceptions of the people involved in each relationship situation. Hopefully, you will be able to identify with *all* the partners in a relationship—sometimes with each in turn, sometimes with several simultaneously. You can actually sharpen your empathizing ability to the point where it is possible to feel not only with the mate of your own sex, but also with the mate of the opposite sex, and even with the children in the situation. Then, by using all available knowledge, by introspective evaluation, by group discussion, and by insight, you can arrive at some solution for the problem acceptable to *you*. Sometimes this may not be the textbook's solution, or the instructor's solution, or even the group's solution. But because it is your own solution, it can constitute important learning.

The empathetic approach is an adaptation of the case-study method used effectively for many years in studying business administration, law, and other people-oriented specialties. The empathetic approach shares two of the major advantages of the case-study method. First, it takes the student out of the role of passive absorber and makes him a partner in the learning process. Second, the empathetic approach opens free channels of communication among students and between students and professors. It enables a student to make a contribution to the understanding of the whole group. This, in turn, encourages all students to think purposefully and to work harder.

But there are reasons for suggesting that the empathetic approach may be even more significant in the study of marriage and family relationships than the case-study method is in many other disciplines. For one thing, marriage and family relationships deal with the extraordinarily delicate but legally permanent interpersonal arrangements between men, women, and children. There is more to it than that, though. To understand fully the significance of the use of the empathetic approach in relationships education, it is necessary to examine the recent history of relationships education itself.

MARRIAGE AND FAMILY RELATIONSHIPS EDUCATION

Courses expressly designed to help students with their own marriage and family relationships—later called "functional" courses—were introduced into American colleges and universities in the early 1920s. Although there was a wide variation in the quality of these courses, much of the writing and teaching of early family relationships educators aimed at perpetuating traditional middle-class customs and attitudes. Richard Kerckhoff pointed out that many of the writers' and teachers' undocumented assertions, both to their students and to their professional colleagues, went unchallenged.[5] Whether there was complete agreement that this was the way things really

[5]Richard K. Kerckhoff, "Value Stance in Family Life Education," *The Family Coordinator*, **19** (July, 1970), 253–260.

were or not, most people generally believed that this was probably the way things ought to be or, at least, that this was the way that young people should be told they ought to be.

But in the 1930s, 1940s, and 1950s, depression, war, and social crises not only turned up glaring value contradictions and agonizing value dilemmas, but also brought about large-scale mixing of people from differing value systems, with a consequent dilution of positive value judgments. Cultural relativism, with its implication of no absolute right or wrong, good or bad (since these vary from culture to culture), became more fashionable, and dogmatic conviction became less so. At about the same time that young adults began to reject and ignore many traditional teachings, their parents and teachers became more doubtful about them, too. As America moved into the second half of the century, traditional value-filled education in the home, in the school, and especially in higher education was clearly on the defensive.

In the hallways of the universities, there was new emphasis on avoiding value judgments. There was also a new stress on creating scientific, value-free knowledge in the behavioral sciences and on eliminating any teaching that smacked of the earlier parochialism.[6]

Furthermore, change had become clearly established as a value in itself—perhaps the highest value. That which was traditional had become suspect. People wanted new things; they wanted 1961 cars in 1960—definitely not 1959 cars. And although there were wide regional and cultural differences, a there-must-be-something-better spirit affected thinking about relationships as well as about automobiles.

A few interpreted "something better" as meaning the rejection of everything old or traditional, forgetting C. C. Bowman's succinct warning: "Noting that the mores contain irrationalities, gross generalizations and many other illogical elements, one may easily fall prey to the unwarranted conclusion that diametrically opposed beliefs will be rational, logical, scientific."[7]

But there were other, more thoughtful scholars who believed that "something better" involved the application of scientific, reliable knowledge

[6]For a good review of the value versus nonvalue controversy in academic sociology, see R. C. Hinkle, Jr., and G. J. Hinkle, *The Development of Modern Sociology,* New York, Random House, 1954, ch. 2. For specific reference to values in marriage and family relationships education and research, see Harold T. Christensen, ed., *Handbook of Marriage and the Family,* Skokie, Ill., Rand McNally, 1964, ch. 24.

[7]Claude C. Bowman, "Hidden Valuations in the Interpretations of Sexual and Family Relationships," *American Sociological Review,* **11** (October, 1946), 543.

gained in a purified, value-free atmosphere to the problems of interpersonal relationships in marriage and the family. Since most reliable knowledge in the behavioral sciences is obtained by statistical investigations, citing research findings on how some other people behaved became the popular *modus operandi* in relationships education. Those students who were seeking academic knowledge as such, without particular reference to its personal significance or usefulness, benefited by this new approach. But for many students faced with individual problems, it turned out to be little more personally enlightening and little more acceptable than the old-style moralizations.

Statistical studies, however well validated and useful in generalizations, can rarely encompass all the complexities of a unique personal situation with enough relevance to clarify an emotional dilemma. For example, knowing the statistics on the number of females who engaged in premarital intercourse at the University of Florida in the 1950s provides very little meaningful guidance for the young woman who is struggling with an immediate decision in a parked automobile in Seattle. Statistical research is extremely useful, but what the Seattle girl's dilemma clearly demonstrates is that *statistical research does not substitute for value judgments in all cases where decisions are needed.* There are at least five reasons why this is so:

Inappropriate actuarial research. The first reason is that much of the social research presently being done is of the actuarial type. Although such research provides dependable predictions in large numbers of cases, it may provide no prediction whatsoever when applied to a single case. It does not follow, for example, that because 75 percent of married couples have trouble with their in-laws, any particular couple has a 75 percent chance of having in-law troubles.[8] A particular couple has a 100 percent certainty of not having in-law troubles or a 100 percent certainty of having in-law trouble. If all the attitudes and feelings bearing on the relationship of a particular couple and their in-laws were known in advance, it might be possible to predict what the outcome would be. The chance of having trouble is determined by the personalities involved and the patterns of the relationship, not by any frequencies found in the population at large.

In relationships as well as individuals, causation is always personal and never actuarial. As Gordon Allport has said, "The only way to make a

---

[8]A physician lecturing to a medical-school class pointed out that in 99 out of every 100 cases, a certain disease was nonfatal. "But," he quickly added, "to each in the other percent, it isn't a 1 percent loss, but a 100 percent loss."

certain prediction of effect from cause is to study the life in which the causes operate and not a thousand other lives."[9]

Allport's statement is especially important in a mobile, changing, heterogeneous society such as ours. In other societies, where patterned role relationships remained relatively stable over hundreds or thousands of years, it might have been possible to predict individual behavior more accurately. For example, in some older societies, a daughter-in-law would have been so rigidly conditioned to be subservient to her mother-in-law that in-law trouble would never have arisen.

Inapplicability to the specific situation. A second reason why any indiscriminate substitution of statistical research for value judgments is often unwise is illustrated by the case of the girl in Seattle. Many of the most quoted research studies are both out of date when they are quoted and unrepresentative of the experience of the people to whom they are quoted. Winston Ehrmann's classic study of premarital intercourse at the University of Florida was made in the 1950s and may or may not have any relationship to the situation on the campus at Gainesville today.[10] Moreover, even if it should still be valid there, the chances that it is descriptive of present conditions on a small midwestern campus or at the University of Washington in Seattle are even less probable. Furthermore, even if Ehrmann's statistics had present validity for college students everywhere, they would have, as Kinsey and his associates have clearly shown, almost no meaning for the vast majority of America's noncollege-educated population.[11]

Conflicting conclusions. A third major problem in the substitution of statistical findings for value judgments in decision-making situations is the question of *which* findings to try to substitute. Reuben Hill, one of the leading advocates and outstanding exponents of family research, pointed out that some of the most highly respected authorities and scholars in the family field have arrived at conflicting conclusions concerning many important family questions.[12] When the research for the decade of the 1960s was

[9]Gordon W. Allport, *The Use of Personal Documents in Psychological Science*, New York, Social Science Research Council, 1942, p. 157.

[10]Winston Ehrmann, *Premarital Dating Behavior*, New York, Holt, Rinehart & Winston, 1959.

[11]Alfred C. Kinsey, W. B. Pomeroy, and C. E. Martin, *Sexual Behavior in the Human Male*, Philadelphia, Saunders, 1948.

[12]Reuben Hill, "Status of Research About Marriage and the Family," address to the American Association of Marriage Counselors, Washington, D.C., October, 1967. Three of his list of eleven propositions on which important scholars disagree are these:

(A.) People tend to marry people like themselves rather than opposites.

(E.) The economic factor is not significant in divorce or marriage adjustment. Burgess and Cottrell (Ernest W. Burgess and Leonard S. Cottrell, Jr., *Predicting Success or*

reviewed, there was a consistent concern that the findings were conflicting because of methodological difficulties.[13] Although such disagreement may be a healthy sign of scholarly growth, it creates severe dilemmas for the student who is seeking personal guidance from research results.

Sometimes it is possible for a sophisticated research specialist to decide which is the more scientifically acceptable of two or several conflicting findings by reference to certain well-established standards of methodology. Often, though, this is all but impossible. So it has become classic in modern relationships textbooks, occasionally even in this one, to cite all the studies that the author can find on both sides of the question and let the student choose for himself which is closer to scientific knowledge and thus, presumably, more helpful to him. This has the seeming respectability of being democratic, permissive, and nonbiased. If one is really dependent wholly on facts (not value judgments) to make his decision, then not knowing which are the facts can be a disaster.

Confusion of prevalence with excellence. A fourth major consideration in the substitution of statistical research findings for value judgments is the problem of confusing prevalence with excellence. It has been suggested that objective discussions of research findings in our contemporary society, although not intended to do so, sometimes lead people to adopt behavior that they might otherwise have avoided or rejected.[14] "Everyone is doing it" and "It's the latest thing" are very convincing arguments in our fad-conscious, security-needing society.[15]

Failure in Marriage, Englewood Cliffs, N.J., Prentice-Hall, 1939) and Locke (Harvey J. Locke, *Predicting Adjustment in Marriage*, New York, Holt, Rinehart & Winston, 1951), *for;* Goode (William J. Goode, "Economic Factors and Marital Stability," *American Sociological Review*, **16** (December, 1951), 803–811), Williamson (Robert C. Williamson, "Socio-economic Factors and Marital Adjustment in an Urban Setting," *American Sociological Review*, **19** (April, 1954), 213–216), and Monahan (Thomas P. Monahan, "Divorce by Occupational Level," *Marriage and Family Living*, **17** (November, 1955), 322–324), *against.*

(G.) American families are becoming democratic companionships. Burgess and Locke (Ernest W. Burgess and Harvey J. Locke, *The Family: From Institution to Companionship*, New York, American Book, 1953), *for;* Hill (Reuben Hill, "The American Family: Problem or Solution?" *American Journal of Sociology*, **53** (September, 1947), 125–131) and Johnson (A. L. Johnson, *A Study of the Applicability of Selected Marital Success Criteria in Certain Population Groups*, Minneapolis, University of Minnesota, 1953, Ph.D. dissertation), *against.*

[13]Carlfred Broderick, ed., *A Decade of Family Research and Action*, Minneapolis, National Council on Family Relations, 1972.

[14]Harold T. Christensen, "The Intrusion of Values," in Harold T. Christensen, ed., *Handbook of Marriage and the Family*, Skokie, Ill., Rand McNally, 1964, p. 982.

[15]James T. Teeven, Jr., "Reference Groups and Premarital Sexual Behavior," *Journal of Marriage and the Family*, **34** (May, 1972), 283–291.

Curiously, this sometimes puts statistical research in the completely unwanted position of being a "bandwagon technique," one of the very anti-intellectual symptoms that those who opposed the teaching of values previously sought to eliminate. This time, however, the presumed values seem to get their authenticity not from being ordained by God or by tradition, but rather from having been statistically blessed by the computer.

Yet even when a certain behavior can be clearly shown to be both practiced by a majority and brand-new to the American scene, its elevation to the status of decision controller only for those reasons is highly questionable. The Nazi debacle in Germany is just one recent confirmation of the historically indisputable proposition that not everything prevalent is good and not every change is progress. This premise is especially true in the area of marriage and family relationships. Some tired old folkways and platitudes may have outlived some of their usefulness, but at least they have the respectability of having been demonstrably workable at one time. In this, they are often more reliable than untested fads and more rational than indiscriminate change seeking.

Emotional impediments. The fifth reason why statistical research is often an inadequate substitute for value judgments is somewhat the opposite of the fourth. Many people, far from being stampeded by new statistical norms, are emotionally incapable of accepting them even when they are relevant and up to date and might well lead to an improvement in relatability. As we shall see repeatedly throughout this book, each individual carries with him the deeply embedded customs, attitudes, values, and expectations that were conditioned into him in childhood. This emotional conditioning frequently takes precedence over any logical reasoning or any statistical research finding in difficult decision-making situations. These inner compulsions to behave in certain ways *are* the person as he exists at the present moment. Any attempt to change him *immediately* by citing what other people have done, however valid the research, often can lead to further frustration rather than to the resolution of a particular difficulty. The person who says "I am in no mood for logic" is probably right.

Despite these five objections to substituting statistical research for value judgments, it should be pointed out once more that the problem is not with the research itself. Moreover, when the behavioral-science research that exists today is properly used, it can be a helpful adjunct to the decision-making process even in specific individual situations. For example, knowing that mixed marriages usually require more difficult adjustments than homogamous marriages may help one to prepare himself even though he decides to go through with a mixed marriage anyway.

The most important function of statistical research is validating generalizations—*when generalizations are important.* Curiously, Willard Waller, one of the most respected figures in the history of family studies, questioned this. Said Waller: "No generalization can be so clearly buttressed by facts as one which is definitely supported by one or two well understood cases; generalization from statistics is ever more tenuous and inconclusive than generalization from persons."[16] A few behavioral scientists are beginning to agree with Waller. But most feel that, ordinarily, dogmatic generalization from one case is extremely hazardous. When generalization is appropriate, it is wise, if possible, to discover its limits of generality by statistical techniques. This does not, of course, rule out initial speculation, without which there would be no research hypotheses to test. Nor does it rule out common sense and the manifest evidence of folk behavior, without which we would face the ridiculous task of proving and reproving billions of commonly accepted premises from one moment to the next.

It is hoped that in this book a neat balance can be achieved by using both case reports for the particularization they can provide and statistical research, where available, to verify the degree and extent of behaviors that comprise our cultural interaction. It is also hoped that you will learn to apply the theory or principles from empirical research rather than to apply specific findings from any one study.[17]

THE CASE FOR THE EMPATHETIC APPROACH

Although the postwar move from advice to statistics may have been a real advance, most students today want something more. They want some definitive criteria by which they can guide their own lives. This has been validated repeatedly, both by research and by clinical interviews. But modern students do not want those guidelines to be presented as dogmatic advice. Nor do they want equivocations or sterile statistics about other people's behavior. Rather they want to find their own criteria and make their own decisions, using their own reflective insights.

This leads directly back to the singular importance of the empathetic approach in studying and improving relationships. The empathetic approach tends to diminish didactic lecturing and preaching markedly. Moreover,

[16]Willard Waller, *The Old Love and the New*, New York, Liveright, 1930, pp. 316–317.
[17]Wesley R. Burr, D. Eugene Mead, and Boyd C. Rollins, "A Model for the Application of Research Findings by the Educator and Counselor: Research to Theory to Practice," *The Family Coordinator*, **22** (July, 1973), 285–290.

while it makes use of reliable scientific knowledge, it avoids the necessity of substituting statistical findings for value judgments when decisions have to be made. The empathetic approach also enables each person to arrive at his own direction and conviction through personal insights that are compatible with the emotional residue of the value system he has carried over from childhood. Such new insights are usually more easily interpolated into the student's own living experience than the admonitions and urgings of other people.

For all these reasons, the empathetic approach seems to offer real advantages in better preparing the individual for a lifetime of relationships with other people—in marriage, in the family, in the community, and in the individual's professional life. It is training in a scientific approach to problem solving that combines the best elements of objectivity and subjectivity. But more, it is practice in "sensitivity," the art and science of perceiving how others feel. As most leaders in business, politics, and human relations will attest, there is no more valuable learning than this.

The idea of using the case method in relationships education is by no means new. In its earliest informal application it antedates all other methods of teaching about family relationships. Willard Waller, as far back as the 1920s, was a strong advocate of the use of personal documents in teaching family relationships. In 1958, Jessie Bernard, Helen Buchanan, and William Smith published an excellent book containing both personal documents and excerpts from fiction that were adapted for case-study use.[18] Stories, novels, and plays are also used as individual situations in marriage and family relationships education.[19]

Some disadvantages of the empathetic approach

The empathetic approach, like the case method, is not without its disadvantages. For one thing, it takes much more time to arrive at a personally acceptable conclusion than it does to adopt and repeat someone

[18]Jessie S. Bernard, Helen E. Buchanan, and William M. Smith, Jr., *Dating, Mating and Marriage,* Cleveland, H. Allen, 1958.

[19]Rose M. Somerville, "The Literature Approach to Teaching Family Courses," *Journal of Marriage and the Family,* **28** (May, 1966), 214–216; Val Clear, "Marriage Education Through Novels and Biography," *Journal of Marriage and the Family,* **28** (May, 1966), 217–219; Laurence Smarden, "The Use of Drama in Teaching Family Relationships," *Journal of Marriage and the Family,* **28** (May, 1966), 219–223; Rose M. Somerville, "Death Education as Part of Family Life Education: Using Imaginative Literature for Insights into Family Crises," *The Family Coordinator,* **20** (July, 1971), 209–224; and Vera Channels, "Family Life Education Through the Use of Novels," *The Family Coordinator,* **20** (July, 1971), 225–230.

else's generalization or conclusion. In the process of classroom discussion, a good deal of time is often taken with statements by other members that are irrelevant, repetitious, or even mistaken. Sometimes students may express feelings about cases that are unacceptable to other members of the class; there will be more about this later.

The long conditioning that many students have had to the traditional notion that their teacher will provide them with the "right" answers to all problems—including their own—is another difficulty in using the empathetic approach. Some students feel that, having once paid the tuition, they are entitled to all the knowledge the teacher possesses regardless of how inappropriate it may be to the solution of the personal problem under discussion. Even if they recognize that there is no right or wrong answer, they would like, at least, to have the teacher's opinion about every case. Sometimes such a request is not altogether unreasonable; a teacher's opinions can be valuable when they enlarge the student's own insight.

There are still other difficulties with the empathetic approach. Sometimes the problems presented are unsolvable, and sometimes the only solutions are markedly less than desirable. Using the empathetic approach occasionally can be shattering to romantic illusions and disappointing to cherished ideals.

Yet using the empathetic approach is stimulating and exciting to the degree that it does make relations between people very honest and very real. For this positive reason alone, using the empathetic approach is an adventure in understanding, communication, and personal growth.

WHAT IS EMPATHY?

Empathy can be defined in two different ways and you can experience it both ways. One is emotional empathy and the other is predictive empathy, or cognitive role taking.

Emotional empathy is a vicarious emotional response to the perceived emotional experiences of others. This type of empathy is usually gained from past associations with that particular emotion.

Predictive empathy is the imaginative taking of the role of the other by accurately assessing and predicting the person's thoughts, feelings, and actions. Although past associations help develop predictive empathy, it may be learned cognitively, through the study and application of principles of human behavior.

Empathy is positively correlated with experience, intelligence, cue sensitivity, and accurate self-perception. Empathy has its beginning during the first year of life when you learn that others have some of the same responses that you have, such as crying and laughing. Later, empathy is more pronounced, when you can actually anticipate another's reaction to a situation, because you too have been in that situation.

People from similar experiences and backgrounds tend to empathize more easily with each other. Role taking is obviously easier when you have experienced many roles or come into contact with many roles. Extensive exposure to people of different ages, different social classes, different conceptual levels, and different cultures promotes increased empathetic ability.[20] However, with the development of a higher cognitive level and through greater knowledge of principles of human behavior you can learn to empathize with others from different backgrounds.

Intelligence is very important in that the greater the capacity to categorize, the greater the ability to understand why different people act as they do.[21] Empathy requires an accurate assessment of the other's definition of the situation, and certain capacities aid in forming this accurate definition.

Cue sensitivity is another capacity which facilitates empathy. Lack of normal sensory development inhibits cue sensitivity, thereby limiting empathy. The person who is very aware of sensory cues can excel in empathetic ability. This highly empathetic person listens to moods and feelings as well as to words.

Empathy extends beyond a simple recognition of affective states. Role taking allows anticipation of the behavior of the other. You learn to project yourself into the role of the other and to determine how you would react if confronted by the same situation. Since not everyone has the same meanings, the more that is known about a person, the more likely that accurate role taking and prediction can be achieved. In order to quickly take the role of another, you learn to stereotype and categorize according to positions in the social structure or according to personality types. Thus, certain roles are stereotyped as appropriate to a doctor, to a teacher, to a nice guy, or to a smart aleck. Stereotyping can quickly lead to accurate behavior predictions, but long-term relations must be based on direct experience with another. In long-term relations, the more experience you have, the more accurate the predictions. Even though long-term relationships offer the poten-

[20]Ezra Stotland, "Exploratory Investigations of Empathy," in Leonard Berkowitz, ed., *Advances in Experimental Social Psychology*, vol. 4, New York, Academic, 1969, pp. 271–314.

[21]E. A. Weinstein, "The Development of Interpersonal Competence," in David A. Goslin, ed., *Handbook of Socialization Theory and Practice*, Skokie, Ill., Rand McNally, 1969, p. 758.

tial for the development of high levels of empathy, this potential is not always realized. Although stereotyping is an efficient way of role taking or predicting behavior, more refined empathy requires being able to discriminate particular behavior of an individual from general behavior patterns. This is where multiple perspectives come into play. You must be able to individualize your stereotypes.

Empathy is also associated with your perception of the self. Since it is believed that the self is a product of social interaction, an interpretation of what others think, then a more accurate definition of self is in fact a more accurate definition of others.[22]

USING THE EMPATHETIC APPROACH IN THE CLASSROOM

When the empathetic approach is used in teaching relationships, both emotional empathy and predictive empathy are used. In fact, the greatest personal learning comes when you perceive a situation to be similar to your own, feel the emotions of the people involved, and yet can interpret and explain the behavior on a cognitive level. Since emotional empathy or perceived emotions may or may not be an accurate assessment of the other's feelings, you learn that your own perception sometimes hinders the understanding of a situation. Three things, then, make up the use of the empathetic approach in teaching relationships: the perceived emotions, accurate assessment of others' emotions, and knowledge of the effect of inaccurate perception of the emotions in a situation.

The objectives of the empathetic approach are these: (1) to become more aware of one's own emotional responses; (2) to understand where these emotional responses were learned; (3) to apply principles of human behavior in accurately understanding another's responses in a situation; (4) to become aware of the influence of one's own emotional responses on accuracy in perceiving another's responses in the situation; and (5) to be able to predict more accurately future behavior of people.

Perceived emotions cannot be taught, but you can be taught to become aware of them and even to express them. Accurate assessment or predictive empathy can be taught. The use of the empathetic approach in the classroom encourages both emotional empathy and predictive empathy, along with a full knowledge of the effect of emotional empathy on predictive empathy. An ultimate goal of the empathetic approach is better human

[22]Leonard S. Cottrell, Jr., "Interpersonal Interaction and the Development of the Self," in David A. Goslin, ed., *Handbook of Socialization Theory and Practice*, Skokie, Ill., Rand McNally, 1969, pp. 547–551.

relationships. It is believed that a higher level of empathy will decrease aggressive behavior and increase helping behavior.[23] A highly skilled empathizer can know how you want to be treated while at the same time knowing full well that he does not want the same treatment.

Read the case of Mary and Al to get the feeling of the empathetic approach.

The first time you read the case allow all your emotional responses to spill out. Say them aloud or at least register them to yourself. Then reread the case and begin to pull out of your memory the times you have had these feelings before. Note the circumstances of the origins of these feelings. Since your ability to do this will sharpen immensely as you use this book, do not worry if explanations for your feelings are not readily accessible. It might be to your advantage to write these feelings down and even to note later why you think you had them.

During the second or third reading begin to bring in explanations for why people act as they do in certain situations. Even though you may not yet be as knowledgeable as you would like to be in the sociological and psychological explanations for behaviors, you have quite a repertoire of your own about why people behave as they do. At this point, brainstorm about the reasons. Speculate about what may have taken place that is not included in the case.

Then try your hand at empathizing with *each one* of the persons in the case—Mary, Al, Mary's mother, Al's mother, Mary's father, Al's father, a guest at the tea. If you have experienced any of these situations you will have emotional empathy. Whether you have experienced the situation or not, you can have predictive or cognitive role-taking empathy. You probably will have some of both.

CASE 1 MARY AND AL

Mary is now twenty and Al is eighteen. She comes from a well-to-do banking family in Spokane; he is from an ex–coal miner's family in Black Diamond, Washington. He is a freshman and she a junior at the University of Washington. Al and Mary knew each other for only three months when they decided to get married. Mary's family, shocked and disappointed, forbade them to marry. So Al and Mary went to Coeur d'Alene, Idaho, on a weekend and were married anyway.

[23]A. Mehrabian and N. Epstein, "A Measure of Emotional Empathy," *Journal of Personality,* **40** (December, 1972), 525–543.

After they were married Mary's parents seemed to become resigned to the idea. Al wanted to drop out of school and go to work in Black Diamond, but Mary's parents offered to pay all the college expenses for both of them and even to provide money for an apartment in Seattle if they would both continue in school. Al didn't think much of that (the truth was that he was failing in several subjects anyway), but because it seemed to be what Mary wanted, he agreed to it.

Al is very close to his family. Al's mother, a plump and friendly woman, has always done everything for the men in the family, picked up their clothes and kept her little house immaculately clean. She feels this is a woman's role, as do her menfolk. Al's mother goes to church regularly and she talks a great deal about religion and what's right, although her grammar is poor and some of her ideas are a little vague. Al's father is a quiet, bashful man who works hard and doesn't like to dress up in city clothes, but who believes in being the boss in his house.

For the first few months of the marriage everything seemed to go well. On the weekends when Al's folks didn't come to visit, Al and Mary traveled the 20 miles to Black Diamond to see them. (Mary's parents rarely came, because Spokane was 290 miles away.) But Mary began to get a little tired of Al's folks and their talk about hard-shell religion. Besides, when Al's mother was around, Mary always felt as if she didn't do enough for Al. His mother would scrub the apartment when she came, and bake and sew for Al. Al's people never offered to help pay any of the young people's expenses, even though Mary felt they could provide a token now and then. Whenever Mary mentioned this to Al, he got quite angry and told her he was going to quit school and go to work in Black Diamond.

A month ago, Al reminded Mary that his mother's birthday was coming on the twenty-first of the month and said he had invited his folks over for that weekend. He gave Mary a little money and asked her to buy his mother a fancy nightgown. Mary was fed up by this time and said some ugly things about Al's people coming over all the time. But she got the gown with the money Al had saved, and Al didn't say much more. A week later Mary's people wrote that they would be in Seattle on the twenty-first en route to a resort in Las Vegas. Since the apartment was small, Mary asked Al to uninvite his folks. "After all," she said, "they come all the time." Al refused. Mary got the nightgown and tore it to shreds. Al stamped out.

Three days later, Al came back. He said he had talked with his mother, and she had sent him back to apologize and resume his Christian duty to his wife. He also said that his folks would not be coming to stay overnight. Mary was relieved and immediately invited some of her college friends to meet her parents on the twenty-first.

On Sunday afternoon the twenty-first, just as Mary was serving tea, Al's folks pulled up in their 1964 Plymouth. Al had told them it wouldn't be convenient to stay overnight, but he hadn't said they shouldn't come at all.

Mary blew her top. She screamed at Al's folks and told them exactly what she thought of them. Al told her to shut up. This made her even more furious and she kicked him. Al didn't say any more; he just took his mother by the arm and walked out.

In using the empathetic approach, several additional guidelines may be helpful. First of all, in making your own private analysis, it is very important to analyze the cases, using, *all* the feelings and facts. Avoid, if you can, reading the cases too lightly; stop and make a note of the significant factors as you go along. Remember that using the empathetic approach requires thoughtful concentration and much self-guided reasoning. The following steps are adapted from a list of E. Jackson Baur's techniques for analyzing and interpreting case material in the social sciences.[24]

1. Become as familiar as you can with the concepts and theories of the general field in which you are working. The empathetic approach draws most heavily on concepts from family relations, child development, psychology, and sociology. Many of these concepts will be discussed in this book before cases involving them are presented, but outside reading is helpful. Also see the Appendix for generalizations about human behavior.
2. After you have read the case carefully, mull it over. Play with the ideas that flow through your mind, and imaginatively manipulate the facts without rational restraint; generate a "brainstorm."
3. After the preliminary free manipulation, critically sort out the tenable from the untenable insights. Retain those that fit and are consistent with the other facts in the case.
4. Look for hidden meaning in people's statements. Words may conceal unconscious feelings. They may not express what the person really intended. Try to "put yourself in his place" and "feel out" meanings.
5. Distinguish facts from inferences. No case ever contains all the facts that

[24]E. Jackson Baur, "A Student Guide for Interpreting Case Material," *Improving College and University Teaching*, **8** (Summer, 1960), 104–108.

are needed for conclusive interpretation, so to complete the interpretation you may have to make some assumptions about things that are not reported in the case. Interpolate or extrapolate from the facts that are present or add hypothetical facts that you imagine are probably there because they seem reasonable and plausible. But be careful to identify these as assumptions or inferences.

6. Write out an interpretation for yourself relating the abstract ideas to the concrete events reported in the case. Whenever you use a concept or theory, refer to the concrete facts in the case to which it applies.

7. If the case is very complicated, break it up into smaller units. Then analyze each unit separately and later bring them together. Draw general conclusions from these separately related parts of the case.

A second major guideline for using the empathetic approach is to try to empathize *completely* with all the people in the cases. In the beginning, you may have a tendency to identify only with the person of your own sex or of your own age group. If you continue this, you will be reinforcing old patterns of thinking and relating, and you will be learning nothing new. Practice taking the other's point of view.

A third major guideline is to reemphasize constantly to yourself that rarely, if ever, is any one participant in the situation wholly right or wholly wrong. Even if it were possible to determine it, discovering who is right does not solve a problem. The only constructive analysis of a situation leads to a decision about *what can be done about it now.*

A fourth guideline is to avoid jumping to conclusions. Very often a case will contain some revealing implications toward the beginning that will trigger an immediate insight. There is a temptation to fix judgment at this point and to go no further. Yet there may be other points later in the case that are not so obvious but that must be taken into account.

It is also important to avoid premature approval or disapproval of a participant in the case. This includes labeling someone's behavior with a common psychiatric term. It doesn't help, for instance, to characterize one of the participants as, say, paranoid. The important thing to know is *why* the person is disturbed and to figure out what can be done to help him.

The fifth guideline is to remind yourself constantly that, in analyzing and discussing cases, although it is wise to know the facts of the particular case and as much as you can about what authorities have said, it is also important not to overlook the value of common sense. Common sense is one of the important tools in the empathetic approach. Fritz Heider, a leading scholar in the field of social psychology, points out in his book *The Psychology of Interpersonal Relations* that

In interpersonal relations, perhaps more than any other field of knowledge, fruitful concepts and hunches for hypotheses lie dormant and unformulated in what we know intuitively. . . . Actually, all psychologists use common sense ideas in their scientific thinkings; but they usually do so without analyzing them and making them explicit.[25]

The sixth guideline leads toward case-study maturity which is largely based on speaking up when the time comes for class discussion of the cases. At first you may find this difficult. Students who have been accustomed to a lecture format and who have been expected only to receive and repeat facts and ideas contained in the lectures and textbooks are often at an intellectual and emotional loss when they must do all the thinking themselves. Professor Charles I. Gragg of Harvard, one of the strong advocates of the case-study method in business administration, has put it this way:

Many people will always prefer to have answers handed to them. . . . The inherently dramatic and challenging character of the case system, however, although it may produce anxiety and confusion for the newcomer, also arouses his deep interest and leads him to make the effort required for adjustment.[26]

Case-study maturity, as in other case-type learning situations, is usually made in three progressive steps. The student discovers that he is unable to think of everything that all his fellow students can think of. He may find it very discouraging to have spent time, thought, and effort considering a particular case and then realize, in listening to his fellow students, that there were many angles that had not occurred to him.

This problem usually corrects itself quickly as the student recognizes the need for accepting help from others. As each student gains security, he derives more and more pleasure from cooperative discussion and analysis.

Later growth toward case-study maturity comes with the recognition that other students and instructors do not necessarily know the "best" answers. Even when they do, each student is still free to disagree. This is

[25]Fritz Heider, *The Psychology of Interpersonal Relations*, New York, Wiley, 1958, p. 5.

[26]Charles I. Gragg, "Because Wisdom Can't Be Told," in Kenneth R. Andrews, ed., *Human Relations and Administration*, Cambridge, Mass., Harvard University Press, 1955, p. 9.

especially true in analyzing interpersonal relationships. Because relationships are highly individual matters governed by the values of the individual, the "best" answer for any particular individual is the best answer for *him*. Even though others may see different things than you may see, those that have significance for you are, in your frame of reference, the best.

In class discussion or in your own private discussion with yourself, do not be afraid to make your values explicit. Throughout history, people who have believed strongly in something have accomplished a great deal more than people who did not. Often the believers also had better relationships with other people, for regardless of how we may disagree with someone else, we are usually made more secure by knowing the other person's patterns of thinking and feelings (provided, that is, that those thoughts and feelings do not threaten us directly). Although you have a social responsibility not to monopolize the class hour, you also have a responsibility to contribute your unique viewpoint to the learning experience of the whole group.

Moreover, you can learn much about your values by restating them. You can also learn much about yourself. Why did you feel compelled to contradict at one point? Why were you afraid to speak up at another point? Why did you feel hostile when somebody said so-and-so? Why were you privately gratified when somebody else said such-and-such? Think about it after each class.

In addition to making your values explicit, it is also important to make your assumptions explicit. In no case, either in this book or in real life, will you ever have all the facts about a particular situation. It will be necessary for you to speculate a great deal about how other people involved in the case might be thinking or feeling. But when you use these assumptions, you should clearly recognize that they are assumptions and so label them for the people with whom you are discussing the case.

Most of the cases that will provide the largest amount of practice in the empathetic approach will be found in the latter chapters of this book. Preceding them will be significant background information and discussion of the cultural environment in which people live in a contemporary society. This too is part of the empathetic approach, because a "frame of reference" and a store of accurate information are, along with insight, necessities for recognizing and evaluating possible solutions to relationships problems.

You will find a list of generalizations about human behavior in the Appendix that will be invaluable for understanding the behavior in the cases. You may want to study one or more of the theories of human behavior in depth so that you will be even more competent in cognitive empathy. The knowledge of theories and generalizations as well as knowledge of what is happening to marriage and the family will give you a better basis on which to make decisions.

2
WHAT'S HAPPENING TO MARRIAGE AND THE FAMILY?

Relationships can best be understood when they are examined in the context of social history and the predisposing cultural experiences of the individuals concerned. So before examining more cases, let us take a look at what has been happening to marriage and the family.

All the professional observers of the American family agree that there have been many changes in recent times in family experiences and family roles. There, most agreement ceases. As America approached the middle of the twentieth century, William Ogburn and Meyer Nimkoff asked eighteen of the best-known family experts to list the most significant changes in the American family in their professional lifetimes.[1] The lack of unanimity in the replies was impressive. The group reported a total of sixty-three changes, but only one change, the increasing divorce rate, was reported by all. Only eight changes were mentioned by at least half of the experts.[2] About two-thirds of the reported changes were mentioned by only one or two persons. Said Ogburn and Nimkoff, "That so many changes should be reported is not surprising because the family is a complex social institution with many inter-relations with other institutions, all of which are undergoing extensive changes in our time."[3]

Many of the changes that Ogburn and Nimkoff's experts proposed in the late 1940s appear to be still in progress. These include the decline in the authority of husbands and fathers, the increase in nonmarital and extramarital sexual intercourse, the increase in the number of wives working for pay, the increase in individualism and freedom of family members, the decline of religious behavior in marriage and the family, and the transfer of family functions.

The decline in family size, which the second largest number of experts mentioned, did not materialize as expected, and the birth rate continued to rise until 1956, when it reached a peak and began to decline. By 1972, the rate in the United States had dipped to the lowest level recorded in modern times.

[1]William F. Ogburn and Meyer F. Nimkoff, *Technology and the Changing Family*, Boston, Houghton Mifflin, 1955, p. 4.
[2]The eight changes were (1) increasing divorce rate (mentioned by all eighteen); (2) wider diffusion of birth control and/or decline in family size (mentioned by twelve); (3) decline in authority of husbands and fathers (mentioned by twelve); (4) increased sexual intercourse apart from marriage (mentioned by eleven); (5) increase in the number of wives working for pay (mentioned by eleven); (6) increasing individualism and freedom of family members (mentioned by ten); (7) increasing transfer of protective functions from family to state (mentioned by ten); (8) decline of religious behavior in marriage and family (mentioned by nine), Ibid., p. 7.
[3]Ogburn and Nimkoff, Ibid., p. 6.

The divorce rate, the only item universally cited by all of Ogburn and Nimkoff's experts, is now on a rising curve after dropping markedly from an all-time high at the end of World War II. The divorce rate per thousand population rose from 2.2 in 1957 to 2.7 in 1967—more than a 20 percent increase in the rate in the decade. In 1972 there was a 3.9 rate of divorce, and in 1973 a 4.3 rate of divorce per thousand population.[4] This substantial increase has been attributed to the trend toward no-fault divorce. This ignores the fact that while the rate per thousand population rose slowly in the past decade, it has risen sharply in the last two to three years, and the percentage of divorces involving people who have children is up dramatically.

Moreover, there are significantly more separations, more desertions, and more annulments than ever before. In many large American cities (Los Angeles, for example), more people seek to break marriages legally than seek to make marriages legally in most months out of the year. In some recent years such diverse areas as Oklahoma County in Oklahoma and San Mateo County in California have actually reported marriage "deficits," because more people did get divorces, annulments, and separations over the entire year than got married. Neither of these places was a "divorce haven" with easy laws designed to encourage out-of-state divorce. San Mateo County, just south of San Francisco, has many of the characteristics that epitomize affluent suburbia. Such figures from an area reputed to be where the fad-makers live is an ominous sign for family stability.

Even so, divorce could be viewed as reorganization of the family rather than disorganization. Families are and always have been in a constant state of change, not only in age and composition but in life-style. To say that there are now varying family forms in the United States implies that there was only one form prior to this. But the notion of only one form —the nuclear, conjugal, neolocal, patrifocal—came from a model rather than a reality. To be different from the model implied deviance and was treated as pathological. The fact that we are now writing and talking about varying family forms as acceptable and about the nuclear family as a possible arena of disturbance indicates a freedom to live in other self-fulfilling ways.

When the family is viewed as a system of roles rather than a system of specific sexes, and when it is seen that various people of either sex or age may be able to fill the roles, disturbances will be lessened. Individuals will not be labeled as deviant, families will not be labeled as broken or

[4] U. S. Department of Health, Education, and Welfare, *Monthly Vital Statistics Report*, October 25, 1973.

incomplete, and discrepancies between the real and the ideal will not be there to cause stress within the person.

Kingsley Davis speculated that girls are more willing to enter a marriage early because of their knowledge that it can be broken.[5] If the marriage is not satisfactory, these girls realize their chances of remarriage are better if they do break the unsatisfactory marriage while they are still young. Subsidization of early marriages in various ways by parents and the government makes the step to marriage a less fateful commitment and therefore easier to break. More nearly equal opportunities for women to make their own livings, coupled with relatively successful birth control methods, have also added to the loss of commitment to lifetime marriage.

SCHOLARLY ANALYSES OF THE CHANGING FAMILY

The changes in modern marriage and family life have been defined, classified, and explained in many ways. Well-known scholars have written erudite books and developed elaborate theories. Notable among them is the cyclical theory of Carle C. Zimmerman, who traced the life cycle of family systems throughout the history of Western civilization. He described a regular pattern or movement from the "Trustee Family," in which all individual rights are subordinated to the welfare of the family group, to the "Domestic Family," in which family control is weakened, although the family remains essentially a strong unit. From the Domestic Family there is a predictable movement to the "Atomistic Family," in which familism is is replaced by individualism. The Atomistic Family is both the cause and the effect of decay in social life. In its latter stages, there is little real meaning in the marriage ceremony, widespread extramarital relationships, acceptance of sexual permissiveness, easy divorce, childlessness, and delinquency.[6]

Zimmerman clearly believed that, like Greece and Rome before us, the United States is in the final stages of the evolution to the Atomistic Family. The best hope for renewed greatness, or even survival, he thought, is to swing back toward the Domestic Family and toward the social strengths associated with it.

Another of the classic theories of family change is the structure-function theory, for which Talcott Parsons is a well-known spokesman. In-

---

[5]Kingsley Davis, "The American Family in Relation to Demographic Change," in Charles F. Westoff and Robert Parke, Jr., eds., *One: Demographic and Social Aspects of Population Growth*, Washington, D.C., GPO, 1972, p. 81.

[6]Carle C. Zimmerman, "The Future of the Family in America," *Journal of Marriage and the Family*, **34** (July, 1972), 323–333.

stead of believing that we are headed toward destruction as a result of recent changes in our marriage and family behavior, Parsons has suggested that the changes are functional adaptations to the increasing specialization of other institutions in our society. He believes that the modern family is doing the only thing it can to meet the requirements of a changing society.[7]

Although these comprehensive systematic theories of marriage and family change have important usefulness to the professional sociologist, the student interested in practical problems of modern relationships needs a more limited and more directly applicable explanation.

It seems that much of what has happened to the marriage relationship in this century can be subsumed under one of two headings: (1) the change in determination to stay married or (2) unrealistic marriage expectations. We will examine each of these areas in detail (determination in this chapter, expectations in the next), because they will provide a frame of reference for the entire empathetic approach. Although the emphasis will be on the changing relationship between the marriage partners, some discussion of family structure and function will be involved as well.

THE CHANGE IN DETERMINATION

It is probable that the primary reason for the continuing increase in the fragility of marriage is that happiness has replaced stability as the major goal of marriage partners. Since happiness is more elusive and less easily measured than stability, it is now easier to convince oneself that a marriage has failed.

A hundred years ago the most important values in marriage were staying married, producing children, and continuing to exist in spite of merciless natural forces that made existence difficult. Generally, both partners took satisfaction and pride in this.[8] In those days a man needed a wife. She was an economic asset to him in many ways. Not only did she cook and clean, but she also put up the vegetables that made it possible for him to live until the next harvest. Additionally, she produced children, and they, too, were economic assets. It was said that a good catch for a young bachelor before the Industrial Revolution was a healthy widow with six children, for he would suddenly have acquired fourteen hands to help him.

[7]Talcott Parsons, "The Stability of the American Family System," in Norman W. Bell and Ezra F. Vogel, eds., *A Modern Introduction to the Family*, rev. ed., New York, Free Press, 1968, pp. 97–101.
[8]Not always, though. William Goode warns against the tendency to stereotype the "good old" American farm family of the past. The interested student should read William J. Goode, *World Revolution and Family Patterns*, New York, Free Press, 1963, ch. 1.

For the woman, too, there was a satisfaction in a stable marriage relationship and in working hard to make the marriage stable. A woman's very existence depended upon her husband, and her emotional satisfaction came from serving him and seeing to it that he had cleaner shirts and better food than the neighboring husbands.

Today, the marriage ideal is "happiness" for each of the marriage partners, and this happiness is often expected to come with the marriage. Since it is no longer absolutely necessary for people to spend their entire lives grubbing out a marginal existence, happiness *is* a more realistic goal than it ever was before. The important question, though, is how that happiness is achieved. If each partner is expecting to receive bountiful happiness from the marriage without giving anything to it, someone is bound to be disappointed. For marriage is a giving relationship—especially after the children arrive. This has not changed. It is as true today as it was a hundred years ago.

In every relationship between two people, inevitably there will be some less ecstatic moments. In the past, these were more often tolerated or shrugged off, but today they have become moments for decision about whether or not to continue the marriage. With divorce as an easy alternative, the modern couple's toleration level has declined dramatically.

This change in determination to stay married has been greatly increased by some recent and often overlooked social changes. For example, now we live in a society where a woman is not dependent upon some man, be it husband, father, or brother, for her very existence. Today a woman can leave her husband, settle down a thousand miles away, and support herself in some culturally approved activity. Often she can make more money than the man she left.

This has given women the same kind of tacit threatening power that men have always had. A wife *can* with relative security, say to her husband, "If you don't behave like the lover I want, I will leave you." And usually a permissive society will allow her to do just that.

The contemporary woman's relative lack of determination to stay married has been explained this way:

What underlies the failure of so many mature marriages is not a new form of friction —but a new unwillingness to tolerate the old frictions.[9]

Here is a case in point.

---

[9]"The Divorced Woman—American Style," *Newsweek*, **69** (February 13, 1967), 65.

CASE 2 ROB AND TINA

"I tried to make it clear to Rob from the very beginning that if I wasn't happier—or at least as happy—after we got married as I was before, I just wasn't going to stick around. It's not that I'm unhappy with Rob—he's a dear, really, and he is good to me—but I've lost that exhilarated feeling I used to get when I was with him. I expected married life to be full of romantic thrills and excitement, but all that died after the first few weeks we were married and we settled down into a rather humdrum existence. I don't have anything to complain about really, but I want happiness—true happiness, not just contentment—out of life and I'm not getting it.

"My parents divorced when I was five and I lived with my mother most of the time while I was growing up. Mother is a very independent woman and she taught me to be the same way. She always told me, 'Tina, never depend on anybody but yourself and nobody will ever disappoint you.' I found from experience that those are very good words to live by. Rob doesn't understand that I want to be able to take care of myself. He tried to make me quit my job after we first got married, but I wouldn't, because that would make me dependent on him for money. He wanted to open a joint checking account too, but I wouldn't do that either. What I earn is mine, to do with as I please. He's the husband—he can pay the bills and buy his own things. I buy the things I need and if I helped him pay the bills I wouldn't have any money left to save in case I ever need it."

"I don't understand Tina at all," Rob told the counselor. *"It's almost as if she's afraid to become Mrs. Rob Fields. Do you know she's never signed her name that way once since we've been married? She still uses her maiden name sometimes, and when she doesn't, it's Tina Stroud Fields. She never signs Mrs. to anything. You'd think she's afraid to let anybody know we're married. About the only time she ever wears her rings anymore is when we go out together.*

"I suppose she told you I tried to get her to quit work after we got married. I make plenty of money, and she would never have to work another day of her life if she didn't want to. It's not that I mind her working; it's the people she works with. Lots of them are men and women who are divorced, and they are forever talking about the joyfulness and freedom of single life.

"Everything we own is either hers or ours—the car she drives to work is her car, the one I drive is ours; it's her stereo and our color TV. I don't really mind, but I wish she'd act more like a wife and less like a roommate.

"I suppose she told you how strong and independent her mother is.

Well, let me tell you, she's independent because she has to be. She lived with Tina's father for seven years, then decided that she wasn't as happy as she thought she ought to be. She's remarried three times since then. She's been living with her last husband for almost two years now; the other ones didn't even last that long.

"I wish Tina could have lived with her father more when she was growing up. It took him quite a while to get over Tina's mother's leaving him, so I understand, but he remarried about ten years ago and he and his second wife have been living together ever since.

"Oh sure, before we were married she told me that if she ever became unhappy she would leave me. I could understand that—there's no sense in two people making each other miserable. Now she tells me that she isn't unhappy with me, but she isn't as happy as she wants to be."

THE INCREASE IN INTERSEX CONTACTS

There are other reasons, too, for the modern loss of determination. One is the more frequent contact of married partners with friends and co-workers of the opposite sex. Today a young wife who works outside the home may see more attractive men in a week's time than her great-grandmother saw in a lifetime. Moreover, the modern young woman may work side by side with some of these men at a task requiring close cooperation that is more interesting than the routine work she must do (with or without the presence or assistance of her husband) when she returns home tired at the end of the day.

The following case illustrates the possible effect of more intersex contacts.

CASE 3 MOLLY AND CHUCK

"My marriage is breaking up," Molly told the counselor, "and I don't seem to be able to do anything about it.

"I married Ross, my first husband, while we were both in college. With a little help from our parents, we both managed to finish. Then he got a job in personnel work at a department store and did fairly well. We decided not to have a family right away so we could have some fun for a while. We had a nice apartment in a big complex in Los Angeles where there were a lot of other young couples. There were many expenses, though, especially because of the weekend parties and skiing trips.

"At first I didn't work. I cleaned up the apartment for an hour or so

in the morning and spent much of the rest of the day around the swimming pool. But after a while I got very bored. Most of our friends began having babies and moving away. So when I was offered a job with a broadcasting network as a typist, I decided to take it. We needed the money right then.

"I started working in the typing pool. But I did very well and soon was assigned to be Chuck's private secretary. He was a rising young executive, married, with two children. He was a fine, straightforward, clean-cut guy and he still is. At first, our only interest in each other was that he was the boss and I was the secretary. But he was a hard worker, and he knew just how to handle me. Before I knew it I became terribly interested in doing my work well and in working with him. Inside of a year I had more to talk about with Chuck in the eight hours we spent together each day than I did with Ross in the few hours we had together before bedtime.

"I met Chuck's wife several times. She was mostly interested in talking about her children and what she did at the bridge club. She didn't know very much about what was going on at the office, and she didn't seem at all interested.

"Well, you can guess what happened. Before long I fell in love with Chuck and he with me. So we each asked for a divorce. Ross didn't raise much of a fuss. I think he was already interested in a girl at his office, because he married her within a few weeks after our decree became final.

"But Chuck's wife threw a fit. She threatened to contest the divorce, and she said an awful lot of nasty things about me and about Chuck's lack of responsibility. He wound up having to pay her a lot of alimony and child support. I don't think the money part bothered him as much as having to give up his children, although he never talks about that now.

"But the money part bothered me. Now that we are married I resent having to give up a large part of our income to keep that woman. Moreover, now Chuck and I have three children of our own, and I have to deny them some things because Chuck's first wife is too lazy to support herself.

"The worst part about all this is that now I see it happening all over again. Chuck and I don't have very much in common anymore. I stopped working at his office five years ago, and he stops listening when I talk about children and the things that happen to me at home. But that's all I have to talk about now. I know that some women can't talk about anything else besides their children, but I don't think I'm that bad. I try very hard to keep up with current events and the news. But I have a feeling that I'm losing out to his new secretary. I've met her several times, and the same things that attracted me to Chuck are attracting her to him. He's a leader, and she's married to an inadequte, mousy little guy. I've confronted Chuck with my fears several times, but he just tells me I'm imagining things."

What were your immediate emotional reactions to this case? What have you experienced or known that may have prompted these personal emotional reactions? How did Chuck and Molly define happiness in marriage? Why do people imagine marriage to be a constant state of happiness when their premarital happiness was in an entirely different setting? How has greater intersex contact changed the willingness to tolerate old frictions? Does a wife at home with three children have any way to make marriage more tolerable? Could a wife who has experienced an intraoffice relationship be just imagining that her present husband is interested in the women in his office? What are the sociological explanations for determination to do anything?

How do the following generalizations about human behavior apply in this case? (See the Appendix for a more complete list.)

When a person gets greater reinforcement for a new behavior than an old behavior (for example, attraction to a different person or divorce), then this new behavior is likely to be repeated.

When a behavior (for example, marriage or parenthood) is idealized by a society, then members of the society are reinforced to try that behavior even though the behavior is known not to be satisfying to many.

When a person experiences negative reinforcement for a behavior (Molly's lack of attention from Chuck), then he or she attempts to stop that behavior (being the housewife).

CHANGING LAWS AND ATTITUDES

The liberalization of the divorce laws and changing public opinion about divorce have contributed to the increasing fragility of the marriage relationship in modern times. In the past, some people were obligated to stay married because they had no legitimate grounds for a divorce in their state and no stomach for deserting their spouses. Ordinarily the legal problems could be surmounted, either by manufacturing evidence (as was common practice in New York State before 1967, when the only grounds was adultery), or by moving to a state where more easily proved grounds, such as incompatibility or mental cruelty, were accepted. Nevertheless, the stricter divorce laws in some states were probably a deterrent to divorce, if only because it was expensive to move or to manufacture evidence.

Public opinion was also a deterrent in times past. As recently as two generations ago, divorce was looked upon in some areas as a sin, and mothers lowered the shades when a divorcee walked past the house so that the children would be protected from the sight of evil. There was a case as late as

1966 in which a high-school principal in a modern industrial city suggested to one of his teachers that she not tell the students that she had been divorced lest the parents protest that their children were being taught by a divorcee.

The "no-fault" divorce laws now becoming acceptable in many states are evidence of the changing attitudes and laws. Many people have urged a reversal in the usual pattern of easy-to-get-into marriage and difficult-to-get-out-of marriage. Since no new marriage laws requiring more capabilities for living in families have been passed and since society is not pressing for any capabilities, it would seem that rather than a reversal, an easing on both ends is happening. However, this very easing may be necessary before a realization of the need for preparation for marriage comes. Some people are already advocating more stringent laws for entering a marriage, particularly where children are likely to be involved.

In general, however, today's new ease and casualness about divorce have led many, especially many young people, to take a "let's-try-it-and-see" attitude toward marriage. Determination to make it work is downgraded from the very beginning. It is tacitly understood by both partners that, if their happiness is not increased—or at least maintained—by marriage, they will end the relationship.

In her remarkable book *Advice from a Failure*, Jo Coudert made a strong plea for some reversal of this trend.

The worst piece of advice I have ever been given was: "Go ahead and get married. If it doesn't work out, you can always get a divorce." It made marriage sound so easy, like accepting a job that has been offered because if you do not like it you can quit and do something else. Even at nineteen, I should have known better, but alas. . . .

Marriage is not a job, and divorce is not two weeks' notice and out. There is no hell like a bad marriage; divorce, although it may be a relief when it comes, is a highly public and painful admission of failure; and after divorce, you are not simply single again, back where you were before marriage. If a nineteen-year-old were to ask my advice now, I would say the opposite of what I was told, that is, that marriage should be contemplated as though there were no such thing as divorce. The possibility should be shut out of mind completely, and all the years of life with this person envisioned: locked in, no escape hatch, forever committed. Is it a bearable thought, or is the prospect of marriage only intriguing because there is a way out if the going gets rough?

If the latter, remember this: until you can squeeze through the trapdoor, you are locked in, and two people can do each other serious and lasting damage in the enclosed space of a marriage. Wounds are inflicted the scars of which are borne for a lifetime. Far more anxiety and depression are involved than could have been predicted. There is ugliness. There is unexpected trauma. It is impossible to escape unscathed, or even lightly scathed, from a marriage. Between in and out, there is a bruising road to travel, and it is infinitely preferable to reconnoiter the road sanely before setting foot on it than to embark on it casually and take a chance on what lies around the bend.[10]

It is important to note Coudert's deliberate reference to the relief some get from divorce. There are people who *are* manifestly happier when they are released from intolerable relationships. But without arguing the merits of any particular divorce action, the importance of avoiding a "try-and-see" attitude before marriage can be emphasized. Consider the following case.

CASE 4 JOHN AND MARGARET

John and Margaret were persuaded to come to the marriage counselor by her mother, even though Margaret thought it would be simpler just to continue with the divorce. They had been married for three years and had two little children. "It's very simple," Margaret said. "We just don't love each other anymore. I guess the marriage just never should have been. As a matter of fact, I had some doubts about it even before we got married, but it just seemed simpler to go through with it and try it out."

Then she went on, "We just don't like to do the same things. I like to go out to exciting places and do things in the evening, and all he wants to do is sit at home and watch television. In the beginning I tried to interest him in modern art and music, but he just brushed me off, and I soon decided it wasn't worth it. Why bother? I have seen lots of attractive men. As a matter of fact, I know one right now who is very interested in me. He works where I do and we have a great deal in common. He's exciting when he talks and he's interested in almost everything.

"I have a very good job and it's never dull," she continued. "I get paid well enough so that I can easily support the children, and with the child-support money the court will make him pay, I can have enough household help so that life will actually be easier than it is now. He never did make very much anyway, and he isn't very ambitious. I guess I married him because I felt a little sorry for him. It seemed like the whole world was against him and I wanted to help him. But I soon found that he really didn't want my help; he just wants to live the way he wants to.

"I really don't know what I'm doing here talking to a marriage counselor. I don't love him anymore, and it would be silly to continue the marriage. I think it would be best to get out now while I am still young and

[10]Copyright © 1965 by Jo Coudert, from p. 200 of the book *Advice from a Failure.* Reprinted with permission of Stein and Day/Publishers and Hodder and Stoughton.

still attractive and can easily get another husband if I want to. If we went on living together, we would just compound our problems and might even have more children to hurt when we finally did separate."

Now his side of the story: "She's got that fancy job and all sorts of social life at the office where she works," he said. "She's constantly nagging me to do things that I don't want to do and, believe me, it's just plain hell. I'm not opposed to going out if there's any good reason for going. But she doesn't want to do the things I want to do, like going to football games. I'd even take her to her stupid old operas once in a while, but that isn't enough for her. She says I have to enjoy it or it isn't worthwhile for her. I want a good old-fashioned wife who stays home and takes care of the kids and lets me do the providing. Instead, I get a wife who wants to go out all the time and expects me to come home and help her with the housework.

"You know," he went on, "she wasn't at all like this when we were going together. She let me think that she wanted to do all the things that I wanted to do, and that all she wanted to do in life was to help me. I still love her and I love my children. I don't want a divorce."

In how many different situations has Margaret used the excuse of doing something because it was easier or simpler? Where might she have gotten this pattern? How did John and Margaret get such differing views about marriage? How can a "try-and-see" attitude be disastrous in a marriage?

How do the following generalizations about human behavior apply in this case?

When a relationship becomes both legal and inclusive of many others (in marriage and family or in an organization), then it no longer can operate on simple rules.

When a complex relationship is entered into with no preparation for skills management, then catastrophe is probably inevitable.

When the culture relaxes its unwritten codes about marriage and divorce, people also tend to relax personal responsibility for a better relationship.

When a person has been reinforced many times for the same behavior, that behavior tends to continue.

THE EFFECT OF CHANGING FAMILY FUNCTIONS

Of the many social changes that have affected people's determination to stay married, none is more important than the loss of the traditional family functions. It is classic among family sociologists to point out that the family has lost or greatly diminished its production function, its educational function, its protective function, and much of its recreational, governmental, and child-care function.[11]

Practically everything consumed in the family in our early agricultural society was produced in the family—food, clothing, and shelter. Today, however, relatively little is produced in the urban or suburban family, except on a hobby basis. Sewing, baking, and woodworking, which used to be regular responsibilities of the family members, have now been turned over to bakers and manufacturers. Today, the bread mixes and do-it-yourself kits are often more recreational than functional.

The educational function has also dwindled to a shadow of its former self. Formal education has been turned over to the school, and vocational education is now often the responsibility of industry. In this technological age, very few parents are equipped to prepare their sons and daughters for the profession in which they will earn their living. Religious education has been turned over to the church (if, indeed, the child gets any religious training whatsoever). Even family-life education, including sex education, has tended to become a province of other institutions because of family default in this area.

There has been a transfer of the protective function outside the family as well. In the early days, the father protected the family from intruders, human and animal, with his rifle, and the mother's home remedies were the only protection the family had against disease. Without police and without many doctors, this was the way it had to be. Now, most families rely almost exclusively on outside professionals for their protection.

The extent to which the family has forsworn its recreational function is debatable. Those who romanticize the "good old days" insist that almost all family recreation occurred in or near the bosom of the home. They think of the nostalgic scene of father and mother and all the children singing around the old parlor piano. It is undoubtedly true that, because of the difficulties in transportation and the sparsity of neighbors, much of the rec-

---

[11]William F. Ogburn authored the best-known exposition of the loss of functions in the American family and the dilemma that was thereby caused. He postulated seven lost functions—economic, status-giving, educational, religious, recreational, protective, and affectional—and indicated that only the affectional remains vigorous in modern times. Recently Clark Vincent pointed out that Ogburn probably had in mind that it was the *traditional content and form* of the functions that were lost; the basic functions themselves were merely changed. For example, the economic production function was changed to the economic consumption function. See Clark E. Vincent, "Mental Health and the Family," *Journal of Marriage and the Family*, **29** (February, 1967), 18–39.

reation did take place in the family. However, in the urban complexes that developed after 1800, there was a considerable amount of visiting to the public house by the male adults and a considerable amount of group activity among the children. In the early twentieth century, as public transportation developed and as such public recreation facilities as the movies began to spring up, more family members sought recreation outside the home.

Since the advent of television and the thirty-five-hour workweek, the typical family (not including the teenagers, who generally want to get away by themselves) may be spending more time at home than they used to. This is not to say that they are spending that time together: They may have three or four different television sets going in different rooms, or they may each be enjoying separate activities. At any rate, the typical modern family is not going to the movies or visiting with friends as much as it was a few decades ago.

Those who do enjoy going outside the home for recreation are doing so much more frequently than formerly, a trend initiated by the two- or multi-car family and encouraged by the wide variety of recreational enterprises available. Attendance at all sporting events is up enormously. This may be accounted for in part by prosperity among socioeconomic groups who formerly could not afford to do anything but sit at home. Moreover, the automobile makes possible quick and easy transportation to the many commercial recreation sites. Various family studies have indicated that the "most enjoyable" recreation for the family is recreation outside the home.

In addition to maintaining and protecting its children, the family has a major function in socializing them. In some parts of the world, however, there is a trend toward more and more public upbringing. Although this is not yet a significant trend in the United States, here there is a tendency toward the lengthening of school hours and the establishment of preschools, day-care centers, and federally sponsored programs that provide both education and outside-the-home care for the children of working mothers. In many communities, because of this lengthening of the school day, outside-the-home feeding has become a part of public education.

Another function of the American family that has changed considerably is the governmental function. As in most other societies, the American family is the first social group exercising control over the individual. However, American families now generally impose fewer restrictions on their offspring than before and deliberately allow them more independence. In part, this may be caused by parental reaction to the confusion over what is right and what is wrong in child rearing, but in part it may be an effort to train children to make decisions and so become self-reliant. Whatever the cause, the immediate effect is apparent: American boys and girls have much more independence and much less control than they did previously.

FUNCTIONS WHICH HAVE BEEN ENLARGED

The same series of technological changes that have diminished the need for some of the traditional functions of the family have also increased the need for other functions. For example, the *executive* function of the family has been enormously increased in recent years. Although it is no longer necessary for the family to produce goods in a direct way, it is now very necessary to plan consumption and make a myriad of quantity and quality decisions.

William Goode has pointed to the family's *mediating* function, in which the family is a buffer between the individual and the larger society. Clark Vincent has suggested that the family has an *adaptive* function. He sees the family as being an important agent for translating the demands of other social institutions into the child socialization process.[12] Vincent points out that because the family lacks the institutional organization with which to resist changes thrust upon it, it must adapt itself and help its members to adapt to a changing society.

It seems reasonable to speculate, however, that the greatest proportionate increase in family function in recent years has been in the affectional function. In our modern, tension-filled society with fewer primary group contacts (that is, contacts with family friends, neighbors, and relatives), the family has in some case become a greater source of solace, comfort, and vital personal attention. Today American men have their wives as friends to a degree that is unusual throughout the rest of the world. In other times and in other places, men more often sought companionship not at home but in the local pub or in the boudoirs of their mistresses. The affectional relationship, both romantic and companionate, is now a major function and cohesive force that provides the determination to hold most American families together.

There are those who believe that the family is finished as a social institution. Barrington Moore contends that the family is no longer function-

---

[12]William J. Goode, *The Family*, Englewood Cliffs, N.J., Prentice-Hall, 1964, p. 2; and Clark E. Vincent, "Family Spongia: The Adaptive Function," *Journal of Marriage and the Family*, **28** (February, 1966), 29–36, reprinted in Joan S. Delora and Jack Delora, eds., *Intimate Life Styles: Marriage and Its Alternatives*, Pacific Palisades, Calif., Goodyear, 1972, pp. 173–184.

ally necessary and that it is probably dysfunctional in a modern industrial society.[13] He thinks that the current theories of the survival of the family are merely projections of middle-class hopes. Since kinship is obsolete, says Moore, there is no longer any obligation to give affection, and there is no reason to fear the transfer of responsibility for the children from parents to professionals. He argues that aristocrats have always turned the responsibility of child rearing over to servants; now, in this age, it is possible for all of us to be aristocrats.

Moore has few followers in modern social thought. Although the experts agree that the family has changed and will continue to change, most authorities see the family as a continuing institution in our society. In fact, there are some who believe that in our modern, computerized, impersonal society, it is more important than ever that each person have someone who is loyally committed to him and who will provide warmth, acceptance, and understanding. Robert Coombs points out that most people desperately need someone who will bandage up a bruised ego at the end of a day and who will genuinely believe that "you must have been right; it was he who was wrong."[14] It is even more satisfactory when the loyal companion is of the opposite sex and the relationship is enriched by the warmth of sexual love. And there is still greater richness when a man and woman have the mutual satisfaction of overcoming difficult problems in guiding dependent children. It is very improbable that Moore or anyone else is going to find an emotionally significant substitute for the biologically and culturally conditioned affectional function in the near future.

A FINAL NOTE ON DETERMINATION

Toward the end of the report of their monumental study, *Sexual Behavior in the Human Male,* Dr. Kinsey and his associates swing away from their in-depth analysis of sexual behavior long enough to make a revealing comment—almost an aside—on marriage. After having examined 6000 marital histories and nearly 3000 divorce histories, and after having laboriously recorded 544 pages of technical data, the sex researchers agree that their research "suggests that there may be nothing more important in a marriage than a determination that it shall persist. With such a determination, indi-

---

[13]Barrington Moore, *Political Power and Social Theory,* Cambridge, Mass., Harvard University Press, 1958, pp. 160–178.
[14]Robert Coombs, "Problems in Mate Selection," address to the Seminar on Family Problems, University of North Carolina, Greensboro, N.C., June, 1968.

viduals force themselves to adjust and to accept situations which would seem sufficient grounds for break-up, if the continuation of the marriage were not the prime objective."[15]

The importance of determination in making marriages successful would be hard to overestimate. A great many successfully married people have reported that, if it were not for a rugged determination on the part of both partners to make it succeed, their marriages would have failed.

What is determination and how do you learn to be determined? Determination is characteristic of those people who have been reinforced to stand pat or stick to a job. It is also characteristic of people who see marriage with all its problems as being less bad than the alternatives. Determination may hold, however, only so long as there is cultural support for determined behavior. Determination to stay married may have less reinforcement than it used to. In fact many expectations in marriage have changed over the years. Those changes are discussed in the following chapter.

[15]Alfred C. Kinsey, W. B. Pomeroy, and C. E. Martin, *Sexual Behavior in the Human Male*, Philadelphia, Saunders, 1948, p. 544.

3
EXPECTATIONS IN MARRIAGE

Despite the present dedication to the pursuit of happiness in marriage, many people appear to lose satisfaction when they marry. Understanding why this is so becomes much simpler if you accept one postulate: In order to achieve satisfaction in anything (and especially in marriage), you must first know what you expect, and also what is expected of you; then you must do what is expected better than others expected you could. If too much is expected, if what is expected of you is not made clear, or even if not enough is expected, it is not probable that you will get very much satisfaction. All three of these conditions—too-great expectations, confused expectations, and inadequate expectations—are present in modern marriage and family relationships. We will take a look at each of them in turn. (See the Appendix for generalizations about human behavior.)

TOO-GREAT EXPECTATIONS

Most young men have always had to compete with a variety of fantasy heroes for their true love's affection. But in the past, the competition has never been as it is now. Today the typical young husband is constantly compared to the best athlete's manliness and the finest gentleman's manners. Television and the broad contacts of modern social living make this inevitable. Unhappily, however, relatively few of our young males can consistently stand up to this kind of comparison. Although this expectation problem usually develops after marriage, it has its roots in childhood and adolescence, when some of the marriage expectations are formed.

This very evening, for example, millions of girls and young women all over the country will watch the latest television hero perform in an idealized setting and act in a manner deliberately calculated to stir emotions. As they watch, these young women will be developing attitudes and ideals. They will be consciously or unconsciously developing expectations about the men they will marry and the marriages they will have. In these fantasies, *their* men will have all the resoluteness, decisiveness, intelligence, perception, good looks, and desirable attributes of the girls' fathers. Almost imperceptibly these dreams will become internalized—that is, they will become fixed expectations—whether the girls know it or not.

Clearly, it is not only television that creates all the expectations, nor is it only females who develop unrealistic expectations. All over the country tonight young men will watch glamorous television heroines and will dream about the wives they will one day have. *Their* wives will be paragons of beauty, charm, poise, and elegance; they will be sweet, kind, tender, and loving, and, in addition, they will have unquestioned skills as homemakers, mothers, and sex partners. They will also be fine cooks, appliance mechanics, chauffeurs, purchasing agents, accountants, child psychologists, and psychiatrists for their husbands. Moreover, they will be warm and tender, submissive, agreeable, and adaptable, and their goals in life will be to fulfill their husbands' every wish.

The fact that these attitudes and expectations are acquired in childhood increases the importance of their effect on later satisfaction in marriage, for childhood expectations—like childhood attitudes and values—have a way of becoming conditioned to the point where they attain emotional dominance over later intellectual learning. By the time many young people are in high school, their expectations for the roles and behaviors of their prospective mates are already established.

Marie Dunn, in her study of high-school boys and girls, found that in her sample it was not uncommon for high-school boys to have expectations of how their wives would behave that differed markedly from the way in which girls in the same high school expected to behave as wives. Likewise, the girls had expectations of the way their husbands would behave different from the boys' expectations of how they would behave as husbands.[1] Obviously, the seeds of marital discord were already planted.

Discrepancies in role expectations will affect a marriage, but Wesley Burr found that it is not the mere fact that there is a discrepancy. Rather it is the importance placed on the discrepancy that makes the difference.[2]

If television were the only source of internalized attitudes, its effect might be only to create similarly unrealistic expectations in both boys and girls, because both would be exposed to some of the same playacting. But expectations derive from a randomly ordered combination of highly emotional attitudes and values gained from one's family living *and* peer-group experiences, as well as from the world of make-believe. An overindulgent family, for example, can create as many—if not more—unrealistically high expectations as can the picture tube and the printed word.

How expectations affect marriage

Often, marriage dissolution starts with the early disenchantment that results when a partner first discovers that his mate is incapable of meeting his expectations. Peter Pineo has pointed out that men often suffer dis-

---

[1]Marie S. Dunn, "Marriage Role Expectations of Adolescents," *Marriage and Family Living,* **22** (May, 1960), 99–104.
[2]Wesley R. Burr, "An Expansion and Test of a Role Theory of Marital Satisfaction," *Journal of Marriage and the Family,* **33** (May, 1971), 368–372.

enchantment earlier in marriage than women, perhaps because their expectations are more unrealistic in the first place. But which is the first to be disillusioned is unimportant. Sooner or later one partner's disillusionment will affect the other, and the entire relationship will suffer.[3]

If disenchantment is seen as almost inevitable, then there must be some antecedents to this disenchantment. People who become aware of the cause-effect relationship and who change the causes, and ultimately the effect, are the ones who gain by "planning the unplannable."[4] That is, they plan to alleviate those things which are not yet there.

In this same general vein there seems to be an overrepresentation of beautiful women wanting counseling for marriage problems. The hypothesis was developed that the plain or average-looking young women might have possessed more realistic expectations of what the marriage relationship would provide them in terms of attention from *one* husband, because before marriage they had not been accustomed to a great deal of attention from large numbers of males.

DOWNGRADED MARRIAGE ROLES

Satisfactions in marriage have been decreased, not only by unrealistically high expectations, but also by the downgrading of the respective roles of husbands and wives. The typical young father today, while still having responsibility for the welfare of the family, often finds that he has responsibility without much authority. His pride in being a "good provider," which was a strong motivating force in bygone generations, has been undermined by a frantic effort to "keep up with the Joneses." This is always a frustrating game, because there are always higher-statused Joneses to keep up with.

Many young fathers have also lost the ego-building satisfaction of knowing more than anyone else in the family. Today the wife is liable to have had more schooling than her husband, and even in well-educated families, the children are often better informed than the parents, as a result of watching television and the increasing emphasis in the schools on current events and social problems.

The status of many young fathers today might well be summed up in the tongue-in-cheek statement of the teenage girl who said, "We always try to make Father feel as if he were a member of the family."

[3]Peter C. Pineo, "Disenchantment in the Later Years of Marriage," *Marriage and Family Living,* **23** (February, 1961), 3–11.

[4]Hilda S. Krech, "Housewife and Woman? The Best of Both Worlds," in Marcia E. Lasswell and Thomas E. Lasswell, eds., *Love, Marriage, Family: A Developmental Approach,* Glenview, Ill., Scott, Foresman, 1973, pp. 309–318.

Within the same society that has downgraded the role of the husband and father, there has been a simultaneous upgrading of both the status and the rewards of the bachelor life. In colonial times, bachelors had a comparatively greater disadvantage economically. Not only did they not have wives to help them, they were even taxed for being bachelors.

Not so today. Now the marriage resister is apt to have a plush apartment and an easy life with multiple rewards, both economic and biologic, unavailable to the married man. Once scorned, the bachelor is now envied not only by married men but by young women as well. Even though some of his pleasures may be illusory and in the long run self-defeating, his way of life represents something of a threat to the American marriage tradition.

The wife-mother role

The role of being *just* a wife and mother has also been downgraded. Some of the neofeminists complain that a smaller percentage of college women are now getting advanced degrees, a smaller percentage want full-time careers, and many more educated women appear to be settling for the traditional wife-mother role. This is true. But it is also true that being "just a housewife" is still somewhat demeaning.

In recent times, an increasing number of women have been able to combine homemaking with outside employment. In 1920, only about one-third of the women working outside the home were married; today about two-thirds are. How many of these women are really more satisfied and "fulfilled" because they work outside the home? Those who have stimulating professional jobs and cooperative husbands may have found additional satisfaction. But there are millions of other women with routine jobs in offices, factories, laundries, and restaurants who dislike working and who feel guilty because they may be doing a less-than-adequate job at home besides. For these women, the "feminine mystique" has a very hollow ring. On the other hand, women who do not work outside the home often suffer a loneliness for adult social interaction as they find themselves tied down to a small apartment or house with one or more young children, day after day, and week after week.

Moreover, some direct satisfactions have now been eliminated from homemaking. For example, the joy of competing for blue ribbons at the county fair is now limited to a small proportion of the population. Even the competitive satisfaction of being the first woman on the block to get the wash out on the line on Monday mornings has been eliminated by the automatic dryer.

Thus, as the expectation of the role that the other person will play in modern marriage has greatly increased, often the satisfaction that is provided by one's own role in marriage has considerably diminished for both sexes. This is not to say that there are not many creative partnerships in which the partners have found increasing satisfaction. There are. But these days this requires both more realistic expectations and more creative initiative from both oneself and one's mate.

In addition to too-great expectations of the marriage partner's performance and too-great expectations of one's own role satisfactions, in recent years difficulty has resulted from too-great expectations of marriage itself. Some individuals expect marriage to provide the happiness that they have never before had in their lives. In many cases, young people go into marriage expecting that they will find new freedom, or new security, or an escape from whatever problems had plagued them before marriage. Usually, though, such people find that marriage only adds to their problems. Marriage is a status, not a cure. It provides an opportunity to give love; it is not a remedy for unhappiness.

CONFUSED EXPECTATIONS

Social roles have been changing so rapidly that it is sometimes difficult to identify what are the proper expectations for role performance. This, too, diminishes satisfaction. For example, today many women are unsure whether or not they should work outside the home, especially if they have children. This is a far cry from the old days when woman's role was highly structured. Elizabeth Cady Stanton, Lucretia Mott, and the others who gathered in 1848 to draw up the manifesto for women's rights did not foresee that once women got the right to work outside the home they might be expected to do so most of the time. Nor did they foresee that the very need for making a choice in a world with less highly structured roles might create emotional difficulty. Today, because of confused expectations, some women feel guilty if they do work outside the home; some others feel guilty if they do not. This kind of confused expectation leads to psychological ambivalence, which, in turn, can preclude marital satisfaction.

Of all the confused role expectations that plague marriage, though, none is more difficult than the family-leadership problem. Most American women are intellectually conditioned to expect a husband to be reasonably democratic, permissive, and equalitarian. He will consult them about important matters, solicit their advice, and sometimes look to them to make decisions.

But the *emotional* conditioning of some of these same young women is very different. They grew up in homes where Father was the undisputed leader, and emotionally they are conditioned to expect that they will marry a resolute, courageous leader who will tell them what to do and make them like it. It is not that they expect the husband to be the boss because he is a man, but rather that he should earn the right to be boss by demonstrating his superior leadership ability. Not uncommonly, many of these young women give their new mates a little harder time than they need to just so that they can enjoy the feeling of his having earned the right to dominate.

Another confusion occurs from the contradictions between the early concept of the ideal family as one in which "one man and one woman should marry and contract to satisfy all of the other's emotional and physical needs" and a later verbalized approval of freedom, autonomy, independence, and occasional deviance in a family.[5] In the individual conditioned early in life to the above idealized family, "concepts of sexual infidelity were unconsciously extended to include all the personal feelings of the two individuals involving outsiders."[6] Such early conditioning to this idealized marriage supersedes the later learning of liberation of the individual and inevitably causes great emotional problems when the "liberated" man or woman finds that his or her spouse is also "liberated." This may very well be one of the greatest problems of the generation now entering marriage.

Confused expectations are often a result of one partner's not knowing why he feels the way he does about his expectations, or it can be a result of misperception of the motives of his spouse. Danny exhibits confusion as he makes his overt demands. Beverly is showing her demands but somewhat more subtly in the following case.

CASE 5 DANNY AND BEVERLY

Danny's father became an invalid when Danny was ten. This forced his mother to find a job in a factory, and led to her becoming the ruler of the household. The reversal in parental leadership upset Danny not only because it demeaned his formerly strong father, but also because he was the only person in his peer group whose mother was the boss.

Beverly's family was generally happy and healthy. They were not particularly wealthy but had enough money to be comfortable. Her mother taught school and felt fulfilled at her job. Although it was not necessary for

[5]Ray L. Birdwhitsell, "The Idealized Model of the American Family," *Social Casework*, **51** (April, 1970), 195–198.
[6]Ibid., 196–197.

her mother to work, her father saw the need for her fulfillment and cooperated in every way. Beverly's parents always believed in equal sharing even though her father made the final decisions.

"Sometimes I feel like Beverly wants to take over," complained Danny, "like this working business. The only thing she does is teach children but by looking at the number of clothes she buys, you'd think she wanted to tell the world that she is a married working woman and can get along perfectly well financially without me. Every night, she tells me about her successful day at work as if to let me know that she is as good a 'man' as I am. Not only that, but she expects me to discuss my job with her! I'm a business manager and that's one area of my life where I refuse to let her rule me with her suggestions or remarks. In my house, the woman will never be the boss; I didn't get married for competition. While we were dating, we always had fun together going swimming, hiking, and even being in charge of ten-year-olds at camp. She'd watch me play football and always cheer me to victory. We'd study together at school and encourage each other when grades got depressing. Of course I knew she was going to teach school after our marriage, but we didn't really discuss how we felt because our life seemed so perfect then."

"Danny has changed so much since we got married. I never knew he'd be like this," retorted Beverly. "I think all of the trouble started when I began to teach school. I had to buy several dresses because my college clothes were impractical for teaching and he pitched a fit. When I bought them with my own money, I didn't know he'd think I was trying to show him up! I try to tell him little things that happen at school every day so he'll become interested in my job, but it seems to irritate him. I thought a married couple was supposed to share everything but he won't even mention a word about his job to me, regardless of how many times I ask. Before we were married, he'd discuss all of his grades, hobbies, and so forth with me. I believe a wife should have a say-so in all aspects of marriage, but the way things are now, I feel very left out."

In present-day marriages, the two sets of conditioning sometimes come into conflict. Sometimes a wife wants recognition as her husband's equal in decision making and planning, and sometimes she wants him to make the decisions and carry them out. Sometimes she does not know what she wants. If she is confused, think how much more confused her husband is. If marriage partners had substantial agreement on role expectations, most marriages might be more stable than they are.

INSUFFICIENT EXPECTATIONS

In recent times, some family members have been denied satisfaction because their roles have not provided *enough* expectation. Medical doctors are familiar with cases of both men and women who, without children or responsibility, have too much leisure and too little challenge. People with too much time on their hands sometimes become introspective and may develop psychosomatic illnesses.

Although there are relatively few idle young adults in our society, there is a much larger group of family members for whom expectations are too limited to provide adequate satisfactions. In our present culture, we have no structured role for Grandmother. In other cultures and in other times, Grandmother received satisfaction in her role as household administrator, wise old counselor, or, at least, babysitter. Today, however, the young married couple usually establishes a separate household and one that may be many hundreds or even thousands of miles away from the grandparents' home. This leaves Grandmother (and sometimes Grandfather) with no role to play in the young people's household, and it leaves Grandmother, because she is often a widow, without much of a role in her own home either.

To understand the magnitude of the change in the Grandmother role, it is necessary to look back only a few generations. As recently as a hundred years ago, the typical woman married at about age twenty-two. She had her children more or less spaced throughout her childbearing period. Because of high mortality rates, and because the last child was often born late in her childbearing years, the typical mother frequently died before her last child left home. She had the structured role of mother right up to the end of her days.

In recent times, however, the typical woman has married at about age twenty, has had her two or three children early in marriage, and is through childbearing by age twenty-six. She is a grandmother by age forty-four. She then has a life expectancy of some thirty years, of which for the last eight or ten she will probably be a widow.

How to get satisfaction in this last thirty-year period is a problem that is causing many women great difficulty. One answer is, of course, to go to work outside the home. The large increase in employed women in recent years has resulted in great part from the needs of young grandmothers.

But the kinds of work outside the home for which older homemakers are qualified, because they often have neither the education nor the experience with which to compete with career women in the business world, are often unacceptable to them. Volunteer work is always a possibility, but it can have the appearance of routine busywork. Until our society finds some more creative use for their talents and energies, many of our younger grandmothers are going to want for feelings of satisfaction and of fulfillment.

Another major group to miss satisfaction because of not enough role expectation is the children. Years ago, when children were working members of the family team with the full knowledge that they were helping to provide for the common welfare, there was far more opportunity for them to develop the adult-type satisfaction. Today, satisfaction through achievement, if any, is more often associated with activities outside the home, such as athletics, schoolwork, and recreational groups.

In today's child-centered homes, the child is often delegated the role of family pet, with the expectation that his major satisfaction will come from receiving *things*. As parents lavish more and more material things on their children, the children learn to get all of their satisfactions from receiving. In addition, the children see on television and read in magazines that marriage is a wonderful state from which they will one day *receive* additional satisfactions. When they grow up and marry someone who was conditioned in the same way, both partners expect that they will continue to *receive* satisfactions as a result of the behaviors of their mate. But, as has been pointed out earlier, marriage is a *giving* relationship. Unless either one or both of this newly married pair learns to make the transition from getting satisfactions through receiving to getting satisfactions through giving, their marriage is in trouble. It is conceivable that a man or woman who does not need to get married to fulfill himself or herself will make the best marriage partner.

THE MARRIAGE PARTNERS' DIFFERING EXPECTATIONS

Too-great expectations, confused expectations, and not enough expectations are only a part of the expectations problem in modern marriage. Of equal importance is the problem of the *differing* expectations that the partners bring to the marriage relationship. These differing expectations sometimes cause not only misunderstanding, but also a complete lack of understanding between the marriage partners.

Because of the differential conditioning given male and female children, men and women have always had a difficult time understanding each other's behavior in the marriage relationship. It is not unusual for a young man to say to the marriage counselor, "I don't understand the woman I married. She expects me to do things for her that she could easily do for herself, she expects me to do things for her that she hasn't told me she wanted me to do, and sometimes, in fact, she expects me to do things for her that she has denied she wanted done." One young man described being away from his new bride on a business trip. Each night he called her from the city where he was staying. One night she said to him, "Now let's try and save money so that I can go with you on the next trip. Don't call me tomorrow night. All right?" The young man, pleased with his wife's thrift and foresight, agreed. When he did call her two days later, she was angry. Why was she angry? He hadn't called her the night before!

The classic example of this kind of behavior is often seen in the sexual relationship. Typically the young man complains to the marriage counselor that he does not understand the woman he married. "I wanted to make love to her last night and she rejected me. So, being a considerate fellow, I turned over and tried to go to sleep. Then she sat up crying half the night." When the marriage counselor talks with the young lady, she claims that she should have been so irresistibly fascinating that he would have persisted despite any obstacles she put in his path. "Obviously," she said, "he doesn't love me enough."

The young man was quite right when he said he did not understand her. He did not understand the conditioning that made persistent reassurances of her desirability so important to his wife. This conditioned need, in its extreme form, causes some young women to continually be asking their husbands, "Do you love me?" or "Are you sure you still love me?" It is a product of competition in the love-oriented society that most girls experience. To be successful is to be loved and to be irresistibly desirable. The young man has not ordinarily experienced this kind of security-need to the same degree. And to add to the difficulties, the woman has learned that "true love" means that the man never thinks of another woman in any way.

Lack of understanding of the opposite sex is by no means limited to men. Often a marriage counselor will see a young woman who will say, "I don't understand the man I married. He went out and bought a brand-new automobile when we could hardly pay for the good car we already had."

What she is saying in effect is that she does not understand the depth and extent of conditioned need for prestige and the symbols of success that were built into that particular young man in the success-oriented male society. Perhaps if she had been raised as a boy in his home she would have understood it. But she was not. This is what the empathetic approach is all about.

This kind of lack of understanding between men and women probably goes back to the caveman, but social change has given it a new dimension. In our mobile, cosmopolitan society, people are marrying other people from widely differing backgrounds—differing nationality backgrounds, differing ethnic backgrounds, differing religious backgrounds, differing socio-economic backgrounds. Each partner brings to the marriage not only his conditioned male or female expectations, but also an entire series of internalized customs, attitudes, and values that are sometimes extremely important to him emotionally whether he is aware of it or not. Yet these customs, attitudes, and values may be so foreign to his mate that they are looked upon as silly whims or notions that are quite unreasonable.

CASE 6 SUSAN AND RUDOLPH

"I've been married to Susan for seven years," Rudolph said to the marriage counselor, "and in all that time she's never been able to hold on to a nickel for more than a few hours at a time. Money goes through her hands like water, and she can't save either. She won't even mend a rip in a torn sheet!"

When the counselor talked to Susan, she said, "Rudolph is the cheapest, the tightest, the most miserly man there ever was. Why, he even expects me to mend torn sheets! Can you imagine that?"

Rudolph volunteered the following information: He was the son of a widowed mother from New England. He grew up with his four brothers in a small, semirural community whose values were "use it up, wear it out, make it do." His mother constantly impressed upon the developing consciousness of her five boys that a good husband—not a wastrel and a profligate like their late father had been—should save his money for the inevitable rainy day.

In due course, Rudolph grew up, went into the army, was sent to California, and there met and very quickly married the happy-go-lucky daughter of a happy-go-lucky Glendale family. In Susan's neighborhood "gracious living" was an important value. The popular attitude was "spend your money, that's what it's for." It was important to keep up with the Joneses. Moreover, those people who did spend (sometimes beyond their means) for houses often made a substantial profit in the California real-estate market and therefore had even more money to spend.

"But I'm only trying to save it for my family's future," Rudolph said emphatically. Susan pleaded, "We are entitled to some kind of adequate living now when we are young enough to enjoy it."

Which philosophy do you ascribe to? When the goals of a marriage are to live together in a relatively satisfactory way, why do specific avenues for reaching these goals make so much difference? Empathize with the person whose philosophy is most different from your own.

How do the following generalizations about human behavior apply in this case? (See the Appendix.)

When people are conditioned to respond in discriminant ways to specific situations, it is difficult for them to generalize these responses to other situations.

When people are faced with a situation that differs from their internalized beliefs, they attempt to change either the situation or the belief.

Although Susan and Rudolph came from very different sections of the country, this regional difference is often far less important in the United States culture than the attitudes of the family in which the marriage partner grew up. Consider the following case:

CASE 7 JOE AND CAROLYN

Joe and Carolyn were both from Illinois. Joe was the son of a prosperous downstate farmer. Joe had three brothers. The men in his family worked hard. When they wanted recreation, they went off together for days at a time hunting and fishing.

Joe's mother was a hard-working farm wife who took pride in keeping the house spotless. She left all the decisions to her husband. Joe's father was the boss, and she wanted it that way. Spending decisions were made on the basis of what was the best for the farm without overspending.

Joe went off to the University of Illinois after he had completed his army service. There he met Carolyn, the daughter of a Chicago banker. They fell in love and were married.

Carolyn had grown up in a large, well-appointed suburban home. In her family, "recreation" meant that Father and Mother would go off to the theater or a concert together, and the children would gather for Ping-Pong or tennis at a friend's house. Father consulted Mother on the major decisions and often accepted her suggestions on what should be done. Spending the family income was never much of a problem, although Father sometimes did have difficulty in deciding which was the better investment opportunity.

Joe and Carolyn had been married only seven months when she came to see the marriage counselor. They had had a fight, and Joe had left home two weeks before. She wanted the counselor's help in inducing Joe to return. Joe talked to the counselor reluctantly. "I sure don't want to go back now, and I'm not sure that I ever do," he said. "Our honeymoon came to an abrupt end early last fall when I wanted to go off on a few days' hunting trip with my brother. 'What!' she screamed. 'You're going to leave me at home all by myself?' In the end I didn't go; it wasn't worth it to fight with her. But now I kick myself all over the place. I should have been man enough to go anyway. She wants to control me. I can't go out with a friend for a glass of beer by myself. She always wants to know how much money I have, and she thinks she ought to manage the checkbook. That isn't right. And even if it were right, I couldn't trust her with it. She spends money for almost anything. She went downtown and bought a coat at a fancy specialty shop and paid $150 for it when they had the same coat—I swear it was the same coat—at Sears for $85. Why should I go back to that?"

When Carolyn came back to see the counselor, she cried profusely. "I just don't understand it," she said. "He doesn't even want to talk to me about it. Do you think it was right for him to go away and leave me in a strange house all by myself after we'd been married just three weeks? I don't like hunting (that is, I don't think I like hunting, though I've never been), but the least he could have done was to offer to take me along. Besides, it wasn't only those two days. Sometimes he's away for a whole evening when he's just told me he's going to see a friend for a few minutes. And then he doesn't want to explain where he's been when he comes back. I admit that I'm not a fussy housekeeper, but I do a lot of volunteer work at the Junior League, and he doesn't even want to help me with the housework.

"I know he thinks I'm extravagant," she continued. "But it pays to buy a good thing. That coat I bought will last me for years, and a cheap coat would have fit me poorly and gone out of style quickly. I want you to try to make him understand."

Why is the selection of a specific but different way to relieve one's tension such a threat to another person? Compare your method with Joe's and Carolyn's. How can people fail to get a full picture of each other's views on life when both are on a college campus? Why is it expected by society that a person will change after marriage? How can the discrepancy of differing expectations before and after marriage be explained?

ROLE THEORY AND SYMBOLIC INTERACTION

The theory that differing role expectations account for all or most of the difficulties in marriage has fascinated sociologists for many years. One of the early expressions of marital role theory was by Leonard Cottrell.

. . . Marriage adjustment may be regarded as a process in which marriage partners attempt to re-enact certain relational systems or situations which were obtained in their own earlier family groups. . . . Maladjusted marriages may be regarded as the results of the failure of the marriage situation to provide the system of relationships called for by the roles which the marriage partners bring to the marriage.[7]

Many theoretical ideas in role theory were integrated with empirical research by Wesley Burr.[8] He concluded that ease of role transitions is related to availability of resources either to begin or stop taking a particular role. For example, if a person must move from the role of nonparent to parent, then the resources that would aid this transition are knowledge of infant development, experience in child care, knowledge of the need to keep the husband-wife relationship viable, and sufficient resources (money or people) to give the parents some time free from child care. It is also believed that indefiniteness about the role of parents is a detrimental factor in making the transition. In addition, when parents have differing conceptions of the parent role, it is more difficult to take that role.

Equally as important is the transition out of a role such as from child to adult. For example, the skipping of the single independent adult stage may make the transition from the child-at-home role to the marriage role difficult. However, the lack of role clarity for the single independent female is causing much role conflict among both men and women.

Closely related to this role theory of marital adjustment is the sociologic conceptual framework of *symbolic interactionism*.[9] The interactionists make important use of the individual's "self-concept" and "definition of the situation," in addition to his perception of marital roles. In general, it is postulated that the greater the congruence of the perceptions that each partner has of himself and his marriage roles with the perceptions of his mate, the more satisfactory the marriage.

Testing these concepts, A. R. Mangus hypothesized that marriage problems resulted from the presence or absence of "harmony, consistency, and congruity among the role expectations of those participating in mar-

[7]Leonard S. Cottrell, Jr., "Roles and Marital Adjustment," *Publications of the American Sociological Society*, **27** (May, 1933), 109.

[8]Wesley Burr, "Role Transitions: A Reformation of Theory," *Journal of Marriage and the Family*, **34** (August, 1972), 407–416.

[9]As Sheldon Stryker suggests, there is some disagreement over the exact differentiation between "role theory" and "symbolic interaction theory." Some writers use them interchangeably; other writers insist on distinction. Stryker has an excellent chapter for the interested student on "The Interactional and Situational Approaches" in Harold T. Christensen, ed., *Handbook of Marriage and the Family*, Skokie, Ill., Rand McNally, 1964, pp. 125–170.

riage." He concluded that "It is believed that the most pressing, inter-personal problems in marriage arise out of the disparities among the role concepts and self concepts that are pertinent to the marriage situation."[10]

Eleanore Luckey reported that in her studies she had indeed found a significant and positive association between marital satisfaction and the congruence of perceptions of self and the perception of self by spouse.[11] Robert Williamson went even further. He said: "In fact divorce may be considered basically the outcome of role conflicts. There is a breakdown in the image of the other person and in his or her ability to personify the role desired."[12]

Recently it has been noted that the postulate of greater congruence of the perceptions of partners may vary differentially for men and women. Marital happiness, in Robert Stuckert's study, seemed to have a greater association with the similarity between the husband's own role concepts and his wife's expectations of him than a congruence of the wife's own role concepts and her perception of her husband's expectations of her.[13]

Bernard Murstein[14] and Richard Klemer[15] both found evidence that self-concept is related to accurate role perception and eventual satisfactory progress in relationships. Murstein found that the more positive self-concept a person has, the more likely he is to perceive his own and the other's roles accurately. Klemer would agree with this in that self-concept seems to be positively correlated with mate selection, which affects later adequacy in role taking. An adequate self-concept is so important that the entire next chapter is devoted to the importance of personality.

[10]A. R. Mangus, "Role Theory and Marriage Counseling," *Social Forces*, **35** (March, 1957), 206.

[11]Eleanore Luckey, "Marital Satisfaction and Its Association with Congruence of Perception," *Marriage and Family Living*, **22** (February, 1960), 49–54.

[12]Robert C. Williamson, *Marriage and Family Relations*, 2nd ed., New York, Wiley, 1972, p. 522.

[13]Robert P. Stuckert, "Role Perception and Marital Satisfaction—A Configurational Approach," in Lasswell and Lasswell, eds., op. cit., pp. 377–380.

[14]Bernard I. Murstein, "Stimulus-Value-Role: A Theory of Marital Choice," *Journal of Marriage and the Family*, **32** (August, 1970), 465–481.

[15]Richard H. Klemer, "Self-Esteem and College Dating Experience as Factors in Mate Selection and Marital Happiness: A Longitudinal Study," *Journal of Marriage and the Family*, **33** (February, 1971), 183–187.

4

THE IMPORTANCE OF PERSONALITY IN RELATIONSHIPS

It sometimes appears that the concept of unmet role expectations may be stretched to cover any malfunction in human relationships, especially in marriage. It could be said, for instance, that a wife who divorced her alcoholic husband did so because he did not meet her social expectation, that a husband who left his frigid wife did so because she did not meet his sexual expectation.

Frequently, there is more to it than this. "Expectation" usually connotes accurate awareness by the individual of his own motivations and attitudes. But not everyone really knows why he behaves the way he does, because some behavior is directed by unconscious feelings and conflicts. For example, a wife who urges her husband to take a Sunday afternoon nap because this satisfies her unconscious need to feel martyred would find it hard to define her unmet expectation. She probably could not tell you whether she "expects" that a wife should play the role of a self-abnegating helpmeet who is subservient to her husband's pleasures or whether she "expects" that a husband should be an energetic, aggressive fellow who will not take naps on Sunday afternoon even if he is urged to do so.

When unconscious needs are involved, as they often are, it is important to look beyond the individual's present role expectations to those patterns of thinking and behaving that formed his personality. The concepts of role expectation and personality needs exist side by side, and, in any one case, one concept may provide a more satisfactory explanation of the situation than another.

Personality is the configuration of an individual's characteristics and behaviors. It is the pattern of thinking, feeling, and behaving that usually (but not always) predetermines and preselects an individual's way of adjusting to the pleasures, frustrations, and insults of living. Some marriages result in the harmonious synchronization of two personalities. Some marriages exist in spite of (or, as we shall see later, perhaps *because* of) the differing personalities of the partners. Some marriages are torn apart by the irreconcilable attitudes and living patterns of the marriage mates. To understand the working of any marriage relationship, it is necessary to know something of the personalities of the individuals concerned.

THE IMPORTANCE OF PHYSICAL STRUCTURE IN THE DEVELOPMENT OF PERSONALITY

Personality develops from physical structure, cultural conditioning, and unique individual experience. Any human being's physical structure affects his personality in several ways. Characteristics such as the ability to talk and smile permit him to develop the individual expressiveness that promotes the differential reactions of other people to him and thus initiates the process of personality development. Equally as important are the basic physical needs—to eat, to sleep, and, later, to have sexual activity—that each person is born with. The individual's unique adaptation to these physical needs both conditions and may be conditioned by his personality. Thus, while some people are grouchy because they are hungry, there are others who eat because they are unhappy.

Another way that physical structure affects personality is through the individual differences in bodily activity that result from one's genetic structure. For example, a man who has inherited an unusually active thyroid gland from his great-grandfather will be more active than other people and will tend to have a lively temperament. If, on the other hand, he has inherited an underactive thyroid from his great-grandmother, he may well be a lethargic and submissive personality type. A person who inherits a tendency toward dyspepsia may have a low frustration tolerance and thus a grouchy disposition.

Still another way in which physical structure affects personality is through body image. (See the Appendix for generalizations about human behavior from a self-concept and perception point of view.) In our culture, a tall, lean, athletic man usually will have greater feelings of self-respect than his short, fat, clumsy neighbor. These feelings often help the athletic-type male to have better relationships with other men as well as with women, who admire not only his physique and athletic ability but also his self-confidence.[1]

Types of body build and consequent social relationships condition personality even in the child. J. R. Staffieri and Boyd McCandless reported in 1966 that even some four-year-old children know what their body build is. If it is short and thick, they tend to describe it unfavorably and in a socially rejecting way.[2] The theory of body image and its effect on the development of personality was developed by William H. Sheldon.[3]

Body image can be even more important to a female. A beautiful girl will develop a different personality from a plain girl. She may also have living experiences that make her life a much more pleasant one and conse-

[1]Ellen Berscheid, Elaine Walster, and George Bohmstedt, "Body Image," *Psychology Today*, **7** (November, 1973), 119–131.

[2]J. R. Staffieri and Boyd R. McCandless, "A Study of Social Stereotype of Body Image in Children," paper presented at the fiftieth annual meeting of the American Educational Research Association, Chicago, February, 1966.

[3]Calvin S. Hall and Gardner Lindsey, *Theories of Personality*, 2nd ed., New York, Wiley, 1970, pp. 338–379.

quently make her personality more pleasing. A beautiful girl may also feel so sufficiently admired that she can afford to reject compromises with her value system.

THE IMPORTANCE OF CULTURE

The second major influence on the development of personality is the culture in which the person grows up. This includes both the large national or regional culture and the subculture of the family unit.

A classic example of the effect of culture on personality is the legend about Quaker parents traveling in New Guinea who became separated from their infant son. The child was found and raised by a tribe of headhunters. Would the boy turn out to be a gentle Quaker or a headhunter? The answer is obvious: He became a headhunter, with all the aggressive personality characteristics of his foster family. A Japanese girl is taught to be submissive and self-abnegating, whereas a middle-class American girl is taught to be independent and self-expressing. The effect of these cultural conditionings on the personalities of the individual concerned is both large and relatively permanent.

Within the larger national culture we have many subcultures that have an important role in the development of any child's personality. A boy from a disadvantaged group may learn to be aggressive in order to exist in the slum; a young woman raised in genteel Southern society may learn to be demure. The disadvantaged boy was not necessarily born aggressive, nor was the Southern girl born demure. (See the Appendix for generalizations on human behavior.)

Individual family differences play a large role in the conditioning of the child. A child from a family whose highest value is the accumulation of material things might turn out to be a grasping, clawing individual, even though he might sometimes adopt certain superficial patronizing behavior in order to disguise his ulterior purpose. Another boy, reared in a family where helping other people was the highest family value, might turn out to be a social-work type whose satisfactions are derived through altruism. Of course, it does not always follow that every child adopts the family values as his own; some children reject them completely. Ordinarily, though, the family is a powerful conditioning factor.

In every period of life, and especially in childhood, parental and family teaching is modified by outside groups. If the child plays with other children who are from families where similar customs, attitudes, and values are observed, much of his role learning will be reinforced. When someone says, "Let's play house," a boy knows that he is expected to be either the father or the brother. If he makes a mistake in his role-appropriate behavior, he will quickly be corrected: "No, no, silly. The father doesn't bake the pie; the mother does!" If his playmates come from various cultural backgrounds, he may start learning for the first time that different families have different customs, attitudes, and values. Then he is in for a long period of agonizing effort in reconciling what his peers tell him is proper and what his parents have prescribed. He soon learns that his relationships both with his parents and his peer group may be affected by the kind of adjustments he makes to these ambivalent expectations.

In earlier times, it is probable that parents and peer groups played a greater part in establishing a child's behavior patterns than they do today. In present-day America, parents are much more permissive, often, as will be seen, because of their own perplexity in a changing society. Moreover, play groups are often more temporary. Considerably more of the child's behavior is subject to confirmation and modification by other influences—especially by the school. It is also often subject to challenge and confusion by television, radio, newspapers, and magazines. The child learns from his parents, for example, that guns are "bad," but on television, people do shoot guns. He also learns that, although the gunslinger is ordinarily the "bad guy," under certain circumstances he can become the "good guy." More important to future marriage and family relationships, however, are the differing patterns of family-role behaviors the child learns. A girl child, for example, may observe that in her home her father is invariably the boss and makes all the decisions, but on television millions of other homes are represented in family dramas in which the mother has the dominant role or is at least equal, in fact as well as in fancy, to her husband.

How well the child accepts his early socialization and how carefully he integrates these cultural standards into his behavior depends in some measure on other aspects of his personality. If, for example, he is aggressive and hostile, he may reject prescribed patterns. If he is mischievous, he may pretend to reject them. If he is obsessive or insecure, he may overreact to all the prescribed patterns in a frantic endeavor to conform absolutely. All of these ways of behaving not only affect the child's current relationships but also have a manifest effect on his later dating, marriage, and family relationships.

THE IMPORTANCE OF UNIQUE EXPERIENCES

A third major determinant of personality is the unique experiences of the individual. Two children raised in the same family in the same culture may turn out very differently. An undeterminable part of these differences is the genetic, but another and possibly more important part is that each child had different environmental influences with which to contend. (See the Appendix for generalizations about human behavior from a behaviorist point of view.)

The first child born into a family is exposed to different parental attitudes than the second one, if only because the first was first. A second child arriving in a family has a differing living experience because he already has a sibling with whom he must share attention and affection. Moreover, most siblings have different playmates, different teachers, different accidents and experiences along the way.

Other circumstances can intervene, too. A child who grew to age ten in a poverty-stricken farm family in Oklahoma might have entirely different attitudes about himself and an entirely different self-image than his brother who was born after a rich source of oil had been found on their little farm. There are different self-esteem levels among girls raised in wealthy homes and those raised in poverty. Rich girls are more poised, aggressive, and self-confident, in part at least because their fathers' financial security has transferred feelings of worth to them. They were born somebody.[4]

Having examined the development of personality in general, we should now look closer at two vital aspects of it: self-image and needs. All three of the major determinants of personality—physical structure, culture, and individual experiences—affect the development of any individual's self-image and his emotional needs. Self-image and needs are the prime effectors of both a man's behavior and his relationships with other people.

THE SELF-IMAGE

A newborn infant makes no distinction between himself and the things outside himself. As he grows, however, self-perception is one of his earliest achievements. He becomes aware of the imaginative ability to get outside his body and look back at himself. This phenomenon was described by sociologist Charles H. Cooley as "the looking-glass self," because the individual perceives himself as he assumes other people perceive him.[5] This is the beginning of self-image or self-definition. Soon the child begins to make cer-

[4]David A. Schulz, *The Changing Family: Its Function and Future*, Englewood Cliffs, N.J., Prentice-Hall, 1972, p. 118.

[5]Charles H. Cooley, *Human Nature and the Social Order*, New York, Scribner, 1902, pp. 152–153.

tain very important assumptions about what he is like, and he tends to structure his behavior in accordance with those assumptions. (See the Appendix for generalizations about self-concept.)

In the earliest years, it is the family group that provides the experiences, in the form of both praise and criticism, that give the individual some basis for his self-image. If a child's parents make him feel loved and wanted and treat him as if he is acceptable and good, he more often comes to see himself as adequate, competent, and lovable in a world that is friendly and secure. Later he is likely to turn out to be an emotionally healthy person who has the self-confidence to undertake new experiences, and the flexibility to modify his behavior and learn from those experiences. William Morrow and Robert Wilson found that a child who is given self-confidence by accepting parents tends to be a high-achieving adult.[6]

If, on the other hand, the childhood home is deficient in either love or security, and if the child is not helped to develop adequate self-confidence, he may grow up with an inadequate self-image. Unloving or inconsistent parents may make him so confused that he loses all confidence in his ability to interpret experiences. A child who is constantly belittled may grow up feeling that he is incapable of dealing with his relationships and so will avoid new experiences, because he is afraid they will always turn out to be bad.

Robert Coombs and Vernon Davies, after citing W. I. Thomas's classic observation, "If a situation is defined as real it is real in its consequences,"[7] suggested that, in the context of the school world, a student who is defined as a "poor student" (by significant others and thereby by himself) comes to conceive of himself as such. He gears his behavior accordingly, and the social expectation is realized.[8]

In the process of developing a self-concept, a child may, and often does, make false assumptions about how other people—especially his peers—feel about him. Sometimes these are in a positive direction: I love myself; therefore others must love me. Sometimes they are in a negative direction—

[6]William R. Morrow and Robert C. Wilson, "Family Relations of Bright High-Achieving and Under-Achieving High School Boys," in Gene R. Medinnus, ed., *Readings in Psychology of Parent-Child Relations*, New York, Wiley, 1967, pp. 247–255.

[7]William I. Thomas, "The Persistence of Primary-Group Norms in Present Day Society," in H. S. Jennings et al., *Suggestions of Modern Science Concerning Education*, New York, Macmillan, 1917, pp. 159–197, and *The Child in America*, New York, Knopf, 1928, p. 572.

[8]Robert H. Coombs and Vernon Davies, "Self-Conception and the Relationship Between High School and College Scholastic Achievement," *Sociology and Social Research*, **50** (July, 1966), 468.

often as a result of the ideas that the child himself has about *other* people. For example, the child who is insecure about his own appearance is often critical of others. Then he turns around and assumes that others are criticizing him, even though this may not be the case at all. This tendency to assume that other people will be critical is pronounced among those who have an inadequate self-image. (See the Appendix for generalizations about human behavior from a transactional analysis point of view.)

Adequate self-image development is even more difficult for the person (male or female) with some uncorrectable body impairment or physical difference. He *has* to learn to live with whatever physical handicap he has. Often this leads him to withdraw from social contacts and drastically affects his ability to relate to others. Acne, for example, can be one of the most serious tragedies to afflict the young human being, for it is a damager of self-image at just the time in his social development when he needs all the self-confidence he can get.

There is, however, no one-to-one relationship between the actual physical impairment and the attitude that the individual has about it. It is not how bad the handicap really is that matters; nor is it how bad the impairment really appears to others. It is how bad the individual himself *thinks* it is that causes all the difficulty. This will be illustrated by a case in the next chapter.

A damaged self-image can result from feelings of inadequacy as well as from physical handicaps. A poor self-image may result from a disadvantaged home situation.

In the process of developing his accepted self-image, the child also develops an *ideal* self-image. This is the self the child wishes he could become, and he frequently judges his actual appearance and conduct against this ideal self-image. If his real self closely approximates his ideal self, he is likely to be a self-confident, secure person who is well liked by others. If his real self-evaluation is widely divergent from his concept of an ideal self, he is likely to be an unhappy person who is difficult to get along with because his opinion of himself is low.

The child's concept of himself will vitally affect his motivation, both positively and negatively. If, for example, there is a close congruence between his present self-definition and his ideal self, he will be motivated to try to close the gap. A young man who has a secure image of himself as a good student will do everything he possibly can to maintain (and even improve) that self-image. Coombs and Davies, in a study of Washington State University freshmen, found that those who had loftier conceptions of their scholastic ability expected to obtain high college grades and usually did so.[9]

But what happens if an individual overresponds in an effort to live up to his ideal? He may be always on the defensive, making elaborate and unnecessary explanations of any behavior on his part that he feels falls short of the high standards he sets for himself. Many highly motivated individuals are constantly trying to prove to themselves and to others that their real self-images approximate their ideal self-images.

EMOTIONAL NEEDS

As a result of his self-image, an individual tends to develop certain emotional needs. For example, if a young man is to maintain or enhance his self-image as a good student, he needs to be constantly reassured by excellent grades. Thus, he may come to develop a rather large need for recognition. If he has any doubt about his self-image, he may have an even greater need for recognition. Or if, in growing up, a woman develops a self-image of being inferior and subservient, she may also develop a masochistic need for abuse in order to fit her low self-image. The satisfaction of being congruent with her self-image gives her greater emotional pleasure than the physical or emotional punishment gives her pain. Thus, we have the woman who is happy when her husband beats her, because this gives her the security of having conformed to her image of herself as the abused wife. (See the Appendix for generalizations about human behavior from a transactional analysis point of view.)

Needs are important aspects of motivation. Although they may grow out of self-image, they have an independent status in almost all theories of human motivation and behavior.

Men and women are motivated—indeed impelled—by incessant inner proddings that have been variously labeled as wishes, desires, drives, and, more recently, needs. Some have made a distinction between these impulses. For example, drives are sometimes spoken of as "pushes" from within the individual, whereas needs are goals or objectives or, you might say, "pulls." But in the end, the effect is the same whether it is from within or without. Needs, as we shall call them, are the motivational factors in human behavior. They develop concurrently with the self-image.

First of all, and earliest of all, the human being manifests his physi-

[9]Ibid.

ological needs. The sucking reflex and evidences of hunger appear almost immediately after birth. So does the need to sleep and the need for sensory stimulation.

Although young children have sex feelings and impulses, no one is exactly sure when the sex impulse can be defined as *need*. The time most observers assign to it is the onset of puberty.

As the child develops, and as his self-image develops, he acquires even more needs. He *needs* to feel secure both physically and socially in order to protect his self-image. He *needs* to be publicly recognized in order to promote his self-image and perpetuate its integrity. He *needs* to be constantly and consistently loved in order to reassure himself of his worthiness.

Throughout this century, there have been attempts by various psychologists to define and classify human needs. William I. Thomas proposed a very simple list of what he called "wishes" in his classic study of unadjusted girls.[10] He suggested that human individuals, in our culture at least, have needs for security, response, recognition, and new experience.

This list has severe limitations, because it obviously ignores some of the more complex needs, like the need for power and the need for self-abuse, but it does have the advantage of simplicity.

Abraham Maslow postulated that all psychological needs subsume from three basic needs very similar to Thomas's.[11] Maslow suggested that the basic psychological needs are for safety, love, and self-esteem. Directly from these needs, he said, comes a fourth need—the need for self-actualization—the need to fulfill the best that is in you.

Just how these needs affect the behavior of individuals in relationship situations will be pointed out in the next chapter. Here it is sufficient to suggest that an individual's needs are basic to the reasons why he behaves as he does in any relationship. The young man who shows off on a date has a basic need for recognition. The boy who is shy and retiring has a great need for security. There is a wide variation in the intensity of needs. Some men spend every waking hour seeking response from other people; other men willingly go off alone to hunt or to prospect for days, weeks, months, or even years at a time.

Although a person's needs tend to fall into precedence patterns, one special need may take overwhelming precedence over another at any particular moment. The young man who feels impelled to show off by driving a hundred miles an hour may be fulfilling his need for recognition at the

[10]William I. Thomas, *The Unadjusted Girl*, Boston, Little, Brown, 1925, p. 4.
[11]Abraham H. Maslow, *Motivation and Personality*, 2nd ed., New York, Harper & Row, 1970.

same time as he is subverting his need for security or safety. At times, physical needs may dominate psychological needs, or vice versa. A person who is hungry may not that minute be interested in recognition, although a need for recognition is one of the main driving forces in his life. A security-needing person who is sexually excited may lose some of his concern for security. On the other hand, an insecure person may endure severe discomfort because he is unwilling to ask directions to the toilet, or a devoutly religious person may take vows prohibiting any sexual activity.

Actually, the relationship between physical and psychological needs is very close. Repeated emotional-need frustrations can have serious physical consequences, just as repeated physical-need frustrations can have emotional consequences. The chronically insecure man may develop stomach ulcers; the starving person may literally go berserk.

The relationship between emotional needs and physical needs is very important in the study of human relationships. It can be demonstrated that physical contacts and emotional relationships between human beings are not only desirable, they are actually necessary to the continuance of life itself. Infants deprived of handling by another human being over a long period of time sink into irreversible decline and often succumb. Adults deprived of sensory stimulus may become emotionally unbalanced. Eric Berne suggested that all humans need "stroking" as a result of their inborn infantile stimulus hunger. In later life, he said, the stroking may consist of subtle, symbolic forms of handling, such as recognition in place of intimate physical contact.[12] Berne saw the infantile stimulus hunger (a physiological factor) as being transformed into something that may be termed "recognition hunger" (an emotional need). As the individual matures, Berne felt, he seeks recognition to replace the original need for physical contact. An actor, for example, may require hundreds of "strokes" per week from anonymous and undifferentiated admirers to "keep his spinal cord from shriveling," whereas a scientist may keep his physical and mental health on one "stroke" per year from a respected colleague.

Because each individual brings to every relationship a series of pre-developed needs, those needs cannot help but affect every relationship into which he enters. This is especially true since needs are often unknown to the person who has them. Even when they are in his awareness, he may deliberately seek to hide them. A basically insecure man may shout and bluster because he knows he is so insecure. Moreover, because many of the needs are unconscious ones, they may serve as channels for all other needs

[12]Muriel James and Dorothy Jongeward, *Born to Win*, Reading, Mass., Addison-Wesley, 1971, pp. 44–56.

as well. As Maslow has pointed out, a person who thinks he is hungry may actually be seeking comfort more than food.[13] A woman who thinks she wants love may actually be seeking security.

Each person, in order to try more perfectly to meet his physical and emotional needs, while at the same time maintaining and enhancing a self-image, develops a series of strategies or defense mechanisms. These protect his tender ego while simultaneously helping him to greater need-satisfaction.

DEFENSE MECHANISMS

Each individual reacts differently to insults to his self-image and to frustrations of his emotional needs. In fact, reactions can differ in the same individual from one situation to the next. Generally, though (and this is the major reason why understanding self-image and needs is so important to the understanding of human relationships), individuals have patterns of behavior that they adopted in childhood and that they continue to use as adults. Sometimes these patterns are neither logical nor problem-solving in a particular situation. But because they were learned in childhood, they are now compelling, even if self-defeating. For example, a girl who learned as a child that by crying she generally got what she wanted may as an adult cry when she is frustrated. Even though her husband is repulsed by her crying and is even more intent on denying her when she does cry, she persists in this behavior. If she were asked why she cries, she would say, "I just can't help it."

Certain defense mechanisms or patterns of adjusting to insults, conflict, and frustration occur so frequently in so many individuals that they have been sorted out and labeled: Rationalization, projection, identification, reaction formation, repression, and compensation are some of these typical defense mechanisms. Before discussing them, it should be pointed out that these reactions are alternatives to either direct aggression, which is probably the most frequent response to frustration, or withdrawal, which is another common method of handling conflict. In addition to direct aggression, such as hitting or threatening, there is also passive aggression, such as negativism or noncooperation. There are also indirect withdrawals. The most common way of withdrawing is through fantasizing or daydreaming, but there are other ways, such as denying response and inattentiveness.

Classic defense mechanisms involve ways to maintain or enhance

[13]Maslow, op. cit.

self-esteem and at the same time to escape or defend against anxiety without using either direct aggression or complete withdrawal. They were emphasized by Sigmund Freud in his account of the unconscious ways in which people react to conflicts and frustrations. All of the defense mechanisms have in common the quality of self-deception, and all are found in the everyday behavior of normal people. Most people probably could not live with themselves without them. It is only when one of the mechanisms is used so frequently that it interferes with the individual's ability to function adequately that it becomes an impairment to his emotional health. Only when people realize they are using these behaviors can they change them.

Rationalization. Rationalization is the process of assigning logical reasons to (or plausible excuses for) behavior that we do not wish to acknowledge to ourselves in its total reality. Examples of such self-deception are legion: "I didn't get good grades because the teacher didn't like me." "I wouldn't have gone to the dance even if I had been invited, because I heard they were having a terrible combo."

Projection. Projection is assigning one's own undesirable qualities, in exaggerated amounts, to other people. This justifies one's own tendencies and removes the stigma of bad qualities by minimizing them in oneself and exaggerating them in others. Typically, a person who is critical or unkind to others but who has a self-image of being a "good guy" will convince himself that those around him are critical and unkind and that the harsh treatment he gives to others is based on justifiable retribution, not on any bad qualities of his own. The classic projection in marriage is that of the unfaithful husband who accuses his innocent wife of having been unfaithful. His emotional mechanics operate something like this: "I have been unfaithful and I feel bad; but if I, who am so good, have been unfaithful, then my wife might also have been unfaithful." It is a very short jump from "might also have been" to "has been" when such a projection will relieve the guilt of the unfaithful husband and so protect his self-image.

Identification. Instead of assigning one's own bad qualities to other people, in identification one often takes other people's desirable qualities as his own. To polish up his own self-image, an individual will identify with important groups or well-known people and by such association (actual or fantasied) improve his own self-stature. If you have ever watched another couple in the theater audience, you have probably seen identification at work. When the hero bent forward to kiss the heroine on the stage, you may have seen both of the audience partners purse their own lips.

In a marriage, one partner or the other often identifies with his childhood family group in an effort to buoy up his own position in his marriage. Or one mate may identify with the hero or heroine role in a television serial in an effort to get his mate to behave like his opposite number on the serial.

Reaction formation. Reaction formation is concealing a strong motive in one's self by giving a strong expression to its opposite. Women who are secretly consumed with passionate desires are sometimes overstrict in curbing any sexual impulse in their children. Feeling guilty over their own sex desire, they seek to atone by downgrading sex. In other family relationships, this tendency toward reaction formation is not uncommon. A mother with an unwanted pregnancy may later be overindulgent with the child in order to assure herself that she is a good mother. The parent who has chosen to be away from home a great deal may also be overindulgent with a child.

Repression. Repression is the mechanism of protecting the self-image from ideas and impulses that are incompatible with it. Repression is different from *suppression* in that repression is unconscious control, whereas suppression is a conscious control that keeps impulses and tendencies in check. A person is aware of a suppressed idea or impulse, but he may go for years without recognizing his repressed thoughts and desires. Usually, however, repression is not complete, and thoughts and impulses find indirect expression.

A classic but oversimplified illustration of repression is the case of a twenty-five-year-old woman who was walking along the street and was suddenly troubled when someone looked her in the eye. Later, being looked in the eye became so upsetting that she actually fainted in the street. After several years of psychotherapy she was finally able to recall a repressed incident that took place in her early childhood. She had been to visit her aunt for a week. Her aunt had told her that she might look anywhere in the house except in the bottom drawer of the bureau in the front bedroom upstairs. As soon as Auntie was out of sight, the little girl went upstairs and into the bottom drawer of the bureau. There, on a piece of gauze in the corner, was a glass eye. The child was frightened.

If she had not been forbidden to go to the drawer and had just stumbled on the glass eye accidentally, the little girl might have run downstairs and told her aunt what she had found. Her aunt would have reassured her and reduced some of the traumatic anxiety. At the end of the week, she might have gone home and told her parents what she had found. They too would have reassured her, and her anxiety would have been further reduced. Then she might have told all her playmates about it. By the time she had told her last playmate, she would have completely reduced the fright and tension that accompanied the incident. She might even have been able to laugh about it for the rest of her life.

But she was not able to do any of these things because she thought she had done something wrong. Therefore, instead of being able to extinguish the fright and anxiety that went with the original incident, she compounded it with guilt. Since she was unable to cope with all of this emotional trauma, she did the only thing she could: She repressed it, pushed the incident down deep inside her. Later it returned to trouble her in the form of the street fainting. She was able to do in psychotherapy what she should have done as a child. She was able to repeat the incident over and over again to another person and so reduce her anxiety and her guilt about it.

Every person brings to his relationships with other people a great many repressed thoughts, ideas, and behaviors. Some minor repressions will trouble some individuals more than some severe repressions will trouble others. There is no rule about the intensity of the repression versus the intensity of the reaction. But those who must live with other people, especially in a relationship as intimate as marriage, must recognize and accept the existence of repressed and unconscious thoughts and behaviors—their own as well as their mate's.

Compensation.   Compensation is the effort to make up for a deficiency in one area by excellence in another. The classic example is the boy who fails in athletic events and so studies diligently and achieves recognition through success in schoolwork. Usually this defense mechanism is the process of making up for weakness in one activity by excellence in another. However, there is another kind of compensation in which the individual attempts to deny or correct his inadequacy by continuing to try to excel in that particular area. Theodore Roosevelt, sickly as a child, showed tremendous determination to become a physically rugged outdoorsman. Often, weak, poorly developed men are spurred by their own weakness into building themselves up to superior performance. In such cases, overcompensation has a positive value, but there have been many instances throughout history in which overcompensation has led to an undesirable result. Many power-mad dictators, for example, were overcompensating for their lack of power in childhood.

As pointed out earlier, defense mechanisms are regularly used to salve and protect the tender self-image. Ordinarily, a person has well-developed patterns of defense by the time he marries. He brings all of his defense mechanisms with him to the new relationship. Often, as we shall see when we come to further examination of cases, these defense mechanisms are fairly easy to spot in someone else's behavior. But the individual who is using them may have had them for so long that now he is almost as un-aware of his defenses as he is of the original unconscious feelings that caused him to adopt them.

PERSONALITY DISORDERS

To use the empathetic approach effectively, it is often necessary to remember that there are some people who are repetitively maladaptive. If they can change at all, they can change only after long-term psychotherapy. Their problems and relationships cannot be solved either by changing their environment or by telling them what they ought to do. These individuals are usually diagnosed by psychiatrists as having character or personality disorders. Psychiatrist Joan Hampson has described four classic examples, which are designated as the psychosocially immature personality, the hysterical personality, the sociopathic personality, and the obsessional personality.[14] Using labels does not aid the process of empathy. Knowledge of what they imply does increase understanding, however.

Psychosocially immature personality. As an example of psychosocial immaturity, Hampson suggests the case of a woman who was "fixated" at the childish level. She had a weak sense of responsibility that could be superseded by any reasonably acceptable excuse. People at this level expect complete reliability in others but alibi for themselves. They are obsessed with achieving praise or fixing blame. Hampson illustrates as follows:

An attractive . . . woman complained that . . . she felt sexually unresponsive because her husband was not "romantic." . . . She was only mildly surprised when [a] guest seduced her. Later she rationalized . . . "After all, my husband won't be romantic, no one can blame me if I fall for a guy who will be."[15]

Clearly, she was not psychotic (out of touch with reality) or so neurotic that she needed to be institutionalized. Equally clearly, although she knew she needed help with her marriage, the underlying problem was her persistent and immature personality patterns—a problem unlikely to be resolved either quickly or easily by attending to the alibis she gave.

Hysterical personality. The hysterical personality is described by Hampson as an immature and shallow person, self-absorbed to the point of egocentricity. Some such individuals can be singled out by their flair for the

---

[14]Joan G. Hampson, "The Effect of Character and Personality Disorders on Marriage Relationships," in Richard H. Klemer, ed., *Counseling in Marital and Sexual Problems: A Physician's Handbook*, Baltimore, Williams & Wilkins, 1965, p. 44.

[15]Ibid., p. 45.

dramatic in manner, dress, and speech. They are emotionally capricious. A female hysteric is often a caricature of the "sexsational"—dressing and acting in a sexually provocative manner but, paradoxically, becoming frightened and perplexed when her behavior provokes a masculine response. Such women are often highly suggestible and are often adept at presenting fantasy as fact.

Sociopathic personality. Under the heading of the sociopathic personality Hampson describes a person of average or sometimes unusually high intelligence. He often has great personal charm and an easy social manner. His freedom from the socially inhibiting effect of anxiety allows him to excel for a while in all of his human relations, including his work and studies. Inevitably and repeatedly, however, he manages to sabotage his life, lose his job, alienate his friends, and often appear in the office of the doctor or the marriage counselor on the verge of losing his wife and children as well. Some sociopathics are passive and inadequate, but others repeatedly commit aggressive and antisocial acts. They are the thieves, check forgers, and swindlers who become involved in common-law marriages, bigamy, and sexual escapades. Sometimes they are involved in more shocking crimes, usually with little or no provocation. Also in this classification are the childbeater, the wastrel, the alimony evader, and the irresponsible nonprovider.

Obsessive-compulsive personality. The fourth in Hampson's categories of personality disorders is the obsessive-compulsive person. These people are overmeticulous, overorderly, and sometimes overpersistent and inflexible. They live by routines and are upset if the routine is disturbed; they are fond of discipline, adhering to a set of regulations themselves and expecting the same precise performance in others. They are perfectionists and are never able to leave well enough alone; some are always busy, others are procrastinators because they feel that they cannot perform well enough. Fearful of error, such people are often indecisive, insecure, hesitant, and dependent upon the opinion of others, even though they try to hide their uncertainty and, paradoxically, may give the illusion of being self-possessed and confident to the point of appearing smug.

The effect that people in any one of Hampson's four categories can have on a marriage relationship is readily apparent, even to the casual observer. Unhappily, it is not always so obvious to the young person who believes he is in love and who is willing to believe that the other person will change after marriage ("I can *help* him!"). It is difficult enough to establish deeply congenial relationships with relatively normal people. With those who have psychological problems, it is often impossible.

Before turning to a case illustrating the importance of personality factors in marriage relationships, it might be well to point out again that even people who are psychologically normal, relatively mature, problem-solving individuals have self-images, needs, and defense mechanisms. Moreover, many people who are motivated by unconscious repetitive impulses are not automatic candidates for the psychiatrist's couch. The test of psychological health is whether the individual maintains and improves his relationships or whether he persistently deteriorates them by his behavior.

Behavior also depends on the situation

In using personality concepts in the empathetic approach to relationships problems, one should remember that, although personality patterns forecast that an individual will act *more or less* predictably in most situations, this is not always true. In interpersonal situations, behavior is frequently the product of the reciprocating interaction between the two people involved. A person may behave differently in the presence of one person than in the presence of another. An army sergeant may be very tough in the presence of men in his squad, very submissive in the presence of the captain, and very gentle in the presence of his wife. Is the "personality" of the army sergeant, then, tough, submissive, or gentle?

Both the relationship between the individuals concerned and the situation in which they find themselves can set aside usual patterns of behaving. Two people who might easily get along in a relatively calm social situation may have violent difficulty when they are placed under extreme emotional tension. In other words, personality factors, while they are usually predictive of tendencies, are not absolute predictors of behavior.

Now it is appropriate to look at a somewhat complex case that illustrates many of the personality dynamics we have been discussing. Try using the empathetic approach, applying all that has been discussed up to now.

CASE 8 RICHARD AND LINDA

Richard came to see the marriage counselor less than three months after he had been married. In the very first interview, he said emphatically that he no longer loved his wife, he couldn't stand to touch her sexually, and he wanted the marriage counselor to tell his wife that she should divorce him. Richard said that he couldn't take the initiative in getting the divorce, first of all because his wife had never done anything to hurt him and, secondly, because he belonged to an evangelical church that would frown on his breaking up his marriage. This was the beginning of a long series of counseling interviews for Richard during which the following facts emerged.

Richard was an unwanted child born to an alcoholic mother who had severe personality difficulties and who despised her husband. From his earliest recollections Richard felt rejected. This was even more true after a brother was born whom his mother obviously favored. Despite repeated rejections, Richard continued to try to win his mother's affection.

As he grew, it soon became apparent to everybody—including Richard—that he was an ugly duckling. He had poor vision and consequently had to wear thick-lensed glasses. Other children laughed at him and called him "four eyes." Moreover, he had very poor muscular coordination and wasn't very good at games. When the teams were chosen, the other kids would say, "Aw, do we have to take him?" Since he rarely got a chance to play, he was very fumbling and unskillful when he did, and his ineptness provoked further critical comments from the other children. Soon he began withdrawing from games whenever he could. He invented all sorts of reasons, from illness to excuses about his mother needing him. When he got away from the group, he hid in a dark corner and fantasied that he was the game's hero, defeating all the other children.

At home, however, he read and studied a good deal and was proud of his stamp collection. He also took a very great interest in Sunday School activities at the evangelical church. He came to believe that, even if no one else loved him, God did, and this was comforting. His strong religious orientation made him even more curious in the eyes of the other children. He ate a very great deal, especially between meals. This, too, was comforting. He soon grew overweight; this compounded his difficulties in relating to the other children. Now they taunted him even more, and they were less willing to let him play with them.

When he got to high school, Richard encountered more social problems. The girls didn't want to be with him any more than the boys did. He had almost no social skills and consistently embarrassed any girl he was with even for a moment. He had almost no opportunity for dates or participation in intersex activity. Here again, after several awkward experiences he withdrew to his reading, his stamp collection, and his church activities.

Finally, his unhappy high-school days behind him, he went to the university. Although the studies and the environment at the university were a little better than they had been in high school, his social life remained poor. He continued to overeat, which not only increased his obesity but aggravated a poor complexion as well.

Richard did exceptionally well in university classes and was admitted to medical school. Here he had his first opportunity to relate to people in a protected, professional relationship. Although his bedside manner left a great deal to be desired, at least he began to learn some of the fundamentals of social interaction. After completing medical school, he was inducted into the army as a medical officer.

Then things began to happen to Richard in rapid succession. First of all, the army slimmed him down with some basic-training exercises. As he lost weight, he gained motivation to lose more, and he dieted his way down to normal. As a matter of fact, he cut a rather handsome figure in his army uniform. When he added contact lenses, the results were astonishing. Not only did other people look at him differently, he began to look at himself differently. Soon he was seeing a great deal of the women who frequented the bars near the army base. His relationships with them provided some of the social experience he needed, for these women, less discriminating than most of the girls he had known previously, gave him a kind of acceptance that built up his self-confidence.

In due course, his army tour was completed, and Richard accepted an offer of a residency in pathology at a large metropolitan hospital in San Francisco. In this particular hospital there were almost 200 young women of marriageable age and marriageable inclination—nurses, technicians, dieticians, secretaries, and others—all of whom were excited and interested in the arrival of the new young resident in pathology.

Richard found himself the center of a great deal of attention. He was smiled at, flirted with, and courted as he had never been before. In one large rush he tried to make up for all the time lost. His diary now began to report a quantity of social and sexual activity that would have made Dr. Kinsey blanch.

Richard, like so many other people, was able to pigeonhole and rationalize his moral values. His activities at the hospital were not allowed to interfere with his church work—and of course, vice versa. He never missed a Sunday at church, and he soon became one of the pillars of the local congregation.

As time went by, the older women of the church began to suggest—at first subtly and later insistently—that it was time he found himself a nice girl, married her, and settled down to the sober family life the Lord had intended for him. Richard didn't really want to do this, but at length he was persuaded that it was, in fact, his Christian duty.

He picked out a demure young nurse named Linda, who had a reputation for wide-eyed sexual innocence, and set about courting her. She was immensely flattered, for it was obvious to everybody that she had won the prized male. It was also obvious that he had a kind of reverent esteem for her and her presumed sexual innocence that was far different from the attitude he had toward most of the other girls he dated. She was very careful to foster this image by appearing incensed at the slightest off-color remark and by actually walking out of a slightly risqué movie. Before long, Richard proposed marriage, and a wedding date was set some six months in the future.

Long before the wedding date arrived, Richard had second thoughts. One night, three months or so before the ceremony, he told Linda that he really didn't think he loved her, and he suggested that perhaps it would be better if they didn't get married. She couldn't bear the thought of telling the other 199 girls that she had lost the prized catch, so she explained to Richard that all bachelors get cold feet before marriage, and even if he didn't love her now he would learn to love her as their marriage progressed. Besides, she emphasized, she loved him in a way that his mother never had. She tried to do everything for him that she could possibly think he might want done. Richard thought he ought to feel reassured and went ahead with the wedding plans, even though he had a nagging, half-conscious suspicion that he would like it better if she let him try to please her more often instead of trying to please him all of the time.

On the appointed date, they were married, and after the marriage they moved into his former bachelor apartment. From the beginning, their life together was difficult. In most of the sexual relationships that Richard had previously had, the women had taken the initiative, and this had given him the security of feeling that sex was "all right." His new bride, however, was still playing the demure innocent, and she wanted Richard to be the aggressor. When she coyly rejected some of his timorous advances, Richard began to feel ashamed and guilty, and before long he didn't want to touch her. The madonna image of her he had built up made sexual relationships impossible. When she tried to correct this by being a little more aggressive, he was even further repulsed.

Other aspects of their married life were equally distressing. She continued in her job and was often up early and gone until late in the afternoon. When she came home, she had little energy left for homemaking chores. Consequently, his married life was not much different from his bachelor life.

Although he had few of the pleasures, he now had all of the responsibilities and restrictions of a married man. Before long, he began to think of the "good old days" when all the girls were crazy about him. Soon he came to the conclusion that he had made a bad mistake and that all he wanted to do was to get out. However, he recognized that he had no real complaint against his new bride except, perhaps, that she wouldn't stop working and stay home. Linda argued that not only did they need the money, but also that she needed to keep her job more than ever, since he was hinting that their marriage might break up.

In this dilemma, Richard tried several ways of solving his problem. He thought of applying for reinstatement in the army, but he almost immediately abandoned that idea, for it occurred to him that he would assuredly be sent to Vietnam. Then he tried leaving his unexpurgated diary out where Linda could find it. His hope was that she would read this diary, which she did, and then divorce him as a cad. However, Linda still could not admit that she had failed and lost the prize. Besides, she still believed she loved him, even if he did not want her.

In desperation, Richard went to a marriage counselor, hopeful that the counselor would tell his wife that she should divorce him.

5

RELATABILITY: THE BASIS OF LOVE

Relatability is the skill and know-how involved in developing close relationships with other people. For some it seems almost natural, as if they had been born with it. The chances are, though, that they learned it.

It is true that some marginally genetic factors, such as intelligence and temperament, are involved in relatability. One has to be perceptive enough to be able to see how to interest other people and active enough to want to.

Since much of relatability is learned, the quality of it can usually be improved by almost anyone who is motivated to work at it. There are many ways of doing this. In order for an individual to know how to improve his relatability, he needs to know something about how people learn to love.

WHY SHOULD THEY LOVE YOU?

In our culture, love is the predominant factor that creates families and holds them together. Most textbooks in the field of family relationships have a chapter on love that either starts or finishes with a definition. Love is not easy to define, because, like electricity, love can be described by its results but it is hard to pin down exactly *what* it is. Almost every author tries, though. Love is looked at sociologically, psychologically, physiologically, anthropologically, psychoanalytically, romantically, and even cynically.

Robert Bell gives a modern and brief definition of conjugal love as a "strong emotion directed at the opposite sex and involving feelings of sexual attraction, tenderness and some commitment to the other's ego needs."[1] Robert Winch defines love as the

positive emotion experienced by one person . . . in an interpersonal relationship in which the second person . . . either (1) meets certain important needs of the first, or (2) manifests or appears . . . to manifest personal attributes . . . highly prized by the first, or both.[2]

Most students are not really very much interested in knowing more about what love is. Again the analogy to electricity is cogent. Most people, even very knowledgeable people, are not concerned by science's inability to define exactly electrical energy: It seems far more important to them that they be able to use it to light and improve their living experiences. Besides,

[1]Robert R. Bell, *Marriage and Family Interaction*, 3rd ed., Homewood, Ill., Irwin-Dorsey, 1971, p. 104.
[2]Robert F. Winch, *The Modern Family*, rev. ed., New York, Holt, Rinehart & Winston, 1963, p. 579.

William Kephart reports that the great majority of college students already think they know what love is.

However, although most students may not be too interested in pursuing any elaborate philosophical discussion of the intrinsic characteristics or meaning of love, almost all of them are eager to participate in it. The real burning issue is not "what is love?" but rather *how does one obtain love?* What are the characteristics of true attractiveness that cause people to be popular lovers and others to be romantic rejects? In other words, why should they love you?

People love you when you make them feel important, when you listen to them, when you fit their picture of sex-appropriateness, when you share their goals, when you respond to them, and when you help them meet their need to respond to you. Not everyone, however, is motivated to become lovable and loving, or motivated even to relate.

MOTIVATION

Many young people behave in a manner that indicates that other things are more important to them than love. Some college students profess to want romance, but when an opportunity for romance comes along, they are too busy to take advantage of it. Soccer practice or glee club or studying is more important at the moment. Their motivation is not strong enough to push everything else aside. Why not? For many, the answer is fear, conscious or unconscious. Others never achieve the "goal-set" necessary to make love their primary interest. Some of the students develop relationships that provide substitute satisfactions to dating. Still others never learn to love.

Fears

Many women and men who come for counseling know they are afraid of love. Sometimes they realize exactly why they are afraid; sometimes their fears are unreasoned. Sometimes, major fears, such as a fear of sex, has been deliberately built into them in childhood by anxious parents who were trying to control their children's later moral behavior. The parents may have realized that this could inhibit the later sexual life of their children, even after marriage, but they probably believed their proscriptions were more valuable than the problem of some future inhibition. In other cases, parents were completely unaware of the harm they were doing.

Fears are easily conditioned. Many fears are learned by the child before he is old enough to remember how he got them. There are some fears that children acquire that can have an injurious effect on their later social lives. Fears of the other sex or fears of sexual experience can be completely love-inhibiting.

Some of the fears most damaging to marriage chances are often not thought of as fears at all. These are the conditioned insecurities that make a young person overly afraid of doing or saying something improper or inaccurate. Kept within reason, these little fears make the world a livable place, because they predict how other people (who also fear disapproval) will behave. But for some people, the fear of being socially disapproved of—especially by their peers—becomes unreasoned and destroys their ability to live creatively.

Such people have difficulty handling normal human relations. Sometimes they are so shy that they cross the street to avoid meeting other people. Often they are extremely sensitive to criticism, real or imagined. They defend themselves elaborately. Disapproval is traumatic for them, and they may become agitated at the mere hint that their activities are being evaluated. Some overrespond to flattery and reassurance and will do almost anything for compliments and praise. Sometimes they demean others in the hope of appearing superior by comparison.

These fears and insecurities not only destroy present relationships but also lead to other problems. A person who feels unloved will not reach out to love anyone else. In turn, no one will love him. Finally he becomes permanently unloved and a first-class candidate for the psychiatrist's couch.

Goal-set

A nonlove "goal-set," another major reason for lack of motivation, is also implanted early in childhood. It may start when a parent, catering to his own emotional needs, dreams himself into the future life of his newborn infant. For example, parents may envision their infant girl as a great woman of magnificent achievements, a glamorous actress, an important career woman, or even a pious and virginal saint. They may see her as a substitute for a son, as a provider and breadwinner for their old age, a devoted life-long dependent, or in any one of many roles that satisfy their own yearnings. Such parents can often make their dreams come true by consciously or unconsciously downgrading one role and lauding another as the child grows and develops. Consider Roberta: "Nobody actually said I had to be a physician, but my parents made an awful fuss whenever I showed any interest in dolls or in working around the house. I never really tried to oppose them, though. I was supposed to be a boy—that's what my father wanted

—and I did everything I could to make up to them for being the wrong sex. I worked very hard in school. They expected me to! I don't ever remember thinking very much about romance; I was too busy. I didn't date at all. I used to think that going into medicine was all my own idea. But as I look back, I can see that I was gently steered that way from the very beginning."

Certainly the parents are not always solely responsible for a particular goal-set or personality malfunction. Sometimes the best-intentioned parents are thwarted by environmental circumstances or the child's temperament. The three factors, the parents, the child, and the environment, interact to condition the child's development. But the parents are usually the primary influence in the initial development of the attitudes and values that will guide much of the child's later behavior.

Once a particular goal-set is established, it often becomes self-enlarging. The individual "sells" himself on the idea that his present role direction is his destiny. He tends to play his self-conceptualized role to the hilt. He searches out meanings in the comments of others that verify the appropriateness of his performance. (See the Appendix for generalizations about human behavior from a transactional point of view.)

One of the common goal-set problems that diminishes later opportunities for love occurs when the child develops an overwhelming need to demonstrate superiority. "I know," Lynn said. "It isn't really opportunity; it's me, Lynn. I see lots of men and I talk with many of them, but somehow it is more important to me to be superior than to win a friend. I see it in the first-graders I teach: Some of them just have to be first all of the time. I'm like that, too. The only time I'm happy is when I have just shown up somebody. It's ironic that here I am, a woman who is denied love because she is deliberately seeking it. As a child, being superior brought me love and admiration from my mother and her friends. I felt especially good when I was better than my three brothers. I know intellectually that people don't like me when I am openly superior to them. But I still seem compelled to seek satisfaction by being the best. It has brought me competitive success but it hasn't brought me the warm relationships I am hungry for."[3]

Men as well as women have goal-sets that diminish their love and marriage motivation. Sometimes with boys, as with girls, this nonlove, nonmarriage goal-set was not deliberately intended by the parents. It may be, for example, that a reserved atmosphere and an absence of overt affection in the home, the parents' normal pattern, were absorbed into the personality of the developing boy. But at times, there can be a deliberate attempt to

[3]Richard H. Klemer, *A Man for Every Woman*, New York, Macmillan, 1959, pp. 72–73.

steer the boy away from love. To placate their personal emotional needs, some mothers stress the advantages of the boy remaining at home or not becoming involved with women on the grounds that women might injure his career opportunities by insisting on marriage. Unhappily married fathers and unmarried friends can also prejudice the young man against romantic commitment. The free, idyllic joy of the bachelor apartment can be made to appear much more attractive when compared to the responsibilities that follow from love and marriage.

"Why get involved?" Christopher asked. "I've seen a lot of very unhappy men who got tangled up in love and marriage—including my father. So I'm playing it casual. I get all the sex I want with no commitments. If a fellow lets himself get serious and sentimental, first thing you know he has a wife and then he's trapped. A woman can get out easily, but for a man there's a big financial risk. A man can barely support himself and have any fun these days. If he gets burned by one woman, then he might have to pay alimony and lose half his income. It isn't like in the old days when a woman helped you. Women don't want to be housekeepers anymore. Now all they want to do is sit around doing nothing or else to be going out spending your dough."

A normal sex drive is of major importance to a goal-set toward love. Those who have healthy heterosexual interests take a more active part in all kinds of male-female relationships, even if they reject love itself. Romance has no greater enemy than apathy, and there is no greater romantic apathy than that of the sexually disinterested person. As one discouraged young woman put it, "A girl has more trouble with the sheepishness of the sheep than she does with the wolfishness of the wolves."

The hows and whys of sexual interest among men and women will be discussed in later chapters. Here it is enough to note that some people, especially women, who typically realize their maximum sexual drive at a later age than men in our society, do not understand their sexual desire until it is too late. For physical or psychological reasons, as yet poorly understood, some people mature sexually later than others. When at last they are mature enough to have desire, they may have organized their lives around patterns, religious or secular, that preclude sex.

Substitute satisfactions

Closely allied to the nonlove goal-set as a reason for lack of motivation to love is having one's needs—physical, emotional, or sexual—met in other ways. Occasionally, twins, very close siblings, and even warm friends lack interest in finding a partner or a marriage mate because they already have someone who meets many of their needs in some sufficient degree.

Some of these relationships are undoubtedly homosexual. Kinsey and his associates found that, of the men in their sample, 10 percent were exclusively homosexual between the ages of 16 and 55, and 4 percent were exclusively homosexual throughout their lives.[4] The Kinsey group reported that less than half as many females in their sample were exclusively homosexual, at least in their behavior. The researchers speculated that the widespread belief that there are more practicing homosexual females than males probably arises from the more affectional responses of females to each other, which is often interpreted by males as indicative of some deep psychosexual interest.[5]

But many people who lack romance motivation, even if they engage in some homosexual activity, are not homosexual in any permanent sense. The Kinsey group reported that some 50 percent of all the males in their sample and 28 percent of all the females had had some homosexual experience in their lives.[6] Many of these people later develop satisfactory heterosexual relationships.

There are many varieties of substitute satisfactions. One of the major satisfactions of any human relationship is being needed. When this need is met by taking care of an aged mother, a friend, or even a stray cat, motivation to establish a new relationship that might lead to romance is reduced in some degree, however slight. Motivations to love are functions of emotional hunger. Substitute satisfactions reduce the hunger and consequently the motivation.

Those who never learned to love

A fourth major reason for lack of love motivation in many young people is that they never really learned to love someone of the opposite sex. That is, they never learned to love any person other than their parents, relatives, or friends of the same sex.

The ability to love is learned. The learning process starts early. By

[4]Alfred C. Kinsey, W. B. Pomeroy, and C. E. Martin, *Sexual Behavior in the Human Male*, Philadelphia, Saunders, 1948, p. 651.

[5]Alfred Kinsey et al., *Sexual Behavior in the Human Female*, Philadelphia, Saunders, 1953, p. 475.

[6]Ibid., p. 474.

the age of two or three, some of the attitudes that will affect patterns of adult love behavior—and, incidentally, sex behavior—are probably already formed.

The majority of parents do a very good job of teaching their children to love, but some do not. Some children have no good example from which to learn because of hostile conflicts between their parents. Sometimes the parents belittle love and denigrate the importance of affectional relationships with other people. By their reserved attitudes toward each other and toward the children, some parents create a "cold" atmosphere in which a warm, loving response is downgraded.

Parents may go in the opposite direction. Abnormal amounts of highly charged affection from the parents can lead to an excessive attachment and overdependence on the part of the child. Some parents give their children an overabundance of love or attention with a recognized or unrecognized intent that the child will respond with an excessive amount of love in return. In the beginning, this may result in only a little spoiling: The child is unhappy whenever he is alone or when he is not the center of attention. Later, the overdependent child often finds it difficult, if not actually impossible, to form other relationships. Many such parents are delighted that their children continue in a dependent relationship, long after the time has come for them to leave the nest.

Sigmund Freud's theory of the Oedipus complex presumes that a child develops an unconscious sexual love for the parent of the opposite sex as a part of the normal process of growing up. In psychoanalysis, an adult who does not love appropriately is often found to have become "fixated" in this Oedipal stage. If the subject is male, he is believed to be still in love with his mother and to fear unconsciously that his father will castrate him in jealous rage. If the subject is female, it is believed that she still loves her father sexually and unconsciously wishes to murder her mother and have a child by her father.

This theory may be appropriate in some cases, for it is true that there are many romanceless people whose relationship to the parent of the opposite sex is unnaturally close. In many cases, though, there appears to be more reason to suspect that a parent has consciously or unconsciously conditioned his pliable and easily suggestible child to meet some of his own unrequited need for attention and affection than there is to assure that the child had a psychological problem to begin with.

As a matter of fact, in our society, a neurotic need for affection on the part of a parent is not uncommon. Sometimes this need is relatively simple and the damage it does is readily apparent.

CASE **9** STANLEY

"*My father divorced my mother when I was only two-and-a-half,*" Stanley told the counselor. "*I guess I was her only real happiness after that. She never remarried, and I was the only child she ever had. Sometimes when I was little I wasn't sure if I really did make her happy. She cried a lot, and it was very hard for me to distinguish whether she was crying because my father was gone or whether she was crying because she was happy I was there. She was always very 'sensitive.' Things other people said hurt her, and even when I was growing up, she turned to me for solace. It seemed to make her feel better to tell me her problems even though she knew that I, as a child, could do nothing about them.*

"*She tried to do everything she could for me. She went without clothes herself so that I could have everything I needed. She worked long hours, and part of the time she had a second job doing work at home. I used to feel terribly guilty about it, but she would always say, 'There, there, you are my little boy to take care of now, but someday you will be my big man to take care of me.'*

"*We were very close. I started sleeping in her bed soon after my father left. I slept with her until I was twelve. I didn't like to sleep alone any more than she did.*

"*When I got to high school I didn't have many dates. I was sort of shy and not very athletic. I didn't have much chance to play with the other boys. I'd been too busy with my studies because that's what Mother encouraged me to do. The girls didn't pay much attention to me. I turned out to be 'sensitive' too, and my feelings were pretty easily hurt. They still are.*

"*In my senior year in high school Mother started getting sick. I had talked some about going away to the state university. But when I found out that the anxiety connected with my leaving made her even sicker, I decided not to do that, and I went to college right here in town.*

"*But she continued to have some manifestations of illness. The doctors have never decided exactly what it is, but anything that upsets her now puts her to bed for a few days.*

"*While I was in college, I went out with a few girls. I might have gone out more often, but I couldn't stand to think of Mother sitting home alone.*

"*When I got to graduate school I met Ruth, and for the first time I had some real feelings of love. But it upset Mother terribly for me to talk about her. Mother didn't like her. She pointed out to me a lot of things that I probably should have seen myself about Ruth. Ruth was from a different background, and she was very selfish. Anyway, I broke up with Ruth after about a year. That was eight years ago.*

"Mother is much older now, and I am her only source of support—both economically and emotionally. She literally lives for me. Recently I met a girl named Beatrice, and I have been going with her for about six months. Mother is starting to talk about her the same way she talked about Ruth, only worse. Beatrice says that I have to choose between her and my mother. I just can't do that. What am I going to do?"

Good marriages are made when the two people involved know themselves, know each other, and know before they marry that they can adjust to each other's faults. The love that leads to good marriages is a love in which two human beings respect each other and are actually drawn close together, despite their mutual recognition that neither is perfect. But learning to love in this manner involves preparation and practice.

Love is not for cynics, pessimists, or critical analyzers and worriers. Love requires being able to see the best—not the worst—in the other person from the beginning. It includes having a reasonable amount of trust and faith that your partner will turn out for the best—after you are sure you could adjust even if he did not. It demands a kind of courage to put aside the fears of "what will happen" that often distort the vision of those who have seen too much of life's unpleasantness.

Some courageous optimism is necessary, not only for a person to love and marry at all, but also to keep a love and to keep a mate. Positive trust is often rewarded by its own expectation. The man or woman who has faith in his partner's ability may help that partner grow toward the desired goal. The man or woman who lacks faith actually helps to make his worries come true.

No one can really love another unless he has self-respect—self-love in its finest sense. For most people, learning to love means learning to love themselves to the point where they believe in themselves, in their own judgment, and in their own desirableness. Then, and only then, can they love someone else and allow themselves to be loved in return.

FLEXIBILITY

Equally as important as motivation to the individual's chances for love is his flexibility: How willing and able is he to adapt to the realities of the social situation in which he finds himself? Some men are notoriously inflexible, insisting that they will date only a rich girl or only one with a perfect figure. So are some women. Mary Jones had always believed that a girl looked silly with a boy who was shorter than she. As a result, she turned down all dates with boys who she knew in advance were not as tall as she was. Not so with Jane Smith. Jane dated both the shorter boys and their taller roommates.

Intellectual and emotional inflexibility may increase as a person grows older. Moreover, an individual may cling to rigid attitudes and patterns of behavior, even though these attitudes and behaviors do not achieve his objective, as the following illustration makes clear. Susan was a well-educated young woman who had a master's degree in fine arts and a great loyalty to the church of which she was a member. As a matter of fact, she insisted that any man who could really interest her would have to be a member of *her* church and also have a master's degree in fine arts. She maintained this, despite the fact that she had grown up on a prairie-state farm where few people knew the difference between a Picasso and a Cézanne. Several people pointed out to her how improbable it was that she would find a young man with these specific qualifications in the small California city to which she had moved, but she persisted in rejecting the men who did try to be friendly with her because they did not meet her rigid qualifications.

Finally, despairing of ever finding the man she wanted in California, she moved to Alaska on the theory that she would find many more men available there. This was, of course, true, but very few of them had a master's degree in fine arts. However, when she got back to the invigorating, pioneering atmosphere of the wide open spaces, the values that she had held as a girl back on her prairie farm seemed to take on a new importance. Ultimately, she met and fell in love with a young farmer who not only did not have a master's degree in fine arts, but had not even been to college. Because they had similar basic value systems, Susan and her husband had the kind of mutual understanding in which love can grow. Even more important, she was flexible enough to reevaluate her own attitudes.

Certainly there is nothing wrong with having high standards. This is a mark of the self-respect upon which the self-love that makes other love possible is invariably based. Moreover, it is almost axiomatic that the more attitudes, values, and expectations the engaged couple share, the more readily they will be able to adjust to each other in marriage. But the inflexible person who can settle for nothing less than perfection in romance is probably defeating his own objective. He or she could very well pass up potential love and marriage partners because of overly rigid specifications. As in all other areas of human interaction, the individual should attempt to protect his basic values, but he should also allow some latitude for reevaluating his attitudes in order to grow. This is flexibility, and it is one more answer to the question, "Why should they love you?"

LOVE CAN MAKE YOU VULNERABLE

Love is the desire to do something for someone else without asking for anything in return. It is that simple, yet that difficult. For when you give unconditionally you are vulnerable to abuse from others.

It is the vulnerability inherent in loving that causes people to fear a love involvement. A person who is unsure of himself anyway is very reluctant to lay his feelings open for rejection. A person who has a vocational goal to reach may fear a loss of momentum by the "overcomeness" of love. Such substitutions for a culturally sex-appropriate mate as pets, same-sex friends, and work keep one from the vulnerability of openly loving.

Reciprocal loving provides the most comfortable and productive situation for the expression of love. Zetterberg noted that in love, as in all emotions, there is a point at which the person is not in complete control of himself.[7] He called this "overcomeness." If you can love someone even to the point of "overcomeness" with the assurance of not being exploited in your vulnerable position, then the experience of mutual love is extremely satisfying and stimulating.

One of the difficult things to learn is that you can love people and preserve the self. It helps to understand that everyone is capable of loving many people at the same time and at different times. If this were not so, parents could not love all their children, friends could not love their many friends, and several men and women could not love each other. Many people choose a marriage mate from more than one love. Cultural conditioning helps them select by encouraging the choice to fit certain criteria. Yet the probabilities are that the choice could have been any one of them.

Commitment to one mate at a time has been the way most people have realistically handled both the dilemma of vulnerability in loving and the dilemma of managing the time and emotions of loving more than one. This commitment, it seems, is the way societies have maintained themselves.

Once a person is willing to love and be loved, the relationship seems to have a well-patterned progression. The development of a love relationship is discussed next.

---

[7]Hans L. Zetterberg, "The Secret Ranking," *Journal of Marriage and the Family,* **28** (May, 1966), 134–142.

6

THE DEVELOPMENT
OF A LOVE RELATIONSHIP

The process by which a love relationship ordinarily develops has been variously analyzed by many behavioral scientists over the years. One theoretical formulation was made by Ira Reiss.[1] He described a progression to love as starting with rapport (feeling at ease with the other person and being relaxed and eager to talk about oneself and learn about the other person). Rapport leads to intimate self-revelation, which in turn leads to mutual dependency (each comes to depend on the other to fulfill his expectations) and, finally, to personality-need fulfillment.

The process can also be viewed as having the following three steps: First, one must make a good first impression on the other. Second, one must become a "sex-appropriate" friend. Third, one must become emotionally indispensable to the other person.

These steps ordinarily should be taken in this order, for taking them out of order can seriously affect the growth of a relationship. The man or woman who tries to become emotionally indispensable on the first date is probably not going to create conditions conducive to enlarging the relationship. But the person who is still trying to make an impression when the time has come to be emotionally indispensable is not going to succeed either.

THE FIRST IMPRESSION

Usually a good first glance is requisite to a good first impression. Most human beings have been conditioned to *temporal extension*, the process of judging what *will* be by what *is* through attitudes stereotyped over a lifetime. If, for example, one person sees another frowning, he assumes that the other has the full-time personality of a cold fish. On the other hand, if he should happen to catch the other smiling, he is likely to judge him as a warm, friendly person he would like to know.

The importance of the smile in social relationships in America is hard to overestimate. A smile is a gesture of response that immediately makes people feel accepted. If one withholds this symbol of friendliness and good humor, he is almost immediately stamped as an undesirable prospect for a deeper relationship.

Studies in stereotyping demonstrate the often underestimated importance of dress, manner, and smile. The stereotype for what is acceptable or desirable varies, of course, with the previous cultural conditioning of the

[1]Ira L. Reiss, *The Family System in America*, New York, Holt, Rinehart & Winston, 1971, p. 90.

judging person and with the current styles in dress and behavior within the culture. But the principle is the same. If the first impression is a good one, it often meets the other person's role expectations, and this, in turn, is the foundation for a successful relationship. The good first glance is not, however, synonymous with the complete good first impression.

Since more than 90 percent of the population does marry and since not that many people fit the stereotype of beautiful or handsome, it is obvious that other factors affect first impressions. Otherwise, the contact might never be made through which a couple finds out whether they can be compatible. Bernard Murstein found support for his belief that as a result of bargaining, men and women with qualities that are similar will be attracted to each other.[2] The theory holds that a person tends to balance what he has to offer in relation to what the other person has to offer. If he is not particularly handsome, he will not expect to attract a beautiful woman and therefore will look elsewhere. Also, if a woman is not particularly beautiful, a man tends to weigh her other attractive qualities more highly. In the end, the balancing of the total qualities in each tends to result in a similarity of qualities between the couple.

One of the reasons that people with similar qualities find each other attractive has to do with the self-confidence each feels in the presence of one he or she feels equal to. However, a person whose life experiences have lowered his self-esteem may not appreciate his own qualities and may lack self-confidence even when a potential partner is available. The fear of rejection is so great in people with low self-esteem that they either avoid meeting people of the opposite sex or project the expectation of rejection. The relationship of any two personalities is complex, but it is probably safe to generalize that the one thing that epitomizes the total good first impression is the self-confidence of the one who does the impressing.

THE IMPORTANCE OF SELF-CONFIDENCE

In attempting to establish some hypotheses about students' relative effectiveness in social relationships, social scientists made observations of situations in which a young woman was about to be introduced to a young man. The two following composite pictures emerged as plausible descriptions of the emotional mechanics of typical social introductions situations.[3] If the person

[2]Bernard I. Murstein, "Stimulus-Value-Role: A Theory of Marital Choice," *Journal of Marriage and the Family*, **32** (August, 1970), 465–481.
[3]These were reported in Richard H. Klemer, *A Man for Every Woman*, New York, Macmillan, 1959.

who was about to be introduced had self-confidence (see Appendix), he or she was far more likely to be successful in the introduction procedure. For example, a self-confident girl, when she was introduced, did not keep saying to herself all the time, "I wonder how I look? I wonder what he is thinking about me now?" Instead, she was thinking to herself, "I wonder what I can do to make him feel more comfortable?"

Because she was able to do this, the boy *did* feel more comfortable, and because he liked the comfortable feeling, he liked her. In turn, because he liked her, she felt even more desirable and self-confident, and she was able to be even more gracious. Consequently, her popularity tended to pyramid.

But when a young woman who had no such self-confidence was about to be introduced to a boy, she would say to herself, "Now I know he won't like me, so I won't take any initiative or he'll think I'm aggressive, and I won't say too much to him or he'll think I'm dumb."[4] Even with the Women's Liberation Movement, many girls still feel this way.

A young man being introduced to an unselfconfident girl would try at first to be pleasant. He would ask her several questions, but to each of these she would give a one-word reply. Thereupon, he would conclude that she really did not want to talk with him. Feeling rejected, he would slink off to nurse his wounded ego. Then the girl would say to herself, "Now, see, I knew he wouldn't like me!" As she lost more and more of the little self-confidence she did have, her popularity tends to decline.

Robert Coombs did a statistical study of social participation, self-concept, and interpersonal evaluation.[5] Coombs's sample consisted of 220 male and 220 female college students paired by a computer. His observational setting was a college dance attended by all 440 participants. For six months he studied the interpersonal responses of the partners and the effect of previous dating participation and self-concept on those responses. He found validation for all of his six hypotheses: (1) Those who were favorably evaluated by their dating partners, as compared to less-successful persons, more often conceived of themselves as having been successful in receiving favorable ratings. (2) Those who conceived of themselves as having been favorably evaluated by their dating partner, as compared to less-confident persons, more often participated in additional dates with their partners. (3)

---

[4]A classic study by Mirra Komarovsky indicated that many young women feel they have to "play dumb" to attract a man. See "Cultural Contradictions and Sex Roles," *American Journal of Sociology,* **52** (November, 1946), 184–189.

[5]Robert H. Coombs, "Social Participation, Self-Concept, and Interpersonal Evaluation," *Sociometry,* **32** (September, 1969), 273–286.

Those who had had experience in dating situations were more often favorably evaluated by their dating partners than were less-experienced persons. (4) Those persons who were most experienced in dating situations, as compared to the less-experienced persons, more often came to the dance possessing favorable views of themselves as dating partners. (5) Those who were favorably evaluated by their partners, as compared to less-successful persons, more often participated in additional dates with their partners. (6) Those who came to the dance possessing favorable concepts of their own dating desirability were more often favorably evaluated by their dating partners than were less-confident persons. In a way, the sixth hypothesis says it all.

There seems to be a tendency for both very high and very low self-esteem to be inversely related to marital happiness. A conclusion should *not* be drawn that the higher the self-confidence, the more likelihood of attracting a partner and therefore the greater marital happiness.[6]

It is extremely hazardous to describe anything as "human nature." The modifying force that cultural conditioning has on human drives is overwhelming. But in every culture and in every situation, the self-confidence that puts other people at ease, whether evidenced by saying the "right" things easily or by properly passing the peace pipe, is essential to the good first impression. It meets the other person's need for security right from the beginning.

BECOMING SEX-APPROPRIATE FRIENDS

If developing a love relationship with another person is the objective, then making a good first impression and becoming *just* friends is not enough. The buddy-buddy or brother-sister type of friendship may be very desirable for some relationships but it can sometimes actually be detrimental to romance. There must be sex-role appropriateness if the relationship is to move toward romantic love.

It is at this point that this analysis of the love progression differs from Reiss's. Reiss suggests that revealing one's intimate feelings and experiences is the second step in the progression to love. In some cases, this is undoubtedly true; being trusted with another's intimate secrets can be a moving and love-enriching experience, but only under circumstances in which the other has already been identified as a sex-appropriate love object. Many people, both men and women, have close personal friends of the

---

[6]Richard H. Klemer, "Self-Esteem and College Dating Experience as Factors in Mate Selection and Marital Happiness: A Longitudinal Study," *Journal of Marriage and the Family*, **33** (February, 1971), 183–187.

opposite sex who know all their secrets but whom they do not love romantically and would never consider marrying.

The identification of an appropriate other for developing romance, like the good first impression, is culturally conditioned. A female love object in one culture might be obese; in another she might wear a bone through her nose. In one culture, a desirable woman is aggressive; in another culture, she is reserved. This cultural variation is equally true for men.

Appropriate others can vary within the subcultural groups of a larger culture, too. A romance-stimulating woman in Hollywood might be heavily made-up, bejeweled, and aggressive. An ideal love object among the Amish of central Pennsylvania might be unadorned, hard working, and reticent. A love object on a college campus might be a long-haired, raggedly dressed intellectual who disdains the cultural codes of the masses.

The one thing that is universal about the love object is that he arouses the potential lover's romantic emotions. To do this he must be appropriate to the particular other's personal sex-role expectation. In other words, when a woman looks at a potential lover, she should be able both to think and to feel romance. She should be able to suggest to herself that this man is or could be, in fact, her hero. Similarly, the way *she* looks and acts should consciously (or subconsciously) stimulate romantic feelings within her male partner. In the late 1960s, there were some writers, notably Marshall McLuhan, who suggested that we have been moving away from differentiated sex roles and, consequently, away from romantic love altogether.[7] The prevalence of young men wearing long hair and beads and women in tight pants and loose shirts led McLuhan to conclude that being a masculine man or feminine woman was becoming less important in our society. He even suggested that, as sex-role importance decreases, the frequency of sexual intercourse might decrease, because there would be no need for the male to be sexually aggressive in order to prove his masculinity either to his partner or to himself. A decade later we find that this has not occurred.

Many observers, while conceding that there have always been and probably always will be minor fads and fashions in sex-role observances, see no complete loss of sex differentiation in the foreseeable future. Both McLuhan and his critics agree that sex role and romantic love are highly correlated. Those who wish to believe in romantic love and wish to per-

---

[7]Marshall McLuhan and George B. Leonard, "The Future of Sex," *Look*, **31** (July 25, 1967), 56–63.

petuate it, at least in their own lives, are going to find that sex-role appropriateness is a large part of the package.

Until very recently, there has been a tendency for some writers in the family relationships field to downgrade romantic love and sexual attractiveness as sound bases for lasting relationships, on the theory that the violent emotional upsurges produced by such feelings are not conducive to building permanent relationships. It is true that rushing headlong into marriage because of a physical attraction increases the probability of marital failure, but it is also true that the excitement of romantic love is often responsible for enabling the partners to surmount some of the difficult adjustments of the early months of marriage. In many instances, if the partners were not so much in love, they might never survive the first year of living together.

Moreover, it is not necessarily true that all romance must be lost from the relationship as it matures. There are many long-married couples who still have excitement and pride in being together. Although, as we shall see, disillusionment is fairly common after marriage, it is not necessarily universal, nor does it have to be complete.

Having made a first impression and become sex-appropriate friends, there remains for those who wish to establish a deep relationship the most important process of all—becoming emotionally indispensable to the other person.

BECOMING EMOTIONALLY INDISPENSABLE

Some years ago, Oliver Ohmann pointed to a curious fallacy to which many modern Americans cling. The fallacy is that, by dressing up their appearance and manner, they can become so irresistible and fascinating that other people will naturally fall in love with them.[8] It is not that way at all. A person falls in love because he *needs* the other person. The wisest course for the one who wishes love, therefore, is to meet the emotional needs of the other person, thereby making himself emotionally indispensable. Meeting the other person's emotional needs is not only the best way to get and keep another person's love, in the long run it is the only way.

But what *are* the other person's needs? How can you identify them?

Let's go back for a moment to the four needs postulated as universal by William I. Thomas: the needs for recognition, response, security, and

[8]Oliver Ohmann, "The Psychology of Attraction," in Helen Mougey Jordan, ed., *You and Marriage*, New York, Wiley, 1964, pp. 13–39.

new experience.[9] Although this short list is not complete, and although needs vary in intensity from person to person, it and the following illustration can serve as a starting point for our discussion.

Hank was a high-school junior. He had been looking forward for months to the junior prom to which he was going to take his classmate Mary. On the Saturday morning of the dance, Mary's mother called to say that Mary had the mumps and could not go to the dance. Hank was terribly disappointed.

Upstairs in the same apartment house lived Jane, an attractive career woman of twenty-five. She had dates, many of them, with men of her own age. Although Jane thought they had had a good time, the men usually said goodnight to her at her door and never called her again. Jane had a date for Sunday evening, but she did not have one on the night of the junior prom. When she heard about young Hank's disappointment, she offered to go with him to the dance. To say that Hank was surprised was putting it mildly, but the more he thought about it, the more he liked the idea, and soon he agreed.

At the end of the evening, when they got home from the dance, Hank was completely in love with Jane. Yet the next night, when Jane went out with a man of her own age, the usual thing happened. Although she thought they had had a good time on the date, the man said goodnight to her at the door, and she never heard from him again. Why did Jane engender an affectional response in Hank, yet arouse no response whatsoever in the older men?

You could say it was a matter of maturity. But that explains almost nothing. What actually happened was this: When Jane started off to the dance with Hank, she expected—and *expected* is the key word—that she would meet his needs. When he talked about himself and what a good football player he was, she listened intently, thereby meeting his need for *recognition*. When he complimented her, she accepted his praise and immediately returned the conversation to him. When he fumbled with the change at the refreshment stand and spilled his drink all over the table, she was the picture of poise and easy helpfulness. She gave him a *security* in the social situation that Mary, ten years younger, was not yet mature enough to know how to do. Jane *responded* to Hank and met his need for a *new experience*. Thus, it was almost inevitable that he would reward her with his love feelings.

But what happened the next night? The next night Jane expected

---

[9]William I. Thomas, *The Unadjusted Girl*, Boston, Little, Brown, 1925, p. 4.

—and again *expected* is the key word—that since the older man had asked her for a date he would meet *her* needs. Since Jane was intelligent as well as attractive, she knew that the male of the species requires a certain amount of flattering attention, so she perfunctorily complimented him on his accomplishments. But the genuine giving feelings she had had with young Hank were not evident, and the man quickly sensed her insincerity.

After all, Jane thought (and her attitude betrayed), why should *she*, intelligent and attractive Jane, subordinate *her* personality needs to those of the man she was out with? Didn't he ask *her* for a date? Was she expected to be subservient in the manner of a Japanese housewife? No, indeed, Jane rationalized; he should be happy merely to be out with an entertaining woman who was sophisticated and impressive.

But was he? No. Are other men? Generally not, although there are, of course, some men whose personality needs for recognition or new experience could be fulfilled by a coldly impersonal but exquisitely beautiful woman, just as there are some other men who need to be dominated in order to feel secure. Most men, however—and most women, too—have less complex personality needs that are better satisfied by genuine recognition, response, security, and new experience.

Almost always it is a serious mistake to believe that cosmetics or glamour can do more than get a relationship to the sex-appropriate-friend stage. From there on, building a love relationship is a matter of becoming indispensable to the other person by a genuine sensitivity to his emotional needs and a genuine desire to meet them.

It is equally important that a man meet a woman's needs as that a woman meet a man's. There is no sex priority in need-meeting. A deep love relationship follows from a casual acquaintance when there is an unusual ability on the part of one individual to sense and to fulfill the psychological needs of the other. Fancy clothes, expensive automobiles, and after-shave lotion are relatively impotent when compared to the addicting power of being able to understand, reassure, and respond to another person.

This suggests one more definition of love: *An individual is in love when meeting the emotional needs of his beloved becomes an ultimate emotional necessity for him.* When one clearly perceives the other's basic personality needs—some to a fault—and still feels he wants to help that other find satisfaction for those needs more than anything else in the world, then he is in love.

From this definition it is clear why the process of continuing love relationships is as difficult as it is. First, it takes a great deal of perception to know what an individual's needs really are. Although it may be easy to see, for example, that a boastful person has a large need for recognition, it is often more difficult to see that the retiring person has an even greater need: He demands that you meet his need for security before he will even talk with you. What needs are being met in the following case?

CASE 10 BOB AND JENNIFER

"I remember the night Jenny and I met. It was at a party, and I was a little ill at ease because I never did very well at those things where you just float around and meet people. Jenny was not one of the prettiest girls there, and to tell you the truth I really didn't pay much attention to her until I ran out of prospects. She was talking to another guy, and when I walked up he left. I really felt uncomfortable then, but I remember Jenny's smile—she made me feel as if I had been the one she'd wanted to talk to all evening. She started asking about my major, my family, what I wanted to do after graduation—she made me feel as if she cared. I felt important, secure. She told me a little about herself and her goals, and I thought, 'Wow, this is some girl.'

"We started dating the following night and from that point on everything seemed to follow a natural course. She continued to be very attentive, not subservient, and very sensitive to my needs.

"Now, when I want her to stay home after we're married, she says that she spent four years getting an education, and she doesn't want to waste it. She says she'll need some outside interests. Suddenly I don't feel like the center of her universe anymore."

Jennifer tells the same story: "I have never had trouble meeting people; it always seemed to come naturally. The night I met Bob I could tell that he was a little lost, so I began asking about his life and what he planned to do with it. We were very comfortable with each other from the very first and throughout the subsequent courtship the pattern stayed pretty much the same: We talked about him and I did things to make him feel important. You might say that the whole situation was misrepresented on my part, but I found that while I knew it was not on a permanent basis, it bolstered my ego to make him feel that way. Now that I know we're getting married, I can't find it in myself to go under just to make him feel that he is in control, because truthfully, I don't think he is.

"I do love him, but if we are going to live together for the rest of our lives, there are going to have to be some changes made in the relationship."

There are many other examples. For instance, it does not necessarily follow that a man will fall in love with the cook at the luncheonette he patronizes simply because she meets what he feels is his primary need for food. Nor will he necessarily fall in love with a casual pickup simply because she meets what he feels is his primary need for sex.

Another part of the difficulty in recognizing needs results from the fact that, although all people have needs, these needs differ in intensity. For example, some men need response so badly that they spend all their waking hours seeking it. Others can go off for weeks or months at a time without apparently needing or missing response from another person.

Still another difficulty about meeting needs is that not everybody can outwardly express his love feelings in return for having his needs met. The need-meeting may be very satisfying, but the individual whose needs are being met is unable to communicate his pleasure. This inability may betray his greatest need: for someone who will understand how he feels without his having to make it explicit.

There are, of course, people who can absorb need-meeting gestures from others like a sponge and never feel or give anything in return. These selfish people are a dead end as far as any true love relationship is concerned. They are probably still a minority in our culture. Such people can be helped to know and understand love themselves only through psychotherapy.

To illustrate the problems involved in need-meeting, we might consider what happened to Linda. As a young child, Linda worshipped her father but was rejected by her mother. She had no dates until she was far beyond the usual age for starting to date. When she got to college, she met Ted, a handsome young man who, by the very fact that he looked in her direction, seemed to meet Linda's easily discernible needs for affection, recognition, and security. By giving Linda a very little attention, Ted won her undying affection.

But Linda did not know how to go about meeting Ted's real needs. She did not realize that Ted was a demanding, highly self-centered individual, from a different subcultural group where exploitation of another individual was a casually accepted custom. The woman who became a physical outlet for his sex tensions was not, by any stretch of the imagination, meeting his emotional needs. Ted demanded and got submissive intercourse from a large number of women, including Linda. He needed a secure, determined woman who would meet his emotionally conditioned expectation that he would marry only a virgin who refused him premarital intercourse even though he insisted on it. He needed a courageous, aggressive, protecting, and dominating mother-figure who could give him the security that he had known briefly as a child but that had been snatched from him by his mother's early death. Because of her limited experience in dealing with people, Linda never even got to know Ted's real needs, let alone to meet them.

NEEDS CHANGE

The fact that an individual's needs may change as he moves from place to place and from time to time is, as Bernard Murstein, among others, has pointed out, another major stumbling block in need-meeting.[10] Some needs change in well-patterned progression as the person grows older. Typical adolescents want less response from their parents and more recognition from their peers. Older people want fewer new experiences and more security.

But sometimes there are changes in the direction and intensity of needs that, unless recognized in advance by the love partner, can be seriously damaging to the relationship. Consider the following classic case, which has come to be known as the medical-student problem. Actually, medical students are probably no more prone to this need-change difficulty than students in other specialties, but they have gained a widespread reputation for it.

CASE 11 SALLY AND RONALD

Sally and Ronald grew up together. They came from the same neighborhood in a small town, went to school and church together, and started going steady in high school. When the time came, they went off to the same college. By the time they were juniors, they decided that they could no longer wait to be married. After the wedding, Sally quit going to school and took a job as a typist so that Ron could complete his education.

In due course, Ron was graduated from college and admitted to medical school. Sally and Ron moved into a small housing project originally designed for low-income families. Sally, of course, continued to work, but she resented that, besides typing for eight hours a day, the household chores were largely her responsibility as well. In the few hours that Ron was home,

---

[10]Bernard I. Murstein, "The Complementary Needs Hypothesis in Newlywed and Middle-Aged Married Couples," *Journal of Abnormal and Social Psychology*, **63** (July, 1961), 194–196.

he usually had some studying to do. Sally sometimes suspected that he could have done his studying at school, but then he would have missed the cafeteria conversation and the occasional bridge games with the other students.

Finally the great day came, and Ron was graduated from medical school and accepted as a resident at a nearby hospital. There was still very little money to spare, so Sally continued to work, but at long last she persuaded Ron to start a family. Before his residency was complete, they had a child. Sally quit her job and seemed to be very happy with her new life. Getting started in practice meant more lean years. Moreover, another baby was born. With two in diapers and a house to take care of, Sally was always tired. But she loved Ron and she believed Ron loved her.

Within a few years, Ron's practice began to prosper. In fact, before long, Sally and Ron had money for all the material things they wanted. At first Ron worked very hard to pay off the debts and to build up an investment income. After a while, however, he began to take an increasing amount of time off to play golf at the country club. Sally went to the country club once or twice, but she was a small-town girl and felt out of place there. The women there talked about golf and bridge, neither of which she played. Ron kept urging her to try, but finally he gave up. With increasing frequency, he went to the country club by himself.

Meanwhile two more children had arrived, and Sally was ever busier with home-making activities. At the country club, Ron met a great many people, including some attractive young divorcees who had grown up in the atmosphere of the country club. Sophisticated and charming, they had gone to elite Eastern women's colleges and seemed able to anticipate exactly what Ron wanted even before he himself realized it.

One day Ron came home and, in effect, said to Sally: "I have found that the women at the country club meet my needs better than you do. I've changed. I need someone who is gay and sophisticated. I am sure you wouldn't want me to spend the rest of my life with you, knowing that I didn't love you. You are a good woman and would make some other man a good wife, but you and I no longer have common interests. I will always take care of you and the children financially, but I want a divorce."

When did Sally and Ron become emotionally dispensable to each other? Did it happen equally to both at one time? Did it happen in stages? What cultural expectations were reinforced in both Sally and Ron that explain their behavior throughout? How did cognitive dissonance about expectations and realities operate to change Ron's and Sally's behavior? What does this case show about allowing wide discrepancies to develop in education, social behavior, and plans for the future?

How are the following generalizations about human behavior operating in this case? (See the Appendix.)

When needs change in intensity and in rank order, behavior changes.

When a person is conditioned to act in a certain way, that action continues so long as reinforcement continues.

When a person's needs change, the type of reinforcement that satisfies him changes, and therefore old reinforcements do not continue the behavior.

When two people's education and activities begin to be far different, they have a different set of needs.

When a wide discrepancy occurs between a person's expectations and his behavior, cognitive dissonance sets in and the person feels compelled to bring expectations and behavior together.

WHOSE NEEDS COME FIRST?

After all is said and done, the biggest difficulty in meeting other people's needs, and so engendering their love, results from the difficulty of putting one's own needs aside in order to meet the other person's needs first. This can be rather easily illustrated. Suppose a group of young women were asked to list the things they did not like about the young men they dated. The list, which would probably be very long and very thorough, would undoubtedly contain the following:

1. They're conceited.
2. They change girl friends without cause.
3. They make too many sexual advances.
4. They call too late.
5. They suggest the same old places to go.

Now suppose the young women were asked to analyze the needs involved in these complaints and—more importantly—*whose* needs were involved. On the assumption that the frequency of repetition is related to the intensity of need, it might be speculated that the boys who talk about themselves excessively have a deep need for recognition and response as well as a need for the ego security of knowing that they are worthy persons. It might also be a valid deduction that men who change girl friends often have a greater-than-average need for response from a large number of persons. The response need might also tend to explain the behavior of the "wolves," though, in their case, biological drives enter the picture and so does the fact that there is a recognition value accorded to the young man who can report back to his friends that he has been victor in another sex adventure.

But what about the other items on the list? What of the young men who call too late and who always take the girls to the same old places? Obviously somebody's needs are not being met, *but whose?* Not the young men's, but rather the young women's! The men who call too late are neither meeting their partners' needs for security nor recognizing them as popular and important young women. The men who take their dates to the same old places are not meeting their partners' needs for new experiences.

This part of the analysis often comes as a surprise to those who, because they have been catering for many years to their partners' obvious needs, have felt that they have therefore been completely self-sacrificing. Many men and many women do not realize how demanding they are about having their own needs met.

Usually, before he is ready to see how he can be more attractive by placing the first emphasis on meeting another person's need, the romance seeker must have many insights about his own needs. Many people are so conditioned to look to their own status and prestige that they play games intended to make the other person put himself in the giving position first. If the objective is immediate ego satisfaction—and nothing more—that is probably exactly all the winner of the game will net. But if the objective is to promote a real, deep emotional feeling on the part of the other person, then meeting the other's needs first is more logical and more effective. The relationships that continue to grow richer with the passing of the years are those in which each person can recognize and meet both the permanent and the changing needs of the other.

Giving need-satisfaction first is an evidence of strength that only the strong and unselfish can afford. Indeed, it is only those people with superior self-respect, or "self-love" in the finest sense, who can meet the other person's needs at all.[11] The insecure individual is too busy looking out for his own tender self.

It should be made eminently clear that meeting another person's emotional needs does not imply that one should become a jellyfish. A sense of personal worth and integrity is absolutely necessary, or it will be impossible to meet any other person's needs for very long. People want their needs

[11]There is an excellent discussion of self-love in Erich Fromm, *The Art of Loving*, New York, Harper & Row, 1956, pp. 57–63.

to be met by secure, positive others and not by fawning, supplicative, "try-too-harders." Experiments with rats have led some psychologists to believe that most animals, including humans, do not want all of their needs satisfied too easily. As Leon Festinger says it, "Insufficient reward does lead to the development of extra preference. . . . Rats and people come to love things for which they have suffered."[12]

This correlation between insufficient reward and extra preference can also be explained by the theory of cognitive dissonance.[13] A person whose expectation and behavior do not coincide is in a state of cognitive dissonance. The theory is that when there is a state of cognitive dissonance, the person will change either his expectation or his behavior to get rid of the dissonance, a state that is not easy to live with. In the case of the rats, the reward was insufficient and therefore the conclusion was drawn that "expectation" had to change. Love for the things for which they had suffered made up for the insufficient rewards and rid them of the dissonance. It is debatable whether an infrahuman can have expectations or not; however in humans it is a different matter. When a person's expectations of another person do not coincide with that other person's behavior, then dissonance occurs in the observer. To reduce the dissonance the observer has to change his expectations of the other person.

Sometimes dissonance is useful in attracting another person. The person who lacks sufficient self-confidence and gives too much in his attempt to win affection may not attract the one he wanted. He does not allow enough dissonance to occur in that other person to cause the other person to direct behavior toward him.

As we shall come to see in the later chapters on adjustment, the husband who tries to do everything his wife might possibly want him to do is not always the most successful of husbands, for he deprives his wife of the opportunity and challenge of working for his love. Here again, perceptive analysis of a partner's true emotional dynamics is a critical factor in need-meeting.

CASE 12 ROLF AND LAURA

Laura, an attractive, twenty-year-old college junior, had been going with Rolf for about two years. She was beginning to wonder if she loved him enough

---

[12]Leon Festinger, "The Psychological Effects of Insufficient Rewards," *American Psychologist,* **16** (January, 1961), 11.

[13]Leon Festinger, *A Theory of Cognitive Dissonance,* Stanford, Calif., Stanford University Press, 1957.

to marry him, which he was eager that she do. "He's a wonderful fellow and most of the time I enjoy being with him. We have fun together," she said. "But I'm beginning to wonder if I am affectionate enough for him. I come from a sort of reserved family. My father and mother never outwardly express affection toward one another, and I am a little uneasy when I see people mushing over each other. But he is from an excitable, foreign-born family and he expects—in fact he demands—a great many evidences of love all the time. I can't figure out whether he was denied enough response or whether he just got used to having too much.

"Anyway, Rolf is always telling me how much he loves me in such elaborate ways that I am embarrassed. He keeps trying to coax me to say that I love him, and sometimes I just can't. It isn't that I don't think I do (or is it?). It's just that I get embarrassed around that sort of talk.

"He is always coming over to my house, even when I'd rather he didn't. I really don't have enough time to study. He brings me gifts and presents. He almost smothers me. I think the time when I was most happy was when we first started going out together. Rolf was then interested in another girl, and I had to compete with her in order to get him to call me at all. Last week for three days he didn't come over to the house. I began to get a little uneasy, so I went to see him. On the way over I got a sort of a thrill for the first time in a long while. It was nice to be able to do something for him that I wanted to do.

"Now Rolf wants to get engaged. It isn't enough for him to go steady. I've always wanted to have a career after I finished college. Not a long one; I want to get married someday. But I do want to have some freedom. Please don't misunderstand me, though. Rolf is awfully nice, and I would hate to lose him. I've gone with a lot of other boys—some were the kind who push you around—and I wasn't really very happy with them, either. I'm afraid that if I tell him we won't get engaged, he'll find some other girl. He really needs affection, and I think he really wants to get married. What shall I do?"

IMPROVING RELATABILITY

If you are really motivated to improve your relatability, and if you accept the theoretical formulation that real love develops in steps from the good first impression to becoming sex-appropriate friends and is brought to completion by becoming emotionally indispensable to the other person, then perhaps the following suggestions will help you. They smack of being a simplistic "how-to" guide unless you have become good at applying principles or theories to ordinary behavior. Your needs may be better met by a complete understanding of the underlying theories and generalizations on which these suggestions are based. Take some or all of them and support them with acceptable psychological and sociological principles.

Most of the easy generalizations about the good first-glance impression have already been made: Smile, respond easily, and keep your appearance within the expectation tolerance of those you wish to impress. In connection with the last point, find out all you can about the group you are preparing to enter and about the people you are about to meet. The more you know about the group's (and the individual's) expectations, the more confidence, poise, and relaxed security you can have.

Since self-confidence is so important to the total first impression, anything that can be done to build your self-confidence and reduce your initial tension will be helpful. Some of the following suggestions may work for you; some may not: (1) Many people find that they can make a better impression by *trying* to be calm and relaxed. Practice "loosening up" beforehand. (2) Remembering that the other people are probably just as concerned as you are may help. If you can understand that they are quiet not because they do not like you but because they are tense too, perhaps you can get the courage to take the lead in the conversation and thus win their friendship. (3) Not trying too hard sometimes helps, too. You may feel that you must impress the other people with your accomplishments. The less they seem to respond, the harder you try. Actually, they may have been very impressed, but you may not have given them an opportunity to say so in their own way. Usually, people hear and see you, even when you are not sure they do. (4) Listen carefully. Listen to other persons' names and what they have to say. Ask discreet questions and get to know where they are from, what they have done, and what their families were like. All these things can give you invaluable clues in talking further with them. (5) Assume that they like you. As a matter of fact, assume that everybody likes you, until it is proved otherwise. If you behave as if everybody likes you, they probably will. (6) Think of other persons' needs and their *likes*, remembering that this will probably make them want to reciprocate. Do not overdo it; there is a time to receive as well as a time to give. (7) When you can no longer appropriately talk about other people, talk about those things you are most enthusiastic about—with the exception, of course, of other opposite-sex friends. They will be interested in almost anything that really interests you, provided you can project that interest to them by your own enthusiasm. (8) Be positive when they ask for your opinion. Not knowing what you think often contributes to other people's insecurity. For example, if they ask if you would like to go to the movies and you say "I don't know" or "It doesn't matter," you are adding to their insecurity. If, however, you are enthusiastic about your likes and are willing to express your dislikes openly, they can feel contented that they have made the right decision by taking you where you want to go. (9) Try not to worry about your first-impression failures. The first thing a good salesman has to learn is that he cannot make a sale every time. If he lets himself get discouraged over the last sale he did not make, he is sure to muff the next one.

Increasing your relatability in the sex-appropriate-friend stage is more difficult, for it often may involve changing some of your customs, attitudes, values, and expectations in order to accept others' customs. First *can* you change? Second, is it worth changing? Sometimes it is easier and better to find someone whose ideal you can be without too much alteration on either's part.

If you do decide that you want the other person enough to change, remember that it must be an honest change. Usually the only person you can change is yourself, and you cannot do it by adopting a new set of tricks or techniques all of a sudden. Any change in your personality involves a lot of motivation, a lot of self-discipline, a lot of practice, and a lot of patience.

Even if there were techniques and tricks available, using them might be self-defeating. Words and phrases seductive to one person may turn out to be repulsive to another. Pressure techniques that force some people into the desired action motivate others toward undesired behavior.

Moreover, do you want people you can trick? Or would you, in reality, feel a little contempt for them? If, in fact, they have to be guided to a decision, are they the decisive people you want?

In the very process of exploring whether or not you can meet their expectations of a sex-appropriate friend, you may well have started the process of becoming emotionally indispensable, for in order to understand others' expectations, you will have to try to understand their cultural conditioning involved. That very interest on your part may meet one of their most important needs.

But the chances are that they have other needs too, and if you decide that you do want them as friends, you are going to have to determine what those needs are. The best way to do this is to observe and to listen. Some people are trying to tell others about themselves all the time, even when they are being overly quiet.

Merely *knowing* another's emotional needs is not enough. If you want to become emotionally indispensable, you have to be able to meet those needs as well. This is something you can practice, even when you are not trying to develop a deep emotional relationship. The butcher, the baker, and the candlestick maker have emotional needs, too. You can start learning to improve your emotional-needs-meeting ability by analyzing your roommate. Watch closely how he or she reacts. Give him or her medium doses of recognition, response, security, and new experience, and study the results. Then try it on a tougher case: that grouchy person in your lab perhaps.

But, remember that your feelings have to be genuine. If you start developing close relationships, it will be because you have genuinely changed, and others are reacting to that change. Remember, too, that *you have a social responsibility not to encourage a deeper relationship than you are prepared to continue.*

7

SOCIAL FACTORS IN MATE SELECTION

Need-meeting may explain why two people love each other, but it does not necessarily explain why two particular people get married. A person may have many loves. Many other people could meet his needs. Why then does he marry the one he does?

There are usually *many* reasons (and some unreasoned feelings) that control both the opportunity to marry and the final decision to take the step. These reasons and feelings have been divided into sociocultural factors, which sociologists have emphasized, and personal and emotional factors, which are usually thought of as being in the psychologist's jurisdiction. We will presently take a look at the sociological concepts of propinquity, exogamy, and endogamy, and later at the psychological concepts of needs and neurotic interactions.

In any *particular* marriage relationship, however, all these factors together may not answer the question "Why did they marry?" for there are an infinite number of chance meetings, capricious impulses, accidents, coincidences, impressions, *faux pas*, missed opportunities, and deliberate schemes that prevent or encourage the marriage of two individuals. Although most marriage partners are aware of at least some of the reasons why they married, in many cases the deciding factors are unconscious to one or both of them.

It is important, nevertheless, that every student of the empathetic approach give careful examination to factors in mate selection, for, as we shall see when we get to marriage adjustment, the best way to ensure good relationships in any marriage is to improve the choice of the marriage mate in the first place. What can be done to ameliorate marriage difficulties *after* marriage is limited; what can be done to avoid marriage difficulties *beforehand*, by wise selection of partners, is infinite.

PROPINQUITY

One of the reasons why people marry the mate they do is because the mate is *there*. Someone who is close at hand is a more probable candidate than someone who is far away.

Apparently, residential propinquity is not necessarily a *cause* of marital choice but rather the *effect* of social considerations that cause people with like interests and like backgrounds to live in the same neighborhoods. Since most people do choose—sometimes with considerable parental help—mates with similar subcultural backgrounds, in the past they were more likely to find them close to home.

Today people in cities and suburbs are much more likely to have culturally mixed backgrounds. More Americans choose mates who were reared hundreds of miles away. More young people have automobiles, more students go away to college, and 20 percent of American families move every year. People still tend to marry partners who are close in distance, but the closeness is more likely to be as of *right now* rather than as of their childhood. Current job propinquity seems to be as important as residential propinquity.

But even the new closeness has to be somewhat continuous for a marriage to result. J. Richard Udry points to studies that show that separation or lack of propinquity during courtship is one of the most frequent reasons for breaking engagements. He says, "Specifically, the more time a couple spends together during courtship, the more likely they are to marry."[1] It may be helpful to have this authoritative sociological validation, but most lovers have known it for a long time.

EXOGAMY AND ENDOGAMY

Stated succinctly, *exogamy* means marrying outside one's own tribe. In some times and in some parts of the world, members of the same clan were forbidden to marry. Exogamy exists in the American culture in the form of incest laws and taboos. Were it not for those, we might have brother-sister marriage or, at least, more cousin marriage.

In the United States, as in most cultures, we have patterns of *endogamy* (marrying within one's tribe) as well. *Cultural endogamy*, the subtle pressure of group customs and group values, still has a significant effect on our mate-selection patterns.

Current movements toward social integration and ecumenicity in religious thought have given new vigor to an old dilemma for young Americans. Which is the more important value: to maintain the traditional endogamous patterns of mate selection and thus to align oneself with parental desire and a statistically greater probability of marriage success, or to break through cultural barriers in the ultimate demonstration of independence and democratic idealism and have the supposedly exciting experience of marrying someone "different"?

Alert students will immediately point out that very few people have to make this kind of cognitive decision when they are about to marry. By the time people are ready for marriage, they are usually deeply in love, and the decision to marry or not to marry is a matter of satisfying or denying emotional fulfillment with very little reference to any social decision.

[1] J. Richard Udry, *The Social Context of Marriage*, 2nd ed., Philadelphia, Lippincott, 1971, p. 186.

But somewhere along the line, from the first date to the wedding, a decision *does* have to be made. "Endogamy, yes or no" is an intellectual choice (albeit sometimes a gradual and semiconscious one) before it ever becomes subordinated and obviated by love. Disillusioning as it may seem to the romantics, we do not allow ourselves to fall in love until we have established a field of eligibles. For example, except in very rare instances, no one permits himself to "fall in love" with his brother or sister, regardless of how common the bond or how close the relationship. Those who do fall in love with heterogeneous others have allowed this to happen.

There are many mate-selection practices today that could result only from parental pressures, albeit more subtle now. As Robert Coombs puts it, "This more subtle means is not unimportant, for although a child may rebel against domination, he cannot escape the ideas conditioned in him from his childhood."[2]

Most children today, though, are exposed to cross-cultural influences, whether their parents like it or not. Now almost 90 percent of our young people enter high schools, and, even in suburban areas, the high school is more cross-cultural than ever before. Some 40 percent of these young people go on to college. There, too, they find that there is a wide heterogeneity of backgrounds among the students. Campus life today, especially at large universities, often encourages the associations of people with diverse cultural and subcultural origins.[3]

Even so, there is abundant evidence that, among the total American population, endogamous courtship and marriage are still the rule rather than the exception. We will examine just a few of the classic areas in which social endogamy is operative: race, religion, social class, age, and education.

RACIAL INTERMARRIAGE

Race is undoubtedly the most strongly continuing endogamous norm. There are surprisingly few studies of interracial marriage, and many of these are out of date, but there is some evidence that interracial dating and marriage are slowly increasing. The principle explaining this increase is that behavior becomes more prominent when there is greater opportunity and a more permissive attitude and when there is a smaller discrepancy between a person's

---

[2]Robert H. Coombs, "Reinforcement of Values in the Parental Home as a Factor in Mate Selection," *Marriage and Family Living,* **24** (May, 1962), 157.

[3]Gerald R. Leslie and Arthur S. Richardson, "Family Versus Campus Influences in Relation to Mate Selection," *Social Problems,* **4** (October, 1956), 117–121.

value and his behavior. Those who do participate in interracial dating still have to pay the price of peer and community support.[4]

Linton Freeman believed that most of those young people who enter into interracial and interethnic marriages were in overactive rebellion against their parents or against their social group.[5] However, this is not necessarily the reason today.

Although racial intermarriage may have been slowly increasing in the United States in recent years, the future rate of increase is obscure. Udry suggests that it seems unlikely that there will be a large increase in interracial marriage in the near future, and Heer finds it hard to imagine that any large-scale black-white intermingling will take place within the next hundred years.[6]

An Associated Press survey found that, in the first full year after the Supreme Court nullified the states' legal bars to interracial marriage in 1967, less than a hundred interracial marriages took place in all of the seventeen states that previously had laws banning such marriages.[7]

That there is an increase in interracial marriage is supported by a study of such marriages in Hawaii. Although more farm laborers intermarry, professional workers do also. In a ten-year period, interracial marriage for both occupation groups increased by more than 15 percent. The percentage of farm laborers who intermarried was nearly twice that of professional workers.[8] The total number of black-white marriages in 1960 was 51,409. In 1970 there were 64,789—an increase of 26 percent.[9] There may be as many as one million black-white married couples today according to one source.[10] However, black-white marriages continue to constitute less than 1 percent of all marriages.

A study of Los Angeles marriages in both 1952 and 1962 found that the rate for all racial intermarriage (including Orientals as well as whites and blacks) had more than doubled in that period, although such marriages

[4]Frank A. Petroni, "Teen-age Interracial Dating," *Transaction,* **8** (September, 1971), 54–59.

[5]Linton Freeman, "Homogamy in Interethnic Mate Selection," *Sociology and Social Research,* **39** (July, 1959), 369–377.

[6]Udry, op. cit., p. 191; and David M. Heer, "Negro-White Marriages in the United States," *Journal of Marriage and the Family,* **28** (August, 1966), 273.

[7]*The New York Times,* July 28, 1968, 35.

[8]Robert C. Schmitt, "Recent Trends in Hawaiian Interracial Marriage Rates by Occupation," *Journal of Marriage and the Family,* **33** (May, 1971), 373–374.

[9]David M. Heer, "The Prevalence of Black-White Marriage in the United States, 1960 and 1970," *Journal of Marriage and the Family,* **36** (May, 1974), 247.

[10]Bert N. Adams, *The American Family,* Chicago, Markham, 1971.

amounted to only about 1.5 percent of all marriages.[11] But because Los Angeles has a greater variety of racial and ethnic groups than most other cities in the United States, these statistics may be somewhat misleading. Barnett reported that, in all California, the interracial marriage rate was 1.4 percent in 1959, the last year, incidentally, that California law required that race be recorded on the marriage license.

The black-white marriage rate in California is considerably lower than the rate of all interracial marriages. Of all the white California males marrying in 1959, fewer than 0.1 percent married blacks, and of the white California females marrying that year, fewer than 0.3 percent married blacks. The great preponderance of interracial marriages in California was between whites and nonwhites other than blacks.[12] More recent data in the two states for which they are available show the black-white marriage rate to be about 0.1 percent in Michigan and about 0.001 percent in Nebraska.[13]

The following generalizations are adapted from Larry Barnett's 1963 review of the available studies on interracial marriage:

1. Whites appear to be more willing to engage in interracial marriage with Orientals than with blacks.
2. Among whites, it is Protestant and Catholic males and Jewish females who most frequently marry members of other races.
3. Religiously less devout persons more often marry interracially than the religiously more devout.
4. Persons who have experienced disorganized and stressful parental families are more likely to marry members of other races than those who were raised in cohesive and stable families.
5. Persons living in urban areas are more likely to marry interracially than persons living in rural areas.
6. In interracial marriages, most studies found that the spouses more often come from different religions and from different socioeconomic levels, although one study suggests that the majority of mates in interracial marriages come from the same socioeconomic group.
7. In interracial marriages, it appears that the nonwhite male has a higher-than-average economic status, and the white male and female and the nonwhite female have a lower-than-average socioeconomic level.
8. In black-white marriages, the black is more often the male spouse, but in

---

[11]John J. Burma, "Interethnic Marriages in Los Angeles, 1948–1959," paper read at the American Sociological Association, Washington, D.C., August, 1962.

[12]Larry D. Barnett, "Research on International and Interracial Marriages," *Marriage and Family Living,* **25** (February, 1963), 105–107.

[13]Heer, op. cit., 262–273.

Oriental-white marriages, the white male more frequently marries a Japanese female and the Chinese male marries a white female.

9. Among those who undertake an interracial marriage, a greater-than-average number have been married previously.

10. Foreign-born white males more than native white males, and native white females more than foreign-born white females, undertake black-white marriages.

11. In black-white marriages, the family of the black spouse seems to be more willing to accept the couple than does the family of the white spouse.

12. American males and females marrying out of their racial group are generally older than average at the time of marriage.[14]

Most of these generalizations still hold true, but a study of twenty black-white marriages made by Ernest Porterfield in the early 1970s revealed that negative attitudes are far fewer than they once were.[15] Although all of the couples claimed they married for love, some were aware that they were expressing personal desires for prestige or vindictiveness toward society. In Porterfield's study, twelve of the sixteen white brides' families opposed the marriage from the beginning, whereas only three of the sixteen black grooms' families were in opposition. This opposition from the families, more than opposition from the community, was a source of frustration for the couples.

Some investigators believe that the gradual increase in school integration, which will hasten interracial association, will have a considerable effect on increasing intermarriage. E. A. Thomas Barth, a University of Washington sociologist, pointed out in 1967 that "In our segregated society young people have not been in contact with other ethnic groups at the dating period. But contacts have been increasing. We can expect the rate of interracial marriage to increase. People do, after all, tend to marry people they know."[16]

Racial intermarriage will probably increase, but the concerns surrounding these marriages are real because of the long-standing feeling of separateness between blacks and whites. Good marriages between races can take place when there is acceptance by people important to the welfare of the couple and when the pair involved have the resources to meet the problems.

[14]Barnett, op. cit.

[15]Ernest Porterfield, "Black-White Families: A Midwestern Study," Ph.D. diss., University of Illinois, Urbana-Champaign, 1972.

[16]"People Who Intermarry: Pioneers or Protesters?" Seattle Urban League Special Report, Seattle, Wash., April, 1967, p. 6.

Knowing these generalizations is usually little comfort to a mother who is faced with her own beliefs and the imminent marriage of her son to a person of a different race.

CASE 13 JACK

"Jack has always been such a good boy," his mother told the counselor. "He always did what he was told, he went to Sunday School, and he was a good student. I don't know what's come over him all of a sudden, but his father and I are frantic. Ever since he has been at the university, and particularly since he got mixed up with this student civil-rights movement, he seems to have gone wild. He went down to Mississippi last summer to help in the job equality drive, and when he came back he was completely strange to us. He says he is going with a black girl, and he insists that he is going to marry her!

"It isn't as if we're prejudiced against blacks. As a matter of fact, one of the reasons we were delighted when he took such an interest in church work was that we believe in Christian brotherliness. But marriage! Oh dear! Their children will never have a chance.

"If I could be convinced that he really loved this girl, I think I might be better able to accept it, although his father never would, I'm sure. But somehow Jack seems to just want to punish us by telling us that he's going to marry her. He knows how upset it makes us, and yet he persists. He says that we are dreadfully out of step with the times, and that we need to realize that we as white people should atone for the atrocious treatment that blacks have had over the centuries. I declare, I don't know where he gets some of these ideas! His father is so disappointed. He expected so much of him, perhaps a little too much. He used to be very strict with Jack. I always tried to be very good to him. (To tell you the truth, he is my favorite.) I can't understand why he would want to do this to us.

"Jack is enjoying the publicity he's getting from talking about the civil-rights movement immensely. He's invited to all sorts of groups to speak, and he describes very forcefully some of the things that happened when he was in Mississippi. I know him pretty well, and I think that he's making up some of the things. Perhaps it would be better to say that he believes so strongly in what he is doing that he exaggerates. But I really don't know, since I wasn't there. Anyway, the more he talks about it, the more he builds himself up. Now he has announced that he intends to be married to the black girl next month. What are we going to do?"

Interracial marriage success

The studies of success in interracial marriages are meager and few. One old study seems to indicate that the average happiness rating for the total interracial group was very low—in fact lower than the total of all marriages of mixed nationality or mixed religion.[17] Racially mixed couples often encounter severe social pressures from their parents and the communities in which they live. They also face discrimination in the economic and business world, and they find desirable housing difficult to secure. Former friends and relatives sometimes break off relations, or at least introduce an element of strain into the relationship. More recent studies seem to indicate that there is less difficulty in Oriental-white marriages than in black-white marriages. At least one recent study appeared to indicate that all interracial marriages among well-educated people are more successful now than they were in the past. However, the individual case reports cited in the study give small comfort to those who would like to believe that interracial marriages are something less than very difficult. As the report put it, "Over and over again the comments on the questionnaire drew a picture of sometimes hard times, rough sledding."[18]

INTERCULTURAL AND INTERNATIONAL MARRIAGES

The increase in world travel has brought about more contact between people of different nationalities. When the contact is made near the average marriage age and in areas such as college campuses, where people condone and even encourage international camaraderie, the likelihood of marriage is greater.

After World War II there was a substantial increase in marriages between American-born white men and foreign-born Oriental women. One reason purported for this increase was the attraction of American males to the subservience of Oriental women. However, most highly educated men need wives who also meet their social and intellectual needs as well, and therefore are not satisfied for long with mere subservience.

In the United States there are many American-born Orientals who marry native-born white men and women. The American-born Orientals,

[17]Albert I. Gordon, *Intermarriage: Interfaith, Interracial, Interethnic*, Boston, Beacon, 1964, pp. 342–347. Copyright © 1964 by Albert I. Gordon. Reprinted by permission of the Beacon Press.
[18]"People Who Intermarry," *op. cit.*

being reared by native Oriental parents, yet being socialized in the American society, tend to have a dual set of values. During the association prior to marriage the values of the American society tend to be more prominent, but after marriage both sets strongly influence behavior. American-born Oriental women, however, are more likely to take on characteristics of native-born white American women than American-born Oriental men are likely to take on characteristics of native-born white men. One explanation given for this is that Oriental-born women are reared to be more subservient than Oriental men or American men or women. When these American-born Oriental women associate with both the Oriental culture and the American culture, they move toward the American culture because it allows more independence for women. It is said that once freed from subservience, hardship, and an inferior role, women—in fact, all human beings—usually show great determination in avoiding a repeat performance of that role. The following two cases illustrate how people from two different cultures appear to be similar at first but later must face the real differences in their value systems.

CASE 14 CAROLYN AND KEIYA

"I thought I was marrying someone with a similar background when I married Keiya," Carolyn told the counselor. "We went to the same school in San Francisco, and he seemed just like all the other kids at school. He was always very nice and polite to me. He was an Oriental, as I am.

"I grew up in a well-to-do home in San Francisco. I never did live in the Oriental section. My father was a college professor, and we always lived out near the university. We had many friends among Caucasians and I was brought up as a typically American girl. I wasn't taught to reject or hate Oriental things or anything like that. It's just that my family tried to make me as normal to the community as they possibly could. However, they did want me to marry an Oriental boy; they made that quite clear. They said I would be happier that way. Well, it hasn't turned out the way they thought.

"Keiya was the oldest son of older parents. They were both born in Japan, but they came over here before World War II. As a matter of fact, Keiya was born in an internment center during the war. They always spoke Japanese around his house; neither one of his parents spoke English very well.

"Even while he was in school, Keiya had to spend a lot of time helping his father in the nursery business. I don't know how he ever got his

studying done. He worked morning, noon, and night, seven days a week. He always said that, because he was the oldest son, he would inherit the business someday.

"When we were married, I thought that would be wonderful, since it gave us financial security. But it turned out to be terribly wrong. For a while after we were married, we lived in his father's house, and that was absolutely intolerable. His parents criticized me all the time. Besides, they made him work fourteen hours a day, and we never had any time to spend together. Whenever I protested, he would always remind me that, after all, it was to be his business. His father never put anything in writing, though. He just expected Keiya to work with him. He never gave him any overtime pay, either.

"The worst part about it was that they expected me to behave like a Japanese woman. I wasn't supposed to talk when the father was talking, and I wasn't even supposed to eat with the men when they had guests. The absolute end came when they suggested to me that I should be working in the nursery, too. After all, his mother did. I put my foot down then and just about moved out by myself. But Keiya promised that, if I would stay, we would build a house of our own. So I stayed. By the time the house was built, I had a child and then I couldn't leave. I thought moving away from his parents' house might mean that they would leave Keiya alone for a little bit, but it seemed worse than ever. When he wasn't down in the nursery gardens, they would call him up all the time. And then they would come up to the house and criticize the way I was taking care of the baby. It wasn't the Japanese way. I don't know what I am going to do. I've reached the end of my rope."

Keiya told just about the same story, adding, "If only she would be nice to my parents! They aren't going to live forever. As a matter of fact, my father should have retired a long time ago. Then I will have the business, and we can live as we please.

"She insists that she doesn't want to live like a Japanese wife. But then she overdoes it in the other direction. She won't do anything! She thinks she ought to go out and play bridge or do club work like other women in the neighborhood. I want her to do this. I want her to be one of them. But she has to be a little bit discreet about it. She could help a little in the nursery and still have lots of time for bridge.

"She keeps telling me that I don't really know how it is. I know far better than she does. I've been living with it all my life. How do you suppose it was for me when I had to come home and work in the gardens when the other kids were out playing football? And there's a part of this problem

that she doesn't see at all. She doesn't know how my parents give it to me for not being able to be master in my own house. They just absolutely don't understand why I don't just tell her what she has to do and make her do it. But if I try to do that, she'll leave me. She really will, too. She'll take the baby with her, and then we've got an even worse mess."

Although Carolyn and Keiya were both Oriental, they were both reared in the American society. Even so, Keiya was taught to accept the Japanese culture far more than Carolyn was. The next case is different in that the husband and wife are from different countries. Note the similarities and the differences between the two cases.

CASE 15 SARAH AND ABDUL

Sarah was a middle-class Protestant girl from a Bible-Belt town in South Carolina. When she was a sophomore at the University of Florida, she met Abdul, an education major from Iraq. Abdul was a good-looking young man who spoke English well and loved American games—football especially. On one occasion he went to New York for two weeks and saw three professional football games. Sarah and Abdul went steady together for about six months and then decided that they could no longer wait to be married, despite the objections of both his Moslem family in Baghdad and the frantic protestations of Sarah's family back in South Carolina. They were married by a Presbyterian minister, and Abdul joined the Presbyterian church. Sarah dropped out of school and took a typing job. Abdul continued his college work.

Soon, however, Sarah became pregnant, and even though she worked up until the eighth month, the eight weeks she was off having the baby created financial hardship for the young couple. Abdul, however, got a job, and they managed to get by. They seemed fairly happy, and, after he received his bachelor's degree, he went on and got his master's degree. Only then, however, did the full realization come to the young couple that he could not teach in the Florida schools because he was not a citizen. No matter, he got a job in Tampa. Soon a second child was on the way.

One day Sarah and Abdul received a letter that contained what seemed to be exciting news. He was offered a job teaching English in Baghdad. They accepted quickly and within a few weeks were on their way to Iraq.

Less than a year later, however, Sarah was back home. She left

Iraq so precipitately that she merely picked up the children, leaving their clothes and belongings behind. She could stand it no longer. What could possibly have happened?

For the first few weeks after the arrival in Baghdad, everything went well. It looked as if the young couple were finally headed toward success. Soon, however—in fact, very soon—Abdul's friends observed that Sarah didn't act like a "normal" woman. Instead of staying in a corner with the other women, she circulated through the room and talked with the men. When the women began to notice these breaches of custom and tradition, they began to gossip among themselves, saying, in effect, "What kind of woman is this?" Meanwhile, the men were urging Abdul to treat his wife the way a wife should be treated. One day Abdul came home and said to Sarah, "From now on you must behave like an Iraqi woman. I know this isn't the way that you were raised, but when in Rome we must do as the Romans do." At first Sarah tried to go along, but there were too many things that she felt she couldn't accept without compromising her integrity. "He wanted me to live like a poor Arab woman, including sitting on the floor and eating with my bare hands," Sarah said. "When I refused, he got angry and I got slugged, shoved, spat at, and cursed at. In the eleven months I was in Iraq, I lost thirty pounds—both from the food I couldn't eat and from nervous tension. It turned out he wasn't really a Christian at all—he was still a Moslem. The blowup finally came when he insisted that our daughters be raised in the Iraqi manner. I just couldn't take that."

This extreme case is used to show how generalizations about behavior are operating, without your getting too personally involved in the case. First of all, the insularity of college campuses causes the students to reinforce each other and eventually to begin to think alike—mainly that only they are "right." This made Sarah and Abdul possible mates at all. Second, when there is a small number of people of a certain religion or culture living in a larger culture, those people are more likely to marry someone not of their religion. Another thing is that Abdul, having come from the more restricted environment of Iraq to the more permissive environment of a university in the United States, changed easily to be more liberal. Sarah, though, could not move easily from the liberal to the restricted, since this direction takes far greater effort. The pattern of women working to send a husband through school and of more equality between husbands and wives was easy to move into, since their peers were doing much the same in the beginning. The pressure to do as your peers do and to take on the accepted behaviors of those in the area to which you move, especially if it is an area where you have formerly lived, explains Abdul's behavior both in the United States and Iraq. Sarah's behavior of fleeing from Iraq without adequate preparation is explained by the generalization that under great stress a person will respond with regressive behavior. Another generalization in operation is that although some people think their religious orientation is a matter of choice, it really becomes a way of life more than they realize. Abdul's and Sarah's beliefs were not changed by their marriage ceremony.

Children add to the physical and economic hardships of most families, but these hardships are multiplied in a family with few resources. Sarah could not meet Abdul's expectations of her because of social factors far outweighing any psychological factor that might have helped her handle the situation differently.

RELIGIOUS ENDOGAMY AND INTERFAITH MARRIAGE

Next to race, religion seems to be the most decisive social factor that American males and females consider in defining those who are eligible marriage partners. Although almost all investigators agree that marriage within one's own religion is a greater-than-chance occurrence, there now is a great deal of disagreement about the exact nature and degree of religious endogamy. Data in this area are sparse, because only one state, Iowa, asks about religious affiliation on marriage-license applications. When special studies are made, it is usually found that there are wide regional differences in the rate of interreligious marriage in the United States. Deciding which is an interreligious marriage is often difficult. There are greater differences among some Protestants than there are between some Catholics and some Protestants. Then, too, people often change their religious thinking throughout their lifetimes. Should a bride who converted from Protestantism to Catholicism six months before she married a Catholic be counted as a Protestant or a Catholic?

The following generalizations are supported by research evidence:

1. Most interreligious marriages in the United States involve Protestant-Catholic combinations. When Jews enter interreligious marriages, they appear to select Protestants or Catholics with approximately equal frequency.
2. In Jewish-Gentile marriages, generally it is the Jewish male who marries

a Gentile female, but there are no consistent findings for which sex most frequently is involved in Catholic-Protestant marriages.

3. Interreligious marriages are more frequent among persons who are re-marrying than among persons entering first marriages.

4. Interreligious marriages are more frequent among the young and among people who are marrying at older ages.

5. Interreligious marriages are more frequently characterized by an out-of-state residence of the bride and by a civil wedding.

6. There is strong evidence that the proportion of a religious group in any community is probably the single most influential factor for predicting interreligious marriage rates: The smaller the group, the larger the probability of intermarriage. The more a minority-group member associates with people of different religions, the more possibility there is that he will marry someone of a different religion.

7. Attitudes toward interreligious dating are more favorable than attitudes toward interreligious marriage.[19]

8. Young people from lower-status homes (as measured by father's occupation) have more favorable attitudes toward interreligious dating or marriage.

It appears that interreligious marriage is becoming more common. There is strong support for the hypotheses that parents of interreligious partners are less tied to their religion, that the interreligiously married are more likely to report dissatisfaction with their earlier relations with their parents, and that the interreligiously married are more likely to report tenuous ties to the family when they were young. Among Catholics, there is strong support for the hypotheses that the interreligiously married are more likely to report strifeful family interaction when young, and that the interreligiously married are more likely to have been emancipated from their parents at the time of their marriage.[20]

Religion and marriage success

Marriages in which the partners come from different religious backgrounds have received more research attention than the other forms of mixed marriage, probably because there are large, organized religious groups

---

[19]Larry D. Barnett, "Research in Interreligious Dating and Marriage," in Marcia E. Lasswell and Thomas E. Lasswell, eds., *Love, Marriage, Family: A Developmental Approach*, Glenview, Ill., Scott, Foresman, 1973, pp. 150–154.

[20]Ibid.

with a vested interest in protecting religious endogamy. Regardless of the happiness or stability of religiously mixed marriages, the very mixing ordinarily tends to dilute the denominational exclusiveness of one or both of the partners; therefore these religious organizations are probably justified in their fears, whether or not they are justified in their reactions.

For the individuals concerned, however, the problem is much more personal. What are the prospects of happiness and stability in a religiously mixed marriage? Lee Burchinal and Loren Chancellor supported past researchers when they concluded that religiously mixed marriages tend to be of shorter duration than those where both partners were of the same faith.[21] Although the weight of evidence from research appears conclusive —mixed marriages are more fragile—other ways to interpret these research results will be discussed when we will examine the case against endogamy.

The problems encountered in interfaith marriages are *not* usually the result of clashes over doctrine and religious argument. More frequently, they are the outcome of differences in childhood conditioning and general values in living. Religion has an influence over far more than the spiritual life of its adherents, for religious groups usually have some differing customs, attitudes, values, and expectations as well as differing religious beliefs. Young people are often more able to change their religious beliefs (or to abandon them altogether) than the accompanying style-of-life patterns that may have come from the religious orientation.

In the study of the development of the husband-wife relationship, some important style-of-life differences resulting from the varying religious backgrounds of the 850 couples were pointed out. The sample consisted of 175 marriages in which both partners were Catholic, 301 in which both partners were Protestant, 232 in which both partners were Jewish, and 144 in which the partners were of mixed religions or in which one or both partners had no religion.[22] Both-Protestant, both-Catholic, and both-Jewish couples were compared with each other and with the mixed- or no-religion couples on a long list of marital habits and behaviors. When the Protestant couples were compared with the Catholic couples, these were the findings:

1. The Protestants appeared to be more open in their relationship, interacted more often with each other, were more aggressive, were more

[21]Lee G. Burchinal and Loren Chancellor, "Survival Rates Among Religiously Homogamous and Inter-religious Marriages," *Research Bulletin No. 512758*, Ames, Iowa, Agriculture and Home Economics Experiment Station, Iowa State University, December, 1962.

[22]Boyd C. Rollins and Harold Feldman, "Marital Satisfaction Over the Family Life Cycle," *Journal of Marriage and the Family*, **32** (February, 1970), 20–28.

achievement- and ego-oriented, and had more value differences between husband and wife.

2. Catholics appeared to be more satisfied with their marriages than Jewish couples. Their marriages were more conventional, more placid, and less emotional.

3. Jewish wives were more active and Jewish husbands more nurturant (doing things for the spouse and playing with the children), and husband and wife tended to interact more with each other than Catholics.

4. When compared with the Jewish couples, the Protestants had a higher level of marital satisfaction. The Protestant couples' conversations were generally about objective and interpersonal or emotional topics, and the results of these conversations were generally positive to the marriage. The relationship between the husband and wife appeared to be more traditional with familistic values seen as in the wife's sphere.

5. The Jewish couples, in comparison with the Protestants, tended to be more emotional in general but less satisfied with their marriages.

6. When compared with the mixed–no-religion group, the Protestants were more verbal, more likely to suppress their negative feelings, and generally more satisfied and positive toward each other. The mixed-religion group had a lower level of marital satisfaction and more conflict and were more different from each other in their values, putting less emphasis on togetherness and more on their individualistic satisfactions. Religion often appeared to be a source of conflict.

7. In a comparison of the Jewish with the mixed–no-religion group, Jewish couples placed a higher value on marriage and sharing the nurturant values, whereas in the mixed–no-religion group, the nurturant values were perceived as belonging more properly to the wife's role. Individualistic values were more important to the mixed–no-religion group.

8. Catholics were generally happier with their marriages than the mixed–no-religion group. Catholics were much more settled, sedentary, and lower in friction and excitement. They valued the kind of marriage they had: an orderly home, good cooking, and financial security, with husband and wife tending to agree with each other about their values. Religion played a large part in their lives and was a great source of unity.

9. In comparison to the Catholics, the mixed–no-religion group had more conflict, were more self-indulgent, and were searching for more self-fulfillment rather than cohesion in their marriages. Neither the children nor the home nor even their mate, was as important to them as their own personal growth. They gave evidence of more differences between the spouses and more conflict.

The importance of Feldman's study is that it documents and validates the style-of-life background differences associated with religious groups. It is the customs, attitudes, values, and expectations that Feldman has identified, rather than the religious doctrines or dogmas as such, that cause the problems in most interreligious marriages. Clearly, not all Protestants have the characteristics that Feldman associated with them. Nor do all Catholics. Nor do all Jews. Nor do all religion rejectors.

One of the many cases that Albert Gordon, a scholarly Boston rabbi, reported in his well-documented book on intermarriage is that of a man identified as Irwin. A condensation follows:

CASE 16 IRWIN

"After eight years of married life, our interfaith marriage ended in divorce. Neither Ann nor I ever imagined that this would happen, but it has happened and, unfortunate as it is for us, it is still worse for our young daughter," Irwin told the counselor.

"I am a Jew. Ann is a Protestant. Actually she had always been a church-going liberal Protestant. When we married, she retained her religious affiliation and I retained mine. We were quite certain that no force or series of forces, family, friends, church, or synagogue, would ever break up our marriage. . . .

"I come from an Orthodox Jewish family. At least my parents were Orthodox even if my brothers and sisters were not. I have two brothers and two sisters. We are all deeply devoted to one another and since our early years have been close. My father was a learned Jew. He was a highly respected member of the community in which we lived, not only because of his knowledge of the Talmud and other Hebrew texts or even because of his active participation in the Jewish community, but also because he was a very successful businessman. My mother was as sweet and kind a person as one could ever meet. She was a devoted wife and mother and a genuinely religious soul. We, her children, loved her very much. We were close to her as she was to us. . . .

"I had gotten a legal position in the city with a good firm. Ann was a secretary. She came from a lower-middle-class working family. Her father had died about ten years before, so through all of her teens Ann had been cared for by her mother. Ann had graduated from high school, and the pressing financial needs of the family had obliged her to go to a secretarial school and take a job thereafter. Both parents had regarded themselves as Protestant although her mother was now affiliated with a very liberal

church that had no formal creed. Ann had always regarded herself as a religious Protestant.

"Ann and her mother had lived in Peoria for about five years. Prior to that, they had lived in a small town in Missouri. I can only guess that the opportunities for work were greater in the big city and Ann and her mother both needed to work in order to live, that the move to Peoria was prompted by this consideration. I am quite certain that during all the time I knew her, Ann's relationship with her mother was excellent and I remember Ann telling me that it had always been good.

"We met on a double date. One of my friends had a date and he asked his girl friend to bring along someone for me. This was not one of those "quickie" affairs. We actually went together off and on for about two and one-half years before the affair became serious. All this while I was at the law office and enjoying my work, but I was lonesome. I didn't go out very much. Of course, there was my own family for part of the time, but due to another change in fortune, my parents decided to move back to their first home town. So, really, I was pretty much alone. I didn't see the family very often. I wasn't earning too much and things were generally quite tight. My office associations did not bring me in contact with Jewish girls. I hardly knew any Jewish people socially. Then, too, one man in the office had intermarried and he was getting along fine. Ann and I were invited over to their home rather often and I saw that intermarried people could get on very well together. The few people I knew who saw us together all seemed to think of her as a sweet girl. The office in which she worked was just around the corner from my law office, and all of these factors sort of drew us together more and more.

"I knew, of course, that the members of my family would not approve of an intermarriage. I knew that they would try to dissuade me by every possible means, but I also knew that my mother would eventually accept whatever I did. I felt certain about that all the time. Yet it was a difficult decision to make because, even though I had drifted far from my parents' Orthodoxy, I still had some strong feelings about being a Jew and I had no real intention of giving up that identification. I guess that the strongest point was the fact that I knew of at least one successful intermarriage and this helped to convince me that, regardless of what others in the family might say, I knew what I wanted to do.

"I shall never forget the way in which my mother pleaded with me not to marry Ann. She cried bitterly. She talked and pleaded with me, but somehow I didn't feel that she understood me or Ann. When the other members of the family, including my father, talked with me, they were just as anxious as my mother to dissuade me, but, even though I knew that it would hurt them, I felt that they would get over it. I thought that all they needed was to really get to know Ann. But it obviously required more than that.

"I cannot today look upon their pleadings, discussions, and arguments as improper or as wrong in any sense. They were, I think, wiser than I was at that time.

"I think that our marriage ended in divorce not because of my family or Ann's, but because of us. We were really very much different from each other and religion did play an important role in our break-up. But it wasn't the Church or the Synagogue that did it. It's the way we responded to our own religion after we were married.

"We were married by the liberal minister of the community church Ann used to attend. Ann's mother had attended this church, too. In fact, she had worked hard for this particular church.

"But, however liberal I thought I was with respect to religion, I knew that I was a Jew, and I did not want to have my home become a Christian home. Of course, I felt this way much more after our marriage than I had ever realized I would.

"For example, at Christmastime, I would not permit a tree in the house, nor would I allow anything resembling a Yuletide celebration. To Ann and her mother, that was cruel and inhuman treatment, for it shattered the traditions of her childhood. (I forgot to mention that Ann's mother lived with us in our apartment.) Whatever Jewish symbols I tried to introduce into the home after my daughter was born, were made fun of by Ann. Now, lest you think that I was taking advantage of Ann by acting as I did, I want to make it clear that prior to our marriage, we had agreed that any children born to us would be reared in the Jewish religion. But Ann changed her mind about all that. She was disillusioned, I guess.

"I know that my family invited Ann and my daughter up to their home for vacation, etc. She came, mostly because I insisted, but it wasn't very successful for any of us. Ann was quite aloof from the family and I felt that she looked down upon their very Jewish way of life, the ritual observance, the Sabbath meal, with the candles kindled. Where, to me, this was lovely and warm, to Ann it was quite meaningless. Whether or not she thought the family were barbarians, I do not know.

"I spoke before about our differences, but they were not just religious differences. I think they were cultural, educational, and social differences, as well. That came to the fore as time went on. When you marry you actually bring your entire past—religious and cultural—with you and it remains with you.

"It was obvious after four difficult years that we could not remain together. We were separated for about three years, and it was my hope that somehow we would be able to reconcile our differences, but that was not to be. We finally got a divorce.

"Some people think that if things don't work out, you simply get a divorce, but I can tell you that there is much more to it than that. In our case, we had a daughter. Ann wanted the child to remain with her, and so I have been supporting her for the past ten years. But it isn't a question of dollars and cents that is important. It is rather what we have done to a child. I feel reasonably certain that my daughter, who is a very unhappy person, would not have been that way had we, her parents, remained together and had she known what she really was—Jew or Christian. She has been seeing a psychiatrist and has been quite ill for a time, but though neither Ann nor I feel entirely responsible, we cannot help but feel that our unsuccessful marriage was certainly a contributing cause to her unhappiness and illness. I am convinced today that interfaith intermarriage can work out only for people who either do not want or cannot have children. The arrival of a child into a mixed marriage changes the entire scope of the original intention, no matter how emotionally strong the professed love was before marriage.

"I do not believe that the unhappiness that came about in our marriage was the result of the fact that I came from an Orthodox Jewish family while Ann came from a so-called liberal Christian family. Unfortunately the prejudice and deep-rooted intolerant attitudes that one finds in non-Jewish families must be considered, too. These attitudes are often such that nothing can overcome the outside pressure upon the non-Jewish girl. It may be argued that a highly intelligent girl, perhaps one who has a higher university degree or someone like that, can withstand all these pressures quite normally. But I would even challenge that postulate.

"I believe now that the only possible route for a Jewish man who marries a non-Jewish girl, and is determined to make his marriage last, is to gradually give up contact with his Jewish circle of friends. This happens sometimes and I know of such people. While I can recall a few mixed-marriage families who apparently seem happy and who have children, I feel quite certain that they are the exception to the rule.

"I would do everything within my power to convince a child of mine that he was violating every principle of his faith and every standard of his family and, more important, what was best for his own future welfare, if he considered getting married to a person belonging to a different religious group. I have discovered that, if one has any feelings at all about one's own faith and one's family, it is the height of folly to undertake such a marriage.

"In our case both Ann and I had strong feelings about our own religion, even though we did not realize it before we were married. But we found that out soon enough.

"I have remarried. My wife this time is a fine Jewish girl and we have two lovely daughters. I know now what it means to be happily married."[23]

SOCIAL CLASS AND SOCIAL STATUS

Most parents try to get their sons and daughters to marry within their own social class in order to preserve the status and, if a high social class, to control the money.

Over the years, many sociologists have suggested that, when and if social class lines are crossed, the man tends to marry down and the woman tends to marry up. This has been termed the "mating gradient" and is classic in most textbooks on mate selection. A study by Zick Rubin has suggested that such a tendency is not as universally applicable as was previously believed. Rubin found some indication that upper-middle-class women tend to marry up, but found no strong tendency in the lower-middle class and lower class.[24]

Since social mobility is most easily achieved by a woman when she can marry a higher-status male, the idea of women marrying up seems quite logical. A man gains status through his career, but a woman's status is still more often conferred on her by her husband. John Finley Scott puts it somewhat cynically:

Insofar as she responds to the American dream of upward mobility, every unmarried American girl has a bit of the golddigger in her. . . . The pressure for marrying up in women produces a kind of imbalance in marital bargaining, to the advantage of high status men and low status women and the disadvantage of low status men and high status women. A low status man has little wealth or prestige to offer for a wife. In addition, he must compete for wives not only with others in his own station but with higher ranked men as well.

A well-born woman, if she is to maintain through marriage the status conferred on her by her parents, must marry a man at least equally well born but for such men she faces a deadly competition from lower status women who also regard them as desirable husbands. As a result, low status men are more likely to

[23]Gordon, op. cit.

[24]Zick Rubin, "Do Americans Marry Up?" *American Sociological Review,* **33** (October, 1968), 750–760.

remain bachelors, and high status women are the more likely to remain spinsters. This is the "Brahmin problem," so named because it reached its most extreme form among the high castes of Hindu India (but it can be observed among the Boston Brahmins as well).[25]

Social class and marital success

One major way in which Americans differ is in the childhood conditioning they had as a result of the socioeconomic group in which they were raised. From the very beginning, middle-class and lower-class children are reared differently. Some differences in breast feeding, toilet training, and discipline practices, which were earlier identified by researchers, appear to be wearing out.[26] But there are still differences in food, amusement, and aesthetic preferences, and differences in the choice of words and symbols used. Some of the more important differences are in sexual behavior, spending the family income, expressing aggression, and raising children.

Few middle-class children have any idea what it is like to be reared as a lower-class child. As a matter of fact, very few middle-class adults, including teachers, have any real concept of family life in the lower socioeconomic groups. Lower-class children are often equally as ignorant of the real problems middle-class boys and girls face in trying to live up to all the social expectations that confront them. Even television, for all of its seeming realism, fails to portray either the defensive hostility of much lower-class social interaction or the spirit-crippling anxiety that some middle-class children have about violating social expectations.

Allison Davis, in discussing the differences in the aggressive and sexual behavior of lower-class and middle-class adolescents, had some insightful comments.[27] He pointed out that, with regard to most goals, what is rewarding to a middle-class adolescent is not rewarding to a lower-class adolescent. What they fear, what they abhor, what they desire, what they crave, what they will work for, fight for, or consider valuable or sacred differs in almost every area of human relationships.

[25]John Finley Scott, "Marriage Is Not a Personal Matter," *The New York Times Magazine* (October 30, 1966), 70. © 1966/1969 by The New York Times Company. Reprinted by permission.

[26]James Walter and Nick Stinnett, "Parent-Child Relationships: A Decade Review of Research," *Journal of Marriage and the Family*, **33** (February, 1971), 70–111.

[27]Allison Davis, "Socialization and Adolescent Personality," in Nelson B. Henry, ed., *The Forty-third Yearbook for the National Study of Education: Part 1, Adolescence*, Chicago, University of Chicago Press, 1944, pp. 209–210.

In all social classes children are rewarded for aggression. In the lower class it is usually physical attack. In the middle class, aggression is in the form of social and economic skills to enable one to compete.

Davis points out that sexual behavior and sexual motivation are more direct and uninhibited in the lower-class than in the middle-class adolescent. The sexual drives and behavior of lower-class children are not regarded as undesirable. Mothers may try to prevent their daughters from getting pregnant before they are married, but the example that the daughter sees all around her is quite often to the contrary. At a very early age, the child learns about extramarital relationships by observing the men and women in his own family. Anxiety and guilt about physical aggression and sexual intercourse are normal socialization in the middle class.

Although a marriage partner who was reared in a lower socio-economic group may outwardly adopt middle-class norms, he may, under stress-producing situations, revert to earlier forms of behavior. It is not uncommon to see a middle-class wife who previously found psychological satisfaction in the aggressiveness and sexual self-confidence of her lower-class husband become outraged when he hits her and insists that he "has a right to" extramarital relationships. Often she describes this behavior as "crazy" and demands that he get psychological help. But, as Davis pointed out, he is behaving quite normally for the group in which he was raised. The difference, then, is not really a matter of psychopathology but rather a matter of background conditioning.

Social-class differences in attitudes toward spending money and rearing children often appear after marriage, too. Ordinarily, middle-class people were taught as children to postpone immediate enjoyment in favor of accumulating savings for future security. Maintaining (and raising) one's present status is very important to middle-class Americans. In lower socio-economic classes, on the other hand, children learn to spend what little they have today for today's necessities or enjoyment. Marriage counselors often listen to middle-class husbands and wives complain bitterly because their mates from both lower and upper socioeconomic groups cannot seem to curb their impulse to spend. Some disadvantaged people, long starved for things that money can buy, are impelled to spend now, and some upper-class people, never knowing the insecurity of not having plenty of money, spend as a matter of habit. Divorces can and do result from just such differences in conditioned values.

In child-rearing practices, too, attitudes conditioned into parents as a result of *their* childhood experiences can vitally affect their marriage relationship. Moreover, it can also affect the emotional stability of the child, because consistency in parental attitudes has long been held to be an important factor in sound child development. Generally speaking, lower-class spouses tend to be oriented toward physical punishment for the children. Marriage of such a man to a middle-class wife who believes in reasoning with her children rather than spanking them makes some husband-wife conflict inevitable. Marriage counselors listen to wives charging their husbands with unfeeling brutality, while the husbands counter that their wives are spoiling the children beyond belief.

Some sociological studies have confirmed that a similarity of social-class background can be an important factor in marriage success. As long ago as 1939, Ernest Burgess and Leonard Cottrell stated that the more similar the spouses were in social-class family background, the better their marital adjustment would be.[28] Later, Julius Roth and Robert Peck, working with the Burgess and Cottrell data, found that substantially more couples who married within their own social class were better adjusted than those who married outside their own class, and that the greater the difference in class level, the more likely it was that there would be poor adjustment in marriage.[29]

Where class differences do exist, the evidence seems to indicate that a higher-status husband can get along with a lower-status wife better than the lower-status husband can get along with a higher-status wife. The explanation most often given for this phenomenon is that the husband needs to feel superior and the wife wants him to feel so. A higher-status wife may make her husband feel less masculine, and therefore he may come to resent her. At the same time, the higher-status wife may resent her lower-status husband because he is dragging down her standing in the community. Consider the following case:

CASE 17 JACK AND NANCY

"I met Jack when we were in college," Nancy told the counselor. "He was the captain of the football team. Every girl on the campus wanted him. On Saturday nights when our team had won, it was thrilling to be the one he chose. I got excited—yes, even sexually—when I got close to the 'hero.' I felt like the Roman women must have felt when they saw their victorious soldiers coming home from battle.

[28]Ernest W. Burgess and Leonard S. Cottrell, Jr., *Predicting Success or Failure in Marriage*, Englewood Cliffs, N.J., Prentice-Hall, 1939.

[29]Julius Roth and Robert F. Peck, "Social Class and Social Mobility Factors Related to Marital Adjustment," *American Sociological Review*, **16** (August, 1951), 480–483.

"In those days, I had never had any doubt that I wanted to marry him, even though I knew that he was from a background very different from mine. His mother and father were as poor as church mice. His father had been an alcoholic, and his mother never was able to earn very much. They lived in a slum, but I always used to think it was to Jack's credit that he pulled himself up enough to stay in high school and to get a football scholarship to college. It made me love him even more, because I felt sorry for him, I guess.

"My father is the vice-president of a large corporation in San Francisco. I know now that he was very much opposed to my marrying Jack, although he said very little about it before we were married. We had a big wedding, and then we went to live in a little town near our college, where he had a job as an assistant football coach. For two or three years we had a good marriage. Our first child was born there, and at first we were happy. But the friends he brought home were kind of rough, and we had almost nothing in common to talk about. I had majored in fine arts, and Jack knew almost nothing about painting or music. Moreover, we had a hard time of it financially. My parents tried to help out, but he resented the things they gave us. I think he was unhappy in that little town before I was, perhaps because it was such a conservative, family-centered town, or perhaps because he knew I was missing the kind of life I had lived before I went to college, and this made him feel more guilty than he had to be. Actually, I don't think he was any great shakes as a coach anyway. So our marriage got to be a little unhappy, and he took to either staying away or bringing his friends in to drink beer. I got pretty disillusioned. He was a nice dresser before we were married, but afterward he used to sit around the living room in his underwear and watch television. He never wanted to do the things that my father used to do (before Daddy got rich), like cutting the grass and painting the house. He just didn't seem to care what the yard looked like. I had to go out myself and cut the grass.

"Shortly after our first child was born, my father saw to it that Jack got an offer from the same industrial firm in San Francisco that employs Daddy. It was a good job as an expediter. I was delighted, of course. We moved away from the little town and back to San Francisco, where I had grown up and where my parents lived.

"But instead of making Jack happy, this only seemed to make him worse. He didn't like my friends there, and he didn't seem to want to make any new ones. He said that my friends had grown up having everything and that they were snobbish and didn't like him. This wasn't so at all. They tried hard to make him a part of the group. They wanted him to try going sailing and skiing, which he had never done, but he said they just wanted to show him up.

"Before long, he got very depressed and sat around the house in his undershirt watching television, even when there weren't any sports events on. By this time I didn't seem to love him anymore. I couldn't get the least bit excited about this despondent man who didn't seem to know where he was going. Sex relations became an unwelcome tolerance, and pretty soon I began to resent him altogether.

"He never wants to go anywhere with my friends or do anything culturally interesting. What am I going to do?"

When Jack came in to see the counselor, he started right out with the issue of her friends. "She and her snooty friends," he exploded. "When we were back in that small town where we started our marriage, she wouldn't have anything to do with my friends. Now she expects me to like hers. They're the country-club set, and all they can think about is sailing or golf. They're so smug I can't stand them.

"When we were in college, I thought Nancy and I had a lot in common. She used to want to come and watch me play football, and she knew a lot about the game. She liked the people I knew then, or at least she pretended to. They were all in college just like us. She didn't make any fuss about my wearing a T-shirt then. Now she hits the sky if I sit in the living room without my coat on. What's a man's home supposed to be, anyhow?

"She's scared to death of what the neighbors are going to think about us. The grass never gets a half-inch high before she's out there cutting it. She says that I never do it, but the truth of the matter is that she never gives me a chance. Her old man is the rigid type, too. He's so bad that he has to have the points of the pencils on his desk all pointing in the same direction or he throws a tantrum. She says that she wants to be happy, but she's never going to be happy until she relaxes a little and stops worrying about what other people think.

"The most important problem in our marriage right now is sex. She's completely frigid now. When we were first married, I thought she was one of the best sex partners I ever had. But now she doesn't want sex anymore. I can't understand what's come over her. She hit the ceiling when I told her about some of the girls down at the office, and yet she won't extend herself a bit to be sexy with me. Actually, I think she was all tied up about sex as a kid: You know, she was a goody-goody girl. Her parents made her that way. You would almost think that sex wasn't natural the way they didn't talk about it.

"Anyway, if she doesn't start coming around soon, I'm going to step out on her. I've told her that before, but this time I mean it."

The greatest tendency is to marry within the social class of one's parents. However, people can change their own social status after they become adult, whereupon their choice of a mate is more likely to be of the more recent social class. Consider the following case of a man who moved up in social class and married a woman who was already there.

CASE 18 JANE AND SYDNEY

"I don't know what to do," Sydney said. "She went home to that fine father of hers two weeks ago. They got together and decided that she should get a divorce as well as 10 percent of my income for the rest of my life! What do they want—blood? I'll have to say my law practice and senator's salary are considerable and 10 percent would be very large. She came back to the house while I was at work last week and took all the silver. I don't mind that, but I don't like her coming to my house on the sly. I had all the locks changed.

"Speaking of locks, she had locks put on all the bedroom doors about three months ago. She said she was afraid of burglars. The thing is, she's been sleeping in her own locked bedroom ever since. In fact, in the whole ten years we've been married there have been almost no successful—if you want to call it that—sexual relations. That sounds unbelievable, but Jane has always been a very affectionate girl up to a point. Then she would freeze up and talk about not wanting to get pregnant until I finished my advanced degree. She knew how badly I wanted to have a law degree.

"My father died soon after I was born, leaving my mother and me with nothing. My mother was an enterprising woman. We managed well and we became successful in the business. We worked hard, day and night, and saved enough money to send me to the university.

"When I met Jane she was so sweet and understanding and made me feel as if I were the most wonderful man on earth. She took me to some exquisite parties her father was throwing and we went to several parties on his friend's yacht. She loved to introduce me as "Senator." I got an equal pleasure, to be sure, for no one in my family had ever been in politics.

"When we married she was willing to live in a little brick house

in a modest part of town. She and her mother hired an interior decorator to decorate that little four-room house. She acted the part of the housewife for about two months and then demanded a part-time maid. I gave her that. I gave her plenty of money to buy groceries but she still complained that she didn't have enough money to spend. I showed her on paper exactly how much she needed to run a house and I knew she had enough. She still complained that I was penny-pinching.

"I built her a nine-room house two years ago and she still was not satisfied. She was a member of the arts council and the historical society, and I got plenty sick of her talking about those ancestors of hers. She could help me a lot with my work if she'd go along with me.

"My mother and I have continued to invest our money and we've done well. Someday Jane and I will have plenty of money, but she wants to spend it all now. Jane is pretty and knows just how to act around the right people. This is a big help to me. I don't see why she's being so hard to get along with."

Jane's story sounded similar but somehow had a different slant. "Sydney expected me to act like the rest of those women in the neighborhood, with their children and wash on the line. I was the first one to buy a dryer and they all said my wash wouldn't be 'sunshine fresh.' I couldn't take it any longer. There is more to life than hanging sheets on a backyard clothesline.

"Sydney has always thought I ought to be the sensuous woman. I just couldn't be that kind of woman. My mother brought me up to be careful of such things. She told me that men should be more considerate. My father was gone most of the time for his business. My mother loved being hostess for his parties. I think my father was not really demanding at all. He is such a fine man. He always told me that I should always come to him if I ever needed him.

"When I was told I could never have children last year my father was so sweet—but not Sydney. He just sulked, accusing me of being glad I couldn't have any. Can you imagine that? I got so mad one night when he told me to go to bed with him that I just screamed at him and hit him. If he could just be sweet and gentle like my father, we could make it. I don't know whether I could ever live with him now or not. I'll have to admit I admire his ability as a lawyer and his prestige in the community. We have a beautiful home with lovely furnishings, but he doesn't appreciate the time I've spent and the value of the paintings and antique furniture.

"I left him two weeks ago because he wanted to know why I was not home with dinner on the table. I don't like to cook. The maid cooks most of the meals and it's just what he likes, but she was not there that night. I was late getting home from the arts council and I wanted to go out for dinner. He's just unreasonable at times. He just has no feeling for the finer things in life. Don't you think he owes me a little consideration?"

AGE, EDUCATION, AND MARITAL STATUS

Americans tend to marry mates similar in age, education, and marital status. There has been an increasing tendency for the differences in the ages of bride and groom to narrow in recent years, even though a gap still exists. For a period of a few years in the late 1960s, this trend toward age similarity was accelerated. Men who marry at a relatively young age tend to choose women only a few months younger, but men who marry much later are ordinarily considerably older than their brides.

Young women usually marry for the first time between the ages of eighteen and twenty-two; young men usually marry for the first time between the ages of twenty and twenty-four. Over the past twenty years the age at first marriage has been consistently higher for both men and women if they have finished college than if they have finished high school. However, the age at first marriage for men is recently decreasing for both high-school and college graduates.[30] In the early 1970s, there were still more never-married males than females at the same young-adult levels but a marriage squeeze resulted from the fact that the girls born in the postwar boom of the 1940s became of marriageable age (statistically speaking) sooner than the boys.[31]

The marriage age has been declining for men but has been increasing for women in this century. In 1900, the median age for grooms being married for the first time was 22.9 and for brides 20.3, but in 1970 the median age for grooms' first marriage was 22.5 and for brides' was 20.6.

Age

The studies of the relationship of the marriage partners' ages to their marital success are few and show no consistent agreement. Some researchers

[30]U.S. Department of Commerce, *Age at First Marriage*, April, 1973, pp. 77–78, 210, 212.

[31]U.S. Department of Commerce, *Marital Status and Living Arrangements of the Population in the United States: 1970*, May, 1973.

have found that it is somewhat favorable for the marriage partners to be the same age, while others have found that no particular pattern of age differences correlated with marital success, and still others have found that it was unfavorable for the husband to be younger than the wife.

Although there may not be enough consistency in the findings to indicate that age difference between the marriage partners is related to success or failure in marriage, there is considerable evidence to indicate that the age of *both* partners is related to it. Many studies have indicated that the probability of marriage unhappiness and disillusionment is much greater when the husband is under twenty and the wife under eighteen, and that, in general, divorce is more probable for couples who marry younger.

Many of the youthful marriages studied were the result of premarital pregnancies, and the partners had little intention that the union should be permanent. It is still probably safe to generalize, however, that older, more mature partners tend to contract happier marriages than younger couples, even those whose decision to marry is not based on premarital pregnancy. Delaying too long can limit one's choice of marriage partners, but so can marrying too early. There is probably an optimum time somewhere in one's twenties when a person has lived long enough to know what he wants and is mature enough to undertake the close interpersonal relationship of marriage but has not lived so long that all of the most adequate partners have been chosen.

Education and marital status

There is a strong tendency for Americans to select a marriage mate with equal or almost-equal education. This tendency is strongest in the college population, with college men showing an overwhelming preference for women with similar education. As with age, the findings concerning differences in educational background as a factor in marriage happiness are somewhat inconsistent. Generally, it has been found that the more similar the husband and wife are in educational level, the greater is their marriage happiness. But Judson and Mary Landis, in studying 6166 marriages, found no reason to believe that marriage partners who were similar in education had a significantly lower divorce rate than those who had widely differing educational backgrounds.[32]

One thing that almost all the studies agree on is that education is

---

[32]Judson T. Landis and Mary G. Landis, *Building a Successful Marriage*, 4th ed., Englewood Cliffs, N.J., Prentice-Hall, 1963, p. 216.

related to marital success in the sense that the more education a person has, the lower is his probability for divorce and the higher is his probability for a good marital adjustment. It may well be, of course, that education is not really a controlling variable. More likely, people who have the determination and ambition required in getting higher education also have the kind of background conditioning that makes them want to stay married and to make a success of marriage.

Americans tend also to marry people with a similar marital status; that is, singles tend to marry singles, divorced to marry divorced, and widows to marry widowers.

THE POSITIVE CASE FOR ENDOGAMY

Robert Coombs has written several papers on value theory in dating and mate selection and has stated that persons with similar backgrounds learn similar values (and, as we have seen, similar customs, attitudes, and expectations, too).[33] He goes on from there to suggest that interpersonal attraction is enhanced when persons perceive themselves as sharing similar value systems, because then their relationship is mutually rewarding. One of these rewards is the ease of communication that results from a similarity of experience. He says:

Disagreement is more apt to arise between dissimilar persons and to be ego-threatening since it challenges one's values and sense of social reality. Consequently, communication between dissimilar persons is likely to be more restrained and to involve emotionally neutral topics. In short, it is less rewarding.[34]

The second benefit that those of like value systems receive is closely related: Coombs calls it *self-validation*. If a person's values are rejected, he feels rejected. When his values are accepted, he feels secure. Moreover, he feels that his feelings are both vindicated and validated, and that the person who made him feel that way likes him. As a final step in this progression, when he perceives them as liking him, he likes them in return, and communication becomes even easier.

Although these positive reasons for choosing a mate among those

[33]Robert H. Coombs, "A Value Theory of Mate Selection," *Family Life Coordinator*, **10** (July, 1961), 54; "Reinforcement of Values in the Parental Home as a Factor in Mate Selection," *Marriage and Family Living*, **24** (May, 1962), 155–157; and "Value Consensus and Partner Satisfaction Among Dating Couples," *Journal of Marriage and the Family*, **28** (May, 1966), 166–173.

[34]Coombs, "Value Consensus," 168.

with similar backgrounds and values do not necessarily make the case for absolute in-group mate selection in present-day American society conclusive for everyone, it can be seen that, in American mate selection, cultural and background similars, not opposites, attract. But why? Udry identifies three factors that he feels tend to produce marriages that are endogamous with respect to social characteristics.

1. Society is organized into groups with similar social characteristics; therefore those who are socially similar are the most likely to meet and interact with one another frequently.
2. There are social values that encourage persons to marry those with similar values and discourage marriage with those who are socially different; groups holding these values bring pressure on individuals to encourage endogamous selection and discourage exogamous marriages.
3. Differences in behavior, attitudes, mannerisms, and vocabulary tend to make interaction between socially dissimilars difficult and unsatisfying.[35]

MANY MIXED MARRIAGES SUCCEED

One of the major arguments used against endogamy is the fact that there are a vast—and increasing—number of people who are happily married to a partner of a different religion, nationality, social status, education, or race. In a society oriented to accepting success as reason enough for overturning tradition, and in a society oriented to accepting change as a value, this is a powerful argument indeed.

Statistics often cited by those promoting religious endogamy are used by Glenn M. Vernon to refute the implication that religiously endogamous marriages are vastly more successful than mixed marriages. Vernon points to the Landis study which showed that the divorce rate for those people in the sample who married people of like faith was only about 5 percent, but the divorce rate for those who married outside their faith was almost 15 percent. He points out that it would appear from these figures that the rate of failure is three times higher for religiously mixed marriages. However, if you look at these figures another way, Vernon suggests, it might be correctly stated that 95 percent of religiously endogamous marriages survive, and that *85 percent of religiously mixed marriages also survive*. Thus, by marrying outside his faith, one reduces his chance of success by only 10 percent.[36]

[35]Udry, op. cit., pp. 197–198.
[36]Glenn M. Vernon, "Bias in Professional Publications Concerning Interfaith Marriages," *Religious Education*, **55** (July–August, 1960), 261–264.

Many observers feel that the trend in the percentages in the United States has been about the same. In a 1967 report by Victor Sanua of Yeshiva University, there was a clear indication that interfaith marriages were on the increase. The study found that in some parts of the country, as many as 50 percent of Catholics and Protestants married outside their faith. The figure was about 17 percent for Jews.[37]

College and university students appear to be about equally divided on whether or not they approve of interfaith marriage. Albert Gordon found that in his sample of 5407 university students throughout the country, 50 percent of the students did not favor marriage to a person of another religion. In contrast, only 13 percent did not favor marriage to a person of another nationality. Thirty-one percent of the students in Gordon's sample did not favor marriage to a person of another educational group, but 91 percent of the students did not favor marriage to a person of another color.[38] If the number of interracial marriages increases, will these marriages become more successful? There are some who believe so. Even black-white marriages, which, in the past, have been cited as the most difficult marriage mixtures of all, may become increasingly stable.

The fact that many intermarriages, particularly religious intermarriages, are succeeding these days indicates that there are factors other than endogamy that affect the success or failure of marriage. One of these factors is personal flexibility, the personality attribute that permits those who have it to be accepting and pleasantly adaptable in almost any situation and compels those who do not have it to be rejecting and rigid.

Another factor is undoubtedly the strength of the conditioned attitudes and values held by one partner as compared to the strength of the opposing attitudes and values conditioned into his mate. A hard-shell Methodist might not get along well with a staunch Catholic (or with a liberal Methodist either), but a liberal Methodist might easily get along well with a liberal Catholic.

Finally, the strength of the determination of two people to make a go of their marriage can make it successful for two people from almost any background, no matter how diverse. Although an endogamous marriage undoubtedly makes adjustments easier in most cases, perhaps there are some people who are successful because of the challenges implicit in intermarriage.

[37]Victor D. Sanua, "Intermarriage and Psychological Adjustment," in Hirsch L. Silverman, ed., *Marital Counseling: Psychology, Ideology, Science,* Springfield, Ill., C. C Thomas, 1967.

[38]Gordon, op. cit., pp. 36–37.

But since it is still true that the intermarrieds apparently have a higher divorce rate than those who marry endogamously, does this mean that those who intermarry are less flexible, more compulsive and rigid, or less determined than their endogamously married friends? It may be that they are unconventional people in the first place. This leads us into the subject of the next chapter: psychological factors in mate selection.

8

PSYCHOLOGICAL FACTORS IN MATE SELECTION

Endogamy is by no means all there is to mate selection. In fact, in most cases, all endogamy does is to establish the field of eligibles. The real choosing takes place for far more personal and much more emotionally related reasons.

The number one emotional reason for marriage is love. And love, as we saw in Chapter 6, usually results from mutual need-meeting. Therefore, some discussion of the details of need-meeting in specific relation to mate selection now becomes important. It is necessary, though, to point out right at the beginning that love is only one of the psychological reasons for selecting a mate. In many cases there are others: worry over waiting too long, an inadequate self-image, escape, adult identification, revenge, sexual attraction, desire for money and/or higher status. Any one of these or all of them can be controlling factors in who marries whom.

NEED-MEETING IN MATE SELECTION

In selecting a mate, does an individual usually select someone whose needs are unlike his own but complementary, or does he more often find someone whose needs are very similar to his own? The answer is not as simple as it might seem at first. It is logical that one should choose a mate whose psychological strengths make up for any weaknesses he might have, whether or not he is conscious of them, but it is also logical that, to facilitate adjustment in marriage, like should marry like, in psychological characteristics as in social endogamy. Which course do Americans follow in choosing marriage partners? Which might lead to better marriages?

Robert Winch, the leading exponent of the complementary-needs theory, started out with a hypothesis that complementarity of motivation (as, for example, dominance in one partner and submissiveness in the other partner) would maximize gratification. Thus, he reasoned, mate selection should follow a principle of complementarity.

As he developed his hypothesis, Winch decided that there was not one, but two, types of complementary-need satisfaction that led to mate selection. In one type, both partners have the same kind of need, but there is a difference in the intensity of the need, with one partner having a greater and the other a lesser need. For example, if one partner has a high dominance need, he will select someone with a low dominance need. In the second type that Winch identified, if one partner is high in a particular trait, the other partner will be high (or possibly low) in *another* trait. For example, if a man has a high need for recognition, he will select a wife with a high deference need. "It appears," he concluded, "that not all of the variation in mate selection among our twenty-five couples is to be accounted for by complementariness, but it also appears that complementariness is probably *one* of the determinants."[1]

J. Richard Udry suggested that, although a dominant male might choose a submissive female, it is not equally true that a dominant female would choose a submissive male. Rather, a dominant female might look for an even more dominant male, so that the usual sex-role expectation could be maintained.[2] Time and time again the exceptionally dominant woman has only contempt for the mouselike male. What she more often appears to be seeking is a male who is dominant enough to dominate her, despite her effort to make it difficult for him to do so.

After examining all the studies pertinent to the matter of complementary needs versus needs homogamy, Lee Burchinal concluded that "Homogamy studies provide greater predictive power for selection of mates than do studies based on complementary needs. Perhaps the chief value for the complementary-needs theory is to account for some of the residual variations in mate selection. . . ."[3]

In summary, some people do marry those with complementary-need patterns and some do not. Unfortunately, some of the sociological studies of mate selection were designed to provide an orderly theory of mate selection, and their hypotheses could be validated only if a large proportion of the sample behaved in accordance with the theory of the researcher. A "some do, some don't" finding is unsatisfactory for theoretical purposes. But for the purposes of the student of the empathetic approach, it is enough to recognize that people fall in love because of needs and that these love relationships often culminate in marriage, sometimes with people with complementary needs, sometimes with people of like needs.

This, however, begs the question, "But when *I* am trying to choose, which is better?" The answer: The mate for you is the one who will better meet your needs, complementary *or* like, in the long run. The qualification "in the long run" is very important, for needs do change. Sometimes a partner who meets your present needs may very well be inadequate in meeting future ones. We have already mentioned several cases in which women have married aggressive men only to find out later that aggressiveness was

[1]Robert Winch, *Mate Selection: A Study of Complementary Needs*, New York, Harper & Row, 1958, p. 119.

[2]J. Richard Udry, *The Social Context of Marriage*, 2nd ed., Philadelphia, Lippincott, 1971, p. 209.

[3]Lee G. Burchinal, "The Premarital Dyad and Love Involvement," in Harold T. Christensen, ed., *Handbook of Marriage and the Family*, Skokie, Ill., Rand McNally, 1964, p. 669.

intolerable to them over a long period. But does this mean, then, that it is always safer to marry someone who has characteristics similar to your own? Not necessarily. Two very dominant and competitive people will probably spend an inordinate amount of their married life fighting. If they are the kind of people who enjoy fighting, this might be ideal, but for many people it would be devastating to marriage.

At the other end of the dominance scale, the situation can be even worse. Two very insecure people may initially be attracted to each other. But after marriage they often tend to aggravate each other's anxieties. This kind of case is often seen by the marriage counselor, since insecure people, who had planned to lean on each other after marriage, usually find no support at all, and sometimes both partners seek support from the counselor. Moreover, whereas dominant people are usually so secure in their own self-conviction that they go ahead and get a divorce at the drop of a hat (often without proper consideration of other alternatives), less secure people sometimes vacillate anxiously, seeking advice from everybody, until whatever might have been saved of their relationship is lost.

Very many insecure people do marry each other. In the beginning, their mutual shyness binds them closer together, for each partner feels a real sense of understanding of the other's need for security in the social situation. Each feels he is lucky to have the other; each thinks he needs the other in order to survive and be complete, and each is flattered that the other needs him. Sometimes a person will partially recognize his prospective mate's insecurity but believes that he can live with it. After marriage, he has a great deal of difficulty when the full extent of his mate's need for help becomes apparent.

It is worse, though—far worse—when both partners completely deceive themselves and each other about their insecurities. This is fairly often the case, because insecure people tend to disguise their insecurity from others. One of the things they are most afraid of is what other people will think of them, so they act strong and self-confident on the outside, even while they are feeling insecure and frightened inside. When two such people get together, each believes that the other *is* a self-reliant, capable person who will be a tower of strength after marriage.

Prior to marriage people tend to block communication in those areas in which there is probable conflict by using idealized views of each other. Marion Schulman studied this tendency by using a questionnaire on empathy.[4]

[4]Marion L. Schulman, "Idealization in Engaged Couples," *Journal of Marriage and the Family*, **36** (February, 1974), 139–147.

People may think that they are getting married because of complementary needs, if they think about it at all. The old saying that love is blind probably results from the feeling that people tend to see in one another things that they wish to see or that they *need* to see. As Udry points out: What a man sees in a woman is very closely related to what *he* is, but not what *she* is.[5]

CASE 19 CARL AND IRENE

"When Carl and I were going together, I always thought he was socially able to get along with people," Irene said. "He appeared to make acquaintances easily and to talk smoothly in groups. I admired this very much, because I was all tied up inside when it came to meeting new people. He seemed so sure of himself, so able to make decisions. I guess that's what I wanted, because I knew how frightened I always was about everything.

"He had been an officer in the navy, but he resigned when he felt the navy was treating him unfairly. He really doesn't get along well with people, because he's always worried that they're trying to do him out of something. But when he resigned from the navy, I just thought that he was even more wonderful because he had the courage to quit.

"He showed me the letter of resignation that he was going to send in to the navy. I looked at it, and it was filled with hostility and recriminations. It could only have injured him in the long run. I told him that he couldn't send that letter in and I helped him reword one. He seemed sort of grateful for my help, and at the time I was very flattered to think that he needed me in some small way.

"I am terrible for telling you this on him. He tends to believe the worst about everybody else. Yet at the same time he wants other people to like him so much. I guess I know how this is, because I am very sensitive about what other people think, too. As a matter of fact, when I pass two people whispering, I am sure they are talking about me.

"Before we were married, Carl always seemed so optimistic. I am kind of a worrywart and pessimist myself. I always have been. But I didn't let it show then. Actually I tried to cover up a lot of things. I thought maybe Carl wouldn't love me if I allowed him to see how worthless I am.

"I am easily hurt by criticism. Carl seemed to know this and he seemed to be one of the few men who really understood me.

"I know you won't like me for saying this, and I guess I shouldn't

[5]Udry, op. cit.

say it, but he really is a very weak man. I think he wants me to mother him. I don't want to mother him. I already have two children to mother. I want him to 'father' me. He yells a lot at the children. I think he's reacting to all the frustrations he feels from the bosses at the office where he works. He isn't man enough to talk back to the bosses, but he comes home and takes it out on the children.

"My mother always told me that men were self-centered and irresponsible, and I should have listened to her about that. Lord knows I used to listen to her about everything else. That is one reason why I was so fooled by Carl. He seemed to be interested in what I thought, even though he would still make the decisions. Now he not only doesn't make the decisions, he really isn't interested in what I think either. He says all my thoughts are negative, and that I just try to tear him down and spread gloom.

"I know I shouldn't say this, but he isn't much of a sex partner either. He complains that I'm not affectionate enough, but the truth is that he hasn't the courage to be aggressive himself. I don't want to be the one who decides when we have intercourse. He should make love to me and make me feel all warm and loving and then take me. But he expects me to give him some kind of permission. We never talk about sex, because I think he's as embarrassed about it as I am. Sometimes he literally cries when I tell him no, and then he pouts for a week.

"I know you won't like me for saying this, but I have grown to hate him. He isn't the strong person I had hoped for."

When Carl came to see the counselor, he started out by apologizing for saying anything bad about Irene. "Her big problem was that her mother dominated her so and kept telling her how worthless she was. When I met her she was so self-effacing it was painful, and she still can't make a decision.

"She is terribly negative. If I say, 'Wouldn't it be nice to go on a picnic Saturday?' then she is sure it's going to rain and that the children will fall in the river and that the car will break down, and so forth. She wasn't like that when we were going together. Everything pleased her then, so I didn't have to decide how I could make her happy. I know that that's a great part of my trouble. I want too much to make her happy. I try hard all the time to do little things that please her, but instead of pleasing her I seem to upset her. I think it contradicts what her mother kept telling her: Men are brutes who will beat her.

"You wouldn't believe how insecure she is now. She goes downtown with lots of money and won't buy a dress that she badly needs. She always has some excuse. Either she thought I wouldn't like the dress that she picked out, or the clerk who waited on her looked at her as if she was a poor person who didn't belong in that ritzy store, or she couldn't decide between two dresses. It's maddening.

"The worst part about it all is that her anxiety is catching. I think I've made a final decision and then she says, 'Are you sure that's what you want to do?' and then I have to go through the whole agonizing process again, because usually I'm not sure.

"Sometimes she actually says things that increase my anxieties. We have a pony out in the backyard for the children. One morning I got up early and found that the pony had gotten out of the yard. I was so upset I could barely hold my breakfast down, because I was worried about losing that $500 pony. She could have made it easier for me by saying something like, 'Don't worry, I'm sure we'll find the pony.' Did she? No, indeed not! She said instead, 'Oh, dear, I'm sure the pony will get in the way of a school bus and cause an accident and all the children will be killed.' That shows you what kind of person she is.

"If only I could have seen these things before we were married! But I thought she was so sweet and trusting, and she made me feel so important. She said, 'I'd be delighted to do anything you want to do.' I need somebody who will help me make decisions. I'm never going to get ahead unless she has some faith in me and tells me that I'm a great guy.

"I suppose she told you about sex; she would. Everything has to be just right, and I have to say all the right words or she won't let me get near her. Believe me, she wasn't like that when we were going together. She was scared then, but she was warm. I want her to love me and show me that she does. But now she seems to think that it's fun to make me keep chasing her and then refuse me at the end.

"I would have divorced her a long time ago except that I just can't make up my mind to do it. There has never been a divorce in my family, and my relatives would all condemn me if I were the first. Besides, I think of myself as being a good husband. I don't drink, and I don't chase after other women. A good husband shouldn't get a divorce. I just want her to love me more."

The case of Irene and Carl points up the importance of individual emotional maturity and stability in marriage. Although love has its beginnings in mutual need-meeting, those people who are so needful as to be dependent and those who seek satisfaction for their needs so urgently that they cannot meet the needs of their partner sometimes actually extinguish love.

Jo Coudert makes a distinction between needing and wanting. In fact, she feels that wanting is a much better predictor of happy marriage than needing. She feels that in selecting a mate, an individual should ask himself, "What would the other's life be without me?" Then she goes on to say,

If you have a sneaking suspicion that it would be a perfectly good life, go ahead and marry. If you have an equal suspicion that you, too, could manage reasonably well you can marry with double assurance, for you can assume then that you want each other more than you need each other, and wanting is a much better long-range basis for marriage than needing.[6]

The distinction between needing and wanting is thin and arbitrary at best. It is possible to restate Coudert's basic proposition entirely in terms of needs this way. Two self-secure adult individuals who are not so needful themselves that they cannot meet the other person's needs make good marriage partners. Unless a person is prepared to bring stability to the marriage instead of taking stability from it, he is not a very likely candidate for a successful marriage.

Bernard Murstein studied all the theories of mate selection and concluded that there were three stages in the process, and that some of the theories explained one stage and others explained other stages.[7] The first stage is the stimulus stage, in which the original attraction occurs. People tend to be attracted to the person who most nearly fits their cultural ideal of sex appropriateness. However, before dating begins a type of bargaining occurs. If the person himself or herself does not fit the cultural ideal, he is willing to give a little in his expectation of the other. In the end it seems that there is a balance and the couple may begin dating. The second stage is the value stage. If the courtship proceeds, then the couple probably has similar values. At least, they seem to be similar. In the third stage, the role stage, the pattern changes. Here the couple that makes the most courtship progress is the one in which the individuals accurately perceive their own

---

[6]Copyright © 1965 by Jo Coudert, from p. 206 of the book *Advice from a Failure*. Reprinted with permission of Stein and Day/Publishers and Hodder and Stoughton.

[7]Bernard Murstein, "Stimulus-Value-Role: A Theory of Marital Choice," *Journal of Marriage and the Family*, **32** (August, 1970), 465–481.

and the other's role expectations. Those people with a high self-concept perceive their own and other's role expectations most accurately.

The following case is an illustration of the stimulus stage. Follow through with the other two stages and predict the outcome.

CASE 20 NANCY ANN AND BUZZY

"Mother made me promise that I would come and see you," Nancy Ann told the counselor. "When I was home on vacation from college last week, I told them I was going to be married in two weeks. Mother nearly flipped. It's true that I've only known Buzzy for two months, but what really got to her was when I told her who he was. She says that he's from such an obviously different background that the marriage can't possibly work. She's old-fashioned. She doesn't understand that today lots of people from different backgrounds marry each other and have very happy marriages. She insists that it's a terrible mistake, and that I'll be divorced within a year, but I know he loves me. If she doesn't agree to help us, we're going over to South Carolina and get married anyway."

As the counselor listened to Nancy Ann, he recalled having had her in one of his classes the previous quarter. He also remembered that she didn't get along very well with her classmates. She had to be right all the time, and she always had to have the last word. He remembered that Nancy Ann had bragged about having dates, although one of the other girls had told him that she rarely, if ever, dated at all. She was a little overweight and inclined to be argumentative and impertinent.

"Why do you think your mother wanted you to come and talk with me?" the counselor asked.

"She wants you to talk me out of it," Nancy Ann said. "The truth is that Mother doesn't like Buzzy because she's a snob. He grew up out by the mill town and never had any advantages. He's had a hard time, but what could you expect the way they treat those people? He hasn't found himself yet, but he will. I'll help him." Then she added, "He loves me."

"Is that Buzzy in the black jacket out by the motorcycle?" the counselor inquired.

"Yes," Nancy Ann responded.

"May I meet him?"

"No, you'll only make fun of him," she said. Then she thought for a minute. "Do you really want to meet him?" she asked after a while.

"Yes."

"All right, I'll bring him in."

Buzzy was a sallow-faced, stoop-shouldered young man who apparently had suffered some dietary deficiencies as a youngster. He was very defensive about meeting the counselor. He had grown up and still lived on a little patch of ground adjacent to a mill village in a dilapidated frame house with his father, mother, and three sisters. His father farmed, but he was barely able to make enough to keep the family together on the marginal land. Buzzy himself had dropped out of high school and was expecting to be inducted into the army very soon. Meanwhile, he spent his time riding around town on his old motorcycle and occasionally doing odd jobs at the foundry. He wasn't sure what he was going to do after he got out of the army. He thought he might raise farm produce too. "It ain't the way you think it is," Buzzy said. "It ain't because her daddy's rich and lives in that big house down in Florida. I really love her and she loves me and we're fixin' to get married next week."

After Buzzy had gone, the counselor talked again with Nancy Ann and gently pointed out that the differences in their background would make marriage adjustment difficult for them. "I know all that," Nancy Ann said. "But you don't understand, he loves me!" Then she was quiet for a while. "Besides, I don't have to tell him any stories; he really accepts me. He doesn't try to make me feel inferior. I know it isn't going to be any picnic at first, but I'll help him and someday he will be a really important man that I will be proud of. You'll see!"

THE FEAR OF BEING LEFT

Need-meeting is only one of the many emotional factors in mate selection. Others include fear, escape, revenge, desire to appear grown up, sex, and ambition.

Probably one of the most potent fears is the fear of being left without a mate. Both men and women suffer from this fear, but we tend to think of it as primarily a woman's problem on the theory that men, because they do the asking, can always get some female to marry them whenever they want to. However, men *ask* in hopes of not being left out.

For the young woman with a poor self-image, being "left" can be a gnawing source of anxiety that can and does lead to desperation. The problem can become self-enlarging, for as the young woman becomes more and more anxious, she is apt to become less and less desirable.

Statistically, no American man or woman should have to go without a mate. But finding a suitable one, especially in later years, is something else again.

It has been variously estimated that the average college woman has ten to twenty-five dating partners in her mate-selection years. She may superficially assess every one of them as a possible marriage mate, but actually she knows only a few of them well enough to determine the probability of marriage success with them. Several of these young men may propose at one time or another, but only rarely do two or more propose at the same time. If this were to happen, it is even more improbable that both or all of the candidates would be suitable. It seems reasonable to speculate that, in recent years, dating patterns have limited the typical woman's realistic marital prospects to one at a time, when that one is willing to propose.

Thus, hers is not the problem of *choosing* a mate but rather of accepting or declining what is presently offered to her. That decision is too frequently made not on the basis of the intensity of love or the degree of need-meeting but rather on the basis of the young woman's anxiety level about her future possibilities. The young woman who is sure of her desirableness can confidently turn down an offer, believing that she will have other chances. But the young woman who is insecure and inclined to be negative and pessimistic about the future may well "choose" (deliberately or half-consciously) her mate because of a fear of being left. Clearly this is not the best basis upon which to start a marriage.

It would be a great mistake to believe that it is only women who are afraid of being left. Although it is generally thought that fewer men are affected by this fear, there are many men whose poor self-images inhibit them from proposing unless they find some young woman who makes it unusually easy for them. Consider the case of Shawn, as told to the counselor by his father.

CASE 21 SHAWN

"Shawn was the last of four children. He had two sisters and a brother who were considerably older than he was. They were all married when he was still in elementary school. Each of the older children was very popular, and each married before reaching age twenty. There was lots of love and affection around our house.

"Shawn was born with a strawberry mark covering the whole right side of his face. His mother and I were terribly shocked when we first saw him, but the doctor told us that there was nothing that could be done to improve his appearance. As a little kid he didn't seem to mind. He was a

happy tyke and a very affectionate one. He was energetic and likable, and you had to be pretty perceptive to know that deep down he was very self-conscious. As he grew older, the mark seemed to fade some, but it surely must have troubled him inside. He never asked girls for dates, and he had very few social experiences with girls, although he was popular with the boys.

"Anyway, now he is a junior in college. He has met a woman graduate student who is eleven years older than he is. She is the teaching assistant in his history class. She has taken a great interest in him. I think she must be the first woman other than his mother who has ever made him feel that she cares. He thinks he is in love with her and wants to marry her. I'm sure she's a good woman; certainly she's a very intelligent one. She's not very attractive, though, and I don't think she has had many men friends. I wonder about her good judgment in agreeing to marry a twenty-year-old kid.

"As you can guess, I don't want him to marry her—at least not now. In the first place, he isn't ready to be married—no diploma, no job—and in the second place, he's never had any experience with other women to know what he really wants. But I honestly think that he's afraid that no other woman will ever love him again, so he'd better take this one while he can. I've tried to talk him out of it, but he's very determined. What am I going to do?"

ESCAPE

Escape, usually from oppressive parents, is another common reason in mate selection. Throughout the history of the world, some young people have wanted to get away from seemingly oppressive parents. But escape probably never was as possible as it is today. Now many young people, freed from any concern over starving because of leaving their kinship group, can marry almost any time they want to. Often this appears to be an easy way of ending parental domination. Only later does the escaping pair discover that marriage does not diminish restrictions and responsibilities; it increases them.

ADULT IDENTIFICATION

It is possible that there is no stronger psychological drive in the typical young person than his desire to be—or at least appear to be—grown up, and some young people deliberately marry because they desire this adult identification. In order to prove to their parents or to the world that they are adults and should be treated as mature adults, they resort to a simple logic. Adults get married; since they want to be adults, they will get married, too. Interestingly, our whole legal structure supports this notion. Once a girl is married, regardless of her age, she has some legal prerogatives and responsibilities that are denied to a single woman of equal age.

REVENGE AND REBOUND

Revenge (or sometimes a milder rebellion expressed as "I'll show you!") is another psychological reason for selecting a particular mate and getting married now. Since this kind of mate selection indicates that the selector is relating to a third person and not to the individual he or she is about to marry, the results are usually unsatisfactory. Sometimes the person is rebelling against society rather than another person. Marriage is a relationship between the people involved, and, although others have to be considered in making one's choice, allowing those others to be the controlling factor in that choice usually presages unhappiness. While this can be true when a woman marries a man because her parents think she ought to, it is even more true when she lets her desire to "get even" take precedence over her real needs in choosing a mate.

CASE 22 JEAN AND CHARLES

"I don't know how to begin. I'm five months pregnant but Charles doesn't know it. We dated regularly last summer while I was working in Washington, D.C. All my friends there were the greatest. Many of them were from different races and nationalities. We believed in the dignity of all human beings. We wanted to show the establishment how wrong prejudice is." The counselor asked Jean if she had considered an abortion. "Yes, but it's too late now. I really don't believe in abortion. I didn't believe in contraception either. It seemed like a putdown to the man not to want his child." The counselor talked with Jean at length and found that she actually wanted to have the baby. "I neglected to tell you," she said, "Charles is a darker complexion than I and is married but separated. He has sent me a plane ticket to come to Washington next weekend."

When Jean came back she told the counselor that she had talked with Charles who said he would get a divorce immediately and marry Jean. She told her parents about the situation and they were furious. Her father

*demanded an abortion, even at that late date, but Jean refused. Jean grad-
uated from college that spring and went to Washington to work. Charles
still did not have his divorce but he assured Jean that it was forthcoming.
Jean had to have some help when it came time for the baby to be born;
therefore she went home to have it. Later she and the baby returned to
Washington, but Jean got sick and was hospitalized. Charles took the baby
home with him to care for it.*

*Then the truth came out. Charles and his wife were not separated.
They were amused at how gullible Jean had been. In fact, they were holding the baby when Jean called the counselor for advice.*

Tangentially related to the revenge motive is the rebound phenomenon. This is so apparent in everyday life that it needs little explanation. A
person who feels rejected by one love often rushes off to find another—
sometimes to prove to himself that he is desirable, sometimes to prove it to
the person who rejected him. In either case, he is not really relating to the
new lover in any sound, permanent way. Rebound affairs sometimes culminate in disastrous marriages.

SEXUAL ATTRACTION

Sexual attraction is an obvious psychological factor in mate selection. Although the exact components of masculinity and femininity are hard to define, some people are just "sexy." They have an exceptional ability to stimulate the opposite sex merely by their appearance and manner. Sometimes
two rather plain people seem to have a particular attraction for one another.
They create images and fantasies within their partners that are beyond the
objective understanding of most observers.

Sexual attraction is clearly necessary both to mate selection and to
the perpetuation of the species. Problems arise, however, when sexual attraction is the *only* criterion by which a person selects a mate. If there is no
greater cement to bond the two people together than sex interest, then when
the novelty wears off—and it inevitably will—the marriage partners are
easily attracted to other sex partners. Someone who is even more sexy is
bound to come along.

SUCCESS AND STATUS

Finally, still another psychological factor in mate selection is the individual's need for success—social or financial. Sometimes romantic and finan-

cial success are inextricably intertwined. Sociologist John Finley Scott has suggested that if a researcher were so blunt as to ask typical American young women if they would marry for money, the young women would probably feel highly insulted. They would be sure they would marry only for love. However, if the investigating sociologist were to follow up by asking what makes men lovable, he might arrive at a surprisingly different conclusion for his research. For the answers to his "What makes men lovable?" question might include such things as suave good manners, sophisticated good taste, and brilliant intellectual conversation. These characteristics usually depend on an expensive education and are generally associated with wealth. Said Scott, "Money, in short, tends to be despised only in abstract; in concrete form, enjoyed by the unmarried scions of a rich family, it is highly admired."[8]

In another paper, Scott went so far as to suggest that Americans have a highly institutionalized process for achieving the devious, insidious purpose of young women in capturing upper-status males. The sorority house, he said, can be compared to the fatting houses of Nigeria, where women are sent to be specially fattened for marriage, or to the convents of the Canary Islands, where old women teach young women special skills and mysteries in order to be more attractive to potential marriage mates.[9]

If American women are so determined to find high-status husbands, many of them seem to be blissfully unaware of it. Most of them would deny not only that they intend to marry for money but also that they would choose status and prestige over companionship and easy marriage adjustment. It is true, however, that some lower- and middle-class members of both sexes *deliberately* choose marriage mates on the basis of an emotional hunger for the material satisfactions money can bring, just as some upper-class people of both sexes choose marriage mates on the basis of deeply conditioned anxieties about what would happen to their social position and, indeed, their own financial reserves if they were to marry beneath them. Moreover, some subcultural groups place a high value on their daughters' marrying high-prestige men. The intensity of this conditioned desire varies not only from subcultural group to subcultural group but also from family to family within the group. Some families, like some individuals, react to deprivation by struggling in every way (including marriage) to move up; others appear to accept their station resignedly.

[8]John Finley Scott, "Marriage Is Not a Personal Matter," *The New York Times Magazine* (October 30, 1966), 72. © 1966/1969 by The New York Times Company. Reprinted by permission.

[9]John Finley Scott, "Sororities and the Husband Game," in Jacquelyn C. Wiseman, ed., *People as Partners*, San Francisco, Canfield Press, 1971, pp. 64–72.

Motives for marriage such as escape, revenge, and social status are patently in conflict with predictable marriage success. Discussing them should serve to underline for the student who is interested in his own future happiness the importance of thoroughly understanding his own reasons for wanting to marry.

There are good, sound psychological reasons for marrying. The most important one, antiromanticists and cynics notwithstanding, is a warm, close, genuine, and abiding love. This kind of love embraces not only the feeling of joyful exaltation in being together but also the feeling of tenderness that only two people who really care about one another can share. It is brought to its full fruition in a sexual longing. Love like this is usually born of, and nurtured by, the ability to meet each other's deep emotional needs, whether those needs be complementary or similar. In turn, this need-meeting ability is usually enhanced by a similar value background, since similar value systems make an understanding of the other person's real needs more easily perceivable. Here Robert Coombs's value theory is again cogent: A similar value system leads not only to easier communication but also to a validation of self.[10] One mate is pleased, and so is the other, when his customs, attitudes, values, and expectations are confirmed as being "right."

In the end, the vast majority of present-day Americans, like their fathers and mothers before them, will probably turn out to be good marriage prospectors, with normal social and psychological reactions to mate selection.

WHAT ARE THE CRITERIA FOR GOOD MATE SELECTION?

What conclusions can be drawn from this discussion for the person who is about to select his own mate? Three general guidelines suggest themselves. First, study yourself. Second, study the prospect. And third, study the possible effects of the relationship between the two of you.

Studying yourself is not easy, despite the amount of time you have in which to do it. We all tend to deceive ourselves—if only by holding our head at the most flattering angle when we look in a mirror and then assuming that we look that way all the time. To really know yourself, you have to ask yourself the hard questions, the ones that really hurt. What are your needs? Do you have a normal need for love and, more important, to give love? Do you have normal needs for security, recognition, response,

[10]Robert H. Coombs, "A Value Theory of Mate Selection," *Family Life Coordinator,* **10** (July, 1961), 51–54.

and new experience? Are you dependent on someone else for emotional support? Can you accept some insecurity in other persons? If so, how much? Do you need a parent figure as your mate, someone who can tell you what to do?

Besides studying your needs, you also need to study your motives. Why do you want to get married? Panic? Escape? Adult identification? Revenge? Sexual attraction? A desire for higher social status? Will this particular marriage be a solution? Or will marriage only increase your problems?

There are several ways to study prospective marriage mates. One is to listen carefully for the real meanings in what they say (there will be much more about this in the chapter on communication) and objectively observe the way they behave. Could you live with them the way they are? Or do you think that they will change after you are married? The latter is very improbable. A girl who has many psychosomatic complaints before marriage is far more likely to turn into a full-blown hypochondriac than she is to get well after marriage. A man who drinks heavily before marriage is much more liable to become an alcoholic than he is to give up drinking after marriage. Listening to your prospective mate and observing him or her in action are probably your best guides to selecting a good mate.

There are other ways of judging, too. How well do other people like them? Do they get along well with other people of their own sex? This can be very important after marriage, not only to your social life but also to their business career. What do your friends think of them?

There is another important criterion. What are their parents like? They were conditioned by their parents. Sometimes their behavior may seem very different from their parents, but often, under stress, they may revert to the patterns they learned as a child by direction or by example from their parents. Not all children of unhappy parents and broken homes are poor marriage mates, but children of happy and successful parents do have a better statistical probability of turning out to be successful marriage partners.

It is also wise to examine prospective mates' relationships with their parents, for this may tell you something about why they want to marry. Jo Coudert cites the case of a friend who looked closely at her fiancé's mother and thought her to be an unattractively positive woman inclined to demand that her husband and son cater to her:

This was not the image my friend had of herself, of course, but in attempting to cope with the information honestly, she faced the fact that behavior of her own, which she previously defined as an inability to resist taking advantage of her fiancé's good nature, was, in truth, an inclination to manipulate him. At this point, she could say cynically that if that was what he wanted, why should she deny him his masochistic pleasures? Or she could take the long view and curb her own natural propensity in this direction so that, when the fever of love returned to normal, they could transit to steady love; she without contempt for his accommodating ways, he without a sense that he had been taken.[11]

Although it is probably going to make very little difference to two people who are really in love, looking at the prospective mate's parents can also be revealing as far as the future physical appearance of the mate is concerned. Most women are more likely than not to be shaped like their mothers when they arrive at their mothers' ages, and men may look considerably like their fathers when time catches up with them, too.

Another major way to improve your mate-selection ability is to consider the possible effects of the relationship between your personality and that of your prospects. How able are they to meet your needs over the long run, and how able are you to meet theirs? Do they even now really provide what you want? Are they able to communicate with you? Do they talk so much you sometimes wish you were not with them? Are you so flattered by their possessiveness or their tendency to cling to you that you do not recognize that this really represents a pathological insecurity on their part? Can they provide the kind of decisiveness and leadership you want? Can they provide the kind of warm tenderness that you need when you both are faced by adversity? Do they have all the qualities of role appropriateness, personal integrity, and loyalty that will make for an enduring marriage? No one was ever perfect or ever will be. The person who keeps looking for perfection may be left waiting or ultimately may have to settle for even less than he might have had in the first place. Yet, as Jo Coudert puts it, "Most men and women who truly want to marry, sooner or later find someone they truly want to marry, and it is infinitely preferable to come late to a good marriage than early to a bad one."[12]

[11]Coudert, op. cit., pp. 203–204.
[12]Ibid., pp. 211–212.

9

MALE-FEMALE RELATIONSHIPS AMONG THE SINGLES

Y ou are either single or married. The newest personal data forms do not ask whether you are divorced, separated, or widowed—only if you are married or single. You may be divorced and have three children, but so far as the information gained from the forms, you are single with three children.

This change probably came about to rid people of the supposed prejudice against being divorced or widowed. But being single also used to cause raised eyebrows and accusations of "What's wrong?" You might think that this would rarely ever be the case now. But although the single life is gaining status, people still push marriage.

Even though the percentage of people ever married continues to remain very high, the single state is also increasing. How can this be so? Some people never marry and some people are marrying later, causing a longer never-married state. More people are divorcing and divorcing earlier, causing them to have a longer single life than married life. However, at the same time people are living longer and if they stay married, they are producing a longer married state. The propensity for the divorced and widowed to get married again may also overcome some of the statistical gain in singleness.

THE SINGLES: NEVER-MARRIED, WIDOWED, AND DIVORCED

The singles include never-married, widowed, and divorced men and women over fourteen years of age. People in each of these three groups may or may not have children, but they all have one thing in common: They are not married to anyone. This simple fact sets them apart statistically and sociologically. Many people have studied singles as if they were inherently different; others have implied that circumstances made them different. However, we are now willing to say that people may remain single by choice, either by not marrying or not remarrying.

In 1970 there were 149.4 million Americans fourteen years of age and over. Table 9-1 the breakdown of the number of men and women who were classified as never-married, widowed, and divorced is given. There were over 24 million single men and over 29 million single women over fourteen years of age. There were more never-married males than never-married females in every group from fourteen years to forty-four years, but there were far more widowed and divorced women in every age group. Therefore, the actual number of "single" women in each age group (except the eighteen to twenty-four group, where the numbers are nearly equal) was much greater than the number of "single" men.

TABLE 9-1
NUMBER OF NEVER-MARRIED, WIDOWED, DIVORCED,
AND MARRIED MEN AND WOMEN BY AGE IN 1970

	Never-married	Widowed	Divorced	Married
Male				
14 years old and over	20,426,937	2,130,932	1,926,597	44,597,574
14 to 17 years old	8,098,673	7,508	6,614	71,528
18 to 24 years old	7,636,138	16,350	118,893	3,248,080
25 to 34 years old	1,890,462	38,770	378,778	9,369,909
35 to 44 years old	884,372	75,546	405,882	9,464,269
45 to 64 years old	1,285,524	550,809	760,143	16,686,539
65 and older	631,768	1,441,949	256,287	5,757,249
Female				
14 years old and over	17,624,105	9,615,280	3,004,278	44,481,843
14 to 17 years old	7,573,262	17,803	10,585	206,608
18 to 24 years old	5,835,542	67,164	234,960	5,226,687
25 to 34 years old	1,263,803	158,024	585,129	9,973,286
35 to 44 years old	672,255	353,760	646,547	9,578,573
45 to 64 years old	1,331,557	2,930,892	1,155,157	15,550,221
65 and older	947,686	6,105,637	371,900	3,946,468

Source: U.S. Department of Commerce, *Marital Status and Living Arrangements of the Population in the United States: 1970*, May, 1973.

In the group between eighteen and thirty-four years of age, there were over ten million single men and over eight million single women. Of these singles, nearly ten million men and over seven million women were never married. About 55,000 men and 225,000 women were widowed. About 500,000 men and 800,000 women were divorced. Even though there were more never-married men than women between the ages of eighteen and thirty-four, the excess of widowed and divorced women is the reason for women's saying, "There are no single men around."

CULTURAL ATTITUDES TOWARD SINGLES

Do we think that we do not question a person's choice to remain single? This is what we generally suppose until we find ourselves making a judgment after asking a person whether he or she is married. Such a judgment questions the single person's qualities as a human being. Those who are sold on singleness as a choice can sometimes control their culturally conditioned judgment against singleness. Others who have been a part of or close to unfortunate marriages can also control this cultural conditioning. But even they will have a flash of a question.

When do you become a never-married single? Legally, it is when you reach the marriageable age and are still single, but culturally the age used to be when you were past your "prime," or past "hope," or past "persuasion." However, these choice terms have meaning only in the context of the era of which you are speaking. Right now, it is difficult to say what classifies a person as a never-married single. Even if you say not-yet-married single, there is the implication that singleness is somehow less than good.

Young never-married persons today, however, are looked upon with more envy than ever before. They are not as pressured to marry to keep the society stable. They are encouraged to "enjoy life" before settling down. Their ability to make their own living alone is far better than it was even a decade ago.

The need to relate to others in a meaningful way is as great today as ever, and there are more options open for relating without getting married. Men and women can also work and play together in a noncourting or nondating atmosphere. They can date a greater variety of people either sequentially or concurrently. They can live together with or without sexual intercourse. They can relate in groups all of one sex, or in groups of mixed sex, or in pairs, although it is still essentially a couples' world. They can have their own children or adopt children or only work with children.

With more research in adult development, we are beginning to believe that going through the never-married adult stage may enhance the married adult stage and the adult parent stage.[1] Others have repeatedly warned of the problems that come when two or more stages in the life cycle must be managed at the same time (for example, the very young adult stage, the early married stage, and the first parent stage).[2] More recently the older father is being recognized as encouraging more autonomy in his children even though he spends more time with them.[3]

It is also far more possible to fulfill the need to be alone. This is possibly one of the greatest areas of envy by married people. Although most single people can choose to be alone, the widowed and divorced are viewed more as having been "left" alone. Self-imposed solitude is one of the greatest freedoms known.

Some women and men are beginning to reject early marriage and

[1]Frank F. Furstenberg, "Industrialization and the American Family: A Look Backward," *American Sociological Review*, **31** (June, 1966), 326–337.

[2]Evelyn Duvall, *Family Development*, 4th ed., Philadelphia, Lippincott, 1971, p. 121.

[3]Patrice Horn, "The Older Father: Late Is Great," *Psychology Today*, **7** (April, 1974), 26–28.

even marriage itself. Since the 1960s the independence of women has loomed large as a personal goal. Many women would prefer independence within marriage, but they either cannot get their husbands' cooperation with their independence or the men they marry cannot adjust to the partnership marriage. Even though men have traditionally had the name of being in greater control of the family, many of them soon find that the subtle control of the wife's pressure for "togetherness" is suffocating. Greater independence, then, seems to be the impetus for many men and women to remain single.

As the never-married person gets older, the culture, even today, is not as lenient in its acceptance. More pressure is put on him or her to marry. According to the information in Table 9-1, there is a sharp increase in marriages in the forty-five to sixty-four age group over the thirty-five to forty-four group. Usually such pressure is more subtle than it was when they were younger. Such pressures are the fact that promotions may be more likely for married men, that more confidence may be placed in a married person, that a higher quality of character is often attributed to a married person, and that there is an expectation of more dependability in a married person. A married person of twenty is expected to know many times more about human nature than a never-married person of thirty. Yet, look at the encounters the never-married person has had compared to the insulation of the married person. The older never-married man has usually been pictured as being somewhat abnormal. Women have fared somewhat better than this.

Being widowed or divorced has been and still is no easy status to live with. Aside from the probable trauma of death or divorce, after awhile many widowed and divorced people are not often looked to for support and advice as are married people. Widows and widowers are generally more highly accepted than divorced persons because of the assumption that they had no part in the cause of separation. The younger the age of widows and widowers, the more likely they are to reenter the social circles of the never-marrieds. Age at the time of divorce also tends to affect one's ability to return to the never-married social circle—the younger the easier. Probably this is because of the greater number of single people still available with whom to associate. Discussion of how single persons deal with male-female relationships and single parenthood will follow.

It's a couples' world

The available single male or female always seems to be at a premium when you want one. Yet pure statistics indicate that there are many never-married men and women in each age group (see Table 9-1). However, the number of divorced and widowed women far exceeds the number of divorced and widowed men in each age group. Therefore, there is a matching problem.

This excess has traditionally affected the cultural attitude toward single women. Because we prefer monogamous marriage, we also prefer a one-to-one male-female relationship outside of marriage. To control the excess females, certain overt and covert rules are followed. One such overt rule is the preponderance of couples-only activities. One of the underlying reasons for this is protection of the female partner of the couple from having to vie openly for her male companion. It could also be a protection of the male from having to make choices that might be uncomfortable.

The preference for, and the open seeking of, the "extra" male is another indication of the excessive number of single females. When a male is recently divorced or widowed, he is quickly returned to the couples' world. But this is not usually so for the recently and not-so-recently divorced or widowed female.

Being a never-married single also has its unenviable side. If you have not already declared an intention to marry, your friends, relatives, and acquaintances consider it their right, duty, and privilege to see that you are paired with someone—in fact, anyone. If you do not latch on to someone or allow yourself to be paired, then you become somehow an object of pity. The fear of being different is so great that the single sometimes fools himself into believing that he does want to continue a relationship, despite its drawbacks.

Although the promarriage forces are strong in this culture, some of the married people bent on staying married are among those who suggest most strongly that the single prolong his or her never-married life a few more years.

SEXUAL RELATIONSHIPS AND THE SINGLE LIFE

The term *premarital sex* has no adequate meaning and therefore will not be used in this book. At one time it probably meant sexual relationships between young persons who had never been married but who anticipated marriage. This excluded a whole group of single people who were older and not married or who were divorced or widowed. Since sexual relationships between consenting adults[4] is becoming culturally accepted in fact,

[4]Committee on Homosexuality and Prostitution, *Wolfenden Report*, New York, Stein and Day, 1963.

if not always in law,[5] this discussion will concern the *relationship* between the people involved.

In the not-too-distant past (and even now in some places), sexual relationships between single people were discussed from the point of view of morality, psychological deviance, and legality. However, the subject is more likely to be discussed now from an interpersonal relationships point of view.[6]

Probably the greatest concern among older adults for the minors and even very young adults is that the young may be exploited even when they consent. Exploitation has usually meant the taking of something from someone in an unfair exchange. Traditionally this has meant that men exploited women, but this has never been the absolute case. Because women are the only ones who can get pregnant, the traditional assumption has been that they are more likely to be the victims. Even in pregnancy, however, women are not always the victims. When men are conditioned to take responsibility, they can be victimized by women who either encourage pregnancy or who deceitfully lead men to believe they will not get pregnant.

With the availability of contraceptives for both men and women of all ages, it seems singularly unusual that pregnancy outside of marriage still occurs, yet there has been an increase of illegitimate births, particularly among the very young and women in their mid-to-late twenties. Also, since the 1973 Supreme Court ruling that abortion should be a decision between a woman and her physician, it seems that illegitimate births should have decreased drastically. Yet neither the availability of contraceptives nor abortion has made an appreciable decrease in illegitimacy. What then is the explanation?

Several things have happened at about the same time, and it is not known which came first. There has been an increase in the use of contraceptives, in abortion, *and* in pregnancy outside of marriage. Mathematically it does not make sense except for two other factors: more permissive attitudes toward sexual relationships and increased incidence of sexual relationships. Still, we do not know if there is a cause-effect relationship.

Some parents who once did everything they could to hide a single daughter's pregnancy or sexual relationships now not only admit it but discuss it along with her other activities. They do not yet condone it or

[5]Robert V. Sherwin, "The Law and Sexual Relationships," *The Journal of Social Issues,* **22** (April, 1966), 109–122.

[6]Lester A. Kirkendall and Roger W. Libby, "Interpersonal Relationships—Crux of the Sexual Renaissance," in Jacqueline P. Wiseman, ed., *People as Partners,* San Francisco, Canfield Press, 1971, pp. 138–151.

encourage it, but they are reluctant to condemn it, or at least they are reluctant to condemn her. Other parents look at the total picture to explain their daughters' or sons' actions, or they do not feel that any explanation is needed. There are some parents whose concern is that their minor or young adult daughters use contraceptives so that they will not become pregnant. In all societies illegitimacy has been condemned more than nonmarital sexual relationships.

The above categories do not describe all parents, however. Many would prefer that their single minor and young-adult children not have sexual relationships. They go to great lengths to prevent it, for they are caught up in their own moral conditioning, accompanied by the hope that their children will not suffer the anguish that might come from either societal disapproval or personal disappointments.

Probably the most important discussion about sexual relationships between single people has to do with their own personal beliefs and desires. The young adults of today were reared by parents who were born in the forties and reared in the fifties—hardly decades of overt sexual permissiveness. Their beliefs became part of their children's beliefs. Therefore, young adults today are not themselves completely free of any of the former cautions and fears of their parents. Most young people, however, are not sexually promiscuous or blatantly unfeeling about their partners. When there is a sexual relationship, there is generally a commitment to that one at that time and there is usually a very strong affection or love relationship. There seems to be far less guilt today about sexual relationships so long as an affectionate relationship with the partner exists. What seems to be problematic for some young men, and some young women, for that matter, is finding that their partners are having sexual relationships with another person at the same time their own relationship is still in force. Both men and women find this a blow to their self-esteem. They also seem to feel disgust, even today, that they have shared their lover with someone else. This is the situation that most often brings young men and women to the counselor's office. What are the counselor's actions in such cases? Here is a case in point.

CASE 23 VICKY

"Well, it's this way. My boyfriend and I have broken up. That is, I'm considering it. He doesn't want to. But I can't seem to be willing to keep on. I always thought he was a fine man. Now, after this, I don't know."

The counselor listened to a lot more of the story before Vicky's reason for uncertainty came out.

"You see, he's got this other girl pregnant and he doesn't love her. He loves me, or at least I thought so. He says he still does, but how could he if he's been doing that with her? He says he will pay for an abortion for her. In fact, I'd help! No, that wouldn't be right, would it? But he's not sure she'll do it. He's really over a barrel. He doesn't know what she will make him do. I feel so sorry for him. He cried when he told me about it. Should I just break everything off? I don't know what to do.

"What bothers me so is that he would need to have relations with anyone else. I thought our relationship would be enough. Oh, I wasn't going to tell you that. You see, I don't have the buxom figure men like. Do you think he just needed someone else? And after his having had sex with her, I don't see how I can let him touch me now. I'm so mixed up."

No matter what the statistics are or what the laws are or what someone else will think, the major consideration is the relationship between those two people. What are the factors that produce problems today in nonmarital sexual relationships? Essentially they are subsumed under the value-behavior discrepancy of all people involved, the woman, the man, and anyone else who is a significant person to either of them. The value-behavior discrepancy (see Appendix for generalizations about human behavior from a cognitive dissonance point of view) essentially states that there will be greater stress when behavior differs greatly from a person's values.[7]

The effect of basic social changes on
sexual relationships without marriage

Not too long ago it was believed that the most radical change in incidence of sexual relationships without marriage occurred in the 1920s and especially among women. The decade of the 1960s was believed to have brought about a definitely more permissive attitude, but not necessarily a greater incidence of sexual relationships. More recently, however, it is believed that the incidence, especially among women, has increased

[7]Harold T. Christensen and Christina F. Gregg, "Changing Sex Norms in America and Scandinavia," *Journal of Marriage and the Family,* **32** (November, 1970), 616–627.

substantially.[8] This is not to imply that there are not some women and some men who choose not to enter into sexual relationships without marriage. Nine explanations for the increase in incidence and accompanying change in attitudes are discussed below.

Changing technology. The first of the factors pointed to as an explanation of the change in sexual behavior and attitudes is often the changing technology, which has brought the automobile, the "pill," and antibiotics into general use. It is doubtful that any invention has had a greater effect on unmarried sexual behavior than the automobile, for it moved dating from the parlor out into the countryside and away from the prying, protective eyes of parents and relatives.

The wide availability of contraceptives in many different forms has also affected attitudes and behavior. Contraceptives theoretically negate one of the oldest reasons for premarital abstinence. The word *theoretically* is important, for the statistics indicate that the rate of premarital pregnancies has gone up. Venereal disease has also increased drastically, despite, or perhaps even because of, the availability of antibiotics, because some strains of gonorrhea are resistant. The false security of believing that an easy cure was available may have had something to do with the increase in the V.D. rate, especially among teenagers.

Urbanization. A second reason offered for changing sex practices and attitudes is the urbanization of American culture. In rural America, primary-group associations tended to maintain traditional values. That is, there was constant association with relatives, friends, and neighbors, all of whom had approximately the same value systems. As people moved to the urban areas in large numbers after World War I, they found a far greater anonymity and a far greater freedom to behave as they wished. Today, fewer people in the big cities know or care what their neighbors are doing, even though apartment-house dwellers may live physically closer together than farm people ever did. The urban situation not only creates an opportunity for behavior disapproved of in the rural culture, it also creates the loneliness that motivates people to form transitory sexual liaisons.

Secularization. Secularization is another explanation for the new sex attitudes. Adherence to religious concepts and doctrines has been steadily declining.

Commercialization of sex. Another factor that has been pointed to as encouraging the new sexual climate has been the increased promotion

[8]Christensen and Gregg, Ibid.

and commercialization of sex by the mass media. Although there are those who would argue that this is an effect of changing popular attitudes rather than a cause of those attitudes, it is fairly evident that at times, the movies and the magazines are leading public opinion rather than following it. Increasingly liberal court decisions about what constitutes pornography and increasing public acceptance of written material that could formerly be classified only as salacious has played a part in changing attitudes toward sex among the unmarried.

Affluence. Some people have always defied sexual conventions, but prosperity and affluence make it easier for large numbers of middle-class citizens to make discreet visits to local motels or to have hideaway weekends at distant resorts. These people can get away from the control of primary groups and still maintain a "respectable" social or business reputation.

Value dilution. Still another reason suggested for changes in sex attitudes is the continuing increase in cross-cultural associations. America in the early twentieth century was a class- and regionally-divided society. The predominant middle class, which in general had relatively strict and somewhat puritanical attitudes toward sex, had relatively little contact with people from lower socioeconomic groups, who generally had much more sexual freedom.

During the crucial adolescent years, there was little social interchange between students from widely divergent backgrounds. The high school that the upper- and middle-class children attended had almost no students from lower socioeconomic levels. Besides, the lower classes could not afford for their children to continue in school much beyond the required minimum age.

But during World War I there was a large-scale exposure of middle-class American men not only to the greater sexual freedom of other American subcultural groups but also to that of some of the European cultures as well. The results were predictable. Middle-class men absorbed the freer sexual values and brought them home to the middle-class women.

The cross-cultural mixing was increased by the Great Depression of the 1930s, when, for the first time, large groups of lower socioeconomic-group boys and girls were forced by state law and economic necessity to remain in school until they were sixteen or eighteen. Again, it was far easier for the more strictly reared middle-class children to absorb the freer lower-class values than vice versa. World War II also contributed greatly to the decline of the old middle-class standards, as did the postwar upward social mobility that brought about large-scale subcultural group mixing in the housing tracts of the suburbs. The admission of large numbers of ex-G.I.'s, fresh from the wartime years of sexual freedom, to the colleges and universities, completed the decline of some of the older sexual differentials.

Sexual equality for women. Another social change that has been suggested as contributing importantly to the new sexual attitudes is the upsurge in sexual equality for women. Almost everyone believes that women are entitled to as much sexual enjoyment (and possibly more, since they are capable of multiple orgasms) and as much opportunity for sexual variety as men have always had. There are, of course, wide regional and subcultural variations in the application of these attitudes.

The concept that women are entitled to as much sexual pleasure as men has given rise to the notion that having intercourse with an unmarried woman is no longer defined as exploiting her. Most societies have always sought to protect the unmarried female on the theory that intercourse was usually disadvantageous to her. Even our common folk language reflects this—for example, "He took advantage of her." Now, however, many men look upon having intercourse with a woman as a mutually pleasurable experience, if not actually a means of doing the woman a favor. Avoiding premarital intercourse for chivalrous reasons has become almost anachronistic, for most mature women seem to like being free to choose. But there remains the problem of what to do about immature girls who can be impregnated or emotionally traumatized before they are old enough to recognize the consequences of their sexual behavior. Men are also sometimes put at a disadvantage by the sexual demands of women.

Crisis philosophy. There is considerable agreement that the pressures of adversity and disaster can and do affect sexual attitudes and behaviors. Just *how* recent events and circumstances have influenced the move toward sexual freedom is, however, a subject of controversy. Theodore Ferdinand represents one point of view in suggesting that, in the early years of our society, severe adversity gave meaning to the ascetic ideal of severe self-discipline. But, Ferdinand points out, today's young Americans

have never known a national disaster like the great depression or the strong likelihood that a world war would drastically interfere with their lives. . . . For them an ethic of indulgence is more meaningful than one of self-discipline.[9]

Another, and almost diametrically opposed, view is that Americans have been living in a constant state of crisis ever since 1939. One international crisis has followed another in recent years, and war has been an ever-

[9]Theodore Ferdinand, "Sex Behavior and the American Class Structure: A Mosaic," *Annals of the American Academy of Political and Social Science,* **376** (March, 1968), 77.

present threat. Three times in the past thirty years young men have been drafted and sent off to die on battlefields. Since 1945, there has been the threat of atomic destruction, and the consequent atmosphere of perpetual crisis has increased social instability. "Take what you want today, for there may be no tomorrow" seems to have become something of a national motto, according to this view.

American attitudes in the 1970s seem to have changed toward more individualism, more liberalism, and more pessimism. Rather than looking at the future with confidence of prosperity or fear of war, it seems they are looking with uncertainty about the economy.[10]

The self-fulfilling prophecy. Finally, one very important factor in creating the more permissive attitudes may be that the so-called sexual revolution was touted as reality by the mass media writers and disseminated to homes throughout the United States via television, even though its actual existence was—in the beginning, at least—doubtful. Many young people, hearing about this revolution, felt that they had a new norm to live up to. Because young people *want* to be normal, they helped to make real what otherwise might never have existed, by exaggerating their sexual escapades to make themselves appear close to what they thought the sexual-conduct norms were, or by seeking actual sexual experience. In either case, they gave credence to stories that originally had questionable validity, and so tended to convince others that the stories were true in the first place.

Such a phenomenon is called a self-fulfilling prophecy. This prophecy has two possible effects. One is that people will tend to make true what is purported to be true. The other is that some rational people will weigh the evidence and study the outcome and then decide not to allow the prophecy to become self-fulfilling. The prophecy about pollution is an example in point. Instead of allowing everything to become polluted, steps were taken in some areas of the country to eliminate the pollution.

From the evidence reported by our own students, many unmarried college students do participate in sexual relationships. They invariably report that promiscuity and indiscretion are the two phenomena that are most unacceptable. It seems that the self-fulfilling prophecy that "everyone is doing it" caused many of the students to make some clear distinctions about what is actually happening and what is acceptable.

Any one or all of the nine major explanations for the new sexual permissiveness postulated in this chapter may be more or less relevant in the

[10]Otis D. Duncan, Beverly Duncan, and Howard Schuman, *Social Change in a Metropolitan Community*, New York, Basic Books, 1973.

life of any particular person. Taken together they give some measure of the complexity of the factors that have brought us to the present state of increasing sexual relationships without marriage.

SINGLES WITH CHILDREN

All of the six categories of singles—the never-married men and women, widowed men and women, divorced men and women—could have children in their present care. The most likely persons to have children at home are young widowed or divorced women. A person in any of the categories could conceivably have either their own biological children or adopted children. Again the most likely groups are the young widowed or divorced women. It is highly unlikely for an unmarried man to be taking care of his illegitimate children. It is also highly unlikely for an unmarried man or woman to have adopted children, but none of these are impossibilities.

The widower with several children garners the most emotional concern from our society. Why this is so is threefold: the underdeveloped capacity for managing the dual role of homemaker and full-time worker outside; the imputed bereavement of the widower; and the great number of married and single women seemingly eager to help. The divorced father with children to care for would also gain the sympathies of society, although not as much as the widowed father.

The following case of Henry Phillips illustrates the widowed father's problems.

CASE 24 HENRY

"Elizabeth died eight years ago. I've been both father and mother to our seven children ever since. I had a good job at the mill but we had no insurance on her. After paying for the funeral expenses, our savings were shot.

"The children were underage so they were all still at home. The youngest was five and the oldest was seventeen. We all decided not to split up. The sixteen-year-old girl wanted to quit school and run the house but I wouldn't hear of it.

"I hired a widow-woman to come in every day to cook breakfast, get the children off to school, clean house, buy groceries, baby-sit with the five-year-old and cook supper on weekdays. She left after school was out. The oldest girl graduated from high school and moved to another city. We hired another woman and my second daughter helped her. Each of the other five children had some housekeeping jobs to do, just as they had when their mother was living.

"Even with the organization and cooperation, we all missed Elizabeth. I didn't have anyone to talk to and the children didn't have the pleasure of the nice things only a mother can do. I didn't have either the time, money, or energy to go with any other women. You can't even talk to a married woman for fear her husband will think you're getting too friendly.

"I've thought of getting married and always stop when I think about her kids and my kids fighting.

"At first I was just tired and lonesome. Now I'm getting lazy. Ever since the second girl left home, the work is still as big as ever.

"You have your good days and your bad days. I've resigned myself to a life of dull days and endless nights."

What would have been the difference in the home and child management if the one left was the wife? What would have been the difference if the separation was due to divorce? What generalizations are operating in this case? Empathize with four different people in the case: the father, oldest daughter, middle son, and housekeeper.

Dating when there are small children presents the problem of baby-sitters, but dating with older children presents the problems of possible disapproval. If the single parent is recently widowed, the disapproval tends to be even stronger, because the child sees the new person as trying to take the beloved deceased parent's place. Another problem develops when the older child of a widowed or divorced parent is the same sex as the parent. This problem is that of jealousy, especially if the child does not have as many dates as the parent or if the older child has to baby-sit with the younger ones while the parent is out on a date.

Sexual relationships are not as inevitable among the divorced and widowed as might be expected, but when there are children, discretion is even more necessary. The use of the parent's home for intimate relationships is usually out of the question.

RESEARCH ABOUT SEXUAL RELATIONSHIPS WITHOUT MARRIAGE

Much of the research pertaining to sexual relationships without marriage has attempted to measure the percentage of people who have had premarital sex. No matter what figure was obtained it was probably neither valid nor reliable. The percentage was not valid because the question, "Have you had premarital sex?" cannot possibly have had a correct answer. Does the answer "yes" mean one time or a hundred, one person or several, penile-vaginal intercourse, masturbation, mutual masturbation, or oral-genital sex? The percentage was not reliable because the same questionnaire means something different each time a person takes it and means something different to groups of different ages and locales. Accuracy in who does what, when, how, and with whom is not nearly as important as what the relationship means to the people involved and eventually to their world.

Some researchers have studied just this aspect of sexual relations between unmarried couples.[11] The findings have been essentially the same: the older the couple, the fewer their problems with cultural and personal biases; the more discreet, the more satisfactory the relationship, because when it is known the cultural pressures mount; the greater the emotional attachment, the better the relationship; and the nearer a person's children (especially daughters) approach adolescence, the more conservative the parent becomes.

SHOULD EVERYONE MARRY OR REMARRY?

There is general agreement among mental-health professionals that everyone needs love, but whether or not everyone needs marriage is something else again. There are those whose physical or emotional handicaps make marriage impossible and those who, despite their motivation, cannot increase their marriageability. It is true that if people have not married by the time they are a certain age, they probably will not marry. In a society that values marriage so highly, this may be a real personal tragedy.

In prior generations, the story might well have been different, but today the evidence indicates that some people live out their lives in relative satisfaction with their single status. In a sample of unmarried professional women, Luther Baker, Jr., found that 90 percent expressed contentment with their pattern of living. Said Baker:

> The never-married subjects in this investigation expressed no feelings of frustration, no sense of not being a "whole person" as a consequence of being unmarried. Their sense of personal worth comes not from their biological function as a female but from their social function as a human being. . . .[12]

It has been suggested that many of these women sometimes feel that their greatest problem is to convince their married friends that they are

[11]Kenneth L. Cannon and Richard Long, "Premarital Sexual Behavior in the Sixties," *Journal of Marriage and the Family*, **33** (February, 1971) 36–49.

[12]Luther G. Baker, Jr., "The Personal and Social Adjustment of the Never Married Woman," *Journal of Marriage and the Family*, **30** (August, 1968), 478.

really happy. This is understandable. However, Hortense Glenn and James Walters quite properly suggest that those who value marriage should also value a person's right to choose not to marry.[13]

The age of an unmarried person may well have something to do with his or her satisfaction with singleness. Robert Weiss and Nancy Samelson found in their study of the social roles of American women that whereas almost a third of the older unmarrieds had no feelings of usefulness or importance, none of the young unmarrieds felt that way.[14]

In fact, when interpreting data in a research study using undergraduates who were engaged, Marion Schulman pointed out that marriage may not be seen as an inevitable developmental step anymore.[15] Even the old notion that fewer married than single women commit suicide must be revised. About twice as many married women as single women commit suicide.[16]

Now that getting married is not as necessary as it once was, the decision to seek marriage can depend—and probably should depend—on a large and complex group of personal attitudes, values, and expectations.

[13]Hortense M. Glenn and James Walters, "Feminine Stress in the Twentieth Century," *Journal of Home Economics*, **58** (November, 1966), 703–707.

[14]Robert Weiss and Nancy Samelson, "Social Roles of American Women: Their Contribution to a Sense of Usefulness and Importance," *Marriage and Family Living*, **20** (November, 1958), 358–366.

[15]Marion L. Schulman, "Idealization in Engaged Couples," *Journal of Marriage and the Family*, **36** (February, 1974), 145.

[16]Jesus Rico-Velasco and Lisbeth Mynko, "Suicide and Marital Status: A Changing Relationship," *Journal of Marriage and the Family*, **35** (May, 1973), 239–244.

10

RELATIONSHIPS IN VARYING FAMILY LIFE-STYLES

Inability to cope with difficult relationships in the typical family of father, mother, and children, even with all the cultural reinforcements, has caused many people to try to find something different. Although the idea of varying family life-styles is not new, there has been a recent increase in trying atypical life-styles.

The "typical" and the "ideal" are not one and the same and never have been, however. The "ideal" American family, in which there is a father and mother who love each other rapturously for life and who have three darling children, where the father jauntily goes to work each day while the mother cleans house and cooks their favorite food is just that—an ideal. There is no such family.[1] It has been said that the ideals fostered in this culture are the family's worst enemy, for they are impossible to reach, leaving the family members with a feeling of never succeeding.[2]

The expectation that the nuclear family should care for all the family members' needs has put another impossible task before it.[3] The inability of one man and one woman to earn enough money to provide necessities for themselves and their children along with opportunities for personal happiness and growth for each family member has led to the breakdown of some individuals. It has traditionally been a mark of incompetency if a person or a family needed outside help.

Families have always needed help, however. They received it from close neighbors, who were more than likely relatives as well. Relatives and neighbor families were expected to help and did, for people need to help. No family has ever really stood alone, yet families are made to feel they should. Most people can cope with these expectations, but some cannot or will not. Should they continue in a typical family life-style if another family life-style is better?

When expectations exceed resources, people change something. They change either their goals or their behavior. When the original goal is to meet the impossible expectations of the culturally ideal family, the members can either change their concept of what their own family should be or they can change their behavior in two ways as they continue their belief in the ideal: They can fervently work toward that ideal until they are exhausted, or they can give up and do nothing, while saying, "I know I ought to, but if I can't have perfection, I won't waste my time on mediocrity." The

[1]William J. Goode, *World Revolution and Family Patterns*, New York, Free Press, 1963, pp. 6–7.

[2]Richard Farson et al., *The Future of the Family*, New York, Family Service Association of America, 1969, p. 64.

[3]Richard Sennett, "Brutality of Modern Families," in Gwen B. Carr, *Marriage and Family in a Decade of Change*, Reading, Mass., Addison-Wesley, 1972, pp. 142–158.

major relationship problem comes when each family member has a different goal and consequently different behavior, or has the same goal but responds to it in a different way.

A DIFFERENT FAMILY LIFE-STYLE AS A WAY "IN"

"Something has to be better than this." This statement is made over and over again. The reference is to the person's parents' marriage and family or to his or her own marriage and family.

So long as there were few opportunities to have something different, most people stayed in the traditional husband-wife family. Divorce was almost the only alternative. A few people tried communal living. Many varied their lives through extramarital experiences. Some chose a dormitory-like life, while others chose to live alone. But most of these were ways *out* of a bad situation.

Now there seems to be a different approach. People are looking for a way "in" as much as a way "out." The way in to better family living, the way in to extended personal relationships, the way in to having some time for themselves while having the security of a group when it is needed—these are the changes being sought now.

For these changes to be possible at all, the opportunities have to be there, opportunities for mobility, education, mass communication, employment opportunities, civil-rights legislation (especially for women), child-care facilities, and a concurrent change in societal attitudes. (Needless to say, the change in attitudes will not be wholesale.)

It is still not easy to live in a too-different family life-style. Not everyone can or should try it. This chapter is about the relationship opportunities *and* problems of living in a different life-style. The two broad categories of life-styles we will discuss are self-actualizing marriages and families in shared living.

ACTUALIZING POTENTIAL IN MARRIAGE

This type of marriage is based on the open-systems model of marriage and family, in which each person can expect to continue to develop toward self-actualization[4] while living in a one-to-one relationship situation. Nena and George O'Neill have called this the "open marriage."[5]

[4]Herbert A. Otto, *Guide to Developing Your Potential*, New York, Scribner, 1967, pp. 59–63.
[5]Nena O'Neill and George O'Neill, *Open Marriage: A New Life Style for Couples*, New York, Evans, 1972.

The concept in the self-actualizing marriage is that of synergic build-up.[6, 7] Rather than each person going his own way unmarried, the belief is that the two partners can develop more fully as individuals if they work together as a married couple. This type of marriage is based on some degree of mutuality. This mutuality is not a mere agreement to bilateral growth for each, but rather to support and tolerance as each one grows in his own way.

This concept is not as new as you would think from reading the popular literature. David Mace, a liberal conservative, as he refers to himself, has for years advocated the marriage in which the partners are represented as intersecting circles, not as completely overlapping circles.[8] Robert Blood emphatically discussed the smothering effect of too much togetherness, while holding to commitment.[9] Some married couples themselves have known this and have attempted to find some time for personal growth without upsetting their marriages or offending the sensibilities of society. The difference is that now the process is being described with supporting evidence of its success. Pursuits for personal growth once scorned by law and by societal attitudes are prescribed as acceptable. Even if couples have in the past pursued some of these activities, they usually did so either without mutual agreement or without social sanction.

For a self-actualizing marriage to work, the couple must be aware of their conditioned expectations of the one-and-only love, the male-female roles, the one-household family unit, and the lifetime marriage and career. They must also be knowledgeable about the principles of human behavior (see the Appendix) and how they operate to control and instigate behavior. We will discuss the relationship possibilities and problems in androgyny, living separately, cross-sex friendships, and short-term or long-term careers within the self-actualizing marriage.

ANDROGYNY

With the women's movement increasing and greater egalitarianism more probable, a marriage with no sex-role differentiation is highly possible. A

---

[6]Abraham H. Maslow and John J. Honigmann, eds., "Synergy: Some Notes of Ruth Benedict," *American Anthropologist*, **72** (April, 1970), 320–333.

[7]Nena O'Neill and George O'Neill, "Open Marriage: A Synergic Model," *The Family Coordinator*, **21** (October, 1972), 403–410; and Lawrence Casler, "Permissive Matrimony: Proposals for the Future," *The Humanist*, **34** (March/April, 1974), 4–8.

[8]David Mace and Vera Mace, *We Can Have Better Marriages If We Really Want Them*, Nashville, Tenn., Abingdon, 1974.

[9]Robert Blood, *Marriage*, 2nd ed., New York, Free Press, 1969, p. 107.

lack of sex-role differentiation is called androgyny.[10] Since there is a definite sex-role differentiation in this society, no two people are ever completely free of the notion. But some people can have such a strong goal of ridding their marriage of differentiation by sex that they can make it operable. In this marriage, tasks are performed by the one who has the time, the energy, the desire, and the interest, and possibly the expertise, so long as a childhood background of sex-differentiated jobs does not automatically give them the expertise. It would be foolish, however, to do a certain task just because it is the opposite of the culturally reinforced sex role when one lacks the time, energy, and desire.

The whole point in androgynous task assignment is that the traditional sex role is not the prime deciding factor. Personal desire within a cooperative atmosphere is the factor. It has been said that individualism is such a strong drive in today's young Americans that it is difficult for them to cooperate. Socialization toward androgyny would incorporate both individualism and cooperation. Women may still choose traditional feminine roles, but the key word is "choose." Men may also choose traditional male roles if they desire.

Most of the problems occur because both want to do the same task, neither wants to do some tasks, and because the individuals receive no societal reinforcement to encourage their untraditional choices. However, a couple bent on making androgyny work need little outside reinforcement. Their own motivation is usually sufficient.

Even in these families, people get irritable under pressure, tolerance levels become lower, and the fight to persevere sometimes becomes too great. If the members are not sold on egalitarianism and androgyny, then they may become accusative and hostile. (Family members in traditional families also lose their patience under stress and begin to accuse the members of not doing their jobs.)

LIVING SEPARATELY

When one of the main reasons for getting married is to live together, it seems rather unusual to suggest living separately as a way to increase human potential or reach self-actualization. Yet some couples have found that they enjoy each other tremendously when they live in separate domiciles before they are married and on occasion after marriage. Too much togetherness can be smothering, while separateness can be stimulating. Too much

---

[10]Joy D. Osofsky and Howard J. Osofsky, "Androgyny as a Life Style," *The Family Coordinator*, **21** (October, 1972), 411–418.

separateness can also create such independence in a couple that they have little need for each other. But we are not talking about the ordinary person. This avenue for increasing human potential is only one of many. If your question is, "Why marry if you're not going to live together?" then you have to remember again that marriage has never had a regulation of constant companionship. (Some states, however, have a law that if a couple lives in separate domiciles, this fact can be interpreted as desertion by one of the spouses. Again, though, intention is part of this interpretation. If it is known that the habitation of separate domiciles has another purpose, an interpretation of desertion is hard to make.)

The fact that two residences cost a great deal of money implies that separate domiciles are possible only for couples with sufficient incomes. Couples can be separate at a lower cost, however, by having separate but adjoining apartments, or separate bedrooms in one house, or even twin beds. That society frowns on living separately is shown almost daily by jokes about twin beds and the facial expressions when separate bedrooms are mentioned. Separate domiciles may attract far less talk, however, purely because such an arrangement is not in the framework of most people's thinking.

CROSS-SEX FRIENDSHIPS

Reaching one's potential would be very difficult if the only relationship a person had was with his or her spouse. Besides working with people of both sexes, some people need to communicate and fraternize with both sexes in a nonworking and nonmarital situation. Mutual support by spouses of each other in the pursuit of self-actualization is as necessary here as in any other facet of the marriage that encourages growth.

Even same-sex friendships are scorned in some marriages, not to mention opposite-sex friendships. However, cross-sex friendships are encouraged and tolerated to a limited degree in many traditional marriages so long as there is no sexual relationship. Admittedly, opposite-sex friendships with a sexual relationship do occur without the knowledge of many mates, but this clandestine-type relationship is not a part of the cross-sex relationship described here. If this is a marriage of mutual commitment to helping the mate and self reach full potential, then any sexual relationship must take place with the knowledge and consent of the mate. Very few husbands and wives can tolerate this knowledge, because of the implication that they are not fulfilling their roles if their mates need an extramarital relationship.

Many times, however, a cross-sex friendship without a sexual relationship is all that a person needs. A marriage can still be an open marriage even when extramarital sexual relationships are objected to and restricted.

SHORT-TERM JOBS OR LONG-TERM CAREERS

The traditional marriage model is for the husband to have one long-term career while the wife has either no career or several short-term jobs before, between, and a long time after the children are born. Some wives have worked outside the home all of their lives, taking off only a few weeks when each child was born.

The difference in this facet of the marriage with a mutual contract for increasing human potential is that: (1) the husband may choose the opportunity to have short-term jobs, while the wife has a long-term career; (2) both may have planned-for long-term careers; (3) or both may have planned-for short-term jobs. The key is in planning for that situation most likely to increase one's human potential.

One partner may need the support of the other when there is unilateral growth. That is, one partner may have to stay on a job that he does not like so well if it is necessary for the other one to take time off or work into a better job or work toward escalating in a job. Many husbands and wives do this when they work while the other one gets more education.

CASE 25 VICTOR AND HENRIETTA

"I need to talk to you about my marriage to Victor next summer. He and I both decided that we wanted to have an open marriage. You know, where we are open and honest with each other and where we encourage the growth of the other one. Well, last week he told me he wanted to take a year's vacation the first year we were married, while I worked. He said I could have the second year off and he'd work.

"It all sounded so good and I was so excited about it. Our friends think we're so clever and thoughtful. But Daddy hit the ceiling. To think that Victor was going to 'live off his wife' was more than Daddy could take. I expected that reaction, really.

"What's bothering me is that Daddy's remark brought out my own misgivings. I really do expect to work all my life. Even if I have children I don't want to quit work, just take a leave. But it's been gnawing at me ever since then that Victor isn't going to work and I wonder if he ever will.

"You see, he never has worked, come to think of it. But he has always talked about how human beings should be above digging out a living. I'm not so sure I would be proud of his not working."

"Henrietta is just running scared. I am majoring in the sociology of languages and know what this world is all about. She was all for the idea of trying several things in marriage until last week.

"I've traveled all over the world. Year before last I studied in three different countries. She needs to get to know something about the world before she gets set in some job."

GUIDELINES FOR ACTUALIZING POTENTIAL

The conditioning of people for the typical closed-marriage model presents great obstacles for growth potential. The first factor in creating a marriage that encourages growth is to recognize the barriers this conditioning will present. The second factor is to acknowledge the concept of synergy, an increase in the possibility that each marriage partner will reach his potential when both partners mutually agree and support each other. The third factor is to be realistic in the actions chosen. A fourth factor is to keep communication lines open so that each partner will know where the other stands. It could be that both want to quit a particular action but hesitate because they are afraid the other wants to continue. If lines of communication are open, this does not happen. A fifth factor is to trust the other one.

It is inconceivable that all the possibilities of the open-marriage model can be accepted or tolerated or desired at one time. It may be that one or more may be tried at different times throughout a marriage. It is also inconceivable that once an open marriage is tried, the couple will return to a completely traditional one.

FAMILIES IN SHARED LIVING

There are many ways that several families are grouping together to make life more meaningful and less hectic. These groups incorporate some of the values of the open-marriage model, but differ in that they include support for several families working as a group, rather than being limited to *one* set of partners mutually supporting each other. One way for families to share with each other is in a commune. Another way is in an intimate network of affiliated families.

COMMUNAL LIVING

Communal living in an intentional community with mutual agreement, organization, commitment, and concern for human dignity is probably the ultimate in family living. No wonder so many plans for communes were named "Utopia."

There are many ways to organize communal living. A commune

can be a group of families with monogamous marriages, or a group of families with legally monogamous marriages but open cross-sex friendships, or a group of nonlegally married people who consider themselves married to each other as a group. There are of course other variations of the pairing or grouping.[11]

FUNCTIONALLY RELATED FAMILIES

Community living can involve organization of affiliated families,[12] an intimate network of families who live in separate domiciles.[13] These arrangements were devised to take care of the needs of the nuclear family isolated from close relatives and friends of long standing. Many of these families are isolated as a result of having moved because of jobs. Some move because of retirement, and some do not move but are left after others have moved. About four or five families are the maximum number in a functionally related group. These families value privacy and thus retain their individual homes. Their joint ventures may include social contact, mutual baby-sitting, and other services as needed.

The relationship problems in communes bring out some basic needs. One such need is for a secure relationship.[14] Jealousy is one of the results of sexual experimentation that is not usually bargained for in the search for security in a group. Most people think they can handle a mate's sexual involvement with another person, but if they have never had to face it they do not really know. No matter how intellectually acceptant the parties involved are, someone usually winds up being hurt.

Communal living is seen by Carl Rogers as a transition rather than a complete change in family living.[15] It seems that most people who have lived in communes eventually want to be married and live in a one-to-one relationship. Rogers has suggested that communal living may be a way of transferring from one's own family of orientation to his new family of procreation.

One of the problems in communal living has been that communes

[11]James W. Ramey, "Emerging Patterns of Innovative Behavior in Marriage," *The Family Coordinator*, **21** (October, 1972), 435–456.

[12]Sylvia Clavan and Ethel Vatter, "The Affiliated Family," *The Family Coordinator*, **21** (October, 1972), 499–504.

[13]Frederick H. Stoller, "The Intimate Network of Families as a New Structure," in Herbert A. Otto, ed., *The Family in Search of a Future*, New York, Appleton, 1970, pp. 145–160.

[14]Carl R. Rogers, *Becoming Partners: Marriage and Its Alternatives*, New York, Delacorte Press, 1972, pp. 125–160.

[15]Ibid.

are started by people conditioned to live in separate families that competed with each other. Consider the following case.

CASE 26 LONNIE AND CAROLE

Lonnie dropped into the chair in the counselor's office. His bare feet, bib overalls, long hair, and beard were all dirty. His posture belied his voiced confidence.

"I don't see why Carole won't come with me to Arkansas. I'm going down there to live in a rural commune and I want to take my two little girls with me. She's balking now, saying that's no way to bring up the children. She was all for living in a group unmarried and having intimate relations with several of the men. Of course, I favored two of the women myself and I found that I had great affection for both of them as well as Carole. After the first little girl was born, we decided to get married but still live in the group. But pairing off legally changed the climate in the group, so we moved out. Now we have two little girls and Carole is screaming like a traditional wife—and I thought that was what we were trying to get away from.

"Don't you think a rural commune would be a perfect place to raise children so that they would learn how to commune with nature and love everybody? I really think Carole is sick. Do you suppose I could get the children away from her on those grounds?"

FAMILY LIFE-STYLES OF THE FUTURE

The numerous family life-styles that are actually being practiced are still in a minority. David Mace has said that monogamy will continue to hold as the culturally accepted marriage type, and the nuclear family as the family type.[16] He implies that experiments in different family forms will not make radical changes in the family. The newest changes will come in the reorganization within the present family, and will be similar to the concepts described in the discussion of families committed to human actualization.

---

[16]David Mace, lecture in a course on the contemporary family at the University of North Carolina at Greensboro, April, 1973.

11

INTERPERSONAL RELATIONSHIPS IN MARRIAGE

Almost every American old enough to be concerned about marriage has heard that "adjustments" are necessary to make a marriage work. Marriage adjustments are the subject of countless magazine articles, soap operas, and advice columns in the newspapers. Despite this wide publicity, most young people enter marriage convinced that they are already well adjusted and that they will not have the difficulties other people have had trying to get along with one another.

This blissful optimism may be a good thing, for some good marriage prospects would never marry if they were made apprehensive about all the adjustments that lie ahead. Everybody has to make adjustments, not only in the beginning of his marriage but throughout his married life. For some, the adjustments are so easy that they do not even know they are adjusting. For others, adjusting is a conscious and deliberate process of learning to understand, to accept, and to change.

Speaking of adjusting is another way of saying that the marriage relationship is an interpersonal relationship that requires attention as much as any other interpersonal relationship. The generalizations about human behavior (see the Appendix) are operating in marriage as much as anywhere else. To know why people are motivated to act as they do and to know how to initiate change in oneself as well as in others is to know how to make conscious adjustment. Too many people assume that their habitual state of behavior is adjustment, when it may actually be irritating to the partner and deadening to one's own spirit. To step back and take a look at the effect of one's actions on others may be just what is needed in a marriage.

Most partners adjust well enough both to stay married and to be counted as happily married, although the most recent review of research in marital happiness indicates that "happiness" is difficult to define, and that the results from research may be misleading.[1]

There are, however, many young marrieds unable or unwilling to make even the initial adjustments to married life. Some who accept the idea that they have adjustments to make at the beginning of their marriage are often unaware that many of the most important and most difficult adjustments come many years after the honeymoon. These later adjustments are sometimes more difficult, for some of the romance may be gone, and partners have established change-resistant patterns of reacting to one another. They may also have developed painful individual problems that in-

[1]Mary W. Hicks and Marilyn Platt, "Marital Happiness and Stability: A Review of the Research in the Sixties," in Carlfred Broderick, ed., *A Decade of Family Research and Action*, Minneapolis, National Council on Family Relations, 1972, pp. 59–78.

crease their criticalness and decrease their tolerance. Initial adjustments are hard enough; later ones can be devastating.

In this chapter, some of the typical adjustments that are required of marriage partners throughout their relationships will be discussed. First it is necessary, however, to answer two important questions: (1) Why do partners not realize their differences and either adjust to them before marriage or never get married? (2) Which of the partners does the adjusting?

WHY DO PROBLEMS REQUIRING ADJUSTMENT NOT OCCUR BEFORE MARRIAGE?

A great many adjustments *are* made before the two partners get married. Some potential marriage mates are rejected or drop out during the dating process, because even the very first adjustments are too difficult for one or both partners to make. Others may be rejected during the engagement period, because, as the partners approach the actual reality of marriage, they recognize (or at least one of them recognizes) that they are not really able to adjust to each other.

Even after this selectivity has taken place, there are often many unforeseen difficulties in getting along with one's mate. Some of these difficulties occur because people tend to disguise their idiosyncrasies before marriage, even though they are well aware that they have them. These can turn out to be "tremendous trifles" in a marriage. A young woman may know that she is usually cranky before she has had her breakfast. She is careful, however, not to let her fiancé find this out until after they are married. A young man may know that he does not like to make "small talk" and probably will like it even less after he is married. But before marriage he tries to keep up an entertaining stream of banter with his fiancée.

A second type of adjustment is necessitated by *unrealized* habits. He takes up three-quarters of the bed, but he does not know it since he sleeps alone. She hangs her stockings in the bathroom, but this never bothered anybody because she had her own bathroom before she was married. He is a compulsive towel-straightener; she tends to overlook such minor details of neatness. She is a "night person"; he is a "day person."

More important than these unforeseen habits, though, are the partners' differences in marriage expectations. For example, what happens if a woman who emotionally needs and expects her husband to remember birthdays and anniversaries without being reminded (as her father always did) marries a forgetful man? Or what happens if a man with a conditioned need for an affectionate wife who talks sweetly (as his mother always did), even after a long day of housework, marries a relatively unaffectionate woman who is easily fatigued?

Many difficulties occur because neither partner discovered before-hand the other's concept of husband or wife roles *after* marriage. Murstein has pointed out that accurate perception of role expectation is important.[2] Each person may assume from his knowledge of the other's behavior during courtship that the other will naturally want to do the "right" things after marriage. Differing and undiscussed expectations can have a very serious effect on the stability of the marriage relationship, as the following case illustrates.

CASE 27 JOHN AND ELOISE

"John is ruining our marriage!" Eloise said. "I work hours preparing a nice dinner for him, and he's never on time to eat it. The worst part about it is that he doesn't even call me to let me know that he'll be late. He could be on time every night if he wanted to. He just doesn't want to. He doesn't love me enough. I know he'll tell you that he's a salesman and can't get up and run out of his prospect's office when suppertime comes, but 90 percent of the time that isn't so, and the other times he could at least call me. All he thinks about is himself. When he does get home and the dinner is cold or burned, he complains.

"He wasn't that way before we were married. He had the same job then, but he was almost always on time for our dinner dates. I'm just not going to put up with his selfishness any longer. I'm tired of begging him, and I'm tired of screaming at him; now I'm going to leave him."

John had a somewhat different version of the same story. "If Eloise told you that I can't get home for dinner every night right on the minute, she's right," John told the counselor. "She knew when I married her that I was a salesman. I have to be where the client is when he wants to buy, re-gardless of what time it is. She didn't make any fuss about it before we were married. She conveniently forgets about it now, but I was just about as late for our dates as I am now. There were a couple of big differences then. In the first place, she wasn't cooking the meals. In the second place, it didn't seem to matter to her so much. She didn't give me the stuff she does now about her father being on time! She and that perfect father of hers. He had a nine-to-five job and was never a minute late getting to the office and never

[2]Bernard Murstein, "Stimulus-Value-Role: A Theory of Marital Choice," *Journal of Marriage and the Family*, **32** (August, 1970), 465–481.

*a minute late getting home. Before we were married she seemed to under-
stand how I couldn't always figure out my time to the second. She even
used to smile about it a little and call me 'Johnny-come-lately.' But after we
got married she changed. Now she never smiles; she just screams.*

    *"I admit that I'm not the best one about telephoning. Sometimes
there isn't a phone around. But there's more to it than that. I feel like such
a baby when I have to report to her every five minutes. The other fellows
don't have to go running to the phone to call their wives. When they're late,
their wives understand. My mother used to understand, too. Before we were
married and I was living at home, Mother didn't nag me all the time. If I
was a little late coming, she would just serve supper to the rest of them and
put mine in the oven. In some ways I think my mother loved me more than
my wife does. She wasn't trying to make me out like a bad guy all the time.*

    *"I don't want a divorce; I love my wife and kids. But sometimes I
think it would be better if she did get a divorce. She sure is making my life
miserable the way it is."*

    There are other important reasons why people do not anticipate the
necessity of adjusting in the courtship situation. For one thing, they are together only part of the time. He never gets tired of her talking, because he
generally leaves when he has had enough. She does not get angry or upset
over the number of towels he uses, because she does not have to wash the
towels. Neither one of them gets hurt by their relatives' cuts or slights, because they both tend to stay away from their relatives.

    But after marriage all this changes. They are together perhaps eight
waking hours out of every day, and on some days much more. A repetitious
behavior that once might have been endearing now becomes intolerable.
Moreover, they find themselves drawn into prolonged contact with their
relatives, and they have to deal with crucial conflicts that they once postponed or ignored. It is by perpetualness and enforced closeness that the adjustability of a partner is really tried—sometimes for the first time.

IT IS DIFFERENT WHEN IT IS NEW

Novelty is another reason why adjustments are not anticipated. In the beginning of any relationship, the partners are polite and eager to please. This
is especially true of relationships between men and women. Good manners
and consequent good feelings are especially important to a good first impres-

sion. The novelty of going steady and being engaged is a delightful adult adaptation of the child's game of playing family—"You be the father and I'll be the mother." Some people never get tired of this game. It is a source of enrichment for the rest of their adult lives, and it is actually an aid to unconscious adjusting. But for others, interest in the game fades soon after marriage. Then the long-delayed real adjustments have to be made or the marriage fails.

Probably the most important reason why adjustability is inadequately tested before marriage is the *idealization* that is part and parcel of the romantic process. Idealization is the tendency for those in love to attribute glamorous characteristics and abilities to a prospective marriage partner that that marriage partner actually does not have. This often leads to one of two unreal assumptions. The first is that the prospective partner is such a noble knight in shining armor or such a delicate lady fair that it would be sheer ecstasy to spend one's life adjusting to this ideal person's whims. The second possible unreal assumption is that there will be no need for adjustment in living with this noble creature in the first place.

Idealization certainly is not always bad. Positive trust is often rewarded by its own expectation. The man or woman who has faith in his or her partner may help that partner to grow toward greatness. With this kind of "good" idealization comes complete acceptance, the willingness not only to tolerate but actually to be enthusiastic about the partner, with all possible emphasis on his good points. Complete acceptance is the stuff of which good adjustments are later made.

Complete acceptance was never better described than by a loquacious New York taxicab driver. "I see a lot of good-looking rich dames in the course of a day's work. I carry a lot of them in my cab. But I wouldn't trade any one of them for the wife I got up in the Bronx. You know what? The other Sunday afternoon when she thought I was asleep I heard her hanging out the window talking to the woman in the apartment across the court. She was telling her what a good guy I am. Imagine that! She was telling her how strong I am and what a good husband I am and how good I am to the kids. Most of it was a whole pack of lies, but I think my wife really believes them. I was a little ashamed that I can't really live up to all that stuff, but I felt good that she thought I could. She's a good mother; she works hard, and she gets tired. But she always tries to make the best of what we got, and most of all she tries to make the best of me. Way down deep I know what I am. But I also know I'm a lot better than I would be if I didn't have her. I think she's happy, too. At least she's a lot happier than those dames who get in the cab and don't know what to do with themselves except to spend their husband's money while they squawk about what a bum he is. My wife may not smell as good as them, and she may not have as many clothes, but she's got something a lot more important. And so do I."

There is "bad" idealization, too. It blinds a marriage partner to the real-life need for making constant relationship adjustments. In such cases, early hero images only tend to make later disillusionment that much greater.

CASE 28 GEORGE AND LILA

"I didn't think it could happen to us," George told the counselor wistfully. "I can remember standing in the moonlight near a beautiful lake five years ago holding her in my arms. She was so eager to touch me and be close to me that I could feel her quiver in my arms. Nothing ever affected me like that. To know that she wanted to be near me so badly that she quivered was just about the most exciting thing that ever happened to me. In those days she wanted to do everything and anything for me; nothing was too much trouble. It wasn't that I needed all that much, it was just that nobody ever loved me like that before. Adjustments? What was there to adjust to? We never even gave it a thought!

"But now the quiver is gone. Yes, I think that's what characterizes our relationship now; the quiver is gone. One day last week I got to thinking about that moonlit night and the lake five years ago and I got all slushy. So I went out and bought her a box of candy and some flowers. When I came in the front door at suppertime, I saw her standing in the middle of the living room surveying the carnage that the kids had wrought. So I just sneaked up behind her quietly and kissed her on the back of the neck. Do you know what she said? She said, 'I wonder if I turned out the fire under the peas.' How do you like that?

"Actually, it wasn't that she didn't turn around and want to be close to me that hurt. It's the fact that she no longer really accepts me. Now she is critical of things that I do, little things, like watching the ball game instead of cutting the grass. And she doesn't seem to want me to touch her anymore. I don't know what to do; I sure would like to have that acceptance back—and the quiver that goes along with it."

George's wife Lila was wistful about it too. "It didn't start all at once. But one day a few weeks after we got home from the honeymoon, I began to see some things about George that I had never seen before. He wasn't strong and all-knowing like I had thought he was. He had a lot of anxieties and a lot of peculiar notions. And he wasn't as neat as he had always appeared. He left his dirty socks around, and he didn't hang up his clothes. I don't think I changed at all right then; at least, it didn't seem to me as if I did. But it must have seemed that way to George, because he changed a little in his way of behaving toward me. All of a sudden he got defensive. Then I guess I changed a little more in my way of behaving toward him, and then he changed again, and so I changed again, and the relationship went down, down, down, until it just seems now that I don't care very much.

"I certainly wish that I had had a better idea of what marriage was going to be like before we were married. I had heard you had to adjust, but I thought the adjustments would be kind of fun. I thought it would be nice to try to please him by changing my ways of doing things. Now I don't care. It doesn't seem important at all whether he's pleased or not. He doesn't go out of his way to please me, either. I don't know what we can do about it. I hate to think of spending the rest of my life this way."

WHO DOES THE ADJUSTING?

Which partner should do the adjusting is one of the basic problems of middle-class marriage. It probably always has been a problem, although in other times and in other cultures there were strict expectations of role behavior that, while they may have placed unfair adjustment burdens on women, tended to reduce controversy over what was "proper." In American society today, with its less structured roles for men and women, deciding who defers to whom is more of a trial-and-error procedure. In the beginning, even before marriage, there is often a subtle and unconscious struggle between the two partners to see who will dominate. This struggle sometimes ends the relationship, and not always because one partner or the other loses. Some men and many women want to be dominated, and they become unhappy when their partner insists on *not* being the leader.

Once this initial jockeying for position has been satisfactorily resolved, the relationship often enters into a period of at least temporary stability. As the partners become more deeply love-related, they tend to be "syncratic" (sharing decisions equally). They talk over major decisions and arrive at mutually satisfactory solutions without the dominant one parading his dominance. As Robert Blood points out, even in this period, some aspects of the future relationship are controlled by one partner or the other. This is especially true for the minor routine decisions of early marriage that are linked to generally accepted sex-role behavior. For example the husband almost always makes a decision on what job to take or what auto to buy, while the wife more often makes most of the food purchases and the petty housekeeping decisions. The initial syncratic honeymoon, with its easy decision sharing, does not always persist as the marriage progresses. Blood believes that the longer a marriage exists, the greater the tendency is for decisions to be made unilaterally. Family affairs are generally the wife's specialty; there is a shift from syncratic to automatic decision making to some extent, until decisions become wife-dominated. Wives seldom seize power, but husbands often withdraw from decision making.[3]

Not all and perhaps not even the majority of marriages are readily taken over by the woman. In fact, in some marriages, the woman struggles *not* to accept the responsibility of leadership, insisting that her husband make the decisions. If the marriage is not to be equalitarian, the emergence of the partner dominant in decision making is controlled by a complex series of factors falling into two general categories: personality and the relative bargaining position of the partners.

PERSONALITY'S EFFECT ON DOMINANCE

Although the democratic or equalitarian marriage has been held up as the ideal one by many of the professionals in marriage relationships education for years, many people do not have the emotional conditioning to accept a coequal marriage relationship. In the middle class at least, the male responsibility is still strong even though the male's authority has been considerably diminished in recent years. Moreover, a large number of women still want men who can dominate them—at least to the extent of being resolutely decisive. Such women often test their men, consciously or not, by giving them a little bit harder time than they need to so that the men will be forced to demonstrate their strength. This need for dominance on the part of these women is believed by some to be culturally conditioned from the example of traditional male-female roles in their childhood homes.

Not all men are capable of consistently accepting a dominant position. Some, perhaps because of their conditioning by dominant mothers, have an emotional expectation (usually unconscious) that *they* will be dominated, and so they put themselves in a position of subserviency. Some other men have a self-concept of inadequacy in all relationships for reasons that are complex and obscure. They deliberately take a lower position in the "pecking order" in any group they enter.

The concept of "pecking order" is derived from observations of the hierarchy of status among barnyard hens. In a flock, one hen tends to be

[3]Robert O. Blood, Jr., *The Family*, New York, Free Press, 1972, p. 429.

dominant and pecks all the others first. A second hen will peck all the hens but the top hen. The rest arrange themselves in descending order, leaving one poor hen that is pecked by all the others but that can peck no one. Among animals, size appears to be an important factor affecting pecking order, and since male animals are usually larger than females, they usually have the advantage. Male hormones apparently give the male some advantage, too. Hens low in the pecking order that are given injections of male hormones have been observed to fight their way up the pecking-order ladder.[4]

Among human beings, many psychological factors affect the pecking order. Size alone is not the controlling factor, nor are hormones. Such culturally conditioned factors as a willingness to fight or a readiness to compromise in order to avoid conflict are important. Then, too, conditioned self-images often dictate an individual's pecking order. If one thinks of himself as a dominant leader, he may well become a "take-charge" type. Soon the rest of his group may defer to him, even though he may have no qualifications other than his own aggressiveness. On the other hand, the submissive individual who demonstrates a willingness to accept a lower status is often assigned a low position by the members of his group.

Much has been written about "castrating" females who presumably emasculate their men by dominating them. The result is classic—the "henpecked" husband. When this happens, however, it is often because the husband wants it to happen, either consciously or unconsciously. In such wife-dominated marriages, the husband does most of the adjusting. Some men try very hard to please their wives—perhaps too hard—and get emotional satisfaction from the fact that they *try* to be such good husbands. To the outsider it may look as if they are severely abused, but in reality they are getting contentment from playing the subservient roles.

RELATIVE BARGAINING POSITION

Equally as important as personality in the control of who dominates whom is the relative bargaining position of the two partners. In 1921, E. A. Ross defined the law of personal exploitation: "The thing is common and its rule is simple. In any sentimental relation the one who cares less can exploit the one who cares more. In the man-woman relation and in the mother-child relation we see this plainly."[5] Subsequently, Willard Waller expanded on

[4]W. C. Allee, *The Social Life of Animals*, New York, Norton, 1939, p. 178.
[5]Edward A. Ross, *Principles of Sociology*, Englewood Cliffs, N.J., Prentice-Hall, 1923, p. 136.

what he called the principle of least interest: The person who has the least interest in the continuation of a relationship is able to dictate the conditions of continued association.[6]

These postulates may sound cynical to those young people who are very much in love. And, indeed, in some marriages where neither partner is —or even feels—exploited, they may never have any valid application. But in some marriage relationships, they are all-controlling. The right to dominate is determined by such factors as physical beauty, amount of education, job status, achievement, and the presence or absence of children. The better bargaining position can fluctuate from one partner to the other at various times in the marriage.

There is very little specific research support for the effect of beauty on dominance, but it is common for a marriage counselor to find one partner or the other tyrannizing his mate by using his good looks as a bargaining weapon. The tacit threat "I can easily find another and you can't" is very often sufficient to control any relationship. A good job can raise one's bargaining position, too. Wives who are employed fulltime have more influence in family decision making than those employed parttime, and the latter in turn have more influence than those who don't work at all.[7] The less the husband is employed, the less influence he has. In fact, as Robert Blood points out, when income is derived from both partners, the balance of power is correspondingly altered. The more the balance of participation in the economic system shifts in the wife's direction, the more the husband's power declines.[8]

There are many marriages in the upper-middle class in which the wives' careers are encouraged by the husbands. Indeed, the husbands take pride in acclaiming their wives' successes.[9] However, this recent finding may merely be further support of William J. Goode's assertion that upper-middle-class husbands merely talk a good game and that in fact they hold the power by continuing to make their jobs the center around which the family revolves.[10]

When the prevailing force in marriage is the power of one over the

[6]Willard Waller, *The Family*, rev. ed. by Reuben Hill, New York, Holt, Rinehart & Winston, 1951, p. 191.

[7]J. Richard Udry, *The Social Context of Marriage*, 2nd ed., Philadelphia, Lippincott, 1971, p. 316.

[8]Blood, op. cit., pp. 530–533.

[9]Catherine C. Arnott, "Husbands' Attitude and Wives' Commitment to Employment," *Journal of Marriage and the Family*, **34** (November, 1972), 673–684.

[10]William J. Goode, *World Revolution and Family Pattern*, New York, Free Press, 1963, pp. 21–22.

other, Vivian Cadden believes that love will be greatly diminished.[11] It is not possible, she indicates, to have both power and love as prevailing forces, even if each partner has equal power. The very same behaviors in two different marriages can be the result of different motivations. When a woman becomes subservient to her husband because she wants to avert the vengeance of an irate husband, she is the victim of a power-ridden marriage; whereas the wife who does things for her husband because she wants to is operating in a giving relationship. The politics of relative bargaining position can be devastating to a marriage relationship. Note the effect of the relative bargaining positions in the following case.

CASE 29 MARIAN AND ALEX

"I'd been married to Marian for about seven years," Alex said. "She came from a home where she had a tremendously domineering father, and she was very much afraid of him. When he said she couldn't go out, that was that. For the first five or six years after we were married, she was pretty good about being a good wife. Whenever she went anywhere, she asked me if she could go. Sometimes it even seemed a little silly for me to tell a grown woman exactly what she could do.

"But then she got a job at a television studio. She is a very beautiful woman. At first I was all for it. I was pleased that my wife was so attractive. But pretty soon she began feeling very independent and staying out until all hours of the night. I began to scream and shout about her not coming in until two or three in the morning. Then she began not to tell me when she was going out. I'd get home and find that she'd left the kids at a babysitter's and gone off on some 'public relations' job. About the middle of the evening she'd call up and say she'd be home in half an hour. Then maybe at about two in the morning she'd finally get home. My yelling at her didn't seem to do any good, so I started trying to reason with her. That wasn't any better. She just told me that she'd do as she pleased.

"A couple of weeks ago I got so mad I moved out. I'd thought I'd show her. But now I'm wondering if I didn't make a bad mistake. She has shown no inclination to ask me to come back, and now she gets to go out any time she wants to. Sure, I'm jealous. I don't know what she's doing out late at night. She says she's just either out with the girls or driving by her-

[11]Vivian Cadden, "The Politics of Marriage: A Delicate Balance," in Marcia E. Lasswell and Thomas E. Lasswell, eds., *Love, Marriage, Family: A Developmental Approach,* Glenview, Ill., Scott, Foresman, 1973, pp. 296–302.

self. She says she wouldn't want any other man, and the way our sex life has been I don't think she would either. I think she hates men and sex too.

"What am I going to do? If I go back and tell her she can go out any time she wants to, I'll have lost face. Besides, I don't think that's what she really wants anyway."

When the counselor talked to Marian, she agreed that everything that Alex had said was right. *"He used to carp at me and pick at me an awful lot. At first I tried to do better in every way he suggested. But I never could meet his expectations so finally I just stopped trying. Then I got my job. Everyone is nice to me down there, and I like the people and I have a sense of achievement. Besides, it is very flattering to be told how nice I look. I'm not going to stop working now no matter what Alex does.*

"Yes, it's true that I lie to him. The thing that set him off three weeks ago was that I waited until the last minute to tell him I was going out for an evening show. I told him I'd be home by ten, but I knew that I couldn't possibly be home before midnight. I was afraid to tell him that, because he would have hit the ceiling and been mad before I left and mad when I got home. When I finally did get home at three A.M., he was only mad once.

"Sure, I understand he doesn't like me out until three in the morning. But he goes out with the boys until all hours, why shouldn't I? Actually, I really think I want him to stop me, but to tell you the truth I don't know how he's going to. I'll leave him if he tries to use force. He did hit me once, you know.

"I don't know whether I'm glad or sorry he walked out, but in many ways it's nice to be independent. Yet in some ways I think I still need him. I wish he could find some way to solve this thing."

THE EFFECT OF CHILDREN ON BARGAINING POSITION

The absence or presence of children in a family can also affect the relative bargaining power of the marriage mate. Some infertile women feel inadequate because of their childlessness and are deliberately more patronizing to their husbands, sometimes fearing that he might seek a fertile woman. The coming of children may also affect the power structure of the family. Sometimes, the more children there are, the more complex and necessary the husband's role becomes, increasing his relative power. David Heer believes that each partner compares his present position in the marriage with the situation that might obtain if he were outside the marriage. In this case, the more children a woman has, the lower is her probable bargaining position for another husband or for a good job. Consequently, she accepts her husband's domination.[12]

Some husbands lose power when the children come. This is not only because they may be outvoted in the democratic process but also because they are afraid to get divorces, knowing that in most courts the woman will get the children. This raises the wives' relative bargaining positions and lowers the husbands'. Is has also been suggested that, in some families, the father loses power after the children come because the wife can more easily manipulate the children's attitudes. If she has hostility toward her husband, either overt or latent, she can openly or subtly demean him to the point where he no longer has respect. He must then bargain with her in order to retain a semblance of control in his own household. Presumably, men are not so adept as women in turning their children against the spouse, even when they are so inclined.

THE EQUALITARIAN MARRIAGE

Are there no equalitarian marriages in which neither partner is noticeably dominant? Most assuredly there are. On an imaginary continuum that runs from male dominance to female dominance, there are couples at every point, so it is readily deducible that there must be some at midpoint. Moreover, since the equalitarian marriage has been a cultural ideal in recent times, there are, in fact, many marriages clustered close to that midpoint.

Those who have achieved this ideal kind of marital arrangement believe that it gives a feeling of worth and dignity and an integrity of the spirit to both partners. Robert Blood indicated that, in general, the greater the sharing of decisions, the healthier the marriage.[13]

In an equalitarian marriage, each partner is so satisfied with the joint decision-making process and with his separate areas of decision making that he never stops to question whether those assignments are exactly equal. Thus, the term *balanced marriage* might be more accurate than equalitarian. In fact, an overemphasis on equality can spoil what otherwise might be a perfectly satisfactory arrangement.

[12]David M. Heer, "The Measurement and Bases of Family Power: An Overview," *Marriage and Family Living*, **25** (May, 1963), 133–139.

[13]Blood, op. cit., pp. 431–434.

THE ADJUSTMENT PROCESS

Adjustment in marriage is a continuous process. As the complexion of the marriage changes, the two partners must resynchronize their ideas, values, desires, and goals if the marriage is to run smoothly. At the outset, newly-weds face a multitude of adjustments. Sexual relationships, spending the family income, keeping in-laws happy, relating to new friends and a new pattern of social life, and adjusting to the personal habits and hygiene of the new mate are all very important. In addition, each partner must learn how far he can push his mate in sensitive areas and which things and thoughts he must avoid. But the initial adjustments are only the beginning. Even after the interaction between the marriage partners has been successfully established, new and changing situations, together with the inevitable personality changes that result from aging and maturing, make further adjustments necessary and inevitable.

The arrival of the first child in the family signals the beginning of a whole new era in the relationship of the husband and wife. Some marriage partners who have made every other adjustment easily have trouble at this point, as one partner or the other becomes jealous of the attention given to the baby. The need for disciplining the child and tending to his value education as he grows up necessitates another reevaluation of the partners' attitudes toward each other, toward the child, and toward the complete living experience. The arrival of the second child causes further adjustments, not only for the marriage partners, but also on the part of the first-born.

Another major adjustment occurs when the children go off to school, leaving the mother with time she had forgotten about. Shall she work outside the home? Still further adjustments must take place when the children leave home for good and the mother finds herself without a role. Perhaps the greatest adjustment of all occurs when the husband retires and suddenly faces the insults of old age without the crutch of feeling necessary or the motivation of competition with other men.

The variety of separate stages in marriage requiring new adjustments has led to the development of the concept of the family life cycle. This formulation suggests that marriages proceed from their inception through a regular and predictable series of stages to which readjustments are necessary. Evelyn Duvall has proposed an eight-stage family life cycle:

1. beginning families (married couple without children)
2. childbearing families (oldest child, birth to thirty months)
3. families with preschool children (oldest child, two-and-a-half to six years)

4. families with school children (oldest child, six to thirteen years)
5. families with teenagers (oldest child, thirteen to twenty years)
6. families as launching centers (first child gone, last child leaving home)
7. families in the middle years (empty nest to retirement)
8. aging families (retirement to death of one or both spouses)[14]

In each of these stages, new adjustments have to be made and old ones reevaluated. For example, here is a summary of Duvall's "developmental tasks" (necessary adjustments) for the couple expecting the first baby:

1. arranging for the physical care of the expected baby
2. developing new patterns for getting and spending income
3. reevaluating procedures for determining who does what and where authority rests
4. adapting patterns of sexual relationships to pregnancy
5. expanding communication systems for present and anticipated emotional needs
6. reorienting relationships with relatives
7. adapting relationships with friends, associates, and community activities to the realities of pregnancy
8. acquiring knowledge about and planning for the specifics of pregnancy, childbirth, and parenthood
9. maintaining morale and a workable philosophy of life[15]

Suppose a teenage couple has to meet the developmental tasks of two stages at one time, as would happen if they were expecting a baby in the first year of marriage. Obviously the problems mount. If Duvall's belief holds true that the successful meeting of developmental tasks depends a great deal on how successfully the previous developmental tasks were met, then a couple having to meet more than one set at a time is more than likely to have serious problems. In the case of our hypothetical teenage couple, the following developmental tasks for the newly married couple are added to the developmental tasks for the couple expecting their first child.

1. establishing a home base in a place to call their own
2. establishing mutually satisfactory systems for getting and spending money
3. establishing mutually acceptable patterns of who does what and who is accountable to whom
4. establishing a continuity of mutually satisfying sex relationships
5. establishing systems of intellectual and emotional communication
6. establishing workable relationships with relatives

[14]Evelyn Duvall, *Family Development*, 4th ed., Philadelphia, Lippincott, 1971, p. 121.

[15]Ibid., p. 199.

7. establishing ways of interacting with friends, associates, and community organizations
8. facing the possibility of children and planning for their coming
9. establishing a workable philosophy of life as a couple[16]

To satisfactorily meet all of the developmental tasks in each of these two stages at one time is a monumental feat. But some couples do it and do it well. If the theory holds true, then those couples no doubt had met their previous tasks for adolescent and young adult living successfully and now have the strength to meet this double set.

WHICH ADJUSTMENTS ARE MOST IMPORTANT?

Given the present state of unpredictability in human relationships in general and the almost universal practice of disguising one's real after-marriage expectations from one's friends, one's fiancé, and even oneself, there is probably no real way of predicting which partners will have to make which adjustments or how soon they will have to make them.

Social psychologists disagree among themselves about which of the initial adjustments cause the most difficulty for most people. In 1946, Judson Landis reported that, of 409 couples studied, the fewest number of partners agreed that they had had satisfaction from the beginning in their sex relations, the next fewest, in spending the family income.[17] He did a similar study of 581 college-educated couples in 1967 and reported that "the problems couples face in marriage have changed little with the changing times. . . . 'New' problems listed by the present generation of married people are not the ones they ranked the highest. Their reports agreed with those of the earlier couples in giving highest ranking to problems in the area of sex, finances, in-laws and childbearing."[18]

These areas are still probably the areas of most interpersonal discontent, but with the acceptance of no-fault divorce and women's liberation, the problem areas of sex, money, and in-laws may take a back seat to personal goals in life as a reason for separation.

Many marriage partners who seek marriage counseling report that sex is their problem. This is so often true that much of the literature in marriage counseling deals with handling sex-related difficulties. Sex, how-

[16]Ibid., p. 169.
[17]Judson T. Landis, "Length of Time Required to Achieve Adjustment in Marriage," *American Sociological Review*, **11** (December, 1946), 647.
[18]Judson T. Landis and Mary G. Landis, *Building a Successful Marriage*, 5th ed., Englewood Cliffs, N.J., Prentice-Hall, 1968, pp. 281–284.

ever, can be a convenient peg on which to hang other difficulties. Two marriage partners who have been fighting all day about spending money are not likely to have a very good sexual relationship that night. Asked the next day what their difficulty is, they would probably blame sex.

In any event, which adjustment is the more difficult for the largest number of people is not very important to most married partners who are not getting along. Their adjustments are their own special problems. Even after they know why they are having trouble, they still must perceive that they have only three possible ways of resolving their problem, regardless of what it is. These three ways are accommodation, alteration, or aggression. The theory of cognitive dissonance explains how accommodation, alteration, and aggression are useful in resolving problems. Dissonance may be reduced by changing behaviors, by changing the environment, or by adding a new perception (see the Appendix).

ACCOMMODATION

Accommodation ranges from complete acceptance to the grumbling toleration of peaceful coexistence. The performance that leads most quickly to adjustment is the acceptance of one partner's attitudes and behaviors by the other. This does not necessarily mean that one should be required to be completely subservient to the will of the other; to do so would damage feelings of personal integrity and so develop a need for even further adjustments. But when both partners can and do accept *most* of the attitudes and behaviors of the other without loss of any sense of personal worth and self-respect, adjustment is achieved relatively easily.

There are a few for whom a theoretically ideal marriage would be the one in which each partner completely accepts the attitudes and behaviors of the other *all* of the time. Usually this is impossible. Besides, most people expect at least some opposition and conflict, even from those who love them. They would be disconcerted by someone who always agreed with them and placidly permitted any behavior, no matter how outrageous. Such permissive acceptance would tend to destroy the recipient's ability to discriminate between adequate and inadequate performance. Thus, it would preclude the satisfaction that comes from earning the genuine approval of the other person. Greater satisfaction is obtained when one is accepted most of the time, rewarded by love for good performance, and rejected (in a manner the offender himself feels is appropriate) for obviously inadequate performance.

Many situations in the interrelationships of marriage partners require a "putting-up-with-it" kind of accommodation, which differs from pleased acceptance. The more happily such accommodation can be made, the more successful the marriage relationship. If, for example, either mate is forced by illness or accident to give up his traditional role, the other must learn to live with whatever new arrangements can be made. If the inevitable can be accepted gracefully, both partners will benefit.

There are less dramatic cases, too, in which accommodating oneself to the other person is possibly the most effective way of dealing with the problem. After a young husband has made his feelings clear about his wife's not putting the tools back, he probably is better off not to keep nagging about it. Nagging usually just increases one's own resentment and the other person's hostility. Foolish though it may seem, some people ultimately get ulcers and/or divorces over matters that have no greater significance in the lives of either one of them than a pair of pliers.

The supercharged emotional feelings of love that most people bring to marriage have an important usefulness in making accommodations. Love-inspired desire plus personality flexibility allow some people to make all the initial adjustments without knowing they are doing so.

Moreover, given an understanding partner, such people can often establish, by their own example, patterns of interacting that will both ensure and increase both partners' ability to make future adjustments. These are the marriages that go on to a self-enlarging richness.

CASE 30 AD AND LOUISE

Ad had been married to Louise less than a year when he approached the marriage counselor for advice. Emphatically he made the statement, "I need variety, make Louise understand!" When questioned as to what he meant by variety, he explained that this meant freedom to date others and go on various functions without his wife. From childhood, Ad remembered his mother not showing him affection, and he detested affection from his wife. He prided himself on looking like his father. "People thought we were brothers," Ad stated. During his college years, Ad was a great football player; he was used to dating various girls and prided himself on the number he had been to bed with and how they responded to his love. He thought of himself as the great lover who could conquer all.

"Another thing I don't understand is that she gets upset if I praise other girls on how they look. Lately we have been having trouble with sexual relations. Why shouldn't I want someone else? I must admit I waited until twenty-eight years of age to get married. I was enjoying life,

and women especially. While I was dating her, I dated other girls on her campus. Do you know, she got jealous! Before we were married she was sort of liberal, but after the wedding things changed, she wanted me to spend more time with her. My mother always stressed that I do what I wanted to do: Don't let anyone rule you. I think that makes sense and is easy to understand. Why can't she? All I want is to be left alone to enjoy life. Explain that to her if you can."

"I married Ad when I was twenty-three; everyone said you can't teach an old dog new tricks but up until now compromising has worked. What upset me was when Ad switched jobs. He went from a bank executive to a car salesman. I was displeased but complied with his wishes. After this, he made known to me he wanted variety. I was deeply shocked and hurt but went along as if I noticed nothing. My mother had been divorced when I was young, and my oldest sister had gotten a divorce. I did not want to fall into this same pattern, so I complied. At first it didn't seem to bother me, but later on I felt rejected. Ad began to call me stupid and criticize the way I dressed and looked. He even criticized my housekeeping. Later on Ad began criticizing my lovemaking; he said it was stupid and I should take lessons from someone. I told him that if he gave me some pointers I would follow. He only laughed. I felt very hurt. I tried to hide the truth that something was wrong with our marriage. To keep him happy, I consulted a doctor about our sexual problem. Ad took no interest whatsoever. At this point I had decided maybe it would be better if he had variety. Maybe he'll tire and come home. Nothing I say or do pleases him now. He resents my discussing personal or financial matters with him. Everything is all right as long as his clothes are clean and food prepared. I feel like a slave. I am no better to him than a live-in maid. Please give me some advice as to what to do. I need Ad!"

ALTERATION

The second way to arrive at adjustment in a marriage relationship is through the alteration of attitudes, behaviors, or the situation. Instead of one person either accepting or tolerating the other person's ideas, he seeks to persuade the other to adopt some new thought or course. Given a reasonable amount of openmindedness and good communicative ability, a couple can reach not only an adequate but often a superior adjustment by compromise, rather than by total accommodation on the part of one partner or the other.

Compromise has been the classic solution to disagreements throughout the history of the world. Unhappily, however, compromises are usually solutions in which neither partner gets all he wants. Thus, both partners wind up with a feeling of something less than complete satisfaction.

There is, however, almost always a possibility for "creative compromise" if the partners will seek for it long enough. Creative compromise is a solution in which both partners recognize that a certain compromise represents something better than either of them wanted in the first place. If she wanted to go dancing and he wanted to go to a ball game, they might find a movie playing at a local theater that both are eager to see. Such creative compromise is not always possible. But when it is, it maximizes satisfaction and is probably the best possible adjustment.

Alteration of the situation has merit in that the problem may be eliminated. If he does not like the way his wife squeezes the toothpaste, then they could buy two tubes. If she does not like the way her husband sleeps on both sides of the bed, then they could buy twin beds.

CASE 31 CLAIRE AND DICK

"I'm so fed up I could cry," Claire complained to the family counselor. "Dick, my husband, never pays any attention to me. He leaves me to look after the children (two preschoolers), and even they get on my nerves to the extent that I seem to be screaming at them all day long."

"I can't understand what's wrong with her," Dick said dejectedly. "She's always bugging me, and yelling at me to do this or that, but nothing I do ever pleases her. So I've just given up trying. I used to show my affection a bit, but her constant complaining has turned me off."

"He doesn't understand me at all," continued Claire. "He doesn't even try now to do the things a normal husband does—like giving me a kiss and a hug when he leaves for work or arrives home. He doesn't spend any time with me, except when he is watching television. That silly TV— I could smash it!"

The counselor's empathetic queries elicited further symptoms of strain and tension in their relationship, resulting in frequent verbal battles, long silences, and little effective communication. In fact, they seemed to manage the daily business of living by reflex action, and occasional monosyllabic replies to obvious questions.

Claire and Dick claimed that their sexual relationship was adequate and normal, except that after five years of marriage it was becoming routine and lacking in imaginative innovations.

Claire revealed some difficulty in relating to her mother on an adult basis, but nothing else of major importance emerged from the sessions until she made a statement almost casually during one interview.

"If only Dick would just hold me. I don't want sex always, but I do want to be held in his arms. I need to be held. I'd like us to fall asleep in an embrace."

Dick had some difficulty in understanding that a simple act like holding his wife in an embrace could be any kind of solution to their problems. He was willing to try, and to make the attempt as spontaneous as possible under the circumstances.

AGGRESSION

The third possible way of adjusting is through aggression. This might better be called a nonadjustment process, since most aggression, either active or passive, usually provokes more aggression in return and leads to conflict and hostility rather than to adjustment. Sometimes such conflict and hostility becomes a perpetual pattern of marriage interaction between two people. They may live out their lives in an atmosphere of constant fighting, or they may finally reach a saturation point at which they are so emotionally divorced from one another that legal divorce follows as an inevitable consequence.

Not all aggression is unproductive. Sometimes the aggressive behavior of one partner or the other can force his mate into accommodation. Indeed, sometimes aggressive behavior by one partner is really what is desired by the other. There are many men and women who deliberately goad their mates into aggression. Nor is all aggression violent. In many relationships there is "passive aggression," in which one partner is deliberately obstructionist or negative or tries to manipulate the other by tears and martyr-playing.

Many marriages combine all three types of adjustment: accommodation, alteration, and aggression. There are also other marriages in which the partners change their ways of relating as they mature and move through the family life cycle. For example, some partners who at first accommodate wind up in aggression and hostility. But there are also some in which the partners learn and grow as they go along and move from immature aggressive patterns in early marriage to acceptance and alteration as they grow older.

John Cuber and Peggy Harroff, in their study of a sample of upper-middle-class Americans who had been married ten years and who considered their marriages satisfactory and likely to continue, concluded that there were five distinct "configurations" of interaction: (1) *Conflict-habituated*, (2) *Devitalized*, (3) *Passive-Congenial*, (4) *Vital*, and (5) *Total*.[19]

The Conflict-habituated partners had almost continuous verbal conflict with each other. Efforts were often made to keep the conflict concealed from friends, relatives, and children, but this was seldom successful over long periods. In relationships with other people, many of these same partners were not hostile or argumentative; it was chiefly in the marriage that conflict had become habitual.

The Devitalized partners had marriages in which they had lost the close sharing identification and deep feeling that they had had at the outset. Cuber and Harroff noted that this devitalization often began to be felt when the partners became parents for the first time. Their interaction was characterized by resignation and apathy and rather dogged determination to accept whatever modest gratification they could obtain under the circumstances and to turn to other facets of their lives for their basic fulfillments.

The Passive-Congenial partners resembled the Devitalized partners except that their relationship had never been really vital, even during the courtship, and therefore they did not have the feeling of disillusionment or regret that the Devitalized couple had over the *loss* of closeness. Typically, these people asserted that they did not really want to be close, and they doubted that other "mature" people did either.

In the Vital marriages, the man and woman made deep psychological investments in one another. They empathized with each other. They spent a great deal of time together, but this was not necessarily what made their marriage vital. Cuber and Harroff felt it was more their desire and their need and the successful expression of acceptance that formed the vital bond between them. They were usually able to adjust easily and well to each other.

Those couples in the Total marriage configuration had all the strengths in their marriage that those in the Vital configuration did. In addition, the psychological investment of each mate in the other more nearly encompassed the total needs and fulfillments of each of the mates. Cuber and Harroff believe that this kind of marriage is rare but that it does exist, despite the fact that such a relationship might be utterly incomprehensible to the people in the Passive-Congenial or Devitalized configurations.

[19]John F. Cuber and Peggy B. Harroff, *The Significant Americans*, Englewood Cliffs, N.J., Prentice-Hall, 1965, p. 64.

Cuber has suggested in another paper that it is important to recognize that people in all five of these configurations are satisfied with them to the degree that they stay married. Once a relationship is established, it tends to endure in that form over a long period:

Couples become adjusted rather early to some one of these patterns of gratification, defend it, and don't take readily to changes in it. . . . [A] minority suffers, however, not because the mode itself doesn't work, but only because it doesn't work for them. It manifestly works for many, many others.[20]

ANTICIPATING ADJUSTMENTS

Just as it is important to anticipate the initial adjustments if a marriage is to get off to a smooth start, it is also necessary to anticipate the continuing changes in the relationship that will necessitate readjustment. Each new stage of the family life cycle can best be adjusted to if the partners can anticipate its coming and the changes that will be required of them. Unhappily it is often easier to see in retrospect what should have been done than to look forward in one's own relationship to what might *be* done. Consider the following case:

CASE 32 DON AND ELSIE

"All Don thinks about is business and golf," Elsie told the counselor. "We've been married for twenty-six years now, and for the last twenty-five he hasn't paid much attention to me at all. He stays away from home many nights when I know that he could be here if he wanted to. He says his business needs him, but I think that they could get along without him. He spends every minute thinking about the business anyway, so he might as well be there. And when he isn't down at the plant, he's out playing golf. Almost every weekend he's down on the golf course or in the clubhouse with the other men.

"I thought growing older together was going to be different. Now the children are all gone; the last boy went off to college last year. We have three sons, and he should be very proud of them. I think he is, although you'd never hear it from him. He hasn't paid much attention to them since the day the first one was born.

[20]John F. Cuber, "Three Prerequisite Considerations to Diagnosis and Treatment in Marriage Counseling," in Richard H. Klemer, ed., *Counseling in Marital and Sexual Problems: A Physician's Handbook*, Baltimore, Williams & Wilkins, 1965, pp. 57–59.

"I need more attention from him now. When the boys left home I suddenly felt deserted and very alone. I turned to him for some of the companionship we had when we were first married. But he doesn't seem to want to be bothered with me now. He only takes me someplace when I force him to. He doesn't really fight with me about it; sometimes I wish he would. He just gets that resigned, hangdog look on his face.

"This isn't the way I thought it would be after the children were gone. When I thought about it at all, I just had a sort of nebulous picture of gay contentment, traveling to Europe and to the Orient, and doing all those things I've always wanted to do. Now I'm just terribly lonely and unhappy. I wish you would tell him that he should pay more attention to me."

Don did indeed seem to be resigned when he talked to the counselor. "Yes," he said, "I know that Elsie is my responsibility, that I have an obligation to take care of her. I always will. But we don't have anything in common anymore. I don't enjoy talking with her, because we don't have anything to talk about. Not even the boys, now.

"I remember what happened, and it wasn't exactly the way Elsie said. When the first boy was born, she suddenly turned completely away from me. She gave all her attention to the child; at least that's the way it seemed to me. Sure I was jealous. I knew I was jealous even then. But what could I do about it? After all, he was my son and I wanted him to have his mother's love. So I just kind of pushed it down inside myself and tried to get more interested in my business. That wasn't hard, because I had a lot of problems and a great opportunity to make something out of it. Now my firm is one of the best in its field, and it's that way because I give it a lot of time. I handle every problem personally, and I know all the men and all their troubles. Sure, I like to play a little golf on the weekends. I'm one of the best they've got at the country club now.

"It isn't as if I didn't take Elsie out once in a while. Every time she asks me to go someplace I take her. And it isn't as if there were any other women. I know a lot of fellows play around, but I'm proud of the fact that I've been faithful. After all, I've got enough trouble with the one woman I've got. Why should I want any more? I'll provide a home for Elsie for the rest of her life. What more should she want?"

The marriages that continue to grow richer are the ones in which both mates anticipate the changed needs of their partners. It is not easy, but, with some advance planning, it can be done. It is sometimes easier to plan when you know some of the impediments to marital adjustment.

12

IMPEDIMENTS TO
MARITAL ADJUSTMENT

If you could ask all the unhappy marriage partners in the world why they cannot adjust to each other, you would probably get as many specific answers as there are marriages. But as you begin to inquire more deeply, you might find certain basic patterns of maladjustment cropping up continuously. For example, the "who's right?" argument is one of the classic impediments to good adjustment. Quarreling and passive resistance are two others. There are more patterned behaviors, including manipulation, blackmail, and brainwashing. Since these behaviors can so drastically affect a marriage relationship, it is important to take a close look at them.

"WHO'S RIGHT?"

Of all the impediments to adjustment, none is more insidious or more universal than the "who's right?" argument. The problem itself begins in the childhood families of the two marriage partners. In their early interactions with their brothers and sisters, most partners learned that if there was a dispute or disagreement of any kind, a weary, but impartial, parent would step in, decide who was right, reward the righteous one by giving him the object of dispute, and admonish the loser. In the typical American home, a girl wins these disputes as often as her brother, in fact, sometimes even more often.

   With this pattern of settling differences deeply entrenched in the emotional systems of both partners, it is hardly surprising that they should perpetuate the "who's right?" habit after marriage, even though it is no longer effective problem-solving behavior. After marriage there is no impartial parent to step in and render judgment and so force the loser to do the bidding of the winner. Some partners do not give up trying, though. Either they undertake to act as judge and jury themselves, or they try to find a marriage counselor, either amateur or professional. Often a marriage counselor will be asked by a husband or a wife to tell the other spouse that he is wrong and then to force that other spouse to change his way of behaving.

   The fact that there is no impartial judge in a marriage is only a part of the futility of the "who's right?" argument. Even if each couple had its own private judge, he would find it impossible to render a decision about most questions. In an intimate relationship, many of the points of argument revolve around subjective evaluations. Stuart Chase cites an interesting technique used by Captain James Saunders, U.S.N., in teaching principles of agreement to a class of graduate students. Captain Saunders gives each class member a small piece of white paper and asks him to chew it and then report the taste—sweet, sour, bitter, or salty. A variety of opinions result, followed by much argument and confusion. Actually, the paper is the same for all, but the sensation of taste varies with the individual genetic differences of the students. Until this chemical reaction is explained, the students continue to argue about whose taste discrimination is right and whose is wrong.[1]

Given the different conditioning of today's typical young husband and wife, it is no more surprising that there are unsolvable "who's right?" differences between them than that there were taste differences among Captain Saunders's students.

There is an even bigger reason why the "who's right?" question is so futile: *It doesn't do any good to know the answer.* First of all, most marriage partners won't agree that they are wrong. A troubled wife once showed a marriage counselor a carefully typed list of reasons why she was right. "I am going to show this to my husband to prove that I am right," she said. Would this have solved her problem? Would her husband have accepted her logic? Probably not. More likely, it would only have stimulated him to think of more reasons why *she* was wrong. Moreover, it would have made him even more defensive and less willing to find a solution to the problem.

There is another reason why proving who's right is sometimes self-defeating. Suppose a wife were able to prove that her husband was wrong; would she really want to? Would it make her love him more because she had defeated him, or might she be a little distressed and unhappy because she had won? There are many situations in which wives or husbands cannot afford to lose, but there may be even more in which they cannot afford to win. Many husbands and wives haven't yet learned this. In most marriages, it is far better to protect the other partner's integrity by allowing him to save face and back off gracefully than it is to score an empty victory by proving you can win the "who's right?" argument.

Obviously, there are times when, if one partner has some special information, it does help to present the facts. For example, if a wife knows for sure that one should turn left instead of right in order to get to the Jones's house, she has an obligation to say so, even if a "who's right?" victory then becomes inevitable.

Usually, though, things are not so clear-cut. A young woman complained to the counselor about her prospective mother-in-law. The mother-in-law, after inviting the young woman to her home for a weekend, demonstrated by making the situation socially impossible that she did not really want the girl to marry her son. She did not introduce the prospective daughter-in-law to any of her friends, she embarrassed her by asking her about

[1]Stuart Chase, *Roads to Agreement*, New York, Harper & Row, 1951, pp. 8-9.

complicated recipes, and she asked pointed questions about the girl's family and background. As the young woman recounted these things to the counselor, she said, "That just isn't right, is it?" after each one. Would it have done any good for the counselor to agree with her? Would this have helped her to solve her problems? Telling the young woman that she was right would only have aggravated the situation. Ultimately, the only solution to the problem lies in the young woman finding a way to relate to her prospective mother-in-law. A person can be completely right and still not get what he wants. Consider the following case:

CASE 33 TONY AND JOSEPHINE

"Tony just won't stand up to his mother, even when he knows that I'm right," Josephine said. "His mother is a foreigner, and she barely speaks English. She demands an awful lot of her son and I get sick of the way he waits on her. His father died when he was young, and ever since that time Tony's mother has made Tony her husband as well as her son. He has to run over there all the time. We have to spend every holiday with her. Never with my folks, always with her. It just isn't right.

"When we were first married, I tried very hard to be nice to her; ask Tony, he'll tell you. But she treated me like dirt. One time I bought paint for the kitchen floor and hired a man to put it on. I thought I had done a wonderful thing. But I didn't take the wax off first, and so the paint didn't dry properly. I felt bad about it when I found out and even worse when Tony had to spend hours scraping it off. But my feelings of being ashamed for having made the mistake turned to real anger when his mother told me how stupid I was in front of Tony. She went on and on about how I wasted Tony's money. The worst thing about it was that Tony didn't take my side. He just stood there and didn't say anything. That wasn't right.

"Tony's a good husband and father in almost every respect. He works hard and he's getting ahead. But he gives in to his mother all the time. What good is there in having a man if he won't stand up for you? My father shouted and hollered a lot, and I hated it. I was very glad when I got a man like Tony who was gentle and quiet. But now I see that my father yelled just as much when he was for you as when he was against you. I guess I want a man like that too.

"Last week I let Tony persuade me that maybe I was wrong after all and that I should be nicer to his mother. I have guilt feelings every once in a while because I really want to be a good daughter-in-law. So I invited his mother over to dinner. I worked all day long in the kitchen, and I had a beautiful dinner fixed. And then do you know what she did? At the last

minute she called up and said that she had decided not to come. She was going to stay at Tony's brother's house for dinner. When Tony said, 'Yes, mother, that'll be O.K.' I just blew up. I grabbed the phone and screamed at her. After all, right is right."

When the counselor asked Josephine what she expected to accomplish in counseling, her answer could almost have been predicted. "I want you to tell him that he should take my side when I'm right. When I'm wrong, that's something else again, but when I'm right I want him to admit it and show it."

"And then after you've demonstrated that you are right, do you want your husband to give in to you?" asked the counselor. "Well," Josephine's voice trailed off. "I don't want him to give in all the time, but what is right is right and he should take my side."

Tony was the picture of dejection when he talked to the counselor. "I don't know what I'm going to do," he said. "I know that my mother isn't very reasonable about some things. She's from the old country and she expects a lot. Most of the time she's tried very hard to be nice to Josephine, but Josephine has a real chip on her shoulder. I know it's because Josephine thinks that I love my mother more than I love her. But that just isn't so. But mother is all alone, and I've been responsible for her ever since I was a little kid. I can't just yell at her, like Josephine would like me to do.

"And besides, regardless of what Josephine says, Mother isn't always wrong. Take the other night, for example, when she didn't show up after Josephine had worked all day long trying to fix a dinner. It was because my brother's wife got sick at the last minute and Mother was trying to help take care of his kids. But do you suppose Josephine would listen to that? Oh, no, she just grabbed the phone and started screaming. Actually, I almost think Jo was delighted when my mother didn't show up for dinner the other night because it proved she was right in the first place.

"There are a lot of things that Josephine does that aren't right. She takes our boy over to her mother's house all the time, but when my mother wants to see him, Josephine tells her that she won't leave him there alone because she says my mother doesn't know anything about kids and is too excitable.

"If Jo would only stop worrying about being right all the time, especially with my mother, she could make my mother very happy, and then we'd all have some peace."

The ultimate goal of deciding who's right in marriage is to use the verdict to force the partner into changing his way of behaving. But even if it is possible to determine who's right, it is usually impossible to force the other partner to behave or conform. Curiously, another goal of deciding who is right is that of rewinning love. The marriage counselor frequently sees a spouse who says, in effect, "I am right, so you should tell him that he must love me." Sometimes it is not as obvious as this; sometimes it is merely that the individual wants the other person to give him more affection because he is right. Yet being right is often the poorest way to redevelop a love relationship. Love is given as a reward for meeting needs, not as a reward for being right.

QUARRELING

Some level of quarreling, from placid discussion to violent shouting, is common in marriage. In fact, it is so common that a large number of marriage partners find it difficult to believe that there are some marriage partners who never quarrel at all and still others for whom even disagreement is a rare occurrence.

Most marriage partners who disagree frequently sooner or later settle into some pattern of resolving their differences. The posture that each chooses in this pattern is often either completely dictated by, or at least influenced by, the pattern of handling conflict that was present in the respective partner's childhood home.

People who never quarrel in marriage are usually from homes where quarreling was not acceptable. For them, settling a disagreement without hostility—and in some cases without even disagreeing—is an important value, both intellectually and emotionally. Often these people are repelled and frightened by any kind of deliberate aggressive hostility or even unintentionally aggressive behavior on the part of their mate. Such marriage partners were often the kind of children who hid behind the sofa when they saw any hostility displayed.

On the other hand, there are marriage partners who grew up in a rough-and-tumble home where they learned how to quarrel magnificently and to make up joyously. Such people find it difficult to understand that there are others who get no enjoyment from quarreling. When a partner from a rough-and-tumble background marries someone like himself, they may get along swimmingly, fighting all the time. Neither one of them would be happy if it were any other way. If, however, a person from such a background marries one of the nonhostile people, there is liable to be trauma in both directions. The damage to the rough-and-tumble person, while it may be less evident at the time, is no less real than the damage to the quiet nondisagreer.

CASE 34 MARIAN AND MILTON

"He won't fight me," Marian complained to the counselor. "He just withdraws and sulks, or sometimes he goes off by himself. He won't say what he really thinks, and it drives me wild. He is always trying to placate me, almost to the point of being patronizing. I need someone who will show me that he really loves me by expressing some emotion once in a while. But I can do anything—including staying out all night—and all he does is try to smooth things over.

"There are times when I deliberately do such provoking things that he should take me over his knee and spank me, but he won't. I know it must eat him up inside, but it isn't fair to me either. I need some reaction from him sometimes. If I'd done some of the things in my childhood home that I've done since we've been married, my father would have beaten me up. But at least I would have known that he cared. I don't understand this man I married at all."

"I don't know what to do with Marian," Milton told the counselor. "I try to do everything I can to make her happy but she seems to want to pick fights. You're a marriage counselor; you know that fighting should be avoided. My mother and father didn't ever raise their voices to one another, and it makes me feel very uncomfortable to see a woman all excited and wrought up the way she gets. Sometimes I almost get the feeling that she actually wants me to hit her. But I'm not going to hit a woman, ever. I wasn't brought up that way. I don't want to fight, I want to be happy."

Present-day Americans have been told by many authorities that it is good to vent resentments and hostilities, lest they fester and cause even greater difficulty later on. This, together with the social changes that have brought more independence and social equality to women, has stimulated more and more open conflict between marriage partners.

Ventilation rather than suppression *is* a good thing in many cases, provided the ventilator (1) takes responsibility for his actions, and (2) receives emotional relief rather than emotional satisfaction from ventilation. Emotional relief tends to reduce tension and so lessens the possibility of a need for further ventilation. Emotional *satisfaction* derived from saying hostile things, however, leads to further hostile expression and ultimately perpetuates the difficulties between the partners rather than ameliorating them. This distinction is often overlooked by those who advocate the indiscriminate release of hostile thoughts.

Students of behavior have identified two types of quarreling: constructive quarreling and destructive quarreling. As Duvall and Hill have suggested, constructive quarrels are those that leave the marriage stronger than it was before the quarrel started by redefining the situation that caused the conflict. Constructive quarreling is directed toward the issue and leads to a better understanding of the issue; it emphasizes problems and conditions rather than personalities. Since these quarrels tend to reduce tension, they should become fewer and less violent as the marriage progresses and as patterns of adjusting are more firmly established. In constructive quarreling, people (1) spell out exactly what they do not like and how they want things changed, (2) stick to the point and avoid side issues, (3) stay with it until they thrash things out, (4) go on to some simple next step for improvement, (5) don't let the matter fester, (6) attack their problem rather than each other, (7) avoid dragging in relatives, and (8) give each other cues as the tension is let up.[2]

Destructive quarrels leave fewer assets in the relationship than were present before. Destructive quarrels are directed at the personality of the marriage partner and are intended to destroy the illusions and fictions by which he has lived. Destructive quarreling is belittling and punishing, and it leads to alienation and further quarreling.

Basically, most fights are a product of the individuals and not a product of the situation. People can fight about almost anything if they want to. They can avoid conflict, even in the face of severe provocation, if they have learned how to resolve their differences without fighting and if they have a mutual desire to do so.

CASE 35 CHERYL AND TED

"I've gone more than halfway in all our disagreements," Cheryl told the counselor, "but he still won't see things my way. We've been married for two years now and instead of things getting better, they only get worse. You would think Ted would want to spend more time with me, but all he cares about is his friends. He seems to spend every free moment with them. If I get upset about it he wants to know why. He says I should communicate with him more and tell him what he is doing wrong. But it doesn't do any good. He never changes. I rant and rave and tell him everything that's wrong but he won't argue back. He just agrees that he is wrong and continues in the same old ways. I love him and I feel he should know what's bothering me, but all he does is admit he's guilty and nothing is accom-

[2]Evelyn Duvall and Reuben Hill, *Being Married*, Boston, Heath, 1960, pp. 285–286.

plished. *Sometimes I just keep quiet about what's bothering me, because Ted won't change anyway, so why bother?"*

"Cheryl is a wonderful girl and I love her dearly, but she has such an inferiority complex that it's pathetic," Ted told the counselor. *"She constantly needs to be built up and I do the best I can. After all, we didn't lose our identities when we married so why should I need to spend every minute with her? I guess it hurts her feelings, but usually I don't even realize that I'm doing something wrong until she starts sulking. I practically have to drag any piece of information out of her. When I finally do find out what's bothering her, she goes into a long dissertation of all my faults. She rehashes every bad thing I've ever done. The other day we were talking about my grades and she went into a long speech about how it was time I grew up. I usually just agree with her to make it simpler. It's the same way with my dad. He's always right and it's no use arguing, so I just keep quiet. He can't ever be satisfied anyway, so why waste time and energy arguing?"*

It is, of course, easier to see how the one who is starting the fights can change the climate by holding his tongue than to see how the person who is constantly being attacked can avoid defending himself. Most marriage partners insist that they do not start quarrels but merely maintain their own integrity by defending themselves. But do they really have to be so defensive? Will they really lose their self-respect or the respect of their marriage partner if they let him get away with an insult made in a moment of petulance?

It has been suggested to marriage partners who feel they are constantly being attacked by their mates that they treat their partners *clinically*. For example, if you were an attendant in the seriously disturbed ward at a mental hospital and a patient came up to you waving his arms and swearing violently, you would probably be able to accept his hostility, calm him down, turn him around, and steer him back to his room. This would be treating him clinically, and it would be possible because you did not let yourself become emotionally upset by whatever he shouted at you. You would understand that this represented *his* problem at the moment, and that you only happened to be the person who was closest at hand.

This approach is often a successful way of handling a specific hostility situation in marriage, even though the angry partner is only temporarily upset and in full contact with reality. However, since such clinical treatment is hardly conducive to the development of love, regardless of how successful it might be in specific therapeutic situations, it is not recommended as a permanent pattern of marriage interaction. But sometimes it does help people to help themselves over a rough spot in marriage. Occasionally it does more than that. Some of the help that can be given through marriage counseling when only one partner is available is based on the premise that, if one partner changes his way of behaving toward the other, the other cannot, over the long run, possibly maintain his way of behaving toward the first partner. A person who has been violent may change his way of behaving when his partner makes some change in his way of reacting. People do learn and people do change, even though guaranteeing such change is very risky.

DISGUISED FEELINGS AND PASSIVE RESISTANCE

There is another type of destructive behavior that is as damaging to marriage as destructive quarreling. This is described by the psychologist as passive-aggressive behavior. It is characterized by noncooperation, negativism, quiet hostility, "underenthusiasm," and other signs of subtle resistance. Since approval and acceptance are vitally important to any love relationship, withholding approval and acceptance can be as devastating as aggressive shouting and yelling—if not more so.

These various forms of passive resistance are often generated by unresolved resentments that have been allowed to fester quietly. As was pointed out earlier, it is now generally believed that it is better to "get things out" in most instances, even if some present hurt is involved, than to repress hostile feelings and risk greater hurt in the long run. Again, however, this is useful only when emotional release from tension rather than sadistic satisfaction is gained by expressing the hostile thoughts.

There are some people who have been so damaged by their childhood relationships that they are unable to express normal emotional feelings in normal ways. Some of these people develop devices and stratagems for obtaining the emotional satisfaction or release they need without ever having to admit to themselves that they were the ones who started the hostility. The least harmful of these devices is accusing the partner of "not loving me anymore," in the hope that the partner will have to change his behavior in order to prove that he does. The more harmful stratagems include playing the role of martyr and various forms of emotional blackmail and manipulation.

Martyrdom is also one means of seeking control in the marriage. Traditionally, the martyr role has been more often ascribed to the wife, but in recent times more husbands, deprived of the authority, have been seeking to control by overt or disguised martyrdom. This technique is based on the assumption that the other person will feel sorry for the martyr and, hopefully, change his way of behaving. Even if his partner doesn't change, the martyr gets the emotional satisfaction of feeling abused. Sometimes the martyr can win either or both ways. In fact, martyrdom (often initially learned from a parent) tends to be so effective and satisfying that it is one of the most easily conditioned patterns of marital manipulation. In its milder forms, it may be tolerated over a long period by a mate who is highly motivated to cater to the needs and desires of his partner. But because it is so satisfying to certain personality types, it tends to become self-enlarging, and ultimately it can reach a point at which it becomes intolerable, even to long-suffering mates.

CASE 36 MONA AND DAN

"Dan spends all day Sunday either sleeping or watching television," Mona complained to the counselor. *"He never takes us out anywhere. I work all week long waiting for him to come home, and then he just lies around like a lump. Why can't he be like other husbands who take their families out to nice places over the weekends?*

"I try to do everything I can to be a good wife. I spend every waking minute trying to keep the house cleaned up, watching over the children. I've even taken in dressmaking to help out. All I ask in return is that Dan love and be together with us like a family on Sundays. Is this too much to ask?"

Dan told a different story. "I could hardly believe what was happening at first," Dan told the counselor. "I'd offer to take her places, and she'd never want to go. She always had too much to do. She was a terrible perfectionist about the house. On top of that, she began to take in dressmaking—'to help out,' she said. We were getting by all right before she did that, but somehow she just seemed to be compelled to take on more, even though it meant staying up longer hours to do it. And then she would tell me how tired she was and how she couldn't go out.

"I got sick of asking her to go out on Sundays. She was always very sweet and self-sacrificing about just having too much to do, and she would urge me to either nap or amuse myself. So I got in the habit of watching television and snoozing. Mind you, she encouraged me to do it! Then she began to complain bitterly to the neighbors about what a bum I was and how I abused her. I tell you, I couldn't believe it the first time I heard her say it, but now she says it to me, too. She seems to get a lot of satisfaction

out of feeling abused. Sure it makes me feel like a heel, but what can I do about it? She still won't go out, even if I ask her."

The case of Mona and Dan has some similarities to the "If It Weren't for You" game in *Games People Play*.[3] In this typical game, the wife complains that her husband has so restricted her social life that she has never learned to dance. Later on, when her husband permits her to take dancing classes, she discovers that she has a morbid fear of dance floors and abandons the project. Although she may not have been aware of it, she had picked a domineering husband so that she could complain that she could do all sorts of things "if it weren't for him." Actually, of course, her husband was helping her, by forbidding her to do things that she was afraid of and by preventing her from even becoming aware of her fears.

But there is more to it than that. His directness and prohibitions, along with her complaining, frequently led to quarrels that seriously impaired their sex life. These quarrels aroused his feelings of guilt, which he assuaged by bringing her gifts that might otherwise not have been forthcoming. Since they had little in common except their household worries and their children, these quarrels stood out as important events and were emotionally satisfying. Moreover, they allowed her to prove to herself one thing that she had always believed: that men were mean and tyrannical.

Berne insists that the solution to the "If It Weren't for You" game is permissiveness. As long as the husband is prohibitive, Berne says, the game can proceed. If instead of saying "Don't you dare!" he says "Go ahead!" the underlying phobias of the wife are unmasked, and she can no longer castigate him.[4]

BLACKMAIL AND BRAINWASHING

Not long after some marriages begin, one partner or the other finds that he can manipulate his mate by using subtle pressure techniques—very much like blackmail and brainwashing. All sorts of coercion, both subtle and obvious, both gentle and arm-twisting, are used in marriage. The wife who says, "If you want to have a nice party for your sister, dear, you'll have to help clean up the house," and the husband who says, "We could buy your mother a decent Mother's Day gift if only you'd take back that silly-looking

[3]Eric Berne, *Games People Play*, New York, Grove, 1964, p. 50.
[4]Ibid., p. 53.

hat," are practicing fairly common forms of marital blackmail. But the wife who threatens to withhold sex and the husband who threatens to withhold money are practicing more crippling forms of legalized extortion. So are the wife who threatens divorce, knowing that she will be awarded the children, and the husband who reminds his wife that she had to marry him.

Like all threats, extended blackmail can lead to brainwashing, the technique of making certain behavior of the mate so painful that he foregoes it rather than accept the punishment that it provokes from his mate. Typical punishments are little unpleasantnesses rather than grandiose threats. Tears, sulking, and refusal to communicate can be enough, when repeated over and over again, to condition a mate to concede. As Jessie Bernard has pointed out, before long the anticipation of the punishment is enough to make the mate compliant.[5]

OTHER MANIPULATIVE TYPES AND TECHNIQUES

The forms of manipulating people are legion. Everett Shostrom, who believes that nearly all people some of the time, and some people nearly all of the time, manipulate other people with whom they have either business or personal transactions, has compiled a roster of "types of manipulators." His eight types are as follows:

1. The *Dictator* exaggerates his strength. He dominates, orders, quotes authorities, and does anything that will control his victims. Variations of the Dictator are the Mother Superiors, Father Superiors, the Rank Pullers, the Boss, the Junior Gods.
2. The *Weakling* is usually the Dictator's victim, the polar opposite. The Weakling develops great skills in coping with the Dictator. He exaggerates his sensitivity. He forgets, doesn't hear, is passively silent. Variations of the Weakling are the Worrier, the "Stupid-Like-a-Fox," the Giver-Upper, the Confused, the Withdrawer.
3. The *Calculator* exaggerates his control. He deceives, lies, and constantly tries to outwit and control other people. Variations of the Calculator are the High-Pressure Salesman, the Seducer, the Poker Player, the Con Artist, the Blackmailer, the Intellectualizer.
4. The *Clinging Vine* is the polar opposite of the Calculator. He exaggerates his dependency. He is the person who wants to be led, fooled, taken care of. He lets others do his work for him. Variations of the Clinging Vine are the Parasite, the Crier, the Perpetual Child, the Hypochondriac, the American Demander, the Helpless One.
5. The *Bully* exaggerates his aggression, cruelty, and unkindness. He controls by im-

[5]Jessie S. Bernard, "The Adjustment of Married Mates," in Harold T. Christensen, ed., *Handbook of Marriage and the Family*, Skokie, Ill., Rand McNally, 1964, p. 693.

plied threats of some kind. He is the Humiliator, the Hater, the Tough Guy, the Threatener. The female variation is the Bitch or Nagger.

6. The *Nice Guy* exaggerates his caring, love, and kills with kindness. In one sense, he is much harder to cope with than the Bully. You can't fight a Nice Guy! Curiously, in any conflict with the Bully, Nice Guy almost always wins! Variations of the Nice Guy are the Pleaser, the Nonviolent One, the Nonoffender, the Noninvolved One, the Virtuous One, the Never-Ask-for-What-You-Want-One, the Organization Man.

7. The *Judge* exaggerates his criticalness. He distrusts everybody and is blameful, resentful, slow to forgive. Variations of the Judge are the Know-It-All, the Blamer, the Deacon, the Resentment Collector, the Shoulder, the Shamer, the Comparer, the Vindicator, the Convictor.

8. The *Protector* is the opposite of the Judge. He exaggerates his support and is nonjudgmental to a fault. He spoils others, is over-sympathetic, and refuses to allow those he protects to stand up and grow up for themselves. Instead of caring for his own needs, he cares only for others' needs. Variations of the Protector are the Mother Hen, the Defender, the Embarrassed-for-Others, the Fearful-for-Others, the Sufferer-for-Others, the Martyr, the Helper, the Unselfish One.[6]

It is often very difficult for new marriage partners (or any two young people in love) to believe that they would manipulate each other. They may remember that they manipulated their brothers and sisters and fathers and mothers, but the possibility that they would ever manipulate their mate or future mate is almost unthinkable, especially at the beginning.

The change from acceptor to manipulator in marriage does not happen all at once. Most young people idealize and completely accept each other at the time of their marriage. They are filled with joy, the quiver of sex eagerness, and the anticipation of living together. But soon, one or the other begins to recognize that his mate is not without fault. No matter which partner gets the insight first, the other is bound to feel the subtle changes in his partner's attitude toward him. Then a reaction takes place.

Let's say it's the woman who first perceives that her new husband is neither omnipotent nor omniscient. He loses his temper, leaves his dirty socks on the floor, has an aversion to large family gatherings. She does not get hostile or begin to manipulate him at the moment of her realization, but her *attitude* toward him changes, and consequently her way of behaving toward him changes, perhaps unconsciously and perhaps only slightly. But he senses the change and so changes his way of behaving toward her in order to protect his ego. Then she has to change her way, he has to change his, and, in the end, they may wind up in the marriage counselor's office, a hostile and manipulating couple.

[6]Everett L. Shostrom, *Man, The Manipulator*, Nashville, Tenn., Abingdon, 1967, p. 36.

CHANGING THE ADJUSTMENT PATTERNS

Is there no hope, then, that people who have difficulty in adjusting can improve their adjustment? Certainly over a long period people change. The personality of a twenty-year-old is not necessarily the personality that the same individual will have at forty. The problem is in controlling the direction of that change, so that the individual's life becomes more successful and more self-enriching, rather than less so.

It is not easy to change or to help people change constructively. Cuber points out that to suggest that the Conflict-habituated couple "talk it over" is simply to continue an already pointless procedure.[7] Moreover, the common suggestion that the partners spend more time together and involve themselves more deeply with each other can actually worsen the situation for the Passive-Congenial and the Devitalized, who in their own intuitive way have already made the important discovery that the way for them to live with a minimum of inconvenience and frustration is to avoid each other as much as they possibly can while still carrying out their other life needs. Nor, says Cuber, is it necessary to tell the Devitalized to "act their age" or to "be mature"—they already have been pulling this off with remarkable adroitness. Sexual advice that might be appropriate for a Vital couple—who almost never need it anyway—would be almost impossible for the Passive-Congenial to understand, much less carry out. An attempt to do so would likely be seriously disruptive.[8]

USING BEHAVIOR MODIFICATION

In general, there are three ways of improving marriage relationships, and they are inextricably interrelated. One is to get the marriage partners who have been focusing on the negative aspects of their relationship to begin to reemphasize what is positive in their relationship. A wife who has been complaining that her husband is always late for dinner is looking at the negative side of the fact that her husband is working very hard for her and the children. By just switching her own emotional focus, the same behavior becomes a family strength rather than a family problem. As one partner begins to change his responses the other will gradually allow himself to let down his own built-up ego defenses and begin to be more positively appreciative himself. For some people, a step-by-step upward rebuilding of their

[7]John F. Cuber and Peggy B. Harroff, *The Significant Americans*, Englewood Cliffs, N.J., Prentice-Hall, 1965, p. 46.
[8]Ibid., pp. 58, 59.

relationship can make it even better than it was in the beginning. For others, the best that can be said is that it will be better than it is now.

A second way to change behavior is to reinforce what you like about a person's behavior and not to reinforce what you do not like. This is essentially what is known as behavior modification. The basic procedures in modifying anyone's behavior are these:

1. Keep a record over a short time to be sure what a person likes and what a person dislikes.
2. In this record, note what the situation was and what stimulated the person's action.
3. After you are rather sure what reinforces the partner, begin to use these rewards (such as a smile, attention, or a pat) every time the partner does what you want (assuming that what you want is conducive to a workable relationship).
4. When the partner does things you dislike (such as nagging, yelling, sulking, or even talking too much) ignore the behavior. Reinforce only that behavior that is appropriate.
5. This reinforcement will have to be constant for the first few weeks or the behavior will not be changed. Reinforcement most of the time thereafter, but not necessarily constantly, will continue the behavior you want.
6. In your attempt to change your partner's behavior, your own behavior will have changed.

The third thing that can be done to help those with adjustment problems is to help them to improve their communication. Communication is the *only* way to understanding. Although there is some controversy over whether understanding one's mate really improves a marriage relationship, there is every reason to believe that understanding is a necessary first step to acceptance, which *does* improve marriage relationships. In the communication-understanding-acceptance progression, it is necessary to start by improving the ability of the partners to communicate with each other.

13

COMMUNICATION AND INTIMACY

Great effort in caring for and getting someone to care in return is expended in courtship. The eagerness to reveal intimate feelings and thoughts to each other, using care not to hurt the other, makes it easier, however.

People respond in a more positive and caring way when they feel good about themselves. The more self-concept-building comments you make to another person, the more likely that person is to be willing and able to respond positively. Obviously, years of childhood experiences that constantly lowered someone's self-concept cannot be completely overcome in a relationship with one person—even if it is you. But skilled communication will be your best method of letting someone know that you care and want to be cared for in return.

It has been our continuing observation that communication tends to fail because of a *lack of ability*, a *lack of desire*, a *lack of security*, a *lack of selectivity*—or sometimes because of two or more of these. Since adequate communication is so important to a relationship, it is appropriate to look at each of these factors individually.

THE ABILITY TO COMMUNICATE

There *may* have been some mates whose communication was less than perfect because they literally did not know the meaning of some of the words their partners used. However, denotive meanings of words cause very little —if any—communication trouble in marriage. Most people in our society are regularly exposed to the mass deprovincialization of modern television. If words are the problem, it is their *connotative* values rather than their denotative meanings that cause the difficulty. Connotation implies emotion and conditioned reaction. If, for example, the word "yellow" is mentioned in a mixed audience, almost all the women in the group will get a pleasant feeling. They will remember a party dress or a waving field of daffodils or something else that has delightful meaning for them. But what about the men? Most of the men in the group will probably get an unpleasant sensation and an association (either conscious or unconscious) with some earlier challenge to their masculinity. After hearing the same word, one person will be pleased and the other upset.

These connotation difficulties in communication are greatly magnified in such areas as sex and death, where most of the words are circumscribed by taboos. Some people have queasy feelings inside whenever *any* sex words are mentioned. Others react only to the words and symbols that they were taught were "bad." Many parents are unable to talk to their children about sex because their hands shake so badly at the mere mention of some of the words that all that they are able to communicate is nervous confusion, rather than factual information and helpful attitudes.

Failure to communicate because of different word connotations is not uncommon. But communication more often fails because of one's inability to communicate genuine attitudes and meanings—with or without words. In fact, words are sometimes unimportant. It is possible to say "I hate you" so lovingly that the person addressed recognizes almost at once that this is not an expression of hostility but rather one of tenderness. On the other hand, as many longtime husbands and wives know, it is possible to say "I love you" in such a flat monotone that it expresses nothing.

There are many other illustrations of the sometime superfluity of words. Young lovers make up their own words of endearment, especially in such emotionally sensitive areas as sex, where childhood inhibitions form barriers against using the scientifically correct terms. When this private language better permits the individuals to express their real feelings, it is an important aid to communication.

Some of the best communication takes place without the use of words at all. A gentle touch can be more meaningful than a thousand words. A look or a movement can communicate an indescribable feeling. Important ideas can be made explicit by a gesture. Emotions can be set on fire by a single glance.

But in all communication, whether by word, touch, gesture, or glance, there is a need not only for the communicator to project meaning and feeling; there is also a need for the receptor to perceive and accept that meaning and those feelings. Good communication depends upon the ability of the receptor to understand the *intent* of the communicator. It requires the skill to sense feelings by inference and to hear meanings rather than just words. Theodor Reik has called this "listening with the third ear."[1]

An example of the need for this kind of feeling-inference is when the hostess, carrying a cake, comes in to her assembled guests and loudly exclaims, "This is the worst cake I ever baked!" Obviously, she does not want anyone to agree with her. She is deliberately using words directly contradictory to her meaning. Similarly, in many of the most significant relationships of marriage, people will say things they do not mean. "I guess we had better not make love tonight; it might disturb the children," may be a deliberate effort on the part of the wife to be assured by her husband that he *will* make love to her and it will *not* disturb the children.

[1]Theodor Reik, *Listening With the Third Ear*, New York, Farrar, Straus & Giroux, 1954, p. 144.

Sensing what people mean from what they say can often be a very difficult task. Consider the following illustration:

"I see now what I should have seen last night," Myra told the counselor. "But it's too late. It's just three weeks ago since Tod was told by the doctor that he had Hodgkins disease and probably has less than a year to live. Last night he sat up crying in the bed. I was still half asleep when I asked him what was wrong. 'Oh, my darling,' he said, 'I'm so worried about what will happen to you and the children after I'm gone!' I just didn't think, I guess, because I said to him too quickly, 'Oh, we'll be all right, darling. I can take care of the children!' It didn't seem to help him a bit. Now that I have thought it over, I know why."

Sometimes people will go to extreme lengths to avoid saying what they really mean. In psychology, the concept of "reaction-formation" is used to describe a situation in which a person subconsciously, but elaborately, denies his own true feelings and openly disavows that which he really wants. For example, a young woman who has a deep desire for sexual activity might be a vociferous prude who crusades against sex in any form.

Other illustrations of disguised meanings are legion. Feelings of severe insecurity are commonly masked behind dogmatic assertions. Feelings of hostility sometimes appear as thoughtfulness and consideration. For example, a wife might say to her child, "Don't bother your father. He is too busy to play with you." To know whether this was a considerate wife or a deliberately hostile woman bent on downgrading the father in the child's eyes, one would have to know much more about the relationships involved.

There are times when communication can be expedited by ignoring the words that the communicator uses. The wife who says, "You always think you're perfect, don't you!" does not really want to talk about her husband's perfection. Rather, she may wish to let him know that he is not really as good as he thinks he is, or she may want him to deny that he is perfect in order that she may win her point. In either event, the argument has nothing to do with whether he really is or is not perfect. The experienced husband will see this and not be trapped into a defensive rebuttal.

Another important aspect of the ability to communicate is sensitivity, the ability to anticipate reaction. This involves an emphathetic ability to prejudge how the feeling that the communicator wishes to express will affect the receptor. Consider the following illustration:

Sally and Tom were a young couple struggling to complete their educations after marriage. They lived in a small apartment in a nice neighborhood largely populated by older, more established couples, all of whom had washing machines, which Sally and Tom couldn't afford. One day, Sally, an eager-to-please young bride who was intent upon showing that she could keep her husband's clothes clean just like any other wife in the community, washed clothes by hand all day long. When Tom came home that night she said to him, "Oh, darling, I'm so tired. I spent all day washing!" She was shocked and startled when Tom shouted, "Well, damn it, I'll buy you a washing machine in the morning." Sally dissolved in tears. "I can't understand what he got so upset about," she said later.

Awareness of intentions and patterns of communication

Recently many techniques for analyzing communication have emerged. These have been taught in workshops for couples and in formal relationships classes. One such program is the Minnesota Couples Communication Program.[2] The significant aim of this program is for both persons to become more aware of what is being said, the intention behind the words, the emotions accompanying the words, the actual meaning of the message, and the personal responsibility for the thrust of the message. To study this more easily, four patterns of communication were noted. We will discuss these patterns later in this section.

It can be very difficult to know others' intentions from their spoken message. This program teaches how to clarify messages in order to convey the intended meaning. To clarify your own message, you can say it in other words, you can spell out your intent, and you can describe the emotions that are involved. For example, when a man asks a woman, "Where were you when I called around six o'clock?" he may need to give some accompanying clarification such as, "I needed to ask whether you would like to go to the game, and had to make reservations right then." Otherwise the message may come across as, "Why weren't you there at six o'clock? You should have informed me if you were going to be late! I have a right to know where you are! You put me on the spot!" An unmarried couple may break up if unclarified messages continue. A married couple may stay together, but may become openly hostile as they cover the resentments. Unintended messages are by far worse culprits than clear messages, even if the intention of a clear message is that you do not like something about the other person. Intended nonaccusative messages are the best for good relationships.

Another aspect of the Minnesota Couples Communication Program

[2]Sherod Miller, Elam W. Nunnally, Daniel B. Wackman with Ronald Brazman, *The Minnesota Couples Communication Program, Couples Handbook,* Minneapolis, Minn., The Minnesota Couples Communication Program, 1972.

is that of making people aware of the communication patterns they tend to use. The four patterns that have emerged are these: (1) small talk, (2) accusative or manipulative communication, (3) factual and documented communication, and (4) communication of personal feelings. All four patterns have their uses, according to the situation and topic. A problem arises when a pattern and situation are not compatible. For example, when a man first meets a woman, it is highly inappropriate for either of them to move into an accusative or persuasive pattern, whether they want the relationship to continue or not. When a wife wants to let her husband know some misgivings about a decision, his choice of small talk would be ineffective in clarifying the situation and helping her work it through. Accusative responses would be devastating, while factual, computer-type suggestions may be the most logical. But logic is far from what is needed when she intends to say, "Listen to me as I spill it all out; comfort me in my distress; yet help me live through it and plan for the future."

Sometimes a wife sends a mixed message. Usually it is unintentional and it may be unconscious, but there are times that it is subtle and intentional. A joke about her husband's clothes, said as part of small talk, may be purely small talk, but if it is an attack covered by small talk, then there is a mixed message, which leaves the husband with discomfort. It is also possible for the husband to misinterpret his wife's comment as a mixed message or slur when there was no such intent, however. He has the responsibility of repeating the message received in order to clarify it. Clarifying unintended messages is one way to keep hidden resentments from festering. Even clarifying intended messages brings them out into the open, where they can be handled.

Obviously sensitivity to intentions, misperceived intentions, how a person is feeling at a given moment, and understanding why another said what he did and thus choosing not to retaliate or even to clarify it at that moment are all a part of the empathetic approach.

To communicate, both parties need to arrive at what is called *shared meaning*. You can do this by asking what the other person meant or by expressing what you think was meant and asking whether or not there was a shared meaning. Connotations and intentions are both clarified this way. An error in word denotation is also cleared up by this method.

THE DESIRE TO COMMUNICATE

It is almost axiomatic that, in order for there to be good communication between two people, those two people must want to communicate. As we pointed out in the last section, this involves something more than just wanting to talk. Genuine communication involves not only the desire to project feelings but the desire to understand and accept feelings as well.

Not everyone has an equal desire to talk, let alone to listen. Mirra Komarovsky found in her study of working-class marriages that dialogue is frequently cut short by disinterest or grudging response. She said:

If it is one of the functions of modern marriage to share one's hurts, worries and dreams with another person—a large number of couples fail to find such fulfillments. Moreover, breaks in the marriage dialogue are not a matter of preference. They result from abortive attempts at communication; attempts frustrated by what is felt to be the mate's lack of interest or an unsatisfactory response.[3]

Some people seem to be "naturally" quiet. Actually, though, the inclination to talk or to be silent is probably conditioned into the individual as the result of both his cultural and subcultural experiences. Men are said to be less talkative than women. Girls tend to talk more and to start talking earlier than boys.[4] (There are, of course, individual differences.) Many boys soon learn that they come out second best in a verbal contest with a girl.

Not only do girls talk more than boys, they also talk about different things. Girls are encouraged to talk about people and relationships between people—including their own—and boys are encouraged to talk about mechanical and spatial things. This differential conditioning causes several problems in later life. For one, girls expect their companions—and later their husbands—to be interested in talking about social relationships to the same degree they are. Men often are not interested. Moreover, the differential conditioning often creates a situation in which the two sexes have little in common to talk about. It is said that when women are together, they talk about things that interest women; when men are together they talk about things that interest men; but when men and women are together, they talk about things that do not interest either one of them.

Modern urban adult men and women often work in different worlds, so they have very little knowledge of the people and procedures in the world in which their mates live. Few spouses have a conversational understanding of their mate's business difficulties.

There is another problem created by the differing roles of men and women after marriage that tends to dampen the desire for communication.

[3]Mirra Komarovsky, *Blue Collar Marriage*, New York, Random House, 1964, p. 140.
[4]Anne Anastasi, *Differential Psychology*, 3rd ed., New York, Macmillan, 1958, pp. 472–473.

Men more often talk to other adults during their working hours. As a matter of fact, sometimes the men talk all day long for their living. By the very nature of things, they want to be quiet when they get home. On the other hand, those wives who have been shut up in the house by themselves or with small children all day are eager for talk and socializing in the evening.

CASE 37 CAROLYN AND LESTER

"He never talks to me," Carolyn told the counselor. "I spend all day long doing routine things around the house and just waiting for him to come home so I will have someone to talk to. But all he wants to do is sit in that darn old easy chair of his and bury his nose in the paper. When he finishes the paper, he watches television, and then he goes to bed. Big deal! It isn't as if I didn't try to make conversation. I tell him about all the little things that happen around the house. I even try to read the newspapers and magazines so that I can keep up with him. I try to ask him about his work, but he just sighs and says nothing ever happens at his office. Sometimes I get so bored with him that I even try to start a fight for some excitement, but that's even worse. He won't fight at all. He just withdraws. Even when we have some real problem, he won't talk about it. He just sits there like a lump and lets me say anything I want to. Then he gets up and goes to bed. It's maddening! Believe me, it wasn't like that before we were married. He used to talk a lot about interesting things. But now he doesn't care anymore. I guess he has just stopped loving me."

Lester was indeed a quiet man. He even had very little to say to the counselor. At length he did say, "Yes, I guess I don't talk enough. People around my childhood home were very quiet when I was growing up. But it isn't altogether that. Sometimes when I come home she greets me at the door and says, 'What did you do all day?' I would like to tell her. But in the instant before I get it out, I think to myself, 'How am I going to tell her?' Take today, for example. Brown, the plant manager, had an argument in my office with Jones, the production manager, over the placement of the semiconductors in the flyback circuit. Actually, Brown was mad at Jones because Jones overestimated the production figures and made Brown look bad with the big boys back in the home office. That was really what the fight was about—not the design. Anyway, before we were through, we had Green, the foreman, and Kelly, the straw boss in the office, in on it, and it turned out that Kelly's daughter had beat out Jones's daughter in some beauty contest. You can imagine what that did to the discussion. Anyway, that was just the beginning of what happened at the plant today.

"My wife doesn't know anything about any of these things. She doesn't even know what a semiconductor is. When I thought of all the explanation it would take to even make any reasonable sense out of what happened at the office today, I just said, 'Oh nothing, it was just sort of a routine day,' and let it go at that.

"Then she was mad. Heck, I work hard all day. I think I'm entitled to come home and sit down and have a chance to read the paper in peace. If she wants to talk, she can have the neighborhood ladies in for coffee in the morning. I just want to be let alone to make the money for this family so that I'll have something to leave her and the kids. She apparently doesn't understand that. She's always nagging me to talk, talk, talk.

"Sure, I may have talked more before we were married. I did my best to entertain her when we were courting. She did her best to catch me, too. She used to make me cherry tarts and bring them over to the dormitory when I was in college. She hasn't made a cherry tart in ten years. I don't yell about that. I know that she has enough to do being a good mother. But I want her to get off my back, too."

Knowing something about the differential conditioning of people is extremely helpful in understanding why some people do not have the desire to talk or even to have shared meaning. Just knowing some techniques of communication does not take the place of knowing why a person will or will not talk.

Among those couples who do talk to each other, how much do they talk and about what? Feldman, in his study of 862 couples from all age groups, found that the average amount of time spent in conversation was about one-and-a-half hours a day. Their most frequently discussed topics were their work and current events (about once a day) and children and friends (several times a week). Sports, religion, and sex were talked about several times a month.[5] Curiously, most husbands claimed that these conversations were about topics such as homemaking and religion that were of more interest to their wives than to themselves, and most wives thought that more time was spent in talking about topics that interested the husbands, such as news and sports. Feldman found that the wife more often initiated conversations about most of the topics, including her work, the children's problems and accomplishments, her parents, and her personal feelings, whereas the huband's fewer initiations were primarily about his

[5]Harold Feldman and Boyd C. Rollins, "Marital Satisfaction over the Family Life Cycle," in Marcia E. Lasswell and Thomas E. Lasswell, eds., *Love, Marriage, Family: A Developmental Approach*, Glenview, Ill., Scott, Foresman, 1973, pp. 381–383.

work, money management, and his parents. Interestingly, Feldman added that the husband's parents are not his exclusive domain as much as the wife's parents are hers.

It is a fairly common observation that, as marriages continue over the years, some partners appear to talk less and less to each other. Komarovsky verified this in her study.[6]

Statistical proof that marital telepathy (each spouse knowing what the other one will say before he or she completes a sentence) is universal or even common does not exist. One sociologist has cited two studies involving a total of 340 couples (out of approximately 45,000,000 couples in the United States) as reason enough for labeling as "myth" folk beliefs in marital telepathy and the notion that husbands and wives become more alike by living together. These studies, he says, have failed to demonstrate that couples either understand one another better the longer they are married, or anticipate one another's responses, or communicate profound meanings to one another via glances, shrugs, and grunts. Such ideas as marital telepathy are, he suggests, "a part of the myth that marriages get better and better, that couples come to love one another 'more deeply' and that they 'mean more to one another' over the years."[7]

It is probably good that there are those with scientific skepticism to keep some of the older folklore in proper balance. It should be pointed out, however, that, although there is no proof that marital telepathy is a tendency in *all* marriages, it most certainly does exist in some. Again, this appears to be a case of "some do, some don't," which does not commend itself to the social theorist.

SECURITY IN COMMUNICATION

Security may well be the most important aspect of communication. One who is made anxious for any reason will not—and probably cannot—communicate as he should. Feelings and daydreams are fragile things. Once ridiculed or punished for them, their owner may never again reveal them. This is not to say that he will stop having feelings or daydreams; he will merely stop talking about them.

The tragedy about this is that spoiling communication by ridiculing or threatening often represents some basic insecurity on the part of the spoiler. It is almost axiomatic that a person who is disturbed because of

---

[6]Komarovsky, op. cit., p. 145.
[7]J. Richard Udry, *The Social Context of Marriage*, Philadelphia, Lippincott, 1966, pp. 274–275.

what someone else has said is disturbed because he feels threatened. For example, a young husband might come home and tell his wife his idea for an invention. Because his wife's father was constantly spending the family savings on one harebrained scheme after another, the wife immediately jumps to the conclusion that her husband is about to raid their savings account. Before he is half through with his excited description of his idea, she is already planning how she can best talk him out of it. Often there is a very simple way: to laugh at him. So she laughs. Her ridicule has no relation to the merits of the idea. It is, rather, her reaction to a threat that, ironically, might never have come to fruition. She achieves her objective, for he never mentions his idea (or perhaps any other) again, but she loses something infinitely greater: his willingness and ability to talk with her about things that are important to him. Consider the following case.

CASE 38 GLADYS AND HAROLD

"All he ever talks about is the women at his office," Gladys told the counselor. "He pays more attention to them than he does to me. A little secretary can have some trouble with her boyfriend and he listens for hours and then wants to come home and tell me all about it. He never listens to me; he just buries his nose in the television. Other husbands talk to their wives about their work and about politics and business, but not Harold."

"I try to talk to her," Harold said. "At least I used to. But she's so sensitive that everything I say she takes personally. It's especially bad since she got older and put on a little weight. Now every time I mention something that concerns any other woman, she has a fit. I work in an insurance office, and we employ a lot of young women. Most of the things that happen to me during the day have something to do with the problems that the girls get into. I've found that it's easier to keep quiet at home and let her yell about my not talking than to talk to her and have a dramatic scene about the affairs she imagines I'm having with the office girls."

It is probable that fear—fear of many kinds—is the greatest inhibitor of communication. Some fears keep people from talking with their partners. Other fears cause them to reject that which their partners say to them. The fear of offending or of being offended is especially limiting for people who are new in a situation and who gingerly (perhaps too gingerly) control their self-expression. The result is often to make the other person believe that he is unwanted or distrusted. He, in turn, "clams up," and the relationship becomes stilted and mutually insecure.

Another fear that inhibits communication is the fear of starting an argument. Many people will not express their genuine feelings lest they provoke their partner. Then there is the fear that talking will give the other person license to talk also. Many husbands have said quite candidly that they would rather not tell their wives their troubles because that would give their wives the right to talk on indefinitely about *their* troubles. Some people do not communicate for fear of getting an unfavorable reply. They have learned that it is better to assume they are right than to be told they are wrong. And there are still others who have a fear of saying something wrong or improper.

The greatest fear of all is probably the fear that a genuine expression of personal feeling will lose one's partner's love. Many children are conditioned early to remain silent by parents who punish them for expressing unconventional thoughts. A child, perhaps in all innocence, will come home and tell his mother something he has seen or done. The horrified mother may then punish the child either by physical means or by a withdrawal of her approval. The mother's reaction will not curtail or even forestall the child from seeing or doing such things again. It merely means that he will no longer communicate his experiences to his mother.

This provides a serious dilemma both for parents and for marriage mates. Can a parent or a marriage partner permit the errant child or spouse to tell what he has done and then let him "get away with it," simply because he told the truth or expressed an honest feeling? No one has ever found the ideal solution to this problem, but there are many who feel that permitting the expression of genuine feelings is more important in the long run to personality growth, to relationship improvement, and to learning than any hoped-for behavior change that punishment or withdrawal of approval might bring about.

Security in communication has two aspects. The first is, as we have seen, the responsibility of the listener to provide the permissive acceptance that will encourage the speaker to express openly, and with as little fear as possible, his genuine thoughts and beliefs. But there is another aspect of security in communication. It is up to the listener to provide the secure climate in which the speaker can speak, but it is up to the speaker to provide security for the listener as well. A speaker has no license to alarm or ridicule or create anxiety in the listener under the pretext of permissive communication, freedom of expression, or ventilating.

The problem of honesty of expression versus sensitivity to the feelings of the other is very important.[8]

The four patterns of communication described earlier in the chapter —small talk, accusative-persuasive, factual and documented, and personal feelings—are relevant to this discussion of security in communication.[9] The patterns of small talk and factual-documented conversation are called low-risk patterns because the person neither lets himself open for attack nor attacks the other. The patterns of accusative-persuasive communication and expression of personal feelings are called high risk.[10] Why? The accusative-persuasive pattern may strike a retaliatory response from the other one. The personal-feeling pattern makes one vulnerable because he has bared himself.

Both high-risk patterns are useful in communication but they both rest on whether or not one needs security. If either partner is in great need of security these two patterns are of too high-risk; however, if one is secure while the other is in need of expressing personal feelings, the secure one can listen intently without getting upset at what he hears.

Being able to time high-risk communication so that at least one partner is secure helps communication. This leads us to the last point— selectivity.

SELECTIVITY IN COMMUNICATION

Good selectivity in communication involves selecting the right time, the right place, the right things to be talked about, and the right way of talking about them.

Almost every child who has grown up in a family learns that it is better not to approach fathers for favors until after they have had their dinners. Yet, it is amazing how often husbands and wives ignore this simple rule. Some wives (and some husbands of working wives) greet their tired mates as they arrive home with a recital of the day's problems and a long roster of complaints. "The furnace broke down, the television quit, your broker phoned to say he needed more margin to cover your stock losses, I told Junior you would punish him as soon as you got home, and my mother is coming to spend a month with us" is a classic greeting hardly calculated to get an evening's communication off to a glowing start. Some

[8]Murray A. Straus, "Leveling, Civility, and Violence in the Family," *Journal of Marriage and the Family*, **36** (February, 1974), 13–29.

[9]Miller et al., op. cit., pp. 79–81.

[10]Ibid., pp. 98–100.

spouses appear so eager to announce this kind of bad news that it is hard to escape the conclusion that they may be obtaining a sort of sadistic satisfaction from the relationship damage they are causing.

The person who wants to develop adequate communication must choose the time wisely. He must also carefully pick the place. A crowded bus is no place for a discussion of sexual incompatibility problems.

But there are other aspects of selectivity, too. Choosing what to talk about and how to talk about it are also vital to good communication.

Most people would be inclined to say that two people—especially husband and wife—should be able to talk about anything that suits the fancy of either one of them. In practice, though, it really cannot work out that way. There are role responsibilities to be considered. A husband cannot talk constantly about his anxieties if he is to be the leader that his wife and family expect him to be, since the leader must be able to project calm, secure guidance. A wife and mother cannot announce that she does not like one of her children or that she likes one more than another every time such an idea enters her mind if she is to be the loving wife and mother her family expects and needs.

As a matter of common decency, husbands and wives must occasionally forego talking about something that would be aggravating to their mates. There is no point in a wife mentioning how much her former boyfriend knew about automobiles when her husband is sweating over a stalled car. Nor is there any point in a husband going on about his mother's baked beans just when his wife is about to serve her latest effort to their guests. Avoiding sensitive areas can hardly be called repression in any "bad" psychological sense. It is more properly defined as good judgment.

J. Richard Udry wonders if a lack of communication leads to disturbed marriages or vice versa. He believes that *selective* communication is a key to the successful marriage.[11] In selecting a pattern of communication, it is very important to know how the other person is feeling. Before you use the pattern in which you reveal a lot about your personal feeling, you must find out if the other person is in the mood to hear it. Just saying to the other that you have something to talk about later may help the two of you to select an appropriate time. One problem is that this may create anxiety in the other when he wonders what it is you want to talk about. To avoid this, it is good to offer a clue about what you have in mind, such as "I need to talk to you about our schedule for next week. Can you give me some time after dinner?"

[11]Richard Udry, *The Social Context of Marriage*, 2nd ed., Philadelphia, Lippincott, 1971, pp. 218–220.

Appropriate selection of a pattern of communication also refers to selecting one that will be the best for preserving the relationship. It can mean changing to a low-risk pattern when the sparks begin to fly. This takes a strong person, however. The person going full blast with an accusative-manipulative pattern can too easily pull you into the same pattern, even if you want to stay logical and supportive.

No communication stays in one pattern all the time. In one conversation, a couple may move into all four from time to time: moving out of personal feelings when the conversation gets too heavy; moving out of small talk when it gets too trite; or moving out of manipulative expression when it gets too risky. They may change by moving into a discussion of personal feelings when the security of the situation permits; or by moving into manipulative communication when one wants to change the other's opinion and moving out again when the other misperceives him.

Selectivity incorporates a great deal of knowledge. Many people who are experts at selectivity may not be able to express theories of human behavior and communication, but they may know a lot about the need to feel like "somebody."

COMMUNICATION AND SELF-CONCEPT

Since the adequacy of self-concept affects behavior and ultimately the relationship, you need to know how to send messages that imply both that you are worthy and that you think the other person is also worthy. In the Minnesota Couples Communication Program, the descriptive words for worthwhileness are "I count, you count." Messages that express "I count, you don't count," "I don't count, you don't count," and "I don't count, you count" are highly inappropriate for making anyone feel worthy.[12]

A woman who says, "I can't go with you tonight, but I can go another time this week" is surely sending an "I count, you count" message. A woman who says, "You shouldn't have given me this gift; you don't have that kind of money," could be sending an "I don't count, you don't count" message, or it could be an "I don't count, you count" message, if she thinks he should keep the money for himself. A more positive "I count, you count" message in this same situation would be "This is beautiful. Your taste is excellent. You are magnificent to make this selection for me."

Messages are not always easily decoded. Problems occur when the message understood is one that hurts the other and consequently the relationship. Consider the messages in this case.

[12]Miller et al., op. cit., pp. 136–141.

CASE 39 MELINDA AND CHARLES

"When Melinda and I were in college we only saw each other on the weekends," Charles informed the counselor. "There was always something different to tell each other. I never thought we'd have any difficulty. Boy, was I wrong! I come home from work in the evenings anxious to see her and before I get in the door I get a cold shoulder and am in the doghouse the rest of the night. I know I'm late for supper a few nights during the week, but I can't help it. You see, this is my really busy period with the firm. Being a CPA isn't easy work. When a client wants to discuss his account with you, you can't just quit because it's five o'clock, especially when it's a $100,000 account. Sometimes when I see I'm going to be late, I'll call Melinda, but she's already upset because her supper is ruined. But what else can I do? I don't know why it worries her so much. I'm the one who has to eat cold food!

"I try to plan different things for us to do on the weekends so we can be together and enjoy each other. There is a couple at the office our age and we usually get together on Friday afternoons and make plans for Saturday to play tennis, golf, and so forth. When I tell Melinda that night she makes up some excuse for not going. This really makes me mad, because she never has a valid reason. It's usually, 'I'd rather not,' or 'I just don't feel like it this time.' Why? I'll never know.

"Melinda claims we never talk anymore, but every night I ask her how her day was and she tells me about it. I always listen to her, even while I'm reading the paper or watching television, but after all there's only so much a guy can say. I'm always willing to tell her about the happenings at the office but she doesn't seem to care so I don't mention it much. I know she has a lot of work to do with decorating the new house we moved into, but that is part of her responsibility and she always seems to have a problem with it. I told her we'd move back to a smaller house if she wanted but she loves this house and wants to make it beautiful. I told her she could do whatever she wanted, but she always asks me about every little thing, including what color to paint the kitchen! It doesn't make any difference to me but it is always on her mind. She is still babbling when we're ready to go to bed. I don't know how she can say we never communicate, she talks constantly.

"I love Melinda but she can't seem to understand that I'm trying to provide her with everything possible to make her as happy as I can. What's wrong?"

Melinda never denied once to the counselor that Charles had been a good provider, but she was not completely happy. "Sure, he calls me when he's going to be late, but only after he's already an hour late. I've asked him to call by five o'clock so I won't even begin to prepare supper. But no, he can't do that. It's not that I mind Charles not being there on time either, it's just that I take a great deal of pride in my cooking and what good does it do to slave in the kitchen and then have a two-hour-old flop staring your husband in the face. I'd be satisfied if he would call me when he was ready to leave the office, at least he'd get a decent meal and we could sit down together for once. It's such a rushed meal when he comes home late! We never seem to have time to talk anymore.

"If I knew what Charles was planning, things would be so much easier. Sure, he has good intentions for us, but he never considers my feelings. Tommy and Sandy, the couple at the office, they're nice and could be a lot of fun. But when those three get together all they talk about is balance sheets and income statements! What am I supposed to do? I try to mention a few things that I am interested in but the conversation always reverts back to the same old topic. I never learned to play tennis or things like that either. Charles assumes I'll learn by practicing with them. I wish he'd take time to teach me alone, but he only gets frustrated. I can't tell him I don't like being with his friends, because he would only get angry.

"Charles is just like everyone else in his family. They never talk. They've never tried to understand my feelings either, but I'm too scared to tell them what I really think because they would only criticize me, so I keep my mouth shut when I go over to their house."

A person creates security by providing a lot of messages that tell the other person he is worthy. When your message also says that you are secure, the probability of the person's feeling worthy is even greater. A message saying "I count, you count" is of this type. Such things as "I finished that job on time and it turned out just like I thought it would. I really appreciate your moving dinnertime back a little every day this week. It was a lifesaver" make both partners come out feeling good.

The same topic handled in an "I don't count, you do count" fashion will give the other person a mixed feeling about what is meant by such a message as "I finally finished that job. I hope it's all right. I put in enough work, but it was more than I could do. I'm worried about whether I did it right. It looked all right. You helped, though, by setting the dinner hour a little later all week." The listener does not know whether his partner needs some boosting or whether he is going to worry about the results so much that the rest of the night is shot.

"HOW" IS AS IMPORTANT AS "WHAT"

The matter of what one talks about is inextricably intertwined with how one talks about it. Earlier it was pointed out that a person can talk about almost anything he wishes and still keep the other person interested, provided he is enthusiastic and confident. His own enthusiasm and confidence will ordinarily be contagious to the point where the other person will not only become interested but will also feel secure in talking about it himself.

The qualification *enthusiastic* is important, for it implies a pleasantness of tone and manner. There are a great many people who talk about things that interest them (their physical ailments, for instance) but who talk about them in a complaining manner. This can be deadly and depressing both inside and outside of marriage. It is a number one communication destroyer.

Many women in marriage counseling complain because their husbands will not talk about feelings. And yet many husbands point out that they are tired of talking about feelings because this, in one way or another, only gets them into trouble. Either their wives reject their feelings as being inadequate, or else they accept them and use them against the husbands later. ("Five years ago *you* were the one who thought my sister was so great.") Moreover, most men are conditioned by the business and social world in which they move to repress their feelings, not expose them. It is interesting to note, however, that despite these handicaps, there was a tendency of the husbands in Feldman's study to feel that they, *not* their wives, more often initiated conversations about personal feelings.[13]

In summary, it might be said that the essence of good selectivity and therefore good communication is a mutually satisfying way of expressing positive, love-enriching feelings. For some men—and some women—the richness of marriage comes from the quiet calm of the home that their mate provides for them. For these people, talking is not an essential ingredient of happiness. But for others, the pleasure of the marriage relationship comes from the partner's ability to transmit verbally the kind of ego reassurance that makes life worthwhile. This is the need-meeting that creates and nurtures love. In this, as in every other aspect of married life,

[13]Feldman, op. cit., p. 108.

the successful couples are those who can move toward each other until their needs for both communication and quiet reflection can synchronize.

It should be pointed out again that communication can lead to understanding and understanding to acceptance and acceptance to adjustment in marriage. It may not necessarily follow that those who communicate at any level and in any way have the best marriages. But certainly those who will not or cannot communicate at all have little opportunity to either improve or even maintain their relationships.

There is considerable evidence that, in our culture, most couples actually increase their communication and so their understanding by talking with one another. Feldman reports that the more time couples spend in talking with each other, the more likely they are to report a high level of marital satisfaction. He adds that couples who spend more time in talking with each other receive reinforcement for even further conversations, for they feel closer to each other after the discussions.[14]

Those who would have good communication need to improve both their desire and ability to listen, to listen carefully and objectively, and to listen to their partner's meaning as well as to his words. In much of what ordinarily would pass for communication, one partner or the other is so busy rehearsing what he is going to say next, or so preoccupied with other problems, that he really cannot listen to what his mate says—either in words or meaning.

Another thing that is needed for good communication is improved selectivity. It is important not only to choose carefully what one says but also to select carefully from the other person's verbalizations as well. In both of these ways, one can provide security: first, by not threatening the other person, and second, by understanding that usually not everything he says is intended just as it was said. Nor does it necessarily reflect his feelings for all time. No one has ever said this better than Dinah Maria Mulock Craik, an English novelist of the nineteenth century:

Oh, the comfort, the inexpressible comfort of feeling safe with a person, having neither to weigh thoughts nor measure words, but pouring them all right out, just as they are, chaff and grain together; certain that a faithful hand will take and sift them, keep what is worth keeping, and then with the breath of kindness, blow the rest away.

[14]Ibid., p. 29.

14

MALE AND FEMALE
SEXUAL CONDITIONING

Many troubled married couples are convinced that sex is the one and only problem they have in marriage, while many dating couples view sex as the area of no problems. Often, though, while married people blame their sexual relationship for their difficulties, other problems have contributed.

Dating couples may be giving more credit to sex than it warrants. The fact that they are not together all the time, that they are inordinately considerate, and that money and children are not yet a part of the relationship may make the sexual relationship better. A good sexual relationship usually, although not alawys, requires a fairly good total relationship.

But there are some marriages in which sex is *the* cause of a marriage difficulty. Some partners have difficulty in synchronizing their sexual desires—or lack of them—with those of their partners. Sometimes it takes weeks, months, or even years to achieve sexual harmony. Some people never do. Some people start out well and then, as hostilities and resentments set in, lose their sexual empathy completely. Some people develop a better sexual relationship after ten or even twenty years.

In sex, as in most other areas of male-female relationships today, things have changed. Formerly, when the marriage partners said they had a sexual problem, it was fairly predictable that the problem was the seemingly great sexual appetite of the husband. Now, however, some women are disappointed that their husbands do not desire them as often as our current emphasis on sexual intercourse has led them to expect. Moreover, although some men are—as in all ages past—disturbed because their wives are not interested in meeting their sexual needs, there are many other men today who blame themselves because their wives do not achieve an orgasm during every intercourse experience, as some sexual authorities have led them to believe all women should. To understand sexual problems in modern marriage, it is necessary to go a long way back.

THE ROOTS OF THE PROBLEM

Unbelievable though it may seem today, throughout history there have been both religious and civil laws regulating sexual intercourse between married partners. Various authorities, from Zoroaster (about 600 B.C.) to our colonial forefathers, sought to establish either the frequency or the appropriate times for sexual relations even in marriage. In those periods when there were no religious taboos or strict laws, there were often inviolable customs that made one kind or frequency of sexual intercourse right and all others wrong.

Contemporary Americans would undoubtedly view the enforced regulation of sexual activity as intolerably restrictive (after marriage, at least). Yet many of these same Americans are confused about what are the appropriate expectations for postmarital sexual behavior. Although the laws and customs of the bygone eras robbed the individual of some freedom of choice, at least they provided him with some basis for knowing what the standard expectations of sexual responsibility in marriage should be.

Today, people with widely differing religious, national, educational, social, and cultural backgrounds are marrying each other, and their expectations and attitudes about what is "right" in sex behavior often differ considerably. Many partners cannot help but have their sexual expectations frustrated and their sexual sensibilities disturbed. In this confusion over expectations, many young husbands and wives have rushed off to the bookstore for so-called sex manuals. Unhappily, not everyone finds real help in these guidebooks. Sex manuals usually place a heavy emphasis on the techniques of lovemaking. Moreover, the manuals are often contradictory, because they present the expectations and the attitudes of the author, and these have resulted from *their* background and *their* conditioning. Some of the recipes for lovemaking in the sex manuals are so "far out" as to be emotionally unacceptable to conservative people, and some are so old-fashioned as to be laughable. Anyway, sexual techniques are usually better discovered than learned from a book. The spontaneity and pleasure of mutual discovery is a part of the richness of lovemaking.

A sexual relationship is an intimately personal thing. Success or failure often depends upon the complex feelings of warmth that are uniquely created deep within each individual and then lovingly interchanged with his partner. Diagrams and statistics may bolster the argument of the more aggressive partner, but they rarely add richness to the sexual feelings between two people.

In the final analysis, an understanding acceptance of the other person's expectations and attitudes (and sometimes his confusions, too), combined with an ability to communicate more meaningfully about sex, are the primary factors in good sexual adjustment. To achieve such an adjustment, you must start by understanding why your partner behaves the way he does.

WHY DOES A MATE BEHAVE THAT WAY?

Sexual behavior results from sexual expectations and sexual attitudes, which in turn arise from an individual's physical capacities, his childhood environment, his later experiences, and the subtle dynamics of the relationship he has with his sex partner. In any particular person, any one of these factors may be more important than in others.

Just how much effect the basic physical functioning of the body has on an adult's sex interest and sexual capacity is still open to serious question. With rare exceptions, all individuals are born with all the potentially excitable sexual equipment they need. There can be, of course, individual differences in the neurological capacity for that sexual equipment to respond, just as there are individual differences in the capacity to perform any feat involving precise physical control. Moreover, some people have more active thyroid glands and so are more active in all bodily functions. But physical differences among individuals probably account for only a small part of the differences in their sexual responses.

In the past, some investigators believed that the body's production of sex hormones might be the key to an individual's sex interest or lack of it. It can be demonstrated that, within limits, sex responses may be modified by increasing the level of *male* hormone in some males and in most females. (Both males and females normally produce low levels of the other's sex hormones.)

But again, this in itself does not appear to be a wholly satisfactory answer to why some people are responsive and others are not. For even if hormones can perceptibly affect the frequency and intensity of sexual response in some people, they probably do not wholly account for the differences in sexual desire. Nor do hormones have any effect upon an individual's interest in any particular kind of sex activity. Nor do they even control his interest in getting sexual release with a person of the opposite sex rather than a person of his own sex. There is something more than physiology involved.

That something more is the psychological and social conditioning that the individual receives as he is growing up. Almost all adult sexual behavior—or lack of it—is dictated by the way the child was molded in his family and in his peer groups. It is this psychosocial conditioning that causes most of the difference in sexual expectations and attitudes not only among men and among women but also *between* men and women.

To really understand sexual behavior, it is necessary to look into some of the differences in the sex conditioning that is given to males and females, respectively, in our modern society.

MALE SEXUAL CONDITIONING

Men are different from each other in a lot of ways. Some men differ from other men more than they differ from women. This is true not only in muscular strength and mechanical ability, but also in what they like and what they like to talk about. Most women grow up knowing this. But there is one area of male variability—sexual desire and sexual responsiveness—about which some women know very little. This causes a great deal of marriage misunderstanding. For some women, some men appear to have too much sex appetite; for others, not enough.

The sex conditioning of the typical American male is a complex and paradoxical process that involves infant training, parental influences, group pressures, social-class customs, romantic rhapsodies, dilemmas, contradictions, winked-at-behaviors, moral exhortation, experimentation, pornography, biologic information, and intellectual conviction. These can be categorized into four major nonphysical influences that shape and reshape the developing sex consciousness and behavior of the typical middle-class American man: (1) infant love-response patterns, (2) early sex training, (3) sex-role identification, and (4) gang and man-group influence. There are, of course, also those differences occasioned by temperament, physical structure, and glandular output.

Infant conditioning

A boy's affectional conditioning (and so, to some extent, his sexual conditioning) begins at birth. If he is cuddled, fondled, and loved, if affection and the demonstration of affection are intimately connected on every occasion with the pleasurable sensations of warmth and the satisfaction of biologic tensions, his so-called affectionate nature is more likely to develop.

But what if he is emotionally deprived or neglected? Harry and Margaret Harlow demonstrated conclusively that monkeys, deprived of a mother's cuddling, were permanently impaired in their ability to form effective relations with other monkeys. At maturity, few showed normal sex interest or mating behavior. The Harlows reported that case studies of children reared with indifferent mothers or nurses "show a frightening comparability."[1] Adult males who have never been in love tend to have come from childhood homes in which they have been deprived of affection.

Not every man who is denied affection turns into a celibate recluse, of course. The human capacity to adjust is enormous. Some deprived men will be able to experience very normal love relationships. And there are

[1]Harry Harlow and Margaret Harlow, "Social Deprivation of Monkeys," *Scientific American*, **207** (November, 1962), 143.

some others who, because they were denied genuine affection in infancy, may spend the rest of their lives seeking it without success. They may wander from sex adventure to sex adventure, trying to satisfy their desperate need for affection with one sexual partner after another.

Early sex training

There are other early influences as important as affection, and some of these directly affect the developing sexual nature of the boy. His first sexual lesson may come from a horrified mother who is upset by his natural curiosity and his penis handling. She can—and sometimes does—punish him for this so severely that it markedly affects his later sex life. It is difficult to be specific about this one thing, though, for often there are so many other possible causes for any later abnormality that few authorities are willing to say for sure what caused what.

The Freudian interpretation of the results of this early genital play is, however, quite clear. During masturbatory activity, the three-, four-, or five-year-old boy fantasies that he has an incestuous craving to possess his mother and tries to seduce her by proudly showing her his penis. If this brings him into severe conflict, either real or imagined, with his father, the boy develops an intense fear that the bigger and stronger father will punish him by cutting off his genitals. This so-called castration anxiety, it is said, will cause sexual repression and later neurotic behavior.

Whether or not penis handling is a boy's first introduction to sex repression, it certainly will not be his last. By the time he is three or four years old, he knows that sex, like death and excretory functions, is circumscribed by taboos in our culture. He is carefully taught what sexual things he may not do, may not say, and may not even think. The punishment for violating any of these taboos is liable to be more severe than for other misbehaviors. Most parents, who were carefully sex-inhibited themselves, have deep-rooted emotional anxieties about childhood sexuality, regardless of how glibly they may talk about sex or sex education in adult groups. In a classic study of how American mothers socialize their children regarding sex, Robert Sears, Eleanor Maccoby, and Harry Levin found that, when exposing their children to other living experiences, the mothers explained carefully and offered alternatives, but when it came to childhood sexual behavior, they offered no alternatives and hurried off the subject.[2] Whether or not a mother discusses sexual behavior with her children is not nearly as important as

[2] Robert Sears, Eleanor Maccoby, and Harry Levin, *Patterns of Child Rearing*, New York, Harper & Row, 1957, p. 185.

how she handles the subject if she does. The ability to discuss sexual relationships with young teenage children is still difficult for most parents.

The sexual conditioning given a boy from a conservative middle- or upper-class family by his parents is only the beginning. The ridicule of playmates given for a taboo violation are often far more effective reprimands than the embarrassed silences or the blushes of his parent. It may take much group reassurance or biologic urging in later years before he again mentions sexual thoughts or indulges in sexual play. Thus, long before a middle-class boy ever learns the real significance of genital stimulation—much less sexual intercourse—social attitudes about sexual behavior have been absorbed into his personality.

As the typical boy grows up, he probably will learn from his middle-class mother to make a romantic association between sexual activity and love. This notion, too, will find reinforcement among his middle-class age mates, for their mothers also promote the notion that kissing, hugging, and other sexually tinged acts that their children are permitted to see are the special prerogatives of those who are married or at least in love. By the time most middle-class boys from even moderately conservative homes approach adolescence, the sex-love relationship is ingrained in their emotions. For some boys, the very idea of sex activity with a woman they do not love is as dishonorable an act as betraying a friend.

The sexual conditioning of a boy from a lower-social-level home is liable to be considerably different from the middle-class boy's. A study by Ira Reiss added the important qualifications of "liberal" or "conservative" to any generalization about sexual behavior and social class. There are liberal and conservative attitudes about sex in each social class.[3]

CASE **40** BEN AND EVIE

"I just don't understand what she expects of me. I work hard; I always have and I guess I always will. When I was small, my family lived on 'the wrong side of town.' I was determined to be a member of the right group when I grew up. It was hard, but I worked my way out of that hole, served my hitch in the army, and today have a good future in my profession. But I still can't seem to satisfy or please Evie, if you understand what I mean."

Ben sat quietly for a few minutes, then began again.

"My childhood wasn't the greatest. My father wasn't around much

---

[3]Ira Reiss, *The Social Context of Premarital Sexual Permissiveness*, New York, Holt, Rinehart & Winston, 1967, pp. 71–73.

when I was growing up, and as I was the oldest, I had most of the family responsibility. Mom was there, but she worked long hours at the town factory and never was there for me to really talk to about important things, things like girls. So I guess you might say I learned everything I know on the streets, at school, and in the army. At school, everybody used to brag a lot, and even though I didn't have anything to brag about, I joined in. Well, pretty soon afterward, I guess I was fifteen or sixteen, I was actually doing all those things I had been lying about at school. When I went away to college because I had managed to get a scholarship, things weren't much different. I had to study some, but the guys always found some fun and games on the weekends. But the big clincher came in the service."

Ben grinned devilishly at this point.

"I guess I had more girls those four years than any other guy in my unit. In Saigon, you could find them anywhere and they were always willing. They were a lot like the girls from my old neighborhood, always willing to oblige."

Ben paused again. When he spoke again, it was in a much more serious tone.

"When I got back I began working with a local realtor. I had finished working on my degree in business and had picked up some real estate courses along the way, so I was really moving. But nothing great happened to me until the night I took Mr. Jeffries, a new client, out to dinner. That's when I met Evie, his daughter. Mr. Jeffries was a big exec with the factory in town and had just been transferred to our branch. I guess you could say I fell in love with Evie that night, from the moment I first saw her. She was so different from any girl I had ever known before. She behaved so properly, just like you always hear good girls are supposed to behave. She let me chase, and she even teased me into chasing until I finally caught her. Anyway, we got married about a month later, a real whirlwind courtship, and I really thought everything I had always dreamed about was going to come true at last. Picture it: me, from the bad side of town, married to a real society girl. At least that's what I thought—up until our wedding night. I just couldn't come through, if you know what I mean. I guess I froze. It's been six months now and we still haven't had intercourse. I'm afraid to touch her, that it's all a dream and she'll go away. But I want to please her and I know I'm not. Evie is beginning to get pretty uptight about the whole situation. Before now, she was at least tolerant. Now all she does is nag about everything, not just our sexual relationship. She says I don't care about her, that I never will amount to anything, that I'm not good enough for her and *never will be. She's like a total stranger; maybe I married a stranger. All I know is that I'm at the end of my rope. Evie is threatening to leave me and I'm beginning to believe that might be the best idea she ever had. I just can't understand the whole mess; I can't understand why, after so many other women, I can't bear to touch Evie."*

Kinsey found that most lower-social-level males (as measured by education, father's occupation, and later-attained occupation) were far less sexually inhibited and far more familiar with all kinds of sexual behavior at a much earlier age than the boys from middle-class homes. Unbelievable as it may seem to middle-class adults, most lower-class boys had observed their parents and other people engaged in sexual intercourse not just once, but often. They were well aware of the techniques, functions, and pleasures of sexual activity at an age when middle-class boys had only a vague idea that there was such a thing as sexual intercourse. They came to regard sexual intercourse, both inside and outside of marriage, as normal and usual. Any substitute, such as masturbation or petting, was looked upon as perversion. Moreover, many lower-social-level parents, while condemning masturbation, advised their male children how to get sexual outlet through intercourse before marriage and what dangers to avoid.

The outside play group has its effect on the lower-social-level boys, too. But in his gangs, sex is discussed far more freely and with far less restraint than in the middle-class groups. The lower-class boy may learn to want to marry a virgin, but he also learns to take premarital sexual intercourse wherever he can get it.

Few of the lower-social-level men in Kinsey's sample looked upon their intercourse experience as anything more than pure physical gratification. Far from loving their casual sex partners, these men very often had only contempt for them. Most regarded preliminary lovemaking and petting as a waste of time, if not a little abnormal.[4]

Today, there may well be less class distinction in the sexual behavior of men than there used to be because of urbanization, economic prosperity, cross-cultural associations, freedom of women, and mass media. But there are still some wide subcultural differences—especially in the early conditioning experiences—that often set the later patterns of social responsibility as well as sexual behavior.

[4]Alfred C. Kinsey, W. B. Pomeroy, and C. E. Martin, *Sexual Behavior in the Human Male*, Philadelphia, Saunders, 1948, pp. 327–393.

Male sex-role identification

The relative sexual aggressiveness of any particular male may be at-
tributable as much or more to his sex-role-identification conditioning than
to his direct sex training. The process of male sex identification that produces the aggressive or the nonaggressive male begins very early. Since the
mother is the first model readily available, it is probable that in most cases
the boy first establishes an identification with her.[5] But the boy soon learns
that it would be absurd, indeed shameful, for him to grow up like a woman.
As he approaches puberty he rejects the company of girls, lest he be termed
"sissy," and adopts an almost compulsive masculinity. He learns in his competitive play with other boys to be very jealous of his masculine image, and
to be very anxious about any threat to it. Since boys are supposed to be
tough, he guards against any expression of tender emotion.

This anxiety over maintaining a masculine image is carried on into
later life and sometimes has a special relationship to a particular male's sexual experience. There is considerable psychiatric evidence that it is the male
who has doubts about his masculine desirability or about the adequacy of
his sexual performance who goes to elaborate lengths to reassure himself
by ultraaggressiveness or ultrapromiscuity.

In fact, nearly all males are under considerable pressure to demonstrate their masculinity by sexual achievement. Our culture instills in the
male the idea that eroticism is essential to maleness, and that it is the mark
of a man both to make sexual advances and to succeed. Yet, a new trend
allowing men not to be so aggressive is causing many men to be very confused about their own sex role.[6]

The male's concept of the female's role

Much of a young man's later sexual aggressiveness depends upon his
childhood conditioning concerning the female role. If, while he is growing
up, he internalizes the assumption that a man is the virtual owner of
women, and his every whim, sexual or other, is immediately to be satisfied,
he will be a far different young man than if he had been brought up to believe that women are coequal human beings. It is only temporarily surprising to learn that the young man with selfish, sex-demanding attitudes is

[5]David B. Lynn, "The Process of Learning Parental and Sex-Role Identification," in
Marcia E. Lasswell and Thomas E. Lasswell, eds., *Love, Marriage, Family: A Developmental Approach*, Glenview, Ill., Scott, Foresman, 1973, pp. 24–29.
[6]Myron Brenton, *The American Male*, New York, Coward-McCann, 1966.

often rewarded both with sex opportunities and with adulation from the women he dates. After all, most often the young women are brought up in homes with the same cultural background as the young men and are subject to some of the same attitudes and ideas. Aggressiveness in men is admired in our competitive society. Many girls feel that a boy is acting in his appropriate role when he is sex demanding, and they like him better for this appropriateness.

Being rewarded for aggressiveness may begin very early in the boy's life—long before he has had any sexual experience. There is a strong tendency for boys' behavior, in contrast to that of girls, to run in antisocial if not directly destructive directions. Parents tend to admire aggressiveness in boys and reward it with their love. Parents frequently treat an aggressive son as a favorite, instead of the "sissy" brother who acts perfect.

Clearly this does not happen in every case. Some boys, faced with mothers who say, "If you are a good boy, mother will love you," or mothers who overtly withdraw their affection when the boys misbehave, are emotionally conditioned to believe that this is the way things really will be. In this situation some boys are made overanxious and overpassive by this love-withdrawing technique.

It has been speculated that some of the very women who emasculate their sons by implanting exaggerated notions of female delicacy and virtue in them are sometimes the very ones who, in their own secret sex lives, are consumed with passionate desires. The conditioning of their sons is another reaction formation—an effort to atone for the guilt they feel as a result of their own desires. Of course, no one suggests that every mother who distorts the reality of sex in teaching her young son is doing so because of guilty projections. Often there are other motivations—a desire to keep the boy with her, a desire to have him enter the ministry or priesthood, or even a calculated hope that he will not be quite so demanding as his father.

In marriage counseling, it is common to find unhappy and mortified women who blame themselves for their husbands' failures in sexual intercourse, feeling that impotence results from their own lack of charm. Usually this is not so. Although there are many causes of impotence, in some instances the difficulty can be traced to the attitudes mothers inculcate in their sons. Sometimes, childhood conditioning has established a "madonna" image that results in the husband's overromanticized tenderness for his wife, so that he is unable to "defile" her. In other cases, young men have had their future sex lives blighted by an overdose of conditioned anxiety about what people think—to the point where the slightest rejection from a woman sends them into emotional panic.

censure. This creates further inhibitions in the unskillful or unattractive young man. On the other hand, the attractive, "smooth," aggressive individual may be rewarded and encouraged to make further experiments.

Regardless of the ultimate limits to premarital sexual behavior that any young man accepts, his association with the outside man-group usually has an effect on his sex life. In many instances, his misunderstandings of what women really want have their origin in the sexually excited imaginations of his misinformed friends. For example, as a result of the exaggerations and misconceptions they acquired in the locker room, many men are convinced that all women have the same sex appetites as they do. These men are likely to approach women sexually the way they would like to be approached—with direct genital stimulation. Some, because such things are deliberately kept from them when they are boys, never really understand that many women prefer emotional stimulation in the form of tender exchanges of love talk before any specific sexual contact.

This misunderstanding of the other sex's desires works both ways, of course. Some women find it difficult to believe that some men at times have an intense desire for a sex experience, without necessarily any desire for love play either before or after. But again, it should be remembered that there are many men for whom intercourse without tenderness would be impossible. There are some men who want no sex without love, just as there are some women who can take the sex experience as casually as some men —if not more so.

CASE 42 NORMAN AND EDITH

"I read somewhere a couple of weeks ago that a lot of women complain that their husbands don't give them enough love—just sex," Norman told the counselor. "But my problem is that my wife doesn't want sex or love. I like to make love, and I don't just mean to have intercourse. I like to hold her and touch her and tell her how much I love her. But she is some sort of cold fish, and she's always got some kind of excuse from being afraid I'll muss up her hair to worrying that the children might hear us. Maybe once a month or so she'll let me near her. Well, I'm an affectionate guy, and that isn't enough for me.

"I've always liked to hug and kiss and be close. She knew that a long time before she married me. But it was all right then; she even kissed back. I don't mean she was real sexy. I think maybe one of the reasons I finally proposed to her was that I couldn't get her to go to bed with me. I guess I

must have figured she was some kind of angel, and for a romantic guy like myself, that just made it so much better. But back in those days she did try to extend herself to be cuddly, and when we were driving down the road she would move over close. I never dreamed we'd have a sex problem.

"I've always needed a lot of sex. When I was in the navy I guess I had more than any man on my ship. But I was romantic about it even then. It's a funny thing, but I could go to bed with some woman who was initially very repulsive to me. But while we were having intercourse—that is while I was actually touching her—I used to feel very tender toward her. For that period it was almost as if I really loved her. After it was over, though, I used to feel very badly about it. I used to be ashamed of myself, not for having intercourse, but because I let myself feel loving when I knew darn well that she didn't have any feeling for me.

"But that's all over now, and I'm trying to be a real straight husband. I haven't had another woman in years, but I tell you I'm going to unless she stops making excuses. A man has a right to some sexual happiness. He has a right to feel loved."

"Norman must be oversexed," Edith told the counselor. "Or else, he's crazy. We have two young children and frankly they wear me out. I just about fall into bed every night. All I want to do is sleep. But not that satyr I married. He comes storming in every night and wants intercourse. Sure I give him a lot of excuses. Sometimes I go to bed early deliberately, but it doesn't help very much. He's so inconsiderate he wakes me up sometimes and demands that I give myself to him. I suppose a wife has an obligation to let herself be used, but he certainly overworks his rights. I suppose he told you that I won't touch him or pat him or even get close to him. That's true. And for a very good reason. If I give him the slightest encouragement in the early evening, then for sure he's after me when we go to bed. Sometimes he doesn't wait that long. Sometimes he can't even wait until the children are asleep. That isn't right.

"A wife has a right to expect a considerate husband, but Norman just plain isn't considerate. Not only that, he isn't smooth and subtle about lovemaking. He thinks he's affectionate but actually he's corny. He gets all sentimental and overeager. I suppose I will have to put up with this for the rest of my life, but right now I don't see how I'm going to."

Human physical variability and conditioning being what it is, it is doubtful if any two men want the same amount of sex or want it in the same way. The range is from impotence or complete lack of sex interest to complete lack of inhibitions and the desire for great frequency and variety of sexual experience.

FEMALE SEXUAL CONDITIONING

Since sexual adjustment requires mutual understanding, it is equally as important for the man to understand the woman's conditioned attitudes and expectations as for her to understand his.

Biologically, sexual response is often quantitatively—if not emotionally—more possible for women. Masters and Johnson are among the more recent researchers to point out that there is a large (and probably increasing) number of women who are capable of multiple orgasms in a brief period of time, a feat that few males can accomplish.[8]

Despite the greater meaning of sex for some women and the modern emphasis on the female orgasm in sophisticated circles, in the past in our culture not only have most young women been less interested in physical sex than men, many also have been conditioned to avoid sexual thoughts and sexual activity altogether.

This, in itself, is hardly surprising, for the sexual conditioning of young females in this society, as well as in recent history, has been fraught with paradoxes and perplexities. Many of the sexual problems of today's female go back to the very earliest formulations of her psychosexual attitudes, which were influenced in large part by the emotional struggles of her carefully sex-inhibited mother. Such a parent, having read something of modern psychology, was thrown into disturbed ambivalence when she saw early evidences of her young daughter's sexuality—usually genital play. Frequently the mother's reaction to this entirely normal play made a poor beginning for the development of sound sexual attitudes and feelings in the child. Later, such a child's sexual insecurity increases when she begins to understand that traditional sex mores and actual sex behavior in our culture are not necessarily congruent. This confusion continues even into adulthood, when she is perplexed by a new need (if she wants to be sexually successful) to demonstrate an enthusiastic sexual response she may not feel. Sexual incompatibility in marriage grows from just such sexual histories.

This is not true, of course, of all women. Some young females accept their sexuality with a joyful enthusiasm. Some are as eager as their male marriage partners for sexual activity. At the other extreme, there appears to

---

[8]William H. Masters and Virginia E. Johnson, *Human Sexual Response*, Boston, Little, Brown, 1966, pp. 283–284.

be an increasingly large number of women whose sexual desire exceeds that of their male partners. This disparity also creates marriage difficulty. No one knows for sure exactly what portion of the total married population is sexually incompatible or which direction that incompatibility takes. Many marriage counselors are still preoccupied with the older "sex-inhibited woman, sexually deprived man" problem, but some researchers see the opposite situation as the emerging predominant difficulty.

As a marriage continues, the inhibited wife becomes more relaxed and more able to enjoy her sexual life, while her husband becomes more preoccupied with his work and less interested in sex. However, it also can be speculated that many women who are eager to accept their husband's sexual approach at the beginning of marriage become less responsive later on. It may well be that these women predispose their husband's loss of interest in sex rather than become victims of it.

In any event, it is clear that, in modern society, there are some women who want less sex than is demanded and some who want more than is offered. Since it is historically the more important (and still probably the more prevalent) problem, let us further discuss the traditional female sexual conditioning that helps to create the woman who desires less sex than her husband.

The importance of psychosexual conditioning

There is general agreement among those who have studied human physiology and behavior that, except in rare cases, all females are born with a potential capacity for sexual desire. But it is also very clear that, by the time they are adults, there are some women who never have any conscious desire for sexual activity and others who have only a very low desire at the age when most other women have maximum sexual interest.

The causative factors for lack of sexual motivation are subject to dispute. Some investigators feel very strongly that inhibitions deliberately conditioned into the child, as a means of assuring later moral purity, and poor sex-role identification are the two major factors accounting for low sexual motivation. Both inhibitions and sex-role identification are psychological rather than physiological factors. John and Joan Hampson concluded from their studies in the early 1960s that sex-role identification is a result of a learning process that is independent of such physical factors as chromosomes or hormones.[9] But there are other very reputable investigators who

[9]John L. Hampson and Joan G. Hampson, "The Ontogenesis of Sexual Behavior in Man," in W. C. Young, ed., *Sex and Internal Secretions*, vol. 2, 3rd ed., Baltimore, Williams & Wilkins, 1961, p. 1413.

believe that low sexuality has some physical component. In some cases, the relationship between low sex desire and physical abnormality can be demonstrated. However, those who believe in the primacy of conditioning factors could here point out that gonadal function—especially that concerned with menstruation—is sometimes susceptible to psychologic modification and that, therefore, any cause-effect relationship is obscure.

Moreover, even if a physical malfunction causes the delay of sexual interest, it is often a conditioning factor that makes that delay permanent. If a woman in her late teens or early twenties is not physically or emotionally mature enough to be interested in sex, she may later be prevented from accepting sexuality by autoinhibition, for, by the time she does become physically mature enough to have desire, she may have so organized her life around a particular cultural pattern of living, religious or secular, that she will be psychologically unable to recognize the desires she now could have. Research findings are adding new complexity to the controversy over the primacy of physiology versus conditioning in sexual behavior. These experiments seem to indicate that an access or shortage of sex hormones during infancy and childhood may affect later sexual identification and/or behavior.[10]

But whether or not physiologic factors are present, it is clear that the socialization and conditioning that the female receives as a child plays a very large part in the development of her sexual desire and in the fulfillment—or lack of fulfillment—she receives from adult sexual activity.

Female sex-role identification

Sex-role identification for the female child as generally understood by social psychologists appears to be much simpler than for the male. The girl, like the boy, first identifies with her mother. But, unlike the boy, all she has to do is to continue this role identification until she becomes an adult. She carries no such heavy burden to demonstrate her femininity as the boy does to demonstrate his masculinity. As Clark Vincent has said, girls are allowed to be themselves, while boys have to prove they are boys.[11] Even so, however, as she approaches maturity, her own role problem may become more difficult than a boy's. Though no crisis of sex identity is in-

[10]David A. Hamburg and Donald T. Lunde, "Sex Hormones in the Development of Sex Differences in Human Behavior," in Eleanor E. Maccoby, ed., *The Development of Sex Differences*, Stanford, Calif., Stanford University Press, 1966, p. 15.

[11]Clark E. Vincent, *Sexual and Marital Health: The Physician as a Consultant*, New York, McGraw-Hill, 1973, p. 46.

volved, some young females experience great anxiety over such things as being chosen for dating and marriage and the confusion over the limits of sexual activity.

Psychoanalytic theory with regard to the psychosexual development of the female is much more complicated and controversial. According to the Freudians, at about the age of two, a girl, manifesting a syndrome which is similar to the Oedipus complex and which is sometimes called the Electra complex, displays a marked preference for her father that remains dominant until about the age of six. Then she turns back toward her mother, realizing that she cannot replace her mother in her father's affection and that, if she were to continue to try, she would lose her mother's love. From then on, ideally, she tries to emulate her mother. Although incestuous wishes play a part in this "complex," in that the girl subconsciously desires to have a child by her father, it is said that there is no such anxiety-laden fear for girls as the boy child's dread of castration.

In present-day society, even though marriage is still one of their goals, many women are having a different kind of problem with sex-role identification. Instead of trying only to meet the normative female sex-role of wife and mother, many women are also trying to meet the role of being a woman who is a person first. Judith Bardwick wonders if these women will succeed until this society accepts women as persons first.[12]

Infant conditioning and early sex training for females

The beginning of sexual conditioning for the infant female, as for the infant male, is probably the warmth and cuddling that she gets while she receives the biologic satisfactions of nourishment. Learning to associate pleasure with intimate body contacts is a primary source of acceptance of one's own sexuality.

A girl's introduction to sex is liable to vary widely with the kind of home in which she grows up. Differences in toilet training, in opportunities for privacy, and even in the acceptance of talk about sexual activity make for a great diversity in sexual patterns. But despite these early differences, certain fairly definite and widespread expectations exist concerning the sexual attitudes and behavior of the American girl at every age level.

Most very young American females are expected to be almost completely nonsexual. Any indication of sexual knowledge or experience ordinarily earns a severe reaction from parents, and neighbors as well. As the

[12]Judith M. Bardwick, *Psychology of Women,* New York, Harper & Row, 1971.

girl child grows up, she usually is made painfully aware of society's expectations if only by its silence. Although boys are rewarded by their peers for tales of sexual exploits to the point where it may make them exaggerate sexual experiences, girls are often punished by other girls as well as by their parents for admitting to sexual thoughts and behavior. Thus are created in most girls feelings that sexual activity is "wrong" and feelings of guilt about any form of sexual release, especially masturbation.

The female conspiracy of silence regarding sex not only prevents many growing girls from getting the emotional catharsis that group discussion might provide, it also makes inevitable a rude awakening when they come face to face with the realities of teenage sex expectations in our contemporary society.

At the beginning of puberty, expectations regarding female sexual behavior change. Now, to be a successful American female adolescent, a girl is expected to know enough about sexual behavior to make appropriate decisions. At the same time, she is expected to be sufficiently provocative sexually to keep the boys coming back for more dates.

As she enters adulthood, the mature American woman is expected to reorient her sexual emotions a second time. Now she must be responsive, with an invariable ability to achieve complete orgasm, despite whatever inhibitory process was built into her developing emotional system. In contemporary society, it often appears as if cataclysmic orgasm, perceived as taking place in the vagina (where, in fact, all orgasm does take place, even though it is initiated by clitoral stimulation) is the ultimate test of feminine achievement.

Obviously, these complex and sometimes contradictory goals of modern female sexual conditioning, requiring two major shifts in emphasis, would be difficult enough to achieve with any particular female, even if there were precise agreement on how it should be done. Unhappily, however, it is over just this point that the confusion among parents and educators is greatest. As a result of her elders' perplexity and consequent default, a typical young female gets very little more information about the realities of sexual behavior than is provided in whispered conversations, or that she can infer from books and movies.

True, some effort has been made in most schools to provide a film about menstruation, and in some schools a section in a home economics, health, or family-living course is devoted to human reproduction. But even in these few instances, those who are in charge of presenting the material ordinarily bend over backwards to assure themselves and the general public that only "scientific" facts are presented and that such practical problems as how to deal with the excitability of the male or the basics of family planning are not discussed. Often the most important aspects of sex education—attitudes, values, and expectations—are totally ignored. With this kind of preparation, it is a remarkable tribute to human adaptability that as many females turn out to be as sexually well adjusted as they are.

Because of sex taboos, many young women of recent generations learned to sublimate their sex drives and to concentrate on the romantic aspects of man-woman relationships. It was quite all right for them to dream about tender love and to be made starry-eyed by romantic novels, provided they made no display of overt sexual activity. Young women were encouraged by their parents to develop romantic attachments, provided they did not involve *overt* sexual response. Thus, whatever sexuality most young women felt became equated with—or at least indissolubly associated with—tenderness and affection.

As a result of their greater love-sex association, some females found out that the men they married had neither the same attitudes nor the same expectations about sexual behavior that they had. A woman might be appalled to find that her husband no longer felt obligated to woo her. He appeared ready—too ready—for instant sexual activity. Such a woman might also be distressed to find that he became sexually excited by viewing pictures of other women, or that he would go out of his way to look when the woman next door left her bedroom shades up.

Having examined some of the differences in the differential sex conditioning of men and women, let's take a look at a typical adjustment problem arising out of these differences.

CASE 43 HOLLY AND SAM

"I don't know what Sam thinks I am," Holly told the counselor. "I'm busy all day with housework and taking care of the children and he expects to have sex every night. Not only that, but he also expects me to be aggressive and to enjoy it. Isn't that ridiculous?

"I never thought our life would be like this. Before we were married Sam was rather aggressive, but if I said no he would stop. Now he just gets furious. I just can't understand why some men are so interested in sex. I wish Sam were more like my father. Dad was always so gentle and understanding. Everyone said my parents had the perfect marriage. You never heard them argue—especially about sex. They had separate bedrooms and simply put sex in its proper place."

"I just can't believe the change in her," Sam told the counselor.

"Before we were married she was very affectionate. She gave me every reason to believe that she wanted me just as much as I wanted her. That's always been important to me. I'm a loving guy and I like to express my emotions.

"Now all I get is an icy 'No!' and a cold shoulder. I can understand that sometimes she really is too tired, but not every night. She always has some excuse—we haven't had intercourse in over two months. In fact, she won't even let me touch me. She now has her own bedroom. I can't stand this much longer. I love Holly but this is destroying our relationship."

What are the differences in conditioning that could explain this problem?

Not all sexual-incompatibility problems involve women who want more love and men who want more sex. Increasingly, the difference in expectations is appearing in the opposite direction. Some sexually emancipated young women are finding that their expectations and attitudes exceed the sexual ability or sexual aggressiveness of their male partners.

Should a young wife, as a result of her disenchantment, start to believe that there is something wrong with her—that perhaps she is "frigid" —then she adds shame and fear to her other sexual problems. If, on the other hand, she blames her husband for her inability to achieve the ultimate in orgasmic response, and if her husband is already frustrated because he cannot give her the pleasure she desires, she further frustrates him and perhaps destroys whatever potential their relationship might have had in the first place.

There are, of course, some cases of sexual incompatibility where the wife is not just deceived by unreal expectations, but really *does* have a sexual capacity that exceeds the ability of her husband to satisfy. Sometimes this is a matter of quantity—a woman can have multiple orgasms during the same intercourse experience and continue to feel desirous long after her husband has been totally satisfied and gone to sleep. More often however, problems of sexual incompatibility that develop from the wife's greater desire have a qualitative dimension. For example, often the husband fails to provide the aggressiveness (or, as we have seen, the tenderness) that the wife has been conditioned to expect will bring her greater sexual happiness.

Curiously, a man's lack of sexual aggressiveness *before* marriage is often interpreted by an inexperienced female as a sign of his strength and love, to her later regret. Consider the following case.

CASE 44 ANNA AND ROS

"I really don't know what else I can do," Ros told the counselor. "Anna simply refuses to have sexual relations with me anymore. During our first two years of marriage I felt that Anna needed time to adjust to sexual relations, so I didn't push anything and tried very hard to be understanding of her. Instead of her desiring more relations later in marriage like I thought she would, she has become less responsive than ever. Sometimes she acts like she wants me to make love, because she tells me she loves me, and then when I advance she turns right off and either just stares or calls me a typical man. When I finally suggested that maybe she needed a professional counselor, to rid her of her inadequacies, she responded that her problem could be solved if I weren't oversexed. I still love and respect Anna, but women wanted me in college and they still do now!"

Then Anna talked to the counselor.

"Ros's whole idea of marriage is sex! Before we were married Ros wasn't like other guys. He respected my feelings and just worshipped me. Why, he would take me anywhere, and never make sexual demands. Now, sex is all he studies! During our early marriage he never pushed me and he was still the man I married. Now, he has lost all respect and wants me to do crazy things with him sexually. If I tell him that I love him he immediately thinks that means instant intercourse, and he ruins what love I did have for him. Ros had the nerve to suggest that I needed professional help. I agreed to it only because I want you to tell him that he is just oversexed!"

Some men who are sexually underaggressive before marriage remain that way. For the woman who expects and wants more sexual relationships, this can be very disappointing.

CASE 45 IRENE AND HAROLD

"I can't understand it now," Irene told the counselor, "but I think I married Harold because he didn't ever touch me. It was very refreshing. He wasn't like a lot of the other boys who are always after sex, sex, sex. Harold seemed strong and resolute, and I interpreted his self-control as respect for my moral sensibilities and as evidence of his love. I honestly thought that after marriage he would turn into a 'roaring tiger' and be the sexually aggressive strong man that I secretly wanted. Of course, I didn't even let myself believe that I wanted that kind before we were married.

"Anyway, after we were married, he didn't take any sexual leader-ship—at least, not much. He almost literally asked my permission to touch me. I didn't want that. I wanted him to know what to do and to do it, whether I thought I wanted to or not. I found out, though, that I had to reassure him. That wasn't the way it was supposed to be. I don't respond to him anymore, and I don't think I really want him anymore. I want a man."

Then Harold talked to the counselor. "I've always tried to be a nice guy; when a girl said, 'Stop,' I stopped. I wanted to be certain that she enjoyed it before I touched her. If she didn't enjoy it, it wasn't going to be any pleasure for me. But Irene sure wasn't any help after we got married. In the beginning she used to respond beautifully, but then she began to stop responding at all and just would lie there like a lump. After a while I began to figure it out. She was trying to goad me into being more aggressive and into doing it all. Then if she didn't enjoy it, she could blame me. Well, that just made it more difficult for me. Pretty soon when she didn't respond to my first touch, I'd get so mad that I couldn't sleep. I tried pleading with her; I tried begging her; I tried asking her nicely. But nothing helped. She just seemed to get more resentful and less cooperative. What can I do now?"

Although the overly sex-aggressive husband married to the under-responsive wife may still be the most prevalent problem brought to the attention of the marriage counselor, the underaggressive-husband syndrome often presents the greater difficulty. Does Irene really want Harold to turn into a "roaring tiger," ruthless and a little brutal? Would she continue to love him if he did? Sexual behavior is often an expression of an individual's total personality. If the counseling process were effective enough to alter the "nice guy's" personality, it might make him so much more self-oriented that he would turn away from Irene, perhaps even divorce her. Is Irene prepared for that?

The whole process of adjustment involves each partner moving toward the other while at the same time reducing his own needs for having everything completely his own way.

With sex, as with other marital adjustments, there are some men and women whose customs, attitudes, values, expectations, and, in this case, appetites fit together so perfectly that very little adjusting is necessary. There are others whose desires are so far apart that adjustment often seems im-possible. For the great majority of young marrieds, though, the sex-adjust-ment process *itself* is both necessary and rewarding.

15
SEXUAL RELATIONSHIPS IN MARRIAGE

Progress toward some new and better level of interaction for each of the individual partners and for the total relationship is the goal for sexual relationships. What is a reasonable goal for the process of sexual adjustment? In other words, what is "good" sexual adjustment?

Some of the most vocal present-day experts in sexology insist that only when the partners have arrived at a pattern of invariable simultaneous orgasm during frequent intercourse, have experimented with every conceivable kind of sexual activity, and have completely rid themselves of any thought of sexual restraint will they have achieved a good sexual adjustment. Some Freudian psychoanalysts insist that only when the woman perceives all of her orgasmic response as taking place in the vagina (rather than the clitoris, which is on the outside of the body) can she be considered "maturely" adjusted.

If everyone had been given the conditioning (and consequently the attitudes, values, and expectations) of these "experts," these goals might be both desirable and attainable. It is certainly true that those people who have achieved this kind of mutual sexuality believe that they have a richer living experience. But it is probably also true that there are many people who have been conditioned in such a way that only long-term psychotherapy might permit them to attain such sexual ideals. Meanwhile, these people feel constant anxiety that they do not respond the way the "experts" tell them they should.

It seems reasonable to suggest that there might be a better criterion for good sexual adjustment. This would be the melding of both partners' expectations into a single pattern of sexual behavior that is acceptable to both of them, regardless of whether anyone else thinks it is a good pattern or not. If both partners are satisfied with intercourse once a month, that for them is good adjustment. If a husband can accept the fact that his wife will not have orgasm during every act of intercourse and not punish himself for his failure to make her respond, that too is good adjustment. Also it would be better for a woman whose orgasm takes place from clitoral stimulation to rejoice in the fact that she does have orgasm at all, rather than to punish herself for the fact that she does not perceive it as taking place in the vagina during intercourse. When some sort of mutually satisfactory pattern is achieved, then—and only then—the marriage partners together can move, little by little, toward richer sexual behavior.[1]

Although frequent intercourse with simultaneous orgasm has been held as an ideal, some couples have known for a long time that simultane-

[1]William J. Lederer and Don D. Jackson, "Sex in Marriage," in Marcia E. Lasswell and Thomas E. Lasswell, eds., *Love, Marriage, Family: A Developmental Approach*, Glenview, Ill., Scott, Foresman, 1973, pp. 302–308.

ous orgasm may not be nearly as enjoyable as when they can concentrate on hers and then concentrate on his either by coitus or by manual or oral stimulation.

How long does it take to attain good sexual adjustment? There is no rigid time schedule. Some partners whose expectations and attitudes synchronize easily and who understand and accept each other's feelings are relatively well adjusted from the time of their first sexual activity. For others it can take weeks, months, or years. Some adjust and then need readjustment.

Usually, if the partners genuinely desire to make their sexual relationship better, they can. Determination, coupled with personal flexibility and some creative imagination, can improve an already successful sexual relationship as well as a failing one. In fact, because relations between people are never static, it is probably necessary that each partner continue to reinvigorate his sexual participation throughout the life of the marriage.

For people who have never known the stark realities of sexual incompatibility, sexual adjustment may sound very simple and hardly worth discussing. But for those with sexual problems, marriage can become a nightmare of disappointment and frustration that can lead to deep resentment and, ultimately, to divorce.

By the time both married partners realize that they have a serious sex-adjustment problem, three distinct sets of feelings usually have already developed in each partner. First, each partner has coordinated expectations of what is right and proper. Each also feels resentful because those expectations have been frustrated. And each, finally, fears what lies ahead, and such fears make the expectations and resentments seem much more important than they really are.

The initial step toward sexual adjustment in any marriage is greater understanding and acceptance of each partner's expectations and attitudes by the other partner. To do this, it is first necessary for each partner to understand that, however right or wrong his mate's feelings appear, they *are* his feelings. Ordinarily, these feelings have been building up just as strongly and for just as long a period of time in one partner as in the other. Neither partner is able to change his feelings overnight.

The second step that both partners must take to improve their sexual relationship is to explore each other's feeling by talking together.

SEXUAL COMMUNICATION

Lack of experience in sexual communication because of taboos in childhood homes has serious consequences in many marriages. Not only are the partners inhibited about expressing their expectations, needs, and desires to each other; sometimes they actually cannot speak the words. Some women, for example, cannot even let the word *penis* enter their consciousness without getting emotionally upset. Sometimes the words one partner does use are distasteful to his mate. Inappropriate sex words can be devastating to a lovemaking mood. Most people know this, and it is one of the reasons why communication between inexperienced partners is often so inadequate. Given enough time and the right kind of security, though, most people can work through their emotional inhibitions about both hearing sexual words and even about using them.

Many workshops in human sexuality are encouraging unmarried and married couples to learn the same information together. The increased smoothness in sexual communication is unbelievable when together couples hear the same information at the same time.

Some marriage partners, with or without sexual-adjustment problems, find that communication security is better achieved by inventing their own words for sexual activity and sexual parts. As long as both partners understand the meaning of these terms, this is probably harmless and very often can be helpful. But it should alert both partners to the fact that they have deeply emotionalized conditioned feelings that make their own private language necessary. They need to be very sure they are not perpetuating their inhibitions by using this sexual shorthand.

Sexual communication can and should be used for something more than problems. Some couples increase their sexual incompatibility by talking about sex only as a problem. Sexual communication can be, with practice, a deep source of marriage enrichment. As the partners explore each other's feelings and fantasies, they can come to have a depth of understanding that makes it seem as if their very beings, as well as their bodies, can touch.

Talking about sex can be as stimulating as a caress—sometimes even more so. Often, one's own sexual fantasies not only excite the other partner but provide knowledge for him of how he can be even more successful in lovemaking. Only by communication can one partner learn what the other really desires. Yet this is a stumbling block in many marriages. Most wives have no difficulty at all in directing their husbands where to scratch their backs—a little to the left, a little to the right, a little up, a little down—to provide the greatest relief for the itchy spot. But many find it impossible to be so explicit in directing them in sexual activities. If you were to ask one of these women why she does not tell her husband what she wants, she would probably reply, "He's supposed to know that!" Just why he should be expected to know what feels good to her sexually is somewhat obscure, since he has never been a woman, and he has never been that particular woman.

ACTION BEYOND COMMUNICATION

Just being an expert in talking about sex is not enough to assure good adjustment. The partners have to be able and willing to do something about it. Sometimes doing something about a sexual problem means going to see a psychotherapist for either individual or conjoint help with the sexual problem. In many cases of impotence and frigidity, this may be absolutely necessary, and the sooner the partners do it the better. There are other partners, such as those with unconscious repressions and homosexual tendencies, who need professional help, too.

But often, by evaluating their situation, marriage partners *can* help themselves. To begin with, they can deliberately work at being more like the sex partners their mates expect. In some cases, this may mean that a husband will try to be less demanding sexually or more aware of his wife's need for more quiet tenderness before intercourse. In other cases, it will mean that a wife will not deliberately stay up to watch the late show so that she can avoid fulfilling her husband's sexual needs.

For most sexually incompatible marriage partners, reversing their long-established patterns of behaving is not easy. Although each may have been eager at the time of their marriage for the caresses of the other, now their resentment and hostility are so great—often *because* of a poor sexual relationship—that one will not permit the other the satisfaction of meeting his expectations, even temporarily.

At least a part of this problem results from the fact that both partners often had unrealistic expectations to begin with about the marriage relationship. Each had built up in his mind an idealized picture of what his mate could produce, both as a human being and as a sex partner. Soon after marriage, the process of disillusionment sets in.

If this disillusionment begins with the wife, the husband soon senses her change of attitude, even though it may still be unconscious on her part. The realization that he is no longer her infallible hero hurts, so he begins to protect himself, perhaps also unconsciously. In turn, the wife has to adjust to the husband's slightly changed new attitude, the results of his defensive maneuver. Then he has to adjust again, then she does, and so forth. This goes on until both partners are totally hostile, or worse, apathetic, as a result of the constant need to protect their own egos from the insults of their mate's disillusionment.

In this process, no single rejection is important in itself, but ultimately there is one that represents the final denial of expectation, the ultimate disillusionment, the last straw. Not infrequently, it is the man who suffers disillusionment earlier than the woman, perhaps because his expectations are often more unreal. Who is the first to be disillusioned is unimportant, however, for sooner or later disillusionment affects the other partner, too. The following case illustrates how disillusionment affects a marriage.

CASE 46 BETTE SUE AND GARRY

"He just doesn't seem to care about me as a person anymore," cried Bette Sue to the marriage counselor. "He only thinks of me as a sex object. When Garry and I were married seven years ago, he cared about me as an individual. I was working as a nurse in a doctor's office and he was interested in my job and activities. I would come home and tell him about an unusual case or a hypochondriac patient. He would listen with interest then. Now he won't even listen to me when I tell him the new words the baby said today!

"Garry's father left his mother when he was four. His mother was able to provide an adequate living for them. But Garry was never satisfied. He always wanted more. After a disagreement with his employer, he changed one job after another. He finally settled into his present job as a salesman for a medical supply company. We met while I was a nurse and we began dating. I should have sensed then his attitude about women. When we went to a movie, he wouldn't take me to a movie theater, he wanted to go to a drive-in. That way, we could see a movie and have a little fun during intermission. I went along with some of his games, because I was afraid he would stop dating me.

"Now it seems all he's interested in when he's home is making love. My mother died a few years ago and my father had nowhere to go, so he moved in with us. Garry is gone so much of the time, it's nice to have a man around the house. Daddy is so helpful and no trouble at all.

"I'm afraid Daddy will hear us or know what is going on if we are making love. I'm always so nervous that I can't enjoy it. Besides, the baby wakes up occasionally and needs my attention. At night I'm too tired after working all day and in the morning the baby usually needs to be fed. Garry just can't seem to understand my feelings."

"Bette Sue can't meet my needs anymore," Garry said, "either physi-

cal or emotional. I don't think I had a real image of my wife before we were married. I had an image of women, or wives in general, and what they were supposed to be like. You know, she's going to like what I like, be interested in what interests me. And vice versa, of course. Well, it hasn't worked out that way. Bette Sue isn't too interested in my work. And I'm not at all interested in what she does. All she can talk about is the baby and dirty diapers.

"Her father lives with us now. I travel quite a bit and when I come home, our activities are planned around her father and the baby. Her parents always pampered her as she was growing up and have continued it. She doesn't know what it's like to be without anything.

"Now I'm on the road, trying to make a good living for us and when I get home, I'm treated like I'm living in her father's house. Even when we go to bed, I'm put off because her father might hear us. Let him hear us, it's my house!

"Bette Sue was very affectionate and aggressive when we were first married and even when we were dating. Now I have to make all the first moves. Sometimes she'll encourage me and then pretend she hears the baby. She runs to her and stays in her room until I'm asleep. The next morning she acts like she's really sorry we were interrupted, but when it happens time after time, I can't believe her anymore. Sometimes I think she's afraid she'll get pregnant again. I don't know. If only we could have sex more often, I know all of our other problems could be solved."

The only way for this couple to reverse the movement toward further disenchantment is for both mates to concentrate on each other's positive characteristics and so rebuild acceptance. As one partner begins to show joy in just being with the other, the other will gradually allow himself to lessen his own built-up ego defenses and begin to be more positively appreciative himself. The beginning of this process of reenchantment is reselling oneself on what is good about one's mate and his expectations. It is also important to remember that the more meaningful the emotional relationship between the partners becomes in *every* human activity, the more love-enhancing the sexual relationship will be. This, in turn, further enriches their nonsexual life together, which, in turn, reenriches their sex life.

A common complaint, especially from women, is that, although they may *want* to have sexual relationships, by the time they actually go to bed they are so physically tired or so emotionally unready for lovemaking that they reject their husbands either by active opposition—or even worse, by passive noncooperation. The woman who really wants to do something to avoid this pattern can do so. The couple must find some time during the week when they are relatively less overworked that they can give to love-making. After all, most people are too tired to do *anything* after eleven o'clock at night unless they have taken a nap in preparation for it! Most people know what they ought to do to improve their relationship. Sometimes fears and resentments are the reasons why they do not.

FEARS AND RESENTMENTS

Regardless of the exact nature of the incompatibility problem, it is usually fears and/or resentments that prevent normal physical responses from taking place. What often happens to the married partner who cannot physically respond to a sexual approach is that his initial stimulation may have been extinguished by some fear or resentment. These may be big fears or little insecurities; they may be long-smoldering hatreds or passing annoyances. Nevertheless, they are extraneous to the lovemaking, and they sometimes are sufficient to cause the beginning stimulation to disappear. For example, a woman may suddenly be chilled by the fear of getting pregnant, or of being overheard by her children, or even her parents, if they happen to share the same house. An unaesthetic or coarse word or gesture on the part of her husband may repulse her. She may recall some unpleasant sexual incident. Any such distraction, if it occurs in the crucial early moments of sexual excitation, can prevent her from having an orgasm. She can continue on through intercourse, yes; but she may not reach a climax.

Similarly, a man can be so disturbed by the thought that his wife did not respond to him the last time, or winced with discomfort when he entered that he too loses his ability to engage in intercourse. The unconscious (or sometimes conscious) feeling that he might be doing something wrong is a primary cause of both transitory impotence and premature ejaculation in the male. One failure to perform in intercourse creates a fear of further failures and so makes further failures almost inevitable. In some males, as in most females, there appears to be a crucial period early in the excitation process that controls the individual's ability to reach a successful climax. One bad experience just at that moment may condition him to fail on successive attempts.

Reassurance and familiarity are the specific antidotes for fear. The woman who has been inhibited by the fear of pregnancy may find a vastly improved ability to respond once she has some reliable assurance that she will not become pregnant. Similarly, the woman who has been fearful that she would be hurt by sexual intercourse often loses this fear when repeated intercourse experiences have been successful.

Providing real emotional security is a difficult task requiring careful thought. It is not very reassuring for a husband to tell his wife that she is "bound to get over her fears." This may just make her feel that he does not understand the real depth of her problem. Nor is it always helpful for a wife to be sexually aggressive with a timid husband. She may just make him that much more afraid that he cannot meet her desire for immediate intercourse. In this case, perhaps it is better to be warmly seductive without any overt demand for intercourse, and so build up both his stimulation and his security at the same time.

Resentments are equally as hard to work through as fears. Insights into their causes, achieved either by self-introspection or communication, are a helpful beginning. Once one has insight into the causes of his resentments, relief can often be obtained by ventilating the hostilities that have been suppressed. This should be done in a way that does not hurt the other partner, though.

Often the fears and resentments stem from outside the couple themselves. There are some cases in which marriage partners were so traumatized by their childhood sexual conditioning or so deeply disturbed by later fears and resentments that they now have severe emotional damage that can be helped only by psychotherapy. Yet there are other cases in which fears and resentments can be resolved by the partners themselves if they can give enough security to each other. Actually, in the end, the partners are the only ones who can really help each other. In these days, some professional therapists are basing their major treatment efforts in sexual incompatibility cases on that assumption. They see their role as aiding the partners in helping each other. Here is in illustration of the process:

Paul was a good-looking but rather shy chemical engineer. He was thirty-five years old, had been married for twelve years, and had two children. He started out by telling the counselor that his problem was his difficulty in getting stimulated enough to have intercourse. Until a year ago, he had had no problem. But at Christmas of that year he had had a fight with his wife in the presence of his father and mother. Things went from bad to worse, and for the past six months neither Paul nor Mildred had made any attempt to have sexual relationships. Paul said that at the beginning of their marriage their sexual relationship was excellent, but that his wife soon began to refuse him at times when he thought intercourse was appropriate. Paul's resentment had been festering for ten years. From what he said, it was apparent that Paul was a considerate husband. It was quite important to him that he please Mildred, and he did not want to risk offending her by forcing his attentions upon her. He believed Mildred to be a conscientious, kind, and publicly affectionate person. He also thought of her as strong willed, decisive, and sensitive to criticism. He said he had a nervous stomach and an ulcer.

When Mildred saw the counselor she confirmed these facts. After the big fight at Christmas, Paul had had a great deal of difficulty in trying to relate to her sexually, according to Mildred. She had not encouraged him to try sexual intercourse before they came for counseling, and she indicated her remorse at not having been more accepting when they could have had sexual relations in years past. She was very cooperative and very interested in trying to help now in any way she could. She said she had tried to become sexually aggressive but that this didn't seem to help her husband. In fact, it just seemed to make the situation worse.

Over the period of the next three weeks, the counselor saw Paul and Mildred several times each. Paul talked considerably about his relationship with his father, a Baptist minister, and a strict disciplinarian. At thirty-five, Paul had not been able to allow his father to know that he smoked and took an occasional drink. Paul conceded that there were many taboos in his house when he was growing up and that his sexual inhibitions were many. He had had almost no sexual experience before marrying Mildred, other than masturbation.

Mildred talked about her own family life. Her parents were much more liberal than Paul's. She was more creative than her brother and two sisters, and she was the leader in her play group. She had been attracted to Paul because there was something "winsome" about him and because she thought she could help him to get ahead. She reported that Paul sometimes broke out in a cold sweat when sexual intercourse was mentioned now.

In subsequent counseling sessions, some positive approaches to the problem were discussed. Paul began to get out more of his hostilities both toward his wife and toward his own father. At home he began to talk with Mildred about things they had never discussed before. He told her of his guilt over early masturbation and was very much relieved when he found out that Mildred had also masturbated and had also felt guilty about it. This appeared to be the opening of a new kind of communication about sex between the two of them. Before long, they were able to talk warmly and intimately about things that neither one of them had previously been able to discuss. Mildred was able to assure Paul that it wasn't necessary that they have intercourse every time they caressed each other. She was quite happy just to be close to him.

The marriage relationship improved in other ways. Mildred and Paul were able to talk about many of his feelings that he had previously felt he had to suppress. Mildred realized that in the past she had sometimes tried to provoke him into being hostile and forceful with her. She began to understand that this caused him to erect further defenses against her, since he was incapable of fighting with her.

Within the next month, Paul and Mildred found that, when there was no demand for intercourse, Paul frequently became very stimulated. They had several successful intercourse experiences. After the first success, Paul's optimism rose markedly. Before long, there was a more successful relationship between the partners than ever before in the past. Mildred told the counselor that it was the most wonderful time of their marriage. She felt as if they really knew each other for the first time.

After the emotionally satisfying experience of ventilating resentments, the person with a sexual-incompatibility problem faces the more difficult task of deliberate self-reeducation so that the problem doesn't occur again. For many people, this is a continuing adventure in self-discipline that may last a lifetime. Usually, once the initial pent-up resentments have been released, it is easier to dissipate new annoyances before they fester.

WHAT IS NORMAL?

Even for those married partners who have come to want to understand and accept each other's expectations, who have developed meaningful sexual communication, and who are motivated to want to try to do something about their sexual incompatibility, there often remains the question of what is normal sexual behavior.

The simple answer that "what is normal for any particular marriage partner is what pleases him" is not very satisfactory in itself. Some marriage partners need the reassurance that other people do what he and his mate have been doing, since mankind has been conditioned from time immemorial to believe that something is right if most—or at least many—other people do it. It helps some marriage partners to feel more "normal" if they know, for example, that the married women in Kinsey's sample had intercourse 2.8 times per week when they were in their late teens. This dropped to 2.2 times per week by the time they were thirty and to 1.5 times per week by forty. By sixty, the women had intercourse once in about every twelve days.[2]

[2]Alfred C. Kinsey et al., *Sexual Behavior in the Human Female*, Philadelphia, Saunders, 1953, pp. 348–349.

More recently Robert and Phyllis Bell found that when married women are between the ages of twenty-six and thirty, the average number of acts of coitus per week was 2.7.[3] Among women forty-one to fifty years of age, the average per week was 1.5. Bell and Bell also found that 24 percent of the married women studied who claimed to be happy most of the time felt they had too infrequent intercourse. Those women who rated their sex life as very good also indicated the highest average number (ten) of acts of coitus per month. Forty-two percent said they had orgasm most of the time, while only 17 percent always had orgasms. In comparison with 25 percent who claimed intercourse was too infrequent in an earlier study, made by Bell in 1967,[4] 30 percent of the present study made such a claim. Six percent of the former group claimed intercourse was too frequent and only 4 percent of the latter group claimed this. The Kinsey and Bell studies were done nearly twenty years apart, yet their findings are very much the same. However, the slight trend is that women may want intercourse more than they used to.

It sometimes helps some marriage partners to know that a man's sexual desire and/or ability reaches its peak at about age eighteen and thereafter gradually declines, while a woman's sexual interest and desire peaks when she is in her twenties and remains relatively stable. It helps some partners to know that experimentation among married partners in positions and techniques for intercourse and other sexual activity is extremely common but that its acceptance varies with the backgrounds from which the partners come. It also may help some partners to know that sexual experimenting between married partners of all backgrounds has been increasing in recent times. Manual and oral genital stimulation has become widespread, especially among highly educated couples.

But even though there are tendencies in these directions, none of these activities is necessarily important to any one couple's sexual adjustment. Some marriage partners are satisfied with infrequent intercourse. Some men lose sex interest in their thirties. Others continue to be sexually active into their seventies. And it is interesting to note that in Kephart's study of Philadelphia divorces between 1937 and 1950, wife-initiated divorce suits involving sexual complaints frequently blamed the husband's desire for unusual sex practices.[5] Robert Blood, commenting on this, said, "In short,

[3]Robert R. Bell and Phyllis L. Bell, "Sexual Satisfaction Among Married Women," *Medical Aspects of Human Sexuality*, **6** (December, 1972), 136–144.

[4]Robert R. Bell, "Some Emerging Sexual Experiences Among Women," *Medical Aspects of Human Sexuality*, **2** (October, 1967), 65–72.

[5]William M. Kephart, "Some Variables in Cases of Reported Sexual Maladjustment," *Marriage and Family Living*, **16** (August, 1954), 241–242.

some enjoy variety, but respect for the partner's feelings is fundamental."[6]

Often therefore, the best possible conclusion to the what-is-right problem is "what is acceptable to *both* partners is right." This is something quite different from suggesting that everything either partner conceives of is right. In many cases, the value system or religious belief of either one or both of the partners may prohibit many forms of sexual behavior that might seem quite right or normal to the other.

What is done between consenting adults is considered to be their business. Although almost no law books reflect this yet, the attitudes and actions of people do.[7] Practically no divorce cases occur now involving complaints of a spouse's demand for unusual sexual practices, and obviously none when there is mutual consent.

Sexual behavior is the expression of the individual personalities of the sex partners. There are marriages in which both partners agree that gentle tenderness is satisfactory to both of them. On the other hand, there are normal marriages where both partners are more pleased when the mate expresses himself with ferocious abandon. But in any case, the mutual acceptance of each partner by the other is the significant factor in adjustment. Although orgasm may be important, the mutuality of satisfaction is probably even more important. Many men, and some psychiatrists as well, find it difficult to believe, but some women apparently get satisfaction without orgasm.

Again it is important to point out that sexual adjustment in marriage —like all other adjustments—is continuous. Some women finally achieve a sexual climax after twenty-five years of marriage. Sexual desires and expectations are in a constant state of change throughout married life and require new adjustments. There is ample evidence that these changes can be for the better if both partners want it that way. There are many people for whom sex is more exquisite at forty than it was at twenty. But the sexual relationship does not improve for everybody.

CASE 47 MIKE AND ELIZABETH

"Mike says I'm frigid," Elizabeth told the counselor, "and perhaps I am. I know that very often I don't want him to touch me, and I invent all kinds of excuses so he won't. I tell him I feel ill or else I stay up later than he does. Most of the time I just don't feel like it because I'm mad at him. He is a

---

[6]Robert O. Blood, Jr., *Marriage*, 2nd ed., New York, Free Press, 1969, p. 311.

[7]Robert V. Sherwin, "The Law and Sexual Relationships," in Marcia E. Lasswell and Thomas E. Lasswell, eds., *Love, Marriage, Family: A Developmental Approach*, Glenview, Ill., Scott, Foresman, 1973, pp. 221–228.

very intelligent, usually well-mannered man, but sometimes he says such stupid things at a party that I could just scream. Or maybe he won't telephone me when he said he would. Then I just get so angry that I can't make myself let him make love to me. My father was always kind, courteous, and considerate—too much so, I guess. He used to let Mother walk all over him. Finally he became an alcoholic and she divorced him.

"Mike and I were married later than most people. I was a little shy in high school and in college too. I studied hard and got very good grades, but I didn't date very much. I wasn't very good-looking in high school, but by the time I got through college I was very pleased with my appearance. After college I had lots of dates, but the boys were rarely sexually aggressive. I guess I scared them off. They all seemed to try very hard to please me, but I guess I didn't really want that kind.

"Anyway, when Mike came along I was about thirty. He seemed so secure and positive. He appeared to be so at ease with people. Now I realize he really isn't very secure; as a matter of fact, inside he is shy, too. I think he is much more shy about sex than I am. He doesn't talk about it easily, and he says silly things. Every once in a while, though, he tries to be the strong possessive caveman type, and I have all I can do to keep from laughing. If he really would be genuinely aggressive, I think I would love it, but I'm afraid it's too late for that now.

"I remember when we were first married one time he wanted me to touch him. I said to him, 'Oh no, Mike, I couldn't do that,' hoping that he would insist. But he didn't. Actually he started apologizing to me for having asked. I think that was the beginning of my loss of feeling for him right there.

"It isn't as if I didn't have sex feelings at all. Sometimes I wake up in the middle of the night with lots of desire. But he's sound asleep, and he's the one who's supposed to start things, so that's all there is to it. I just go back to sleep."

"I grew up in a very good home," Mike said. "My father was firm, but loving. There were very few conflicts. He was a good churchman and there was no drinking or smoking in my house. I was slow with the girls, and I never went out to wild parties. Sure, I had sex desire like the rest of the fellows, but I used to pride myself in being a gentleman about it.

"When we were first married, she seemed to be almost as interested in sex as I was. She was warm and receptive, and we got along fine. But then somewhere along the way—it seems to me it was soon after Mike, Jr., was born—things began to get bad. All the time there were excuses, and even when we did have intercourse she stopped responding to me. I don't believe she's had a climax in the last two years, and she doesn't even care whether I know it or not.

"I don't want to force myself on her. As a matter of fact, I would like it if she were more aggressive, but it seems to be too late now. I've just about resigned myself to the fact that I'm never going to have the kind of sex relationship with Elizabeth that I would like to have. I've talked to a lot of the fellows down at the office and they don't seem to do much better than I do. Some of them step out on their wives. I could never do that, although it might help me if I did. Some of the guys say that you benefit two ways. First, you get sexual satisfaction outside. And then if your wife finds out about it and if she doesn't divorce you, things get better at home, too."

A good sexual adjustment involves patience and practice as well as passion. It derives its excellence from the complete emotional acceptance of each partner by the other and not from any standardized set of techniques or social norms. To arrive at a better sexual relationship, or to solve a sexual problem, the partners have to understand why their mates behave the way they do and then help each other to achieve greater enjoyment. Only when *both partners* really want to help each other can there be any substantial improvement.

16

EXTRAMARITAL RELATIONSHIPS

Extramarital relationships have traditionally had a sexual aspect. This remains true today with one exception: There are now more numerous extramarital contacts between men and women that do not include sexual intercourse than ever before. This increase far exceeds the increase in extramarital sexual intercourse, even though both have risen in recent years.

These extramarital relationships include a whole host of activities, from incidental encounters as part of a daily job, to very close heterosexual friendships. In fact any activity which a man and woman who are not married to each other engage in together is an extramarital relationship. Jetse Sprey makes this definition very clear in his discussion of extramarital relationships in conflict management.[1]

Ray Birdwhistell has explained the reason for our society's traditional view of every extramarital relationship as being sexual.[2] He says that the ideal married state was traditionally one in which all the emotional and physical needs of the partner were met. Sexual fidelity was extended to fidelity in all activities of the couple. Therefore, when either one of the couple participated in almost anything outside of marriage, the suggestion of sexual infidelity was always there.

There seems to be a continuous searching for love and attention by almost everyone, a fulfillment that monogamous marriage cannot always provide.[3] When a person is determined to be faithful in sexual relationships to his spouse, he manages the monogamous marriage by suppressing any desire for anyone else. Bernard Farber has become known for his thesis that people are permanently available and that only the totality of conditions determines the direction they will choose to go.[4]

Extramarital relationships of all types are now looked upon by some as a new form of human endeavor.[5] These relationships do not necessarily lead to the breakup of a marriage. There are many marriages that are strengthened by the incidence of extramarital relationships as defined in the wide sense.

Nonexclusive sexual partners in monogamous marriages has been a

[1]Jetse Sprey, "On the Management of Conflict in Families," *Journal of Marriage and the Family*, **33** (November, 1971), 722–731.
[2]Ray L. Birdwhistell, "The Idealized Model of the American Family," *Social Casework*, **51** (April, 1970), 195–198.
[3]Gerhard Neubeck, ed., *Extra-Marital Relations*, Englewood Cliffs, N.J., Prentice-Hall, 1969, p. 5.
[4]Bernard Farber, *Family: Organizations and Interaction*, San Francisco, Chandler, 1964, p. 106.
[5]Spurgeon E. English, "Values in Psychotherapy: The Affair," *Voices*, **3** (April, 1967), 9–14.

fact if not a rule in the history of legal marriage. However, to support the legal enforcement of monogamy, societies have had written and unwritten moral codes that expressly condemn adultery. There are some interpretations of the moral codes against adultery that imply that the thrust of the codes was to protect the family as an institution responsible for the primary socialization of children and as an institution through which possessions might be kept intact. According to this interpretation, adultery means anything that might threaten the family, extramarital sex being only one of these. Implicit, but not stated, is that any act that does not threaten the family does not break the moral code against adultery. Furthermore, extramarital sex, it is claimed by such interpretation, could conceivably enhance and not adulterate the family. This view is open to controversy at the moment.

Several writers are now openly expressing the view that extramarital sex should be a matter of personal choice and should not be against the law. That a marriage should break up because of the extramarital sexual relationships of one or both spouses is not necessarily their implication; the opposite is more likely to be their contention.[6] Nevertheless, one of the sex-related problems in marriage even today is extramarital relationships. Today's society, with its new freedoms for women, now provides every wife as well as every husband a relatively easy opportunity to try and solve his real or fantasied problems, be they sexual, affectional, or social, by seeking satisfaction elsewhere.

With extramarital sex, as with premarital sex, no one knows for sure exactly what percentage of today's population is involved. It is certain that there are some who have sex outside of marriage. Clark Vincent has reported a study of extramarital pregnancy in which about 10 percent of the women had been impregnated by someone other than their husbands.[7] It is also certain that there are many women and men, even in today's liberal society, who go through their entire marriages without having sexual intercourse with anyone other than their mates. But there the certainty ends. We will be referring in this chapter to alleged increases in extramarital sex, but it should be remembered that these "increases" could be very small. In fact, they may not even be increases at all, since it is quite possible that the apparently greater rate of extramarital sex means only that more people are now willing to tell that they have participated in it.

[6]Lawrence Casler, "Permissive Matrimony: Proposals for the Future," *The Humanist*, **34** (March/April, 1974), 4–8; and Nena O'Neill and George O'Neill, *Open Marriage: A New Life Style for Couples*, New York, Evans, 1972.

[7]Clark E. Vincent, *Sexual and Marital Health*, New York, McGraw-Hill, 1973, p. 239.

It should also be remembered that the self-fulfilling prophecy is as applicable to extramarital relationships as it is to other sexual behavior. Because one hears in the mass media that "everybody is doing it," some get the feeling that they will be missing something if they do not do it. It is seldom pointed out that some people might be missing something if they do, since loyalty and trust are not only the foundations of the marriage relationship but also two of the "promises that men live by." Some people cannot live with going against traditional ways without internal guilt while others are very willing to be nontraditional.

There appear to be three major trends that are causing alarm among those who see extramarital relationships as a threat to the stability of the family in our society—the increase in the involvement of middle-class men and women and the acceptance of extramarital relationships as normal.

THE INCREASED INVOLVEMENT OF MIDDLE-CLASS MALES

The first of these apparent trends is the larger number of middle-class males who are accepting sexual relationships outside of marriage as permissible and desirable. There has undoubtedly always been a great deal of extramarital sexual experience among men in most of the societies and cultures where the concept of monogamous marriages has been an ideal.

Until recently, the public notion went relatively unchallenged in the United States that middle- and upper-class males upheld their status and their reputations by being faithful to their wives. Extramarital affairs were sometimes punished by the loss of job and standing in the community. Of course, this was never universally true. At the height of Victorianism in the late nineteenth century, the Reverend Henry Ward Beecher, one of the most popular preachers of the times, was publicly accused of extramarital sexual activities. Elizabeth Tilton, a young married Sunday School teacher at Beecher's church, confessed that she and Beecher had been intimate. But, as Arthur Schlesinger, Jr., has pointed out, neither the size of Beecher's congregation nor his popularity and moral influence was perceptibly affected.[8] Still, the very fact that this affair was so newsworthy then, and is still remembered now, points up the general conclusion that it was counter to the public expectation. By and large, marital fidelity for both men and women was an American ideal of no small significance.

In the present culture, however, there is a very real question about the number of people who pay more than lip service to the ideal of marital

---

[8]Arthur Schlesinger, Jr., "An Informal History of Love in the U.S.A.," *Saturday Evening Post*, **239** (December 31, 1966), 34.

fidelity. John Cuber and Peggy Harroff found in their study of 437 upper-middle-class Americans that many of their respondents were involved in extramarital relationships either for one night's thrill or for some deeper, longer-lasting affectional reason.[9]

Cuber and Harroff point out that some business firms now use "total entertainment," including the services of a playgirl for the evening, as a form of sales promotion when customers come to town. Since most middle-class businessmen travel, invitations are said to be hard to avoid. As Cuber and Harroff put it, these practices have passed the stage of being naughty oddities that only a few people know about. They are standardized, understood, and almost institutional. (Some businesses, however, are counteracting this notion by requiring that their executives bring their wives to out-of-town conventions.)

Such practices are, however, probably only a small part of the extramarital sex picture for the average American middle-class male. Equally as important are the many opportunities he has for affairs with the women who work in his office or whom he meets in his suburban neighborhood, perhaps while his own wife is working in somebody else's office. Sometimes these relationships blossom into full-scale love affairs fulfilling needs for both partners that are not met in their marriages.

THE INCREASED INVOLVEMENT OF MIDDLE-CLASS FEMALES

The second trend in extramarital sexual relations is that there has apparently been an increase in extramarital sex among middle-class women, too. As with the males, much of the evidence for this increase is circumstantial. For example, in testifying before a Senate committee in 1966, a manufacturer of electronic eavesdropping equipment reported to the committee that in 1961 he sold more of his bugging devices to women who were checking up on errant husbands, but in 1966 some 80 percent of his domestic clients were husbands trying to find out what their wives were up to.[10]

[9] John F. Cuber and Peggy B. Harroff, *The Significant Americans*, Englewood Cliffs, N.J., Prentice-Hall, 1965, p. 152. Cuber later explained that they were interested in context, not number, and thus did not publish exact statistics in this study. They felt that a mere count would yield a useless and possibly spurious statistic, because any count of adultery would lump together behavior incidents of such diverse character as the action of a man who has had "one too many" at the office party, the tender "mismate" who finds warmth wherever he can, the lecher who seeks every possible sexual variety, and the mate whose marriage is capable of destroying him but who is sustained by an extramarital relationship. John F. Cuber, "Adultery: Reality Versus Stereotype," unpublished paper read to the 1966 Groves Conference, Kansas City, Mo.

[10] "Do-It-Yourself Kits 'Bug' Erring Mates, Senators Are Told," *New York Times*, June 15, 1966, 25.

Occasional newspaper and magazine stories about mate-swapping and suburban housewives caught in call-girl raids do nothing to diminish the popular notion that such behavior is fairly widespread. Again, however, the very fact that it is headlined in the newspapers indicates that it is still news and that the overwhelming majority of the population looks upon it as nontypical behavior.

Robert Bell, among several others, has suggested that in present-day America, many men feel that a wife's extramarital sex is an irreparable blow to their marriage, even though women are often less inclined to view male extramarital sex in the same extreme way.[11] Bell's statement is not wholly congruent with the case histories that Cuber and Harroff report. At least some of the husbands interviewed knew that their wives were having extramarital affairs and continued to live with them.

It has been suggested that American women are not really very good at extramarital sex. Morton Hunt has said that most women eventually want their extramarital sex partners to be their legal mates.[12] On the other hand, there are some American women who can be as casual about their temporary sexual liaisons as their male partners.

CHANGING ATTITUDES AND LAWS

The third trend in extramarital sex is the change in attitude toward it. Until the early days of this century, in our culture it was defined as sin, an abominable evil, and a threat to the monogamous base of society. In the last few decades, as we have turned more away from the concept of sin and more toward psychological and psychiatric behavioral interpretations, some have been inclined to describe the person who participated in extramarital sex as sick, immature, narcissistic, or neurotic, all designations implying a psychopathologic state.

However, Robert Whitehurst has come to the conclusion that extramarital sex is now so prevalent for middle-class males that it can be described only as normal behavior in the social context in which many men live in today's United States.[13]

This is also the conclusion reached by Cuber and Harroff, who feel

[11]Robert R. Bell, *Premarital Sex in a Changing Society*, rev. ed., Englewood Cliffs, N.J., Prentice-Hall, 1973, p. 147.

[12]Morton M. Hunt, *The Affair*, New York, New American Library, 1969, p. 139.

[13]Robert Whitehurst, "Changing Ground Rules and Emergent Life Styles," in Roger Libby and Robert Whitehurst, eds., *Renovating Marriage: Toward New Sexual Life Styles*, Danville, Calif., Consensus Publishers, 1973, pp. 309–320.

that, because much of the evidence about extramarital sex has come from those people who sought help for their neurotic problems, it has been too soon concluded that people who participate in extramarital sex are therefore neurotic. Cuber and Harroff point out that many ordinary people have had the same extramarital experiences as the clinical cases. Cuber and Harroff report that an overwhelming number of their upper-middle-class Americans who had participated in extramarital sex expressed no guilt with respect to these affairs.[14]

Albert Ellis, a psychotherapist, feels that, in this society, there are both healthy and unhealthy reasons for extramarital sex as well as various other kinds of unconventional sex behavior. He cites the "freeing of the human spirit" as a "healthy" reason for extramarital sex. Ellis believes that many people "find that they are freer, more labile and more truly themselves (as distinct from well behaved conformists) when having promiscuous rather than conventional mating relationships."[15] He also suggests that these affairs not only provide sexual variation but also improve sexual techniques and help relieve the boredom of living by the excitement of adventure.

Ellis concedes that there are some unhealthy reasons for extramarital sex too, including the danger of becoming compulsively promiscuous and so destroying existing or potential involvements by hastening from one affair to another. He also includes a neurotic need for ego-bolstering and escapism among his unhealthy reasons for seeking sex outside of marriage. Further, he is not accepting of extramarital sex that involves hostility and rebelliousness, since this prevents people from getting the "real joy and personal growth they might experience from being healthfully promiscuous."[16]

In examining these speculations and opinions about extramarital sex, it should be borne in mind that marital fidelity is still the expectation for most people in the mainstream of American living today. Cuber and Ellis have sampled only an infinitesimal part of the 45 million American couples who, by and large, maintain more traditional attitudes, if not actual behavior, toward marital fidelity. It is probable that most Americans—even those who have had some extramarital sex experience—still think of such behavior as "cheating" and still respect the decision of the husband or wife who does not participate.

Although laws are a reflection of cultural attitudes at the time of writing they do not seem to be rewritten as quickly as attitudes change.

[14]Cuber, op. cit.
[15]Albert Ellis, "Sexual Promiscuity in America," *Annals of the American Academy of Political and Social Science*, **378** (July, 1968), 66.
[16]Ibid, 67.

Laws about sexual activity seem to be among the slowest to change. Legal changes from regulation of sexual activity even within marriage to allowing any sexual act between consenting adults have occurred in only a minute number of states, and have taken centuries to achieve.[17]

THE EFFECT ON THE MARRIAGE RELATIONSHIP

It is extremely difficult to tell how many marriages are affected in any one year by the infidelity of one spouse or another. In the past, adultery has been the third most often used of the legal grounds for divorce, cruelty and desertion being the first two most used legal grounds. Even if it were possible to measure accurately the divorces resulting from broken pledges of faithfulness, it would probably be only a partial measure of the marital disruption caused. In many cases, the matter is quietly hushed up, but not before one partner or the other has suffered mental anguish and self-doubt.

A deteriorating marriage is not a necessary concomitant of infidelity in every case. Nor is philandering always injurious to the mental and emotional health of those who participate in it. There are some marriage partners, especially some wives, who are pleased, either overtly or covertly, when their husbands engage in extramarital sex. Some, who did not particularly care for sexual activity in the first place, are delighted to be rid of their wifely "duty" to satisfy their husband's "animal instincts." Other wives, then relieved of some of their own possible guilt, feel justified in having extramarital affairs of their own. Still other wives receive masochistic emotional satisfaction in finding out that their mates are the reprobates they always suspected them to be.

Not all husbands are unhappy when they find out about their wives' extramarital relationships, either. Cuber has asserted that he found cases in his study in which both wives and husbands knew of their mates' extramarital affairs but in which the marriage remained qualitatively at least as good as the average marriage.[18] Many happily married people who base their love on loyalty find these data hard to believe.

REASONS FOR EXTRAMARITAL RELATIONSHIPS

In the unknown number of marriages in which extramarital affairs are occurring, there probably could be less trauma if the partners would recognize

---

[17]Robert V. Sherwin, "The Law and Sexual Relationships," in Marcia E. Lasswell and Thomas E. Lasswell, eds., *Love, Marriage, Family: A Developmental Approach*, Glenview, Ill., Scott, Foresman, 1973, pp. 221–228.

[18]Cuber, op. cit.

some reasons for their mates' infidelity and then take some rational steps when reacting to it.

Rational action usually requires some meaningful self-evaluation as well as some clear perception and decision making. To make those perceptions and decisions, one needs to know not only something of the nature of extramarital sex, but also something of the nature of the persons.

In order to understand the dynamics of extramarital sex, it is necessary to take a look at some of the different values and attitudes that motivate the person. Later we shall see that the motivation of the unfaithful partner may control the type of reaction and decision that the aggrieved partner will want to make. No one, either male or female, falls into a totally neat classification, but the following are some general reasons:

Liberal beliefs

People, particularly males, reared in a subcultural group in our own society in which the prevailing value system views extramarital sexual relationships as both normal and desirable are not likely to make sexually faithful mates. Such people may argue quite candidly that, in the cultural group from which they came, "every man had sex outside of marriage, and what's wrong with that?" They may look upon monogamous marriage as a curious custom, a mid-Victorian hangup, or a vestige of middle-class prudery. It is highly improbable that such individuals are going to change dramatically in order to conform with any of the notions the tradition-oriented middle-class mates may have about fidelity in marriage. Most marriage counselors would not go so far as to say that reorienting the cultural libertine is altogether hopeless, but most would certainly agree that it is difficult. Although it may be too long for their mates to wait, there is some evidence that, as the libertine grows older, he is inclined to become more faithful. It is also probably true that the young rebel who has "dropped out" of middle-class society in a show of nonconformity may have much less difficulty in returning to traditional conformity than the person who was never conditioned to a monogamous marriage expectation to begin with. Today, more and more men and women who would resent the label of "libertine" can be classified as liberal.

Sexual dissatisfaction at home

There are other large groups of people involved in extramarital sex who have strikingly different motivations. There are, for example, many people of both sexes who feel that they are sexually deprived in their present marriage. Such people often seek—deliberately or unconsciously—an extramarital relationship in order to show their spouses that somebody else desires them, or that somebody else can offer them the satisfactions they desire.

CASE 48 PEGGY AND RALPH

"I don't love my wife Peggy anymore," Ralph told the counselor, "and I'm not sure that I ever did. Oh, I guess I did have some affection for her in the beginning: I'm a kind of a sentimental guy. Besides, she tried hard to please me then. But as time went by, she began to make it very clear that she didn't want me sexually. It got so that if I tried anything, she gave me all sorts of excuses, and if I persisted, she would just lie there like a lump.

"About a year ago I met Claudia. She was unhappily married too, but in all of our relationships she was all of the things that Peggy wasn't. Claudia was warm and eager to have sex. Moreover, she accepted me completely, and she listened to me. I didn't have to try to be something I wasn't with her. I could tell her all my troubles. I didn't have to hold back, as I did with Peggy, for fear that she would get upset. Instead of helping me get over my anxieties, Peggy would just add to them, and then there were two people twice as anxious.

"Some funny things happened after I began sneaking out with Claudia. I found that I wanted Peggy sexually more than I ever had before. As a matter of fact, I never really wanted Peggy until after I had been with Claudia. I don't think our poor married sex life was all Peggy's fault. She was brought up in a strict religious home. She wasn't ever allowed to believe that sex could be good. She was taught that it was something bad or dirty.

"Anyway, I told Peggy about Claudia almost two months ago. Peggy screamed and cried and carried on. But she didn't do anything to try to make our marriage better. I told her I wasn't going to leave her, because of the children. And I won't either.

"I broke off with Claudia last month, though. I'm through with her. She wanted me to stop having sex with Peggy. Claudia thought she could tell me not to have sex with my wife. Imagine that! I was a little amused at first, but she started nagging me about it, and I began to realize why Claudia and her husband don't get along too well. Now I don't know what to do. I don't want Claudia, and Peggy doesn't want me."

"I have always been a little afraid of him," Peggy told the counselor. "He has such terribly black moods sometimes. I suppose I did try harder to

please him when we were first married, but after a while I began to feel that some of his criticalness and moodiness and drinking too much at parties was the cause of our trouble. I guess I stopped trying to please him and started trying to punish him into being the pleasant, considerate, thoughtful man I had thought he was.

"My mother was very critical of me as a child. She was an absolute perfectionist, and I had to do everything just right or she told me about it. It's funny, I just traded a critical mother for a critical husband. I was resentful when she hurt my feelings, and I'm even more resentful when he does.

"Our sex life has never been very good for me. I used to like for him to touch me when we were dating, but I always thought that intercourse was a little dirty and disgusting. I'm not sure where I got those ideas. I don't think my mother ever said it exactly that way. She just made me timid about everything. I think I must have made up most of the inhibitions myself.

"Anyway, I need someone to help me about sex. Ralph was no help at all. He was very boyish about sex; he needed my approval all the time. He couldn't be happy when I just enjoyed it a little bit. I had to have some completely rapturous, earth-shaking response, or he thought I didn't care anymore and then he got in one of those black moods. I thought our sex life had improved recently. He started coming home more. And once in a while he was very eager about sex, and I loved it. He seemed happier, too, on these occasions. When I found out about Claudia I was terribly hurt and angry. I haven't yet decided what I'm going to do. But I'll tell you this: It's going to be a long time before I can respond to him again. Imagine his wanting to touch me after he has been with that other woman! When he tries to make love to me now, that's all I can think about. I get angry all over again just sitting here talking about it! I have a good mind to leave him."

It is not always direct sexual deprivation that makes one mate or the other feel he is so abused that he has a right to seek solace elsewhere, nor is it always the male who feels abused.

CASE 49 SYLVIA AND LARRY

"Larry was an absolute clod," Sylvia told the counselor. "All he wanted to do was to come home and sit and watch television or work on that stupid boat of his. He had no interest in art or in good music. We never went *anywhere. He never wanted to take me out. I really don't know why I married him, since we had nothing in common. It must have been that he offered a kind of security. His family had lots of money, and we have a beautiful home now. He could provide all the things that I dreamed about having as a girl: fur coats, maids, the whole bit.*

"About two years ago I met Roy at a cocktail party. He was handsome in a very masculine sort of way, and I was immediately attracted to him. But more than that, he could talk brilliantly and knew all about good books and music. He was vibrant and exciting, and I wanted to be near him. Roy was married, of course, but very unhappily. I invited him and his wife over to our house, and Larry even took them out on our boat. I would see Roy at the repertory theater. (Larry wouldn't go with me, so I went alone.) Pretty soon it was obvious that Roy was attracted to me. One thing led to another, and before long we were having sexual relations. I just left my children with a maid; it was easy. Roy was a salesman, so it was easy for him too. Sometimes I convinced Larry that I needed to go away by myself for several days at a time.

"The sexual experiences Roy and I had were more exciting than anything I had ever known. He was self-confident and imaginative. I began to find out what real sensual pleasure was for the first time. Now I can't stand to have Larry touch me.

"I'm going to leave Larry and marry Roy as soon as he can divorce his wife. She won't give him a divorce easily. I can't understand that. Why should she want a man who doesn't love her anymore? He says he'll provide for his children.

"I can't make up my mind whether I want to keep my own children or not. They're a real problem to me sometimes. I couldn't stand them if it weren't for the maid and having Roy.

"I see it this way," Sylvia went on. "Human beings only have a short time on this earth, and they're entitled to all the pleasure they can get. They shouldn't be locked up for the rest of their lives with people they don't love. Sometimes I think I would let Larry have the children if that's what it takes to get a divorce. But not unless we settle everything the way I want. The judge will award me the children if I want them. They always give the children to the mother.

"Larry says he wants the children. But I think that's only because he is so conventional and thinks he should protect them. He never plays with them. He just sits there and watches that stupid television."

Larry looked at things very differently. "There is something terribly wrong with Sylvia," he told the counselor. "She is emotionally sick and should be seeing a psychiatrist. Both her sisters and even her parents have told me (and her too) that what she is doing with Roy is very wrong. I haven't done a thing to her. I have always tried to be a good husband. I don't drink, I don't run around with other women. As a matter of fact, Sylvia was about the only woman I ever dated. I guess I was kind of slow in that regard by modern standards.

"I've always tried to give Sylvia everything she wanted. I got her a maid because she thought taking care of three children by herself was too much. When I didn't enjoy something that she liked, I let her go ahead and do it anyway, and I'd make myself happy in other ways. That may have been a mistake. I let her go to the theater by herself, and she thanked me by carrying on with that other fellow.

"There is another reason why I think she needs psychiatric help. She is very moody. She gets to feeling depressed, and then she says she has to go off by herself to 'think things over.' Sometimes she goes for several days at a time. She never tells me where she's going or where she's been. Usually when she comes back things are worse than when she left.

"I really don't know what to do about the situation. I threatened twice to put her out of the house if she saw that other man again. Then she went ahead and saw him again anyway. I don't know what to do now. I don't want to lose her. I still love her, and besides, the children need a mother. I talked with my lawyer about the situation, and he said to wait a while and not do anything that would force her into the other man's arms. Maybe she will come to her senses or get some psychiatric help.

"Our sex life is down to absolutely nothing. When she permits me to touch her at all, she makes it very clear that I may have her body but under no circumstances will she respond to me. She seems to be trying to punish me for something. I can't understand it. She had a very forceful dominating father who always told her what to do. I always thought she would like being allowed to make her own decisions, but that isn't the way it appears to be at all. She doesn't even want to decide anything—even what color dress to wear. She seems to want me to tell her what to do. And I don't make decisions easily myself. I hate to make people angry with me.

"She has offered to stay on living with me at the house in a brother-sister relationship. I don't really want to do that, but I remember what my lawyer said about not driving her out. My cousin thinks I should throw her out, but I just can't do that. Tell me what I should do."

Getting older

Still another reason is that the man or woman feels he is abused not so much by his mate as by increasing age. Much has been written about the so-called male climacteric, which often includes the notion that men, foreseeing the end of their sexual prowess, go out for one last fling. Many mature men do want the ego-building satisfaction of having a young woman sexually attracted to them. The difference in ages and interests usually makes such relationships either exploitative or unrewarding.

Age affects female adultery as well. Infidelity soon after the birth of a baby may indicate that a woman is seeking to reassure herself of her ability to attract men, despite her maternal role. If unfaithfulness occurs later in life, it may represent a desire on the part of the woman to compete with her daughter and so demonstrate to herself that she has not lost her femininity. Some women need even more reassurance of their continued desirability after their menopause. This need sometimes leads such women to take part in adultery for the first time in their lives.

Since it is probable that more males than females are involved in middle-life adultery, let's first take a look at a fairly typical male case:

CASE 50 DELLA AND GEORGE

"I think he's just gone crazy," Della told the counselor. "Here he is, a respectable businessman of forty-five and he's gone off chasing after some twenty-three-year-old sex symbol. She works in his office—or at least she did until I raised such a fuss. I threatened to go to the president of the company and then he would fire them both. There was no excuse for this! My daughters are eighteen and sixteen. When I told them about it, they were shocked, believe me. One of them told him what a terrible father she thought he was. The other, the younger one, just hung her head and said nothing. But I know she thought it was terrible, too, the way he was acting.

"It isn't as if he were some real lover type who needed more than I could give him. Actually, he never was much at making love, and in the last few years there have been times when he wasn't even able to have intercourse at all.

"And of all the people to choose, that flighty little tramp at his office was the worst. I wonder what's the matter with him; he must be sick to take up with her. She's just a little mouse without any brains. Oh, she has a figure all right, but that's all she has.

"I really don't understand it. I tried all my life to make a good home for him. I've always had his dinner ready. I've helped him by scrimping and saving. I've raised the girls so he could be proud of them and he rewards me this way. I really should divorce him. He deserves to be punished for this."

George didn't deny any of his wife's accusations when he saw the counselor. In fact, he enlarged on many of them. "Yes, it's true. From the outside Della was everything a respectable wife should be. She did get my supper. She did scrimp and save. She did take care of the girls. But once they got old enough to talk with her, she never really talked with me again. This girl in the office, Caroline, would listen to me. She understood me in a way that I don't think Della ever did. And when she told me she loved me, I got a thrill I never had before. I felt young again—as if life wasn't really over for me. And when she let me know that she wanted *me to touch her, I was happy for the first time in twenty years.*

"In a way, it was like back when Della and I were first married. It was playing house all over again. Caroline was so neat and tidy, not only in the way she kept her apartment but also in the way she kept herself. She was immaculately clean about everything. I'll tell you, Della has gotten a little careless and dumpy lately. But Caroline was young and alive. She was graceful to watch. I still can't believe that she would really love me. But she did.

"It's over now," George added sadly. "I didn't end it; Caroline did. All of a sudden she seemed to turn cold and unresponsive. I guess it really wasn't any one thing that did it. An old boyfriend of hers came back and she started going with him again. I probably suffered in comparison with him. But I also think she was beginning to see that I wasn't the hero she thought I was. Part of the problem was that I really wasn't *that hero, and I knew it better than she did. I couldn't keep up the pretense forever. I felt guilty about what was going on, and I guess some of my guilt and anxiety was transmitted to her. She didn't want guilt and anxiety. She wanted courage and leadership, so she turned away from me.*

"Now I guess I need Della more than I ever did. But she's mad at me now and she's turned the girls against me. I don't know what I'll do now. I sure need somebody to help me."

Opportunity for involvement

Situational circumstances—some accidental—can often play a part in an adventure into infidelity and in creating a fourth type.

The availability of a large number of young, sexually emancipated women in today's society who are eager to establish relationships with mature men has given the problem a new social dimension. Today's executive is more likely to meet more of these young women in more private situations in one day's time than his great-grandfather met in the course of his lifetime. Moreover, he often meets them at a period in his life when he has lost much of his youthful idealism and at a time in his life when his marriage relationship with his wife has begun to wear thin.

Even so, it is questionable how many married men deliberately set out with the conscious intent of having an extramarital affair. Most have no intention of being unfaithful when they befriend the secretary who works in the office. Extramarital sex is at the end of a long progression. The first step may be talking with the secretary about her desperate financial problems; the second step may be taking her to lunch so that they can talk at greater length about her problems; the third step may be offering to drive her home each night to save her carfare; and so forth. It is possible, of course, that this sweet, kind lovable fellow might have gotten into difficulty with some other girl if he had not with this one. But certainly *this* particular episode would not have occurred had he not met *this* particular girl at *this* particular time.

There are other situational circumstances that can play a part in adultery, as the following case illustrates:

CASE 51 MARTHA AND KEN

"After she started working, Martha couldn't seem to leave the men alone," Ken told the counselor. *"Oh, I knew there was a bunch of wolves at that big industrial plant, but she made it very easy for them. I should never have let her go there in the first place. I wouldn't have if I knew then what I know now. But she changed! When I married her she was a quiet, shy type of woman. She did everything I told her to do. As a matter of fact, sometimes I wished she would have had a little more spunk. I had to tell her what to do most of the time. Sometimes I even had to do the housework. She seemed afraid that she couldn't do it well enough to suit me. She will tell you I criticized her a lot, and she's probably right, but I knew she was capable of doing so much more than she did.*

"It isn't as if there was just one man, now that she's working outside the home. She's had three or four. After the first one, I told her she had to quit playing around. But she wouldn't do it. She threatened to leave me. I put up with it as long as I could, and after the last one I walked out. Now I sort of wish I hadn't, because she didn't come to her senses like I thought she would. Now she keeps telling me she isn't sure she really wants me back. But I want her. And I sure want my kids."

Martha started out by telling the counselor that as a child she'd been shy and always felt a little inferior. "I had crooked teeth and I always thought of myself as rather homely," Martha said. "About three years ago, though, I got my teeth straightened. All of a sudden I began to feel differently about myself. The men began to look at me. Even so, none of this with the men would have happened if it hadn't been that Ken wanted me to go to work. We needed the money, but I sort of resented him pushing me out.

"Anyway, I soon found I liked it at the plant. There are a lot of men there, and they told me a lot of nice things. When somebody flatters me, I'm gone. I didn't think about the consequences, and I didn't care whether the men were married or not. I remember the first man. He really made me feel like something special. I had a kind of excitement inside of me that I had never known before. He made me feel important—not like Ken. Ken was always critical at home. Ken could do the housework better than I could, so sometimes I'd let him.

"When I got to work I felt very independent, especially after I got my first paycheck. Then I knew I could take care of myself and the children, too, if I had to. Up until then I had always been afraid that something might happen to me if I didn't do just what Ken said. I always thought I had to have somebody to take care of me, but now I don't, and I'm not going to put up with Ken's criticizing anymore.

"I'm not sure I'll ever let Ken come home. He keeps begging me. But why should I? I'm still having a good time at the plant. The kids are well taken care of. Ken sends me money in addition to what I make. I don't even think about Ken much anymore. And when I do, I feel a little sorry for him. The only time I even wanted to call him was a week or so ago, when I found out that he had gone out with another woman. It's a funny thing: That made me interested in him for the first time in months. I don't understand it, but that's the way it is."

Fear of missing something

Not far removed from the people who wander into extramarital sex accidentally are the people who arrive there because they are afraid they may miss something. Single women have reported that they regularly encounter married men who want to establish illicit relationships. Some of these men are perennial wolves, but there are also more timid men who make an approach, the single women think, simply because they have heard that everybody else is "doing it," and they do not want to miss out on what they have been led to believe is today's most popular thrill.

Several of the single women report that it is fairly easy to send these men back home by using just a little amateur psychology. There are, however, many men and women who enter an extramarital affair at least once, just so they can say they have not missed anything.[19]

In all of these cases of infidelity, one fact is certain. Each partner decided on his or her own to participate. Some will find this hard to admit.

WHAT DO PARTNERS DO?

Understanding that there are different reasons for extramarital relationships sometimes makes it easier for both partners to know what to do. For if anything at all is to be accomplished in saving or improving a marriage relationship after infidelity has taken place, both partners must achieve some new insights into the dynamics of their own behavior. It is as important for the aggrieved partner to recognize the extent to which he has contributed to the infidelity as it is for the errant partner to come to understand why he behaved the way he did. As a matter of fact, it is frequently the aggrieved partner who must get the insights first, for if he or she does not take the right action, the marriage may be destroyed before anything constructive *can* be done.

Most aggrieved partners do the wrong thing when they initially find out about their spouses' infidelity. For example, some wives who find out that their husbands have been unfaithful seek sympathy from a neighbor or a friend by telling her the whole story. Only later do they realize that revealing the details hurt their pride as much as the infidelity itself did.

Another woman may order her husband out of the marriage bed, only to recognize later that this has perpetuated and enlarged the probability of his infidelity. Another woman may seek a quick divorce, later to realize that she did not want to lose her husband but rather to regain him. She was only trying to threaten him into being faithful again.

Another woman may seek out her husband's sex partner—the "other woman"—and beg her to let her husband alone. Only later does this wife realize that she had added to the other woman's self-assurance and so possibly increased her influence over the husband.

Still another wife may take a moral, judgmental attitude, accusing her husband of "being bad." This undoubtedly will put him on the defensive, but it is very questionable that it will make him regret his infidelity.

[19]Richard H. Klemer, *A Man for Every Woman*, New York, Macmillan, 1959.

Another woman may punish her husband with silence, only to realize later that lack of communication was the problem in the first place. And yet another wife may play the role of martyr with a dramatic ability worthy of Sarah Bernhardt, only to convince her husband that he was right to seek the other woman who did not openly try to manipulate him.

While all these behaviors are unproductive or destructive in *some* cases, they are not necessarily so in *all* cases. Each situation has to be handled on its own merits. The aggrieved partner can best serve himself and his marriage by carefully examining his own role, discussing with his partner the basic backgrounds of the problem, and, with dignity and self-assurance, taking the action that seems most likely to lead to some sort of permanent solution. Consider the following case:

CASE 52 CONNIE AND SAM

"As I look back on it now," Connie told the counselor, *"I know I wanted Sam to find out that I had been unfaithful to him. Ever since we've been married I have been getting less emotional response from him than I wanted. He is the unemotional type who turns his back on feelings. It isn't only that he doesn't know how to enjoy the emotional qualities of music or of art, but I don't think he can even feel love or hate. Do you know what Sam did when he caught me in bed with Harold? He just turned around and walked out. Later on, he came around and wanted to discuss it like an adult. I thought the least he would do was to get a gun and shoot one or the other of us. Not Sam! Actually, I was a little disappointed the way Harold acted, too. After we were caught he stopped calling and didn't come around anymore.*

"The man I want must have feelings. *He must be happy, lively, and animated. He must laugh, and he must cry. I cry a lot, but I always feel even more frustrated after I have. Sam doesn't try to comfort me. He just withdraws. I don't think he has any feelings whatsoever.*

"The funny thing is, he thinks he's a good husband because he stays home and doesn't chase after women and doesn't get drunk. I think he is a poor husband because he allows me complete freedom. He even offers to keep the kids while I go out. I want a husband who cares.

"My mother felt sorry for herself most of the time," Connie continued, *"and she controlled me by making me feel bad. She was a complete martyr. I used to hate it. But, would you believe it, I actually think that even though I hated it, I'm acting like my mother myself. Sometimes I catch myself being happier when I feel abused than I am when things work*

out well. I guess since he won't give me any emotion, I have to create it some way.

"As a matter of fact, that's why I'm continuing to call Harold every once in a while. It isn't really that I want Harold; I just want some excitement. I just want something to happen in my life other than washing dishes and changing diapers. Oh, I know I'm melodramatic. I play little scenes inside my head all the time. But what else am I going to do, married to this unimaginative jerk?"

Sam showed very little emotion when he talked to the counselor. "When I found Connie and Harold together, I was stunned," Sam said. "But I tried to be calm and logical about it. I've always tried to be calm and logical about things, but after a while I began to think that maybe a part of the problem was that I hadn't taken her out very much lately. She's always so busy with the kids, and she makes such a fuss about how bad things are for her when I get home, that I don't feel like taking her out. So anyway, I went to her, and I told her that I would forget all about the thing with Harold if she would, too. I thought she would be pleased that I was going to forgive her. She wasn't pleased at all. She screamed at the top of her voice until the police came. Sometimes I wonder why I married her. I don't think I ever really understood her. She apparently wants something that I can't give her. I don't know why she wants to make such a fuss. I've always thought it was good to be calm. I like to be objective about things, and anger is not using good judgment. There just isn't anything worth fighting about.

"When I was growing up, my father was very strict. He criticized me a great deal, so I try not to be overcritical with her. But she won't discuss things logically. If I try to tell her even very gently that there might be a better way to do something, she just begins to cry and scream, 'Oh I can never do anything right,' so then I have to apologize.

"She gets so excited about little things. I forgot our anniversary a week or so ago, and you should have heard her carry on. I think she got more emotional satisfaction out of my forgetting than she would have if I had brought her a gift. Sometimes I think she is pushing me to fight with her. I don't like to fight. But she keeps pushing and pushing and pushing until she stirs something up.

"She left home last week. She took the kids with her, and she rented an apartment. What shall I do now, let her have a divorce? Seek a divorce myself? Perhaps I would have a better chance of getting the children that way? Or should I try and make up with her? I think after she has had a little more of Harold she will have had enough. That fellow couldn't even *get along with his own wife, and he isn't going to be able to get along with Connie for very long."*

Obviously both partners—aggrieved and errant—have to help each other, through communication, to understand their emotional involvements and psychological needs. They may have to see and admit the satisfactions that the "other woman" or the "other man" has been providing for their mates.

CASE 53 KAY

"I was terribly unhappy with our marriage," Kay stated to the counselor. "Sometimes I think it was because I was somewhat older than the average mother of preschool children, which means I had been independent for a longer period of time. I got so bored, unhappy, and depressed at home that I felt like chucking the whole thing."

Further information revealed that at times she had become uncertain of herself as a functioning person in the home, and that she had a strong desire to punish herself by means of self-accusations.

Her irregular periods of depression had left her easy-going but financially successful husband Bruce feeling guilty about his possible failure to be more serious in his endeavors as husband and father. "But recently," Kay revealed, "I have a new outlook on life and Bruce is the benefactor."

Kay told of an affair with another man, about which she feels somewhat guilty and wonders if she should tell Bruce. Verbally she was able to express her disagreement with society's standards that a person can love only one other person of the opposite sex, and her actions declared the same view. However, her conscience still bothers her.

In spite of her guilty feelings she is able to recognize positive values in the relationship with the other man. "It is a beautiful relationship. We confide deeply in each other. It broadens my outlook on life and helps me considerably," she stated with a clear note of happiness. "Would you recommend that I tell Bruce? I am positive he believes that a couple should have a monogamous marriage."

It is revealing to examine the feelings of one wife who met the woman she knew to be her husband's friend by chance. It gave the wife the opportunity to assess realistically the ability of the other woman to attract the unfaithful husband. The wife soon concluded that, under other circumstances, she herself would wind up liking the other woman, for she found her to be warm and accepting, easy to talk with, and nondemanding, calmly reassuring, and stimulatingly enthusiastic. Far from being a young sexpot, the other woman was in fact a gracious, mature human being who met deep emotional needs within people, regardless of their age or sex. Moreover, the other woman exuded quiet confidence about herself, about her environment, and especially about sexual activities.

As a result of her contact with the other woman, this wife said: "I have learned that I am a taking person. I have placed my needs first and under the guise of not being a nagging wife, I simply turned my back. Lucille—that's the other woman—gave my husband a mature love versus my taking, clinging variety. To be truly mature is to be able to give, and the immature take, cling, and refuse responsibility. I never realized before that this applies to sexual adjustment. Now I can see some of Don's effort to give me a mature relationship. Living with me must be like living with a child in many ways—like a case of arrested development. You can't make love to a child. No wonder my husband chased girls and devoted so many hours to the adult world of business, and no wonder he spent those months with Lucille, who gave him the mature adult love and mature companionship and security that he so desperately needed and still needs."

If aggrieved partners can see the realities of the situation and are motivated to some self-improvement, they cannot help but improve the marriage relationship.

17

MONEY: WHO MAKES IT AND WHO SPENDS IT

Many Americans—and especially many college-educated Americans—have as much difficulty spending money as they do making it. As income levels off and standards of living and prices continue to rise, more and more decisions of ever-increasing complexity have to be made within families concerning how money should be used. In the upper-middle-income brackets, where there is enough income to make a decision difficult, but not enough so that everyone can have everything he wants, a new problem presents itself.

Decisions about money are a common source of conflict between husbands and wives. If it is not the greatest source of friction, it is very close to it.

Given modern society, with its enormous emphasis on the accumulation of material things, with its conspicuous consumption, with its keeping-up-with-the-Joneses, and with its mass-media-stimulated appetites, and given the increased potential in the urban society for marrying a mate who has a value system different from one's own, it is almost inevitable that there will be trouble in many marriages. Many are almost completely unaware of potential differences over making and spending money.

WHEN BOTH PARTNERS EARN

More and more married women are earning part of the family income by working outside the home. About two-fifths of all women employed are married, and many of them have children. About two-fifths of all married women work. More women are working longer and taking less time off the job to care for their children. The expectation that women will work is increasing. Although some upper-middle-class women claim to be working for personal fulfillment, the majority of women working do so because the husband's salary cannot cover the expenses of the standard of living they have set for their families.

It is a curious paradox that women college students inevitably indicate they intend to work only until the children are born, yet observation of these same students later shows they are working longer than they had ever dreamed they would.

The expectation that women will work, combined with an acceptance of self-supporting women, has led many women to demand more voice in how they are to be treated in a marriage relationship. Many women thought they would like having their husbands make the decisions for them and indeed did like it for about five years. But they began to dislike helping earn the income without being given an equal voice in decisions as to where it was spent.

Some of these same women are refusing to move when their husbands have offers of promotion which would require transfer to another locale. This is only a trend, however. By far the most families operate around the husband's job still. Even when husbands vocally support equality of men and women, somehow their families still revolve around the husband's job.

When women choose to work, whether or not their incomes are necessary to meet their freely chosen higher standard of living, it appears that the husband-wife relationship is often strengthened.[1] The explanation for this is that when a wife actually *chooses* to work she is not defying anyone, least of all her husband. She is not implying that he cannot make enough money. She is probably more pleased with the world, and all of this affects her relationship with her husband.

What would happen if *husbands* could choose to work or not with social sanction? They really cannot choose not to work without recriminations from society. Would marriages be better if neither the husband nor the wife had a socially sanctioned choice? One husband announced that he was going to quit work just as many wives do, whereupon his wife agreed, on condition that he give himself a socially accepted title such as "tree farmer" or "consultant" or "philosopher." Both were jesting, yet both were very serious.

In this day of women's liberation and men's liberation, it seems curious to have young men like Harry in the case below still wanting to be the sole breadwinner.

CASE 54 HARRY AND DEB

Harry's mother never worked, although the extra income could have been used. His father was somewhat possessive of his wife and she did all that she could to keep her husband and children happy. Neither of his parents finished high school and they were very proud when he graduated. All of the major decisions in the family were made by his father.

Deb's father was a successful businessman in town and her mother worked in a beauty salon in their home. Her family took long vacations and enjoyed family activities. Most decisions were made jointly by both her parents. When she began to date Harry her parents were somewhat concerned. Since Deb seemed very happy with Harry and had not dated much before this, they did not try to interfere with her happiness.

On her first trip to the marriage counselor Deb was almost hysterical.

[1]Susan Orden and Norman Bradburn, "Working Wives and Marriage Happiness," *American Journal of Sociology,* **74** (January, 1969), 392–407.

"Harry and I met three years ago. He was so nice to me then. I had never dated very much and I was delighted. I knew that we were from really different families, but we were in love and we would not let that create a problem. Things went really well for a time. When I first met Harold's parents they really seemed to like me. After we'd been married awhile, though, they began to criticize me all the time. I couldn't do anything to satisfy them. I spend too much on clothes. My dresses are too short. And you'd think that having my hair done every week was some kind of sin! I tried going to Harold's church with him for awhile after we were married, but I just couldn't take it. Everyone talks at the same time and the whole service is noisy. It really is not reverent at all. Harold's parents were pretty upset when we started going to my church. Now that I want to go over to the community college and take some courses, Harold has hit the ceiling! He doesn't want me to get out of the house. When we were first married I wanted to work, but Harry said no wife of his was going to work. I think he was just afraid that I'd find someone else. I just can't understand why he doesn't want me to go to the community college. He says that he thinks we should start a family. Why can't he see that what we need is money—not a baby?"

When Harry talked to the counselor he seemed very nervous. "Deb just wants everything. I know that I can't give her everything she wants and had before we were married, but I work hard and I just got another raise. She knew that things wouldn't be perfect for a while after we were married. She offered to work when we were first married, but I just didn't want my wife to work. Besides, a woman's place is in the home. She doesn't want to visit my parents because she says they don't like her. Truth is she just doesn't try to get along with them. She dresses a little mod for my parents, but they try not to say much about it. I've talked with her several times about starting a family, but each time she finds some excuse to stall. This time is the limit. She wants to go over to the community college to take some courses so that she can get a job. She knows that I don't want her to work. I think it's time we had a child. After all, we've been married almost two years!"

THE SPENDING PROBLEM

In spending, as in every other sensitive area of marriage, two of the major sources of conflict are, first, the different value conditioning that each of the mates has had in his childhood, and second, the complex of anxieties, attitudes, and behaviors that make up each partner's personality. In addition, a particular family's financial and affectional circumstances at any given time have considerable influence on its spending problems. So too does the spending knowledge that each mate brings to the marriage or acquires as the marriage goes along. Each of these four factors, social conditioning, personality, circumstances, and knowledge, will be discussed in turn.

SOCIAL-CONDITIONING FACTORS

Not everybody who lives in Maine is thrifty, and not everybody who lives in Las Vegas is a wheeler-dealer type. Nor is every Scotsman parsimonious or every foreign prince a wastrel. It is true, however, that there are subcultural group patterns of spending. Saving is more valued in some social circles and conspicuous consumption in others. A woman who expects that she will be able to show what a good provider her husband is by the number of mink coats she has is not going to be very happy married to a man who believes that money is to save and that any display of wealth is unseemly.

Specific buying habits

Both general attitudes toward spending (and earning) money and some specific habits of how and what to purchase are acquired in childhood. A child reared in a family where the acquisition of money and conspicuous consumption are primary values will usually form his attitudes and judge his own performance by these values. Interestingly, both the child who grows up in a very well-to-do home where spending one dollar more or less has little meaning, and the child who grows up in a very deprived home where there is a desperate longing for a dollar to spend, may turn out to be unreasoning spenders. So, of course, may a middle-class child. Ordinarily though, he will have more of a middle-class value system of postponing present satisfaction in order to ensure future rewards. And if he has grown up in one of the more traditional homes, he may have absorbed something of the Puritan ethic that thrift is a virtue and ostentatious spending is not in good taste.

Along with these general values, the child often acquires specific buying habits. Even within the same socioeconomic group (and perhaps within the same subcultural group), two families will spend their money differently. One family believes in buying the best, on the theory that it will wear longer. Another will buy the least expensive because of its low replacement cost. Each of these families would insist that theirs was the more thrifty program. Both might get along exceedingly well with their own purchasing patterns. The only trouble might come when the daughter of one of these families married the son of the other. Even though they shared the common value of thrift, they might disagree violently over the ways to arrive at that objective. She might be outraged to think that he paid $3 for a pair of socks, but he might point out that they will last four times as long as a 75¢ pair of socks. She might then retort that, even if they did, she might have to darn them before they were completely worn out, but if he had bought the 75¢ socks, he could have afforded to throw them away. And so the argument would go on interminably.

In marriage counseling practice, the differential childhood conditioning about money is one of the most common problems brought to the counselor.

CASE 55 CURT AND VIRGINIA

"Curt drives me nutty with his constant penny pinching," Virginia told the counselor. "We have plenty of money now. Yes, it was difficult when he was in dental school and even after he was out starting his practice. But now he makes almost $50,000 a year, and we still fight all the time about spending a dime. He keeps all sorts of records on everything we spend. He grudgingly hands a few dollars to me and the children. The way he acts, you'd think he could take it with him. Whenever I try to talk with him about not being so stingy, he just says that he's trying to build up an investment income for me and the kids later on. And that's a very big laugh. We will have an investment income later on, but it will come from my inheritance. My parents are well-to-do; as a matter of fact, I think that's part of the problem. He's constantly trying to show my father that he can accumulate money, too. Actually, my father really didn't accumulate his; my great-grandfather did.

"Anyway, trying to show my father how good he is is only part of the problem. The real difficulty arises from the fact that Curt's father was always a record-keeper. That's what makes it so funny. Curt's father never really made any money, but he always kept track of everything down to the last penny. And he made his boys do it, too, or he wouldn't give them their allowances. It didn't take on his older son, Jack, but it sure took on Curt. Jack's been in and out of bankruptcy several times, but Curt, who doesn't ever need to think about his future income, keeps track of everything.

"I guess Curt's father got it from his father, too. They came from an old European family where pinching pennies was sort of their religion. I suppose they had to scrimp up until the time they came. But I think there was more to it than that. I once went to a neighborhood meeting where his

father and mother lived. All the neighbors who came from the same background were exactly the same way about money.

"The worst part about all this is how confusing it is for the children. No, I take that back. That isn't the worst part. The worst part is the fights we have in front of the children, because I want to live a little now and because I believe you have to dress well and live well if your children are going to have the respect of their neighbors.

"If he had his way we would drive around in a beat-up old car and we would all wear rags. He can't seem to see that nobody would send their children to him for orthodontia then. Who wants to trust a professional man whose wife and children look dowdy?"

Curt told the story a little differently. "I know she told you I was a miser, and by her family's standards, I guess I am. She's probably told you too that we don't have to worry because she's going to have a great inheritance. Well, let me tell you this. There isn't going to be very much inheritance, if any. Her father never had to work for anything in his life, and consequently he's gone through the family fortune. There's going to be darn little left. I'm sure Virginia must know this intellectually, but she can't believe it emotionally. She still acts and behaves as if she were rich.

"Sure I raise a row when I get a bill for $350 for one dress. I bet my mother didn't spend $350 for all the clothes she had in her life. But it isn't really the amount that upsets me. It's the fact that she doesn't even know how much some of her dresses cost. She just goes down and picks out one and waves her hand airily and says 'I'll take this.' She has absolutely no sense of responsibility. My mother helped my father to save money for what we needed. In fact, she sometimes made the decision that it was better to save the money than to spend it for something we really didn't need.

"I want to provide something for Virginia and the kids. I'm not a rich man. If serious illness kept me away from my practice for any extended period, it could cut heavily into our standard of living. I haven't been practicing long enough to build up complete security. But even that isn't the point. It just plain isn't right to spend hundreds and hundreds of dollars on silly little gewgaws when there are other people who have so little. I wish to goodness my wife could know the problems that some of our patients have. I don't think she realizes that some of the dollars she just throws away may represent a great sacrifice to a patient who paid my bill.

"She feels we have to spend the money in order to keep up with her friends and my colleagues. Well, I don't think so. If the children are upset, it's because she's spoiled them, and I'll tell you I'm not going to have that much longer."

PERSONALITY FACTORS

The line between family conditioning and personality factors is very blurred. But there is enough difference between the spending patterns of children from the same family to make it clear that spending is sometimes a very personal thing. Within the same household, one brother may grow up to be a compulsive gambler and another a tight-fisted saver.

The tendency to worry, which seems to be built into some youngsters very early, has an important effect on later spending patterns. Those who cannot tolerate the anxiety of any form of risk try to spend less and save more. In this, though, they may be self-defeating, if they turn down risk opportunities to make more money that would provide them in the long run with more security.

A chronic worrier about spending may have a difficult time in life even if he never marries, but he is sure to aggravate his problems if he does marry. First, he will have the added responsibility of a wife and children. Worse yet, however, if he marries a woman who is as anxious as he is, they will probably increase each other's anxiety either deliberately or unconsciously by asking each other for reassurances of security. If, by the very seeking of this reassurance, each suggests to the other the possibility of failure, they will both wallow more deeply in anxiety.

CASE 56 JUDY AND CHRIS

"I've had about all I can take from Judy," Chris said. "Here I am owing money to my father, and he doesn't make half of what I do. It's ridiculous. I knew Judy was from a different background when I dated her, but my parents' opposition only made me want to see her more. I didn't mean to marry her, but then she got pregnant and I had to. It was my last year at State and my parents had to support us till I graduated. As an architect I made good money for a beginning salary, but we were in debt, what with the baby and all, so Judy took a job to help out. That's when I really began to find out about her. With her own money coming in, she started running up more bills, so that we were worse off than before. Also, she couldn't hold a job at all because she couldn't get along with bosses. We've been married six years and she's had twice as many jobs. Last year she quit for good, but she didn't quit spending. Our little girl Cindy has three rooms full of toys. She even has her own kitchen, and Cindy and Judy both wear a different dress each day of the year. But that's not the worst part. Judy's got a whole staircase of younger brothers and sisters. Two of her brothers just got out of

reform school and the sixteen-year-old is married and has a baby. Judy's parents are separated, and she tries to support them all—with my money. I've got regular bills coming each month for the house, car, boat, and furniture besides all that. I've told her before she's got to stop it, and she's taken Cindy and left me three times to go live with her mother. This time she can stay."

Judy said, "Chris doesn't know what it's like to be the oldest of five children when both parents are alcoholics. I practically had to raise the other children, and even had to quit high school to provide the care my parents wouldn't. I don't see how I can sit back and enjoy affluence now when I know they're still struggling for enough to eat. If Chris loved me, he wouldn't mind me helping them now. Every cent had to go on food and other necessities when I was a child, and I sure don't want Cindy to have to miss out on all I did. Chris just doesn't seem to realize how important toys and pretty clothes are to children. I still love my family. How can I just desert them when they need me? Chris's parents think my family is terrible because we've been on welfare. That's the whole problem. They hated me before we were married, and now they talk against me when Chris borrows money. Actually, he's sharing investments in things like boats with his father. Chris always sells them for more than he pays and gives his father the profit. I don't see how Chris can say I'm bringing him down when actually he's richer than I ever dreamed to be. I made a mistake when I went home to Mama this time, because Chris doesn't know that I'm pregnant again and we've got to work this out."

It is possible for a chronic spending worrier to marry a woman who is more secure than he. This may be good for him, but sooner or later she may get tired of his constant worrying and become contemptuous of his lack of spending courage. When her reservoir of reassurance gives out, she may start to berate him and thus confirm to him that his anxiety was justified in the first place.

Immaturity

Insecurity is a big problem in spending the family income, but immaturity, another personality factor, is even worse. The marriage counselor often sees young married couples with a chronic pattern of immature spending.

CASE 57 LESTER AND LYDIA

"Lester takes money we need for the baby and spends it on his hobbies," Lydia told the counselor. *"He buys all sorts of fancy chrome parts for his car, and he spends hundreds of dollars on flying lessons and shotguns. Why anybody needs more than one shotgun I don't know, but he has five or six of them. I plead with him and beg him to let me have a little money for the baby every once in a while. But he just doesn't seem to care. We're three months behind with the pediatrician's bill, and sometimes there literally isn't enough for the child to eat.*

"All he says to me is, 'I make the money, and I'll decide how it is spent.' We would have been kicked out of our apartment for back rent a long time ago if it weren't for my parents. When we get too far behind in the rent, my father can't stand it anymore, and he gives me the money to pay it. But it's so embarrassing. Sometimes my family gives me money for clothes, too.

"I knew I couldn't have everything I used to have after I got married. But I don't think Lester even tries to get ahead. He's happy the way he is. He's so busy with the car and the flying that sometimes he's late to work, and he never volunteers for overtime. But even at that, he makes enough money so that we could live fairly comfortably if only he didn't blow it all. My family is getting very tired of bailing us out, and they are beginning to suggest that I leave him. I don't know what to do."

But Lester told the counselor, *"I was a freshman in college two years ago when she came to me and told me she was pregnant. I'll bet she didn't tell you about that. She put on a big act. I loved her, so I said, 'All right, we'll get married.' After we were married, it turned out she hadn't been pregnant at all. But she did get pregnant right away, and the baby came before we had been married a year.*

"Before we were married she used to be as proud as I was of my car. But now all the spending has to be her way. We have to live in an apartment we can't afford because her father wouldn't want her in any average neighborhood. I'm supposed to give up everything—all the things I really enjoy—so she can spoil the baby.

"I don't know what she told you, but we always have plenty to eat and a good place to live, even though it is too expensive for us. But I work hard for my money and I want some fun with it. My father used to tell me, 'You're only young once; don't let any woman take all your youth.'

"Besides, what I spend on my hobbies is only a small part of my income. The real trouble is that she has no sense about spending money. She

went downtown and paid $145 for a baby crib and $35 for a fancy blanket. She doesn't work, but she has to pay a maid one day a week to come in and clean the house so that she can take the baby over to see her mother. Then while she's there, her mother fills her full of a lot of trash like, 'What is that husband doing to you now?' Then she comes home and makes my life miserable about the car and flying. I don't care if she does leave. I used to have a lot more fun before we were married."

Obviously not all immature spenders are teenagers. Some older people do not know how to handle their money wisely, either.

There are some husbands and wives who try to use money to control the other person. Some men do not even let their wives know how much they make. They just dole out little dribbles of money so that their wives can pay the household bills as they come in. Often, even in these times, the male who behaves this way is unsure of his role, and fears that sharing spending decisions with his wife will somehow diminish his male status. Some such males use money as a form of punishment, denying a wife who has not behaved the way he thinks she should some of the things she wants.

The man is not the only one who uses money for control and for punishment. There are the few obvious cases in which women who come from higher income families buy or attempt to buy the affection or the adherence of their less well-to-do husbands. And there are many wives who punish their husbands for some insult, either real or imagined, by just going out and spending. In marriage counseling, this too, is often seen.

CASE **58** CHARLIE AND BETTY

"When I married Charlie he was so determined and motivated," Betty told the counselor. "My father approved of Charlie from the first because he was a hard worker and anxious to prove himself in the business world.

"Now, after a year of marriage, I think that Charlie has set his goals too high. He is determined to make a million before the ripe old age of thirty-five and money has actually become an obsession. He works so long and hard at the office and is already the highest paid worker there.

"Still, he isn't satisfied. Every possible minute is spent on some complicated scheme to make more money. He wants to invest every cent that he earns. He thrives on his work and sometimes is so keyed up that he can neither eat nor sleep well.

"As our income increases, I feel that we can raise our level of living. If we have more money, why can't we spend more? Charlie has a savings complex. He gets more satisfaction out of making money and saving it than he does out of the material things money can buy.

"Charlie gives me a small allowance which he terms 'your money.' The rest is his. I feel that the money in the bank is 'ours.' In the last few weeks I have been charging anything I wanted in the local stores. Charlie's reputation is good and opening accounts was no problem. Last week the bills came and Charlie raised the roof. He was like a wild man. He still hasn't gotten over it and has been a nervous wreck ever since. I had no idea it would upset him so much. I'm afraid he may do something drastic."

Charlie was equally upset over the pattern their married life was taking. "When I married Betty she was the most considerate and understanding woman I had ever known. She was so interested in the plans I had made for our future. I got a good job and began working hard so someday we would have all the money we could possibly want.

"Betty wants money and what it can bring now, without regard for the future. She has no interest in pursuing a career herself and becomes infuriated when I stay at the office past five o'clock. Yet, she certainly keeps after me for some of the money those overtime hours bring.

"I've come up with some really great business deals lately and you would think Betty could show some interest. Instead she harps on me day and night for more money. I've given her an adequate, no, a quite generous allowance but she is never satisfied.

"Well, last week was the clincher! When I started paying the bills, I found that she had opened up charge accounts at every large store in town and had managed to accumulate a large bill at each already. I must admit that the scene that followed was a little wild, but she did go behind my back. I'm not going to let her destroy everything I've worked for so hard."

Closely related to the kind of punishment spending that we saw in the case of Betty and Charlie is *compulsive* spending. This is a form of repetitive neurotic behavior in which the spender's motive is often unconscious. In some cases, it may represent a repressed desire to punish a parent or to punish oneself. In other cases, it may represent a form of sexual sublimation or signal deep feelings of inadequacy. In any case, when spending has become totally irrational and uncontrollably compelling, there is a clear indication of a psychological aberration requiring psychotherapy for treatment.

Before we leave the matter of personality factors in spending, there should be some mention of "his" and "her" money. It is surprising how often individuals bring these feelings to marriage. Sometimes the husband feels that his income is "his" because he earns it. Often a wife who works outside the home believes that the additional income should belong to her and that she should have absolute control over its expenditure, despite the fact that her husband is paying all the family bills out of his income. It is possible that the seeds for many of these "his and her" attitudes are planted in the childhood home. Parents deliberately give *each* child his own allowance and encourage him to spend it on himself. The idea of a brother and sister pooling allowances is almost unthinkable. With this pattern so well established, it is hardly surprising that in later life "his" and "her" money sometimes becomes a problem.

CASE 59 JIMMY AND SHIRLEY

Jimmy came from a middle-class family where the father was a very dominant figure in the household. He made all major decisions and gave his wife a household allowance. His father was very possessive and the family members were expected to account for their whereabouts.

Shirley, too, came from a middle-class family. Her parents frequently went on trips separately. They made all major decisions together and their money was "ours," not "yours" and "mine." Affectional display was free and a great amount of trust was present.

"I don't understand what's wrong," Jimmy told the counselor. "While we were dating and for a while after we were married Shirley was so open in showing her affection for me. It was really wonderful. But lately she doesn't welcome me home with a hug and a kiss. She turns away from me and makes it very evident she doesn't want me to touch her.

"When we were dating I'd let her decide where we'd go eat and we'd discuss what movie to see but those decisions were really nothing. But now she thinks she should have as much to say about how we spend my money as I do. I've provided for her—she has lots of clothes, all the conveniences in the home that she could want. What else could she want? Anyway, what does she know about cars and things like that? Not much. When she starts earning money she can decide how to spend it."

When Shirley came in she was visibly upset. "Jimmy was the sweetest guy I had ever met, or so I thought until a few months ago. He's changed so much so fast. When we were dating and even after we were married he was always asking my advice.

"He really knows how to make me feel like a beggar—and a dumb one at that. He's always talking about 'his money'—I'm just a charity case. And I don't know enough about anything to be able to have a say in how 'his money' is spent. He just went out and bought a new car last week—then came home and told me about it. We really couldn't afford it just now and the color is really awful—purple, would you believe it? And he couldn't understand why I was upset."

CIRCUMSTANCES REQUIRING A FINANCIAL OUTLAY

Some circumstances that are reasonably predictable, as well as some that are not predictable, have an influence on any family's spending problems. Many young couples, even well-educated ones, start out their marriages these days heavily in debt. Because of our affluent society's emphasis on instant gratification and the desire to begin marriages at the same level their parents now have, newlyweds often buy expensive appliances and automobiles. Sometimes they buy these costly items without figuring out the total monthly payments and the relationship of those payments to their income. Even some others who do manage to balance their budgets are perilously close to insolvency. An unexpected pregnancy, an illness, the loss of a job, or any one of a hundred other emergencies can put them on the financial rocks.

If this happens, the damage to their credit rating is bad enough, but the damage to their marriage relationship may be even worse. Soon they may be blaming each other for their financial mess. Consider the case of the young divorcee who was explaining to the counselor how it happened:

CASE 60 VIVIAN AND DAN

"I can see it now, but I couldn't then," Vivian told the counselor. "We wanted everything to be nice when we first got married. We bought a larger house than we could afford, a lot of furniture, a new car, a color television, and we spent a lot of money on skiing weekends. We also had a boat and a trailer. I was working at the time, and it seemed like we could pay for everything easily.

"But then I got pregnant. We still might have been all right except that there were complications with my pregnancy and I had to quit my job. I haven't been able to go back to work since, and that was two years ago.

"Anyway, then we had doctor bills on top of everything else. At first

it just seemed to increase our love for each other—the fact that we were facing difficulty together. But soon (it seemed like almost too soon) the creditors began to call. At first I didn't mind very much, but they began to get unpleasant and I got edgy. Sometimes I would tell Dan about them, and he would get angry. I can see now that he felt terribly guilty, but I couldn't understand it then. Then he began to get angry with me, and he seemed almost irrational. He would accuse me of being a bad manager, and sometimes he would say it was all my fault because I got pregnant. That would make me so mad, and I would say some nasty things, too. They must have sounded much worse than I intended them to, because he went out and got a second job.

"But even that didn't solve all our financial problems, and it made him much more tired and upset. Pretty soon he was yelling and screaming at me most of the time. Then we really said some ugly things to each other. I guess once or twice I told him that if I had married somebody who was a better provider, this would never have happened. I didn't really mean it. Dan was a good husband.

"The thing that hurts most is that after we were divorced he sold the house and most of our beautiful furniture and things. He apparently got himself out of debt and now he's doing very well. He's moving up in his company, and he seems brighter and happier than I've ever seen him. How do you think that makes me feel? I know—in fact I'm positively certain— that if we hadn't had all those debts we could have had a good marriage. But when we got started the way we did, I never had a chance to show Dan how really good a wife I could be."

Spending and the family life cycle

There are some predictable phases that every family goes through in the family life cycle that have an effect on spending the income. The first stage, the honeymoon period, often finds both partners working. The newlyweds are often relatively well off if they do not succumb to the temptation to load up on material things. They may even be able to save a little for the periods of heavier expenditures ahead.

The second stage in the family life cycle often comes very quickly. The first child is born and expenses shoot up. And since the wife ordinarily stops working, income goes down. A second child is born, and the economic pinch is increased. This period is sometimes the most difficult of all financially. Most young husbands' earning power increases very slowly and usually does not keep up with the increase in expenses. This is the stage in which careful money management is most needed.

As the children grow and move on into the upper elementary-school grades and even into high school, the expenses increase further. However, after all the children are in school, many mothers are able to go back to at least part-time work (and by this time many want to). Consequently, in many families, the strain is eased somewhat. Moreover, a college-educated father's earnings will probably be increasing as the years go by.

But there may come another crisis period when the children are in college. Fortunately, by this time, the father's income is approaching its maximum level in many families, and often children themselves can help out. Moreover, some wives are by then able to work fulltime, and total family income may reach its highest level.

The next stage in the financial cycle of the family occurs when the children have left home. At this point, income is usually the highest. Often a college-educated wife is holding a full-time job. Investments are beginning to mature, and surplus income can be plowed back into investments, further increasing them. Hopefully this will be the time in which income for retirement can be built up.

The final stage in the cycle is retirement. Retirement income varies widely. Social Security will provide a bare minimum for some. For others who have had an opportunity to save and invest, retirement is a relatively easy time. Government subsidies in the form of income-tax exemptions and medical programs also help to improve the level of living for older folk. Although there are still many elderly people who live at and below the poverty level, especially those who have no savings and those whose fixed incomes cannot take into account the decline in the value of money, generally speaking the older American is financially better off now than he ever has been before.

It is probably good that many young marrieds believe that they are going to conquer all financial adversity and wind up with security and personal riches. If there were no such dreams, there would be no dreams to come true. On the other hand, this same bubbling optimism often prevents some young couples from realistically assessing the expenses and needs of the next stage in the family life cycle.

SPENDING KNOWLEDGE

The fourth major factor that influences spending decisions is the financial and management knowledge that both of the partners bring to the marriage.

Clearly, those people who have some realistic expectation concerning the value and limitations of money have a great advantage over those who don't.

Most families that are financially successful have some common characteristics. First of all, such families have goals, both long-range and short-range goals. Next, they are able to plan ahead because they are motivated to set aside present desires in deference to long-range satisfactions. If the family is to provide satisfaction as well as success, its members should have a genuine ability to communicate with each other and enough "give-and-take" adaptability to compromise.

On top of these things, however, the financially successful family usually works out for itself some system of spending that is acceptable to its members. The system can be formal or informal. Evelyn Duvall and Reuben Hill suggest that there are five common systems that families use for the allocation of the money:[2]

First, there is the "dole" system, in which one family member hands out the money a little bit at a time to the other family members. If this system is not fully accepted by the partners, it can make for constant conflict—either open or concealed behind trickery.

Second is the "family treasurer" system. Although this may often appear to be similar to the "dole" system, it differs in the spirit and nature of the relationship. Family members get a personal allowance. The rest is turned over to the treasurer, who pays all the bills and does most of the buying.

The third system is the "division of expenses" system. Certain spending is assigned to the husband (perhaps for rent, car, or insurance), and the other spending is the responsibility of the wife (perhaps food, utilities, or clothing). Additional spending is done by cooperative decision.

The fourth system is called the "joint account" system. Earnings of both husband and wife are put in a joint checking account from which either may draw to pay common or personal expenses. Often one partner or the other writes the monthly checks for the household bills. This system works well when both members are responsible and cooperative individuals and when the income consistently runs above the expenses.

The fifth is the "budget" system. Expenses are budgeted in advance by common agreement. Any excess goes into a common fund that is saved or spent only by common agreement.

Although many people think of the budget as a device for saving,

[2]Evelyn Duvall and Reuben Hill, *Being Married*, New York, Association Press, 1960, p. 251.

in reality it is a plan for *spending*. Basically it enables people to decide in advance what they want to spend their money for and then to be sure there is enough left to purchase those satisfactions previously agreed upon. The budget helps families to look at the whole spending picture and weigh short-range satisfactions against long-range goals.

It is probable that only a small portion of American families regularly and consistently attempt to live within a strict plan for spending. There are, though, many marriages in which the partners have turned to planning in order to get them out of some immediate difficulty at some time during the family life cycle.

Many people at all educational levels prefer not to plan, even though they know this may be the wise thing to do. Some argue that it takes all the fun out of spending. They would rather live impulsively, even though they know that in the long run this can only lead to periods of difficulty.

For those who *do* want to undertake a spending plan, all sorts of information about how to go about it is readily available. But in other areas of family finance, knowledge is not so easy to obtain. Moreover, many college-educated people are so busy acquiring knowledge to *make* money that they fail to acquire any that will help them to spend it wisely. Almost all girls have some introduction to buying food and clothing and many boys have some idea of how to buy an automobile, but college men and women ordinarily have very little functional knowledge about the really major purchases they will soon be making—houses, insurance, and investments. Often, less well educated people have a greater understanding of the practical workings of the commercial marketplace than do new college graduates. This is regrettable, for most colleges and almost all universities offer courses in family finance that could be useful.

Current consumer magazines, although they have some shortcomings, often provide information that is timely and readily applicable to the practical realities of family spending. For example, take the matter of buying a house, the largest single purchase most families make. Proper choice of a home can have a very great positive or negative effect on future family relationships. It may interest the prospective home buyer to know what percentage of the family income other people have apportioned to housing, the kinds of mortgage and credit plans available to the home buyer, and the philosophical advantages and disadvantages of buying a home versus renting one. But usually these matters are only tangential to the real buying problem when a couple is faced with actually finding a house in a new community. Often the realities of the market and the individual tastes of those who are buying are far more crucial factors. Specific information about current real-estate values in the local communities and practical tips about the best kind of heating and the closest shopping center are more important to home buyers at the moment of purchase than all the statistical tables and philosophical arguments.

Very practical guidelines are also available for newlyweds who are about to buy the family's two other major purchases—insurance and investments—if they will take the time to look for them and study the alternatives. The more eager the partners are to learn (and to learn together), the more successful the family spending patterns are going to be.

Because each family has its individual preferences, individual desires, and individual needs, it is probable that some learning has to come the hard way, through experience rather than through books. Spending mistakes can often hurt for years, but if the mistakes are not repeated, the lessons can be worth almost any cost.

Sidney Margolius has suggested a checklist of ten common spending errors:

1. constant payment of large finance charges on installment purchases
2. overspending for food
3. high housing and household-operating costs
4. heavy car and car-operating expenses
5. larger-than-necessary expenditures for insurance
6. heavy spending for commercial recreation
7. overpayment of income taxes
8. failure to time shopping to take advantage of opportunities
9. random spending for toiletries, cosmetics, and household drugs
10. failure to make savings produce maximum yield[3]

Checklists such as these can be helpful, but the most important knowledge that a marriage partner can have is his awareness of his mate's personal spending idiosyncrasies. Given an understanding plus a great deal of motivation, a lot of planning, and some intelligent use of readily available information, young marrieds can make up spending-knowledge deficiencies as they go along.

Those partners who can remember that spending patterns and anxieties—one's own as well as one's partner's—were conditioned a long time ago will have an easier time making the spending adjustment. For they are the partners who can, with patience and understanding, gently teach each other new ways and patiently reassure old insecurities. At the same

[3]By permission of Hawthorn Books, Inc., from *How to Make the Most of Your Money*. Copyright © 1968 by Sidney Margolius.

time, they can be flexible enough to learn some different ways themselves and steady enough to stay cool when the molehills seem like mountains.

Trying new things—such as letting the other partner handle all the money for a change—can often help to reduce tensions. But in the end, only when both partners *really* want to find a better way will it be found.

Since so much of one's spending attitudes and knowledge come from one's parents, it is appropriate to study intergenerational relationships next.

18

INTERGENERATIONAL RELATIONSHIPS IN ADULTHOOD

The generations referred to in this chapter are those in adulthood. Neither ages nor labels will be used to designate generations, but it is generally agreed that a generation is about eighteen to thirty years apart.

It is probably as likely that people differ in values as much *within* age groups or generations as they do *between* generations. Far too many people assume differences in beliefs, values, and behaviors to be directly related to an age group. Children are expected to be malleable and developing; adolescents are expected to be searching for identity; middle-aged people are expected to be the bastions of the cultural ideals; and the aging are expected to be looking for a way to give the reins to the younger generation. Some people happen to fit these stereotypes precisely. However, not all people fit this model of "inevitable" sequence of development.

Stereotypes of certain age groups have created biases that are hard to change. Yet you can name several people a generation older or younger than you who do not fit the stereotype of that age group. It is their outlook on life that makes them different. This tells the main point of this chapter on intergenerational relationships: Most problems between generations are value-specific, not age-specific.

BEHAVIOR IS VALUE-SPECIFIC

Age does have some bearing on a person's values. But more than that, the historic eras during which a person was certain ages—combined with his or her socioeconomic level, marital status, job, the ages of his or her children, and crises and experiences during each age—affect his or her present outlook. For example, a man born in the early 1920s to poor parents probably did not feel the impact of either the Roaring Twenties or the Great Depression: His family probably was not aware of the *avant garde* in the 1920s. The depression of the 1930s did not deal his family the devastating blow of losing a good income. Yet this same person may have joined the army in the 1940s, enabling him to receive a college degree and travel all over the world. Another man born in the early 1920s to a well-to-do family may have traveled all over the world when he was young, but lost all his status by the early 1930s due to the depression. He may have been exempted from the army due to a physical defect he was unaware of and worked in a defense plant instead of going to college. In the 1970s, these two men, just from the combination of events in the first twenty-five years of their lives, are going to have differing outlooks on life. The first had an upward movement in his life which built up his ego; the second faced defeat from the age of ten years.

Another man, born in the late 1930s, will have a different combination of historic eras and age categories. By the 1970s his outlook on life may be one of bitter disappointment because he had too little to fight for in his college days, instead of being part of a great national defense as in the 1940s. Historic eras do make their mark on a person.

What we tend to overlook is that everyone of every age is also being affected by today's historic era. Every adult person you know has experienced all the historic eras that today's college-age students have and has been changed by each era. The liberal views of the 1960s did liberalize most adults to some extent, as well as the teenagers who lived through that decade. Today's historic era is also affecting everyone—yes, your grandmother too.

Another thing that affects people as they move from one age span to another is their own personal makeup. A bitter, hard-to-talk-to forty-year-old woman was probably a little, if not a lot, that way as a thirty-year-old woman and as a twenty-year-old woman. A congenial sixty-year-old man probably did *not* develop into that from a tight-lipped, compulsive, thirty-year-old, yet people do change some from their experiences and the era at hand.

Probably one of the worst culprits to an understanding between adults of various ages is a person's own stereotyped notions of various age categories. Students in a marriage and family relationships class once laughed out loud at the notion that an eighty-year-old man could have sexual intercourse. Questioning them about their laughter brought forth the answer that they thought sexual potency diminished well before that—probably in the late forties! It is very possible that a certain eighty-year-old man could be potent and a certain forty-year-old man be impotent. Stereotyping hurts both men.

A belief that one should act a certain way, reinforced by responses from others who think he should act that way, almost assures control of that behavior. You can fall into your own stereotyping trap. You can categorize yourself and therefore be self-reinforcing and punishing as your conscience keeps you in line.

CASE 61 GERALD AND LIZA

"I hope she has suffered. The way she embarrassed me by running off and marrying that old man ten years ago. When people asked me what happened I didn't know what to say. All along she was writing to him while I was going to see her. He died last year after being an invalid the last

years of their marriage. She must have had it hard, though. She's nearly sixty-five now and that took her last years of spirit, I suppose. She says she's coming to see me, but I don't care." Gerald looked both put out and sad as he told this story. He's nearly seventy himself.

"I've loved Gerald for twenty years or more," Liza said. "I never stopped loving him even though I did marry Samuel. But you see, Gerald would act as if I wasn't even alive at times. I'd ask him to dinner and have it ready for him and he wouldn't even show up. He'd tell people we weren't going together, so I guessed he meant it.

"When Samuel suggested we marry because we weren't getting any younger, I thought it a good idea. But I haven't had any sort of marriage at all. Samuel was an invalid for so long. I have told Gerald all of this but he's too stubborn and his pride is too false to let me get through to him. We don't have many years left. We don't even have to get married. If he'd just accept me and welcome me, we'd have such a good companionship. We could fish and talk and cook and garden. But how do you tell a man that old he's got to start making sense?"

EMPATHETIC INTERGENERATIONAL RELATIONSHIPS

"You can't talk to them; they won't understand," could be said by any generation about the other. If the complaint could really be assigned to one generation, then we might take it more seriously. As it is, it shows that each generation thinks the other will not understand. Misperception is probably the greatest block to empathy with another person, no matter what the age. You can generally clear up misperceptions in three ways: first, ask the person; second, apply your knowledge of human behavior; and third, be aware of the combination of historic eras and personality variables of the person. Read the case of Leroy to see how intergenerational relationships are affected by historic eras, lack of knowledge of human behavior, and misperceptions.

CASE 62 LEROY

"I don't know what to do with Leroy," the father told the counselor. "He's twenty-four years old now. By the time I was his age, back down in Oklahoma, I was through college and out working for three years. I already had several thousand dollars in the bank, even though it was the depression. But not Leroy. He's been in and out of three colleges already. He makes

just enough C's and D's to balance his F's, and then he talks somebody into letting him stay on for another semester. I don't think it says much for the university that lets him stay on, but I want him to get a degree so badly that I'm not going to complain. He takes only a few courses each semester. He's pretty good at tennis, though. He gets on the tennis team whenever he's eligible. As a matter of fact, that's all he wants to do: play tennis. It's practically the only thing he does well. He even used to beat me.

"I've tried to cut him off financially a dozen times, but that doesn't do any good. The first time I decided to do it, I didn't send him any money for three months or so. He dropped out of school and got a job in a bar. But pretty soon he began to pile up debts, and I got letters from his creditors. He wrote some bad checks, and they were going to send him to jail. I bailed him out. What else could I do? Having a jail sentence would just ensure his turning into a bum.

"The tragedy is, the boy's got the ability. I know he has. When he was in elementary school, the teachers used to tell us he was bright. I had big hopes for Leroy. Somehow, though, he never seemed to measure up. I think most of the problem was that his mother spoiled him. If Leroy didn't do the work I assigned for him, she would try to wheedle me out of being upset about it. She'd excuse him and let him go off and play instead of sticking to what I'd told him to do. If he didn't do it well, she would say I had criticized him too severely. Maybe I was a little harsh, but no kid should be allowed to do sloppy work when he's capable of doing better.

"One reason why cutting off his financial support never worked was that she used to send him money on the side. I think she tried to buy his affection. I love him as much as she does—more even. I love him so much that I want him to make something of himself. She thinks loving him means doing everything for him. That will only ensure his unhappiness in this competitive world.

"I know what I'm talking about. I came up the hard way. I was a poor kid, and everything I got I had to work for. I sold papers after school, and I worked my way through college. I didn't get to be vice-president of my company by sitting on my hands, either. I went back and worked in the evenings when I didn't have to. Sometimes the other guys thought I was ruthless, and sometimes my wife had a fit, but I got there by using all the brains I had all the time. I want that for him, too. Is that wrong?"

The counselor talked with the mother. "It isn't Leroy's fault," she said. "You wouldn't believe how critical my husband was of our son. Leroy couldn't do anything right, or even well enough to please his father. When he was young, if he got four A's and a B in school, his father raised the devil because he didn't get straight A's. If my husband told the boy to have our enormous lawn mowed by 3:00 and the boy didn't finish until 3:30, he got criticized again. I had to stand by and watch the boy suffer. Finally, Leroy just gave up. It seemed to happen all of a sudden, as if he realized he was going to get criticized whatever he did. As a matter of fact, pretty soon my husband's hollering and criticalness wasn't even a punishment anymore. The boy became almost immune to it. And then something even worse happened. Leroy himself began to believe that he couldn't do the things that other children could do. When his father told him he was 'dumb in arithmetic' because he missed two or three problems, Leroy accepted what his father said to an extent my husband never intended. He believed he was dumb in arithmetic. And so he never tried anymore.

"I don't know what we can do about him now. He feels inadequate, so he is inadequate. I think his father is just going to have to face up to the facts and take care of Leroy until Leroy can find himself again. Leroy is very good at tennis. He can beat his father once in a while, and that's why I think he likes tennis so much. I've sent him money from time to time so he could play. Maybe he will get to be a great professional someday. I hate to see him drop out of school, though, because it's probably his last chance to redeem himself.

"Leroy threatens his father all the time. He says that if he doesn't send him more money, he will quit school and go to work. If he really would do that, it might be the best thing in the world for him, but he won't. He'll just get into trouble, and we'll just have to bail him out again. That's the problem now: He owes money to almost everybody in the university town. I hope you can help him when you talk with him."

The counselor talked with Leroy, who was inclined to be both belligerent and resigned. "All right," Leroy said, "let's get it over with. You're about the twenty-first do-gooder they've made me come to see. Let's see what you can do.

"I know what they both have told you, because they've told it to me often enough. As a matter of fact, they might have been a lot better off if they had never even tried to analyze me. I might have turned out better if Mother had never felt so sorry for me and continually told me what a brute my father was. I might have been better, too, if he hadn't yelled at her all the time about coddling me. If they had gotten along together, the whole thing might never have happened. But you can't tell them that. Both of them still think that they were doing the right thing and that if only the other one hadn't messed me up I would have turned out to be a great success.

"Actually, I may turn out pretty well anyway. I have a lot more fun than many of the eager-beaver bookworm types at the university who will spend the rest of their lives in competition and hostility. And I'm a lot better off than the far-out protester types, who have masochistic compulsions to beat on themselves for humanity's wrongs. I don't polish and I don't protest. I just live, and my old man can afford to keep it that way."

The case of Leroy is probably an illustration of almost every behavior principle you have studied so far. Predict what Leroy and his father and mother will do now based on what you know about generations, individuals, and human behavior (see the Appendix).

Parents are the generation in the middle

The middle child has been described as the one who is frustrated by conflicting expectations. He is expected to wait until he gets older in order to do the things his older brother can do, yet as each year passes he never seems to reach that age. At the same time he is expected to be the big brother to the younger brother, who never seems to have any responsibility.

Parents who have grown children and who also have living parents are likewise caught in the middle. They are still children to their parents and yet must provide for their own. A greater problem arises when their aging parents are also as in need of help as children would be, yet continue to try to rule their adult children.

The common ground between generations

There is more common ground between the generations than any of them wants to acknowledge. The constant, shifting struggle for power makes it appear that there is no common ground, as the young seek power, the middle group fights to hold it, and the older group loses it. The common ground is the basic needs of all humans. Lists of needs have varied from one writer to another, but they are basically these: (1) affection, (2) recognition, (3) context, (4) repeated gratification, (5) stability, and (6) variance in social structure. The gratification of these needs is the very way generations may find consensus. Too often, however, people in one generation see people in another generation as having different needs from their own. The older person wants recognition just as the middle adult and the child do. Empathetic understanding is far more likely when it is remembered that people of all ages have similar basic needs (see Chapters 4 and 6).

The following illustration shows how communication can break down when a wife misinterprets the meaning of a mother-in-law whose interest is in being helpful.

Annie Lee and her husband Jeff and her mother-in-law were discussing the prized grandchild, Mark.

Annie Lee said, "I think Mark, now that he's seven years old, should be doing more to take care of his own room and things. When I suggested he make up his bed, he answered by saying 'Daddy doesn't make up his bed.' I know this, but I still think Mark should do more around here."

Whereupon her mother-in-law said, "Well, you could tell Mark his Daddy works and that's why you make up his bed."

Annie Lee hit the ceiling. "Well, I work too! Or do you not consider my job work? I make as much as your son does—maybe more. Isn't that work?"

The mother-in-law quietly said, "I didn't mean it that way."

THE THREE GENERATIONS IN ALL OF US

We live in our own generation, we are affected by our parents' generation, and we are involved in trying to influence the generation coming behind us. These generations are all linked in every person. If you say you have only one or two generations of relatives living, that does not mean the other generations are not within you just the same. The influence from the older generation has its impact on you, and your own plans for influencing the next are already brewing. When it is thought of this way, the term "generation gap" has little meaning.

Intergenerational understanding becomes even more important when a person of another generation becomes your in-law. Since this is one of the areas that seem to give young married couples some trouble, the rest of this chapter will deal with in-laws.

IN-LAWS: A GENERATIONAL APPROACH

If the notions that problems between generations are value-specific as much as they are age-specific, and that each of us has part of each generation within us, then the conflicts between in-laws from differing generations may be studied in the same way as conflicts between any persons from differing generations.

Mothers-in-law are very much joked about and very little studied.

It is said, for example, that the classic case of mixed emotions is that of the man who sees his mother-in-law about to back his brand-new automobile over a cliff. Some sociologists believe that the jokes themselves have created part of the self-perpetuating stereotype that makes young people fear in-laws and thus creates trouble that might otherwise not have occurred. But the jokes are not all to blame.

How much trouble do couples have with in-laws?

Because of the differing designs of presently existing research studies, it is difficult to generalize about the extent of in-law difficulty. In one study, almost 75 percent of a group of married couples of all ages reported some difficulties with one or more in-laws.[1]

On the other hand, other research findings suggest that only about 29 percent of wives and 21 percent of husbands experience friction with their in-laws, and that most couples have a good relationship with their relatives.[2]

Getting along with one's in-laws appears to be another case of "some do and some don't." As a matter of fact, some partners work out a better relationship with their in-laws than they had with their own parents.

A statistical probability of in-law difficulty does not mean that every marriage is equally affected by this probability. Such a view overlooks the reasons for the difficulty. What should be added to every research finding are the conditions under which the probability will be applicable. For example, in those families where there is in-law difficulty, there are also the personalities, the resources, the perceptions, the attitudes, the expectations, and circumstances that led to the difficulty. If a son-in-law fits the expectation of his parents-in-law and if they in turn fit his expectation, there is almost no reason for difficulty. On the other hand, when parents-in-law are in great need of getting cultural praise from the successes of sons-in-law, these young men are put into the position of having to meet far greater expectations than they can, and in-law difficulty is inevitable.

There is one thing about the in-law problem on which the experts agree: The mother-in-law is involved more often in whatever in-law difficulty there is than is any other in-law.[3] The reason why the mother so often turns out to be the most difficult in-law seems apparent. As Gerald Leslie suggests, mothers' lives, more than fathers', are likely to be organ-

[1]Evelyn Duvall, *In-Laws: Pro and Con*, New York, Association Press, 1954, p. 188.
[2]Robert O. Blood, Jr., *Marriage*, 2nd ed., New York, Free Press, 1969, pp. 261–262.
[3]Duvall, op. cit.; and Judson T. Landis and Mary G. Landis, *Building a Successful Marriage*, 5th ed., Englewood Cliffs, N.J., Prentice-Hall, 1968, p. 331.

ized around their children.[4] When those children marry, the mothers, reluctant to give up the satisfactions of their role, often try to hold on to their former responsibilities and privileges. It also often happens that the children's leaving is coincident with other dissatisfying events in the woman's life, such as menopause and the advent of wrinkles and gray hair. This unhappy series of events has led David Mace to suggest that,

Most difficult mothers-in-law are really middle-aged women unadjusted to life. . . . Their plight is sometimes pitiful. They need, above all, warm affection and understanding. Yet by their irrational, critical behavior they cut themselves off more and more from the very things they most need.[5]

Apparently, wives have much more trouble with their in-laws than husbands do with theirs, although the jokes have it the other way. Duvall found that women are involved in in-law problems six times as often as men. There are probably many reasons for this. For one thing, as Leslie points out, there is greater emphasis placed upon "being a good wife" than upon "being a good husband" in our society.[6] The wife who is in direct competition with the husband's mother fears she will be judged in terms of her ability to keep house, cook, and otherwise cater to her husband's needs. On the other hand, the husband more often feels he is judged in terms of his success in the occupational world. Although he may sometimes compete with his father-in-law for occupational success, usually he is not acutely aware of this competition.

It has also been suggested that the strength of a mother's attachment to her sons may create some of the antagonism between the daughter-in-law and her husband's mother. Less commonly is a father-in-law's close relationship to his daughter so threatening to a son-in-law. Here is a case in the classic pattern.

CASE 63 LUCILLE AND ARTHUR

"Arthur's mother is our major problem," Lucille told the counselor, "He is tied to her apron strings—but tight. I tried to be very nice to his mother when we were first married. But she never did like me. In fact, one time she came right out and told me that she didn't believe that I was the right woman for him and I never would be.

---

[4]Gerald R. Leslie, *The Family in Social Context*, 2nd ed., New York, Oxford University Press, 1973, p. 318.

[5]David Mace, *Success in Marriage*, Nashville, Tenn., Abingdon, 1958, p. 67.

[6]Leslie, op. cit., p. 317.

"The truth of it is that his mother spoiled him badly. She waited on him hand and foot. She was from an old-fashioned family, and she got all of her satisfaction from cooking and housekeeping. I don't keep house very well, and I admit it. But she didn't have to come over and pick things up after me like she did. It made me so mad I screamed at her and told her to get out. And do you know what, Arthur didn't even take my side!

"As a matter of fact, I think that's what hurts the worst. I can sometimes abide his running over there all the time, but I can't stand the fact that he doesn't stand up for me. He never says anything to his mother in my defense. He never talks back to his mother at all.

"His mother keeps working on his emotional system, even more so now that his father has died. She makes him feel like he ought to come and see her every day. He goes over there at least seven or eight times a week. If I try to make him promise not to, he just lies to me and goes anyway. I've caught him at it.

"I want to move away from his mother. He went and bought a house about a block from her place last year. I almost left him then.

"One time when we were first married, he took a good job down in Atlanta. Do you know how long we stayed down there? Two months! He just couldn't stay away from Mama. He'll tell you all sorts of reasons why we came back: It was a poor job, we didn't like the area, his boss was impossible to work with, but those aren't the real reasons at all.

"I always know where I stand with my own mother. When I do something she doesn't like, she tells me about it right there and we can fight it out. But his mother—she just looks hurt and tries to do even more things around my house. It's infuriating. Last month I forbade Arthur to let her come around anymore. And I made him promise again that he wouldn't go down there. I want you to tell him, too, that he has to stay away. If he doesn't, I'm going to get a divorce. And I mean it."

Arthur said, "Lucille is frantically jealous of my mother. She doesn't even want the children to have gifts from Mother. Lucille is younger than Mother, and she could at least try to understand how Mother feels now that her only son and her husband are both gone. Lucille could end this marriage problem anytime she wanted to by just acting decently to my mother. But she won't.

"Lucille is a terrible housekeeper. I think she'll tell you that herself. And really, that's part of the problem. Lucille knows she should pick things up, but when Mother came over here and did it, she began to boil. That's really what started all the trouble.

"I know Lucille says she wants me to take her side, but what it amounts to is that she wants me to punish my mother as a demonstration of my love for her. She has said it almost that way. What am I supposed to do, castigate my mother because she's trying to help? I can't do that. I've tried to make things as easy as I can for Lucille. I used to ask her to go with me to Mother's, especially on the holidays. But now I don't even ask anymore. Every once in a while I take the children by myself. And then does Lucille scream! She says my mother tries to condition the children against her. Actually, all Mother does is give them a little loving care that they rarely get at home.

"Anyway, I don't go down to Mother's so much myself anymore. Actually, Mother has been a big problem for me all my life. Since I was the only child and her only real interest, she expected a lot of attention from me. I know I feel obligated to help her, especially since my father died. Who else is there? You just can't tell her to curl up and die. But Lucille doesn't understand this. Her own mother is an independent type who can take care of herself. She tells Lucille off regularly, and Lucille seems to respect her for it.

"I don't know what I'm going to do. My life is miserable this way. Lucille wants me to move way across town, and in some ways it might be a good thing, although I would never admit that to her. On the other hand, it might just increase the time I had to be away from home, because I know I can't ever abandon Mother altogether."

Other in-laws

Sisters-in-law were named a source of friction by 20.3 percent of one sample, as opposed to 36.8 percent who named mothers-in-law.[7] Since brothers-in-law and fathers-in-law accounted for only slightly over 10 percent of all the problems, it is strikingly clear that in-law difficulty more often has a feminine angle in both directions. Not *always*, however. Consider the following case:

CASE 64 CRAIG AND GEORGIA

"We moved in with Georgia's father about two years ago," Craig told the counselor. "At the time it seemed like the only thing to do. Georgia's mother had just died, and there was no one to care for her father, who is a partial invalid. You wouldn't know there's anything wrong with him to hear him

[7]Duvall, op. cit.

talk, though. He's fiercely independent. But I guess he does need someone near in case of an emergency. Besides, we needed to save money, and he had a very big house. It was just about the time I had realized that the only way I was going to move up at the research laboratory was to go back and get a Master's degree. All in all, moving in with her dad looked like a real good thing—then.

"But as soon as we got in the house, trouble started. Something seemed to come over Georgia. She wouldn't do the housework if her father didn't tell her to. Now she never does anything around the house unless she's absolutely forced to. I'd like to help with the dishes and the housework, but if I do, she lets me take over completely. If I try to talk calmly with her about it, she flies into a rage.

"Sometimes she tries to compete with me like a little child. If I point out to her that we don't have enough money for some of the things she's bought in the last few weeks, she'll say, 'Well you spent money on yourself last month; now it's my turn to spend some on me.' She doesn't want me to give in to her. Apparently what she wants is a kind of a forceful dominating man like her father used to be. He told her what to do and she loved it. She talks to me about how everything should be fifty-fifty, but she really doesn't mean it. She wants the security of having a husband who is sometimes authoritarian and who is always self-confident. I'm not that way and I admit it.

"But her father is, or was. She still looks to him for leadership. Whenever there is a decision to be made, if I try to talk it over with her she says, 'We'll ask Daddy.' If I try to tell her what to do, then she sulks and I know she runs to Daddy after I'm gone. It isn't that the old man doesn't try to stay out of it. He knows there's a problem, too. But she nags and digs him until he tells her off, and then he tells her exactly what she should have done in the first place. Almost always it's just what I said, but she takes it from him and won't take it from me.

"Georgia is quick to criticize me, but she gets petulant and stubborn when I correct her. I don't mind her pointing out my goofs to me in a good-natured way when we're alone, but it sure fries me when she mentions some mistake I made in front of her dad. That's what most of the fights have been about in the last few months.

"I told her a week ago that we're going to move out of that house. But now she insists that the old man needs us more than ever. He doesn't need Georgia; she needs him. She apparently won't leave, and I guess I'm not forceful enough to make her. She say if I go, I'll have to go by myself and she'll keep the child. What can I do?"

Georgia agreed to almost everything Craig had said. "Yes, it's true," Georgia said. "I do trust Daddy more than I trust Craig. But that's because Craig takes such stupid positions sometimes. I can see now that it's often because he wants to make me feel like he's a leader like Daddy was. But somehow he just hasn't got the personality for it. I want him to be the leader—desperately I want him to be the leader—but I want him to show me that he's the leader by accomplishing things. And he needs to prove himself not only for me but for himself, too. He always feels as if I'm comparing him, and I guess often I am.

"Sometimes I don't do the housework and he just does it himself. Daddy would never have done that. He would have spanked me, and I would have felt better about it.

"Now that Daddy is old and not so forceful anymore, I feel sort of lost. I guess really I'm looking for something I had a long time ago. This is a bad situation. I know we should get out of the house now, but I just can't bring myself to go. My father really does need me. But there's more to it than that. I have always felt completely accepted by him even when he was punishing me. When Craig criticizes me, I just get mad. Sometimes I get mad enough so that I wish Craig would leave."

The case of Craig and Georgia may be unusual in several ways. Sheldon Stryker found that, among 104 couples he studied, the husband's adjustment to his mother-in-law tended to be less adequate when his wife was dependent upon her mother, but his adjustment to his father-in-law tended to be more adequate when his wife was dependent upon her father.[8] Research findings, while demonstrating group tendencies, don't—as we pointed out earlier—always apply to individual cases such as Craig and Georgia.

Dependency

Running through many in-law problems is the recurrent theme of dependency. Some studies have shown that marriage at an early age is highly correlated with in-law difficulties, possibly because some young people are not ready to leave home, even if they think they are.

Judson and Mary Landis found in their study of 544 wives that 63 percent of those who married at twenty-four or older reported excellent ad-

[8]Sheldon Stryker, "The Adjustment of Married Offspring to Their Parents," *American Sociological Review*, **20** (April, 1955), 149–154.

justments with their in-laws, while only 45 percent of those who married between the ages of seventeen and nineteen reported excellent adjustments. Only 7 percent of the older group reported only fair or poor adjustments, but 21 percent of those married at the younger ages indicated only fair or poor adjustments.[9]

A very common complaint of the husbands of teenage brides is that their wives spend half their lives on the telephone talking to their mothers. Some young husbands who have moved their wives a long way from their mothers complain that the expense of long-distance calls can be staggering. Often, though, the psychological aspects of this mother-dependence are more detrimental than the financial aspects. Although not all men take an active pride in being good husbands, a surprisingly large number of them do. Such men resent the implication that other people—especially in-laws—can meet their young wives' dependence needs and solve her problems better than they can. Clearly, in such cases, the wife's dependence is only part of the problem. The husband's need for self-esteem is also a part.

Exaggerated independence on the part of one or both of the young partners is as common a cause of in-law difficulty in marriage as is overdependence. Many of the young people who have the most friction with their parents-in-law are rebelling against the influence of older people, symbolized until recently by their *own* parents, and against their own needs to remain in a childlike state of dependence.

Since this kind of exaggerated independence is more characteristic of the young and more characteristic of those who are newly married and still a little defensive about their prerogatives, it is one of the major reasons why age and duration of marriage are correlated to in-law problems.

In-law interference

Not always, but usually, there is something to be said for both sides in any in-law problem. It is true that some young marrieds overreact in an effort to emancipate themselves from in-law domination, but it is also true that there are many in-laws who really do interfere.

Possessive mothers—or fathers—are not likely to stop being possessive just because their children get married, nor are dominating parents likely to stop being dominating. When children have been the parents' primary concern and interest over a long period of years, it is probably unreasonable to expect them to divorce themselves completely from that feeling of responsibility or from that interest overnight.

[9]Landis and Landis, op. cit., p. 338.

But well-adjusted parents who have lived full, well-rounded lives themselves and who are not overeager to run their children's lives can live their own lives after the children have gone. This ideal type of in-law can find ways to help the newlyweds without increasing their dependency or threatening their independence. When there is reasonably good accommodation on the part of both the in-laws and the newlyweds, both of them can afford to relax a little, secure in the knowledge that whenever problems do arise, they will ultimately be resolved, for, as the young people grow older, they will feel less threatened by advice and help. In fact sometimes they wish they could get more of both when they themselves become parents and begin to experience all the problems and frustrations that they so recently looked at from the opposite direction. Stryker found that, in general, married offspring who had children of their own had better adjustments with their parents than those who did not have children. He speculated that this might be because they were more likely to appreciate the problems and difficulties their own parents went through.[10]

There are, though, some compulsively manipulating parents who just cannot stay out of their married children's lives. Consider the following case:

CASE 65 REBECCA AND DAVID

"My mother is doing everything she can to break up our marriage," Rebecca told the counselor. "David has put up with an awful lot, but I don't know how much more he's going to take.

"My mother was against David from the time we started going together. At first she forbade me to see him. She found all sorts of reasons for not liking him. She said he was a jerk and a vulgar lowbrow because he got a little tight one night. Then she caught him in a little fib about where we were going one night, and from then on she wailed about his being a pathological liar. So we ran off and got married secretly. She didn't find out about it until I was pregnant. At first she wanted me to have an abortion. When David refused even to consider it, she screamed at him. But there was nothing she could do about it. She threatened all sorts of vile things. Among other things, she was going to cut me and our baby out of her will. She thinks David is just after my family's money.

"When she saw we weren't going to get an abortion, she tried to

[10]Stryker, op. cit., 153–154.

work on me to divorce David. She promised she would take care of the baby while I went back to school. All of a sudden she began to make noises like a grandmother—but only if I'd divorce David.

"The thing about it that makes it so difficult is that David has been having a hard time finding himself. He's lost several jobs, and we've had a difficult time financially. His mother has been helping us a little bit. My mother could actually help us a great deal if only she would. She says I can come back and live with the baby in the big house anytime I want to, but that she's not going to have David around.

"Last week David gave a bad check in order to get his car out of the garage. Now the garage owner is threatening to have him arrested. Mother could help us out, but she swears she'll see him in jail first. What are we going to do?"

The counselor talked to David. "Rebecca's mother is responsible for all our trouble," David said. "She hates me because I took Rebecca away from a situation that was almost intolerable. When I first met Rebecca, she jumped every time her mother came near her. All she could say was, 'Yes, Mother.' I've gotten her to see that she should lead her own life and not be a puppet on a string. But the old lady sure has made it tough for us.

"I've had some bad breaks in the jobs I've had. At one place I had an accident with the truck the first day I was working, and that finished that. At another place they had an old jerk for the boss who tried to tell me what I should do every minute, so I quit the second day. Then I got a really good job where they had a training program. I might have moved on up, except that it turned out that Rebecca's old lady knew the vice-president, and she began filling him full of a lot of lies about what a bad guy I was— I'm sure that's what happened—and pretty soon the other guys moved up and I didn't. So I quit.

"Rebecca's mother is forever trying to bribe Rebecca to leave me. She doesn't come right out and say, 'I'll give you a thousand dollars if you'll leave David.' Instead she just points out the advantages the baby could have if she'd only divorce me and come home.

"She won't help us when we need it. Last week I had a line on a new job, but I had to have a car to get it. My car was in the shop, and I owed about $150 for repairs. So I called Rebecca's mother and asked if she'd advance the $150. Do you know what she said? 'You're always saying how you can take care of Rebecca. Now let's see you do it!'

"I had to have the car so I wrote a check that I knew we didn't have the money for. It would have been all right if I had gotten the job, because then the garage man probably would have given me time until I got my first paycheck before he called the cops."

The counselor also talked to Rebecca's mother. "David is impossible," she said. "He met Rebecca at a drive-in restaurant when his car pulled up beside hers. He picked her up, to put it bluntly. But Rebecca was just a child. The fact that David was a juvenile delinquent—or at least behaved like one—didn't make any difference to her. Certainly I tried to stop her from going with him. I would have done everything I could to prevent their being married. Yes, I am trying to do everything I can to get her to leave him. Someday she may come to her senses and thank me for it.

"In the first place, he's a liar. I tried to help him three or four times by giving him money when he told me he needed it for job expenses. I always gave the money to Rebecca so he would be sure to remember how he got it. Anyway, he didn't spend it for what he said he needed it for. Sometimes they bought something they didn't need; one time they even took a trip with the money.

"I'd think he would be smarter than that. After all, all he wants is my money. If he were really as clever as he thinks he is, he would try to do something right for a change, and then maybe I could accept him. But he never seems to learn.

"That's why I won't have him back to live in my house. As soon as I started taking care of both of them, he would quit even trying to find a job. Then first thing you know, she'd be pregnant again, and I'd have both of them for the rest of my life.

"Now he's really done it. He gave a bad check the other day, and the man is going to have him arrested. I want to let it happen; maybe it will teach him a lesson. But if I do, my family will have bad publicity. Imagine my daughter being married to a jailbird. Then if she ever does get a divorce, no one will want to marry her again. This is a terrible mess. In the end I may have to bail him out, but I'm certainly going to let him sweat awhile before I do."

Many parents look for opportunities to give money and gifts to the children *without* placing them under any obligation, having learned that the slightest implication of lost independence may produce resentment. But there are still some groups and some situations in which generations clash over expectations of filial obligation. This often happens when the in-laws have come from a different cultural background than the young husband or wife.

In-laws can help, too

As we said in the beginning, some in-law relationships are a great advantage to everybody. There are many cases in which in-laws have provided needed economic assistance. Marvin Sussman studied 195 cases and found that in 154 of them, parents were giving either direct financial support, or help and service to their married children.[11] Moreover, in the majority of cases, today's in-laws also provide large quantities of affectional support that the young marrieds need to work through their own early adjustment process.

Peggy Marcus did a study of seventy-nine marriages and found that several factors were significantly related to good in-law adjustment for both husband and wife: approval by the parents; meeting the families before marriage; friendliness of parental families toward each other; a separate household; happy marriage of the parents; and a happy relationship between the parents and the grandchildren.[12] The findings from Vladimir de Lissovoy's longitudinal study of high-school marriages tended to support Marcus's findings.[13] The kin network of economic and psychological support was claimed to help sustain the marriages.

But what happens when two people fall in love and get married without having all or any of these factors working for them? What can be done when there is trouble? Other than platitudes about doing one's best to understand other people's needs and the importance of cooperative understanding, there probably are very few generalizations that have meaning in any specific in-law situation. In modern America, there are as many millions of complex in-law relationships as there are marriages. An old rule of thumb —that the spouse who is the blood relative is the best one to deal with an in-law problem—may be the worst possible advice in a particular situation, since this particular spouse may be emotionally incapable of solving his or her own problems. On the other hand, the newcomer to the established family group is often at a great disadvantage in trying to change established relationship patterns.

About the best that can be done is to practice patience and deter-

[11]Marvin B. Sussman, "The Help Pattern in the Middle Class Family," *American Sociological Review,* **18** (February, 1953), 23. Reprinted in Marvin B. Sussman, ed. *Sourcebook in Marriage and the Family,* 2nd ed., Boston, Houghton Mifflin, 1963, pp. 380–384.

[12]Peggy Marcus, "In-Law Relationship Adjustments of Couples Married Two and Eleven Years," *Journal of Home Economics,* **43** (January, 1951), 36–37.

[13]Vladimir de Lissovoy, "High School Marriages: A Longitudinal Study," *Journal of Marriage and the Family,* **35** (May, 1973), 245–255.

mination. In some situations, this means inestimable patience and unshakable determination. For many people, the problem does get better. In their study of 909 Michigan families, Robert Blood and Donald Wolfe found that the percentage of in-law difficulties tended to decline as the couples grew older.[14]

A final note to our in-law discussion is provided by Peggy Marcus. She points to one of the "feeling tones" in her study that seemed to stand out most clearly between those with good adjustment and poor adjustment: "Those . . . couples with a good adjustment seemed to be working as a unit, accepting both families as their own and regarding all problems as a common task. Those with a poor adjustment, on the other hand, showed a tendency to blame the spouse's family for friction in all areas."[15]

[14]Robert O. Blood, Jr., and Donald M. Wolfe, *Husbands and Wives,* New York, Free Press, 1960, pp. 247–248.
[15]Marcus, op. cit., 37.

19

AFTER THE CHILDREN COME

In almost every society throughout history, the arrival of children in a family has been culturally valued as a great blessing and as an integrating factor that increases the closeness between marriage partners. Most young Americans think of it that way, too, even though several research studies have shown that a birth often creates a family crisis for which the partners are woefully unprepared.[1]

Whether having a child produces a crisis or not, it will surely bring some change to the marriage. Relationships will never be the same again. Moreover, the changes in the family brought about by the coming of the first child are the prelude to many more. With the coming of the second child, the triangular relationship of the family becomes quadrangular. Then in addition to husband-wife relationships and parent-child relationships, there are child-child relationships to be considered. But the spacing of the number of children in a family has more to do with the relationships than the absolute number does.[2]

HUSBAND-WIFE RELATIONSHIPS DURING PREGNANCY

Changes in the husband-wife relationship often start the minute the wife suspects she is pregnant. Individual reactions to impending parenthood vary widely. For some partners, the realization that conception has occurred is a source of anxiety, hostility, or regret. Such initial feelings are often followed by feelings of guilt, since there is a strong cultural belief that rejecting pregnancy is morally reprehensible. Whether the rejection is by the husband or the wife makes little difference. The marriage relationship is liable to deteriorate either way, particularly if one partner blames the other for not having taken greater precautions against the unwelcome event.

Ordinarily, though, especially with the first child, confirmation of conception brings pleasant satisfaction to both partners. Yet the pregnancy itself will almost inevitably change the interpersonal relationships of even the most delighted marriage mates, for although modern attitudes have drastically reduced some pregnancy problems, some complications of modern

---

[1]E. E. LeMasters, "Parenthood as Crisis," *Marriage and Family Living*, **19** (November, 1957), 352–355; and E. D. Dyer, "Parenthood as Crisis: A Re-Study," *Marriage and Family Living*, **25** (May, 1963), 196–201. A third study, by Daniel Hobbs, found no such evidence of family birth crisis as LeMasters and Dyer reported earlier. Hobbs urged further study with larger and more representative samples. Daniel F. Hobbs, "Parenthood as Crisis: A Third Study," *Journal of Marriage and The Family*, **27** (August, 1965), 367–372.

[2]Harold T. Christensen, "Children in the Family: Relationships of Number and Spacing to Marital Success," in Marcia E. Lasswell and Thomas E. Lasswell, eds., *Love, Marriage, Family: A Developmental Approach*, Glenview, Ill., Scott, Foresman, 1973, pp. 344–351.

living create difficulties that Great-Grandmother never faced when she was pregnant. For example, many contemporary American women are left alone for the first time in their lives in the latter months of pregnancy. Up until that time, they have either been in school or working—always with other people. When it becomes necessary for them to stay at home by themselves, sometimes in small apartments far from their childhood homes, many women need and demand more affection and social interaction with their husbands. Nagging fears and insecurities about the birth process and the normalcy of the developing baby add to this need for closeness.

Physiologic changes in pregnancy can create relationship changes, too. Sometimes a wife's altered hormonal balance can bring about unpleasant changes in her disposition, causing a placid, easy-going woman to become argumentative and moody, which does not improve a marriage relationship. Moreover, some women are tempted to take advantage of their "delicate condition" to get a little more attention and perhaps a little more service from a doting husband than they know they deserve. In the long run this is no help to the marital relationship either.

CASE 66 SARAH AND PHILLIP

"Phillip takes no interest in my pregnancy," Sarah said. "He wasn't even excited when he found out I was going to have a baby. I didn't call his attention to the fact that I missed a period, and I don't think he even knew it. That's part of our problem. He never notices the little things about me. I could dye my hair green, and he wouldn't know it for six months. Anyway, I didn't even tell him I was going to the doctor. I thought it would be a very big surprise. When I was sure, I could hardly wait to tell him. But I wanted to do it big, so I planned a special dinner and had it by candlelight. And when I told him, do you know what he said? He said, 'Oh, is that so?' I thought he would come and tenderly take me into his arms and hold me very close. All he did was give me a routine little peck on the cheek and take his insurance book and go out and make some calls.

"I could have forgiven that if he would at least show some interest now. But he doesn't seem to care whether I feel well or not. I've had a miserable time with morning sickness, and I've had to stay in bed a great deal. I'm sure he doesn't care, and I'm not sure that he even knows how bad it's been.

"Now that I've felt life, I want him to take an interest in the pregnancy. Not him. The only time he's interested in looking at me is when he

wants sex. You'd think he could control himself for just a little while. When he found out we couldn't have intercourse at all during the last three months, you would have thought he had been personally wounded. It was almost as if he thought the doctor had selected him out of all the men in the world to be deprived. He couldn't see that it was to protect my baby. All he thought about was himself.

"There's nothing I can do about it now, of course. I can't divorce him with my baby on the way. But I am thinking about going home to Mother's to stay until after the baby comes. She's very interested in my pregnancy, and I like to talk with her about it."

Phillip told it this way: "If I had known that Sarah was going to carry on like this after she got pregnant, we never would have had a baby, believe me. She cried every day for three weeks because I didn't make a big enough fuss when she told me. I was real pleased then, and I tried to make that clear to her. Sure, I was surprised at first. But when I got used to the idea, I tried to tell her how happy I was. But by that time all she could say was, 'Oh, you spoiled it all!'

"I suppose she told you I don't care how she feels. That isn't so. Since she's been having such a bad time in the morning, I've been trying not to wake her when I go out. I get my own breakfast every morning. But I can't stay home from my job to take care of her every day. And even if I could, I wouldn't be much of a nurse. There have been a couple of Sunday mornings when she's gotten up to go to the bathroom and throw up. She leaves the door open, and I've gotten sick myself. I really feel bad about her being uncomfortable, but there isn't that much I can do about it.

"Besides, I'm beginning to wonder a little about this morning sickness bit anyway. She had it every morning until last Saturday. Then early in the morning—before we were awake—the telephone rang. It was some old friends of hers who were just passing through town. Actually, it was one of her old boyfriends who married another girl. She got on the telephone, and they invited us out to lunch. I couldn't go, because I had some insurance calls to make. But I was around the house until almost noon. You should have seen her rushing around. She washed and dried her hair and did a thousand other things, and she never got sick once. But Sunday morning —oh, that was different—she carried on all over the place again.

"The worst part about all this is that she says I'm not interested in the pregnancy. What she means is that I'm not as interested in it every minute, twenty-four hours a day, as she is. The first time she took my hand and put it to her abdomen so that I could feel the baby move, I was as thrilled *as she was. But, believe me, by the 493rd time it began to get a little old, and I ran out of things to say.*

"She wants me to know every detail, and I'm not sure that I want to know that much. I married a beautiful, romantic woman. Now she's turning herself into a biological exhibition. When I'm out making my insurance calls, sometimes I think of her with tenderness and I think of her with passion. But I don't think of her as some medical sideshow. I don't want to think of her that way. I don't want her to make me think of her that way. There are some things she just shouldn't make me know.

"She threatens me all the time that she'll go home to be with her mother until the baby is born. I'm beginning to wish she would. Maybe it would be better for all of us."

As the pregnancy progresses, many women become less interested in having sexual relations. Although they may not decline intercourse outright, their husbands sense their feelings and feel very rejected. Other women, especially those who are basically insecure about their ability to maintain their husband's sex interest, become ultrasensitive when they begin to feel less physically attractive during pregnancy. Because of their own insecurity, they accuse their husbands of interest in other women—accusations that may or may not have any basis in fact. Some husbands *do* use their feelings of sexual deprivation to seek sexual satisfaction elsewhere, especially in the months at the end of the pregnancy. This, of course, can dramatically alter the husband-wife relationship.

By and large, though, in most middle-class marriages, the initial pregnancy—despite the transient difficulties and inconvenience that go with it—is a time of drawing closer. Some women never feel better than when they are pregnant, and some men enjoy nine pleasant months. In many cases, troubles—if there were any—are forgotten on the birth day. Divorce suits filed by women who are pregnant are often withdrawn after the baby is born.

HUSBAND-WIFE RELATIONSHIPS AFTER THE CHILDREN ARE BORN

There are marriages, though, in which resentments created during pregnancy carry over after the baby is born. There are other marriages in which the time of pregnancy was a beautiful period of bliss but in which the happy world falls apart when the baby comes. The birth of a baby does not in itself necessarily improve a marriage; in fact, the new arrival brings a few new tensions to all marriages and a great many destructive tensions to some marriages.[3]

For one thing, the new baby creates a triangle. In all triangular relationships, there are bound to be some jealousies. In most marriages, it is the young husband who suffers the most from jealous feelings. Used to enjoying his wife's full attention, he often finds it difficult to share. His frustration is compounded by the fact that he feels he has nowhere to ventilate his hostility, since it is not socially acceptable to admit to feelings of animosity toward a tiny baby. His relationship with his wife tends to deteriorate as conflict festers within him.

Jealousy on the part of the mother is not uncommon either. Some women are extremely jealous of their husband's relationships with their daughters, especially when those daughters near womanhood. And, of course, it is very common for the child to be jealous of the attention that one adult partner receives from his mate.

Some young husbands *do* suffer from a loss of marital attention and satisfaction that is very real and more than just jealous fantasy. The coming of a child enormously complicates the wife's role. The amount of physical energy as well as the amount of nervous energy she must spend on her increased duties is usually fatiguing. This is especially true in our American culture where the young mother frequently has no help from another mother, mother-in-law, visiting aunt, or paid helper to make it even a little easier. One of the problems of today's society is that so many emancipated young women who have been raised in relative freedom and luxury find themselves trapped in a chrome-and-porcelain prison with no other adult to talk with when their first child is born. And it goes on 365 days a year. The dispositions that results from this way of life are not always the kind that tend to enhance loving relationships.

Children bring other problems, too. They interfere not only with casual conversations but with the warm moments of mutual need-meeting between the partners. The child is imperious in his demands for immediate attention, regardless of how important the communication between the partners is at that minute. A young father who is excitedly telling his wife about the most meaningful experience of his day is quite likely to be interrupted by a child's screams for nothing more than a toy deliberately thrown from the highchair. Sometimes the one word that could improve the rela-

[3]Mary W. Hicks and Marilyn Platt, "Marital Happiness and Stability: A Review of the Research in the Sixties," in Carlfred Broderick, ed., *Decade Review*, Minneapolis, National Council on Family Relations, 1972, pp. 59–78.

tionship between the partners has to be postponed because something has to be done for the children. And thus the right moment is forever lost.

It is not only conversation that suffers, either. After the children arrive, spontaneous lovemaking usually comes to an abrupt halt. Sexual relationships have to wait until the children are asleep, and by that time the wife is ordinarily so tired that she wants only to go to sleep herself. Even if she can manage to achieve some kind of stimulation, her sexual excitement may be limited by her apprehension that the children may wake up.

In marriage counseling, it is common for a husband to complain that his wife's sexual responsiveness came to an end when the first child was born. Sometimes the wives admit this and are as baffled for an explanation as the husbands are. Some blame the traumatization of the birth canal for their loss of sexual appetite. Others contend that it was just about the time of the baby's arrival that the novelty of sex wore off. Whatever the cause, though, the result of the new mother's sexual disinterest is to make her young husband feel rejected, and so add another burden to their relationship.

Changes in husband-wife feelings toward one another can also result from arguments over how the child should be reared. This is especially true when the partners have come from homes with differing value systems. Traditionally, the male has more often been the authoritarian who tries to maintain stricter discipline by stern punishment if necessary. This is not always true, of course. Many wives complain of husbands who will not take any responsibility for punishing the children or who tend to be too lenient with them.

Arguments over child rearing become especially bitter in the "sensitive" areas of the marriage partners' relationship. Some husbands and wives can manage to compromise on how much allowance the child should have or whether he should be permitted to play football in junior high school, but they may literally come to blows over whether Grandmother has a right to buy the child fancy clothes, whether one partner has the right to insist on the child going to his church, or whether the adolescent daughter in the family may have a cocktail with adult guests.

Despite all the difficulties that children can create in a marriage, they also can be an integrating factor in the relationship between some marriage partners. Ninety-one percent of the respondents in Daniel Hobbs's study indicated that their marriages had been more happy and satisfying since their first child was born.[4]

At the very least, children can provide a sense of achievement and

[4]Hobbs, op. cit., 371.

pride in the later stages of marriage, to those partners who have managed to maintain an adequate relationship up to that point. When 852 couples were asked which stage of the family living experience they thought was most satisfying, the two most-preferred stages were, first, when the children were infants and, second, when the partners became grandparents. The third preferred stage was the period before the children were born, the fourth was when the children were preschoolers, the fifth when the children were all in school, and the sixth when the children were teenagers. The least-preferred stage of all was when the children had left home but had not yet had children of their own.[5]

It is possible, of course, that these data were a little contaminated not only by cultural approval of having children in the home, but also by the same kind of nostalgia for facing difficulties shoulder-to-shoulder that led British air-raid wardens to speak of the "good old days" twenty years after the bombing had stopped.

In fact, it might be the very challenge of working together for a common goal that makes the early child-rearing period so significant in the lives of the married pair. Once there are children, there are reasons—and rationalizations—for sticking to it and trying to get ahead. There is a new basis on which decisions can be made: what is best for the children. There is a new kind of camaraderie with other young couples who are suffering through the same agonies of rearing children in a changing culture. Most important of all, there is a new feeling of responsibility and adultness that is magnified by the dependence of tiny children. The need to be needed is an important human drive. There is no greater fulfillment for adults than to provide happiness for a child. Many ultrasophisticates who laugh at suburbanites become eager proponents of middle-class values once their own children are born. Why should they not? Some of them find real meaning and real purpose in their lives for the first time.

PARENT-CHILD RELATIONSHIPS

The notion that children were conceived in wickedness and sin, and therefore had badness born in them, died slowly. It was not until the early days of the twentieth century and the scientific study of culture and personality that the emphasis changed. When the shift came, however, it was a dramatic one. From placing blame on the child for his actions the pendulum swung

[5]Boyd C. Rollins and Harold Feldman, "Marital Satisfaction over the Family Life Cycle," in Marcia E. Lasswell and Thomas E. Lasswell, eds., *Love, Marriage, Family: A Developmental Approach*, Glenview, Ill., Scott, Foresman, 1973, pp. 381–383.

to placing blame on the parents. Many experts insisted that there really were not any bad children, only bad parents. "To meet Johnnie's mother is to understand his problem" reflected the preoccupation of midcentury psychologists and psychiatrists with the so-called *mal de mère* syndrome. Adjectives such as "anxious" and "rejecting" were freely used by child-guidance specialists. Many parents accused themselves—or each other—of being responsibile for their child's disturbed behavior.

Incidentally, Elizabeth Hurlock refers to studies of mothers' treatment of babies revealing that the way they treat them during infancy is significantly related to the way they treat them as they grow older. Changes are likely to occur in quantity rather than quality of treatment. That is, indulgent parents tend to become more indulgent and rejecting parents more rejecting. Consequently, small frictions in early childhood may well become major disruptions in late childhood.[6]

A good case was often made—and still can be made—for the detrimental effects that some parents have on the conditioning and development of their children. James Coleman has summarized the parent-control conditions that are conducive to faulty parent-child relationships and the possible effects of those conditions on the child's personality (see Table 19-1). Not only can these conditions affect the personality and behavior of the developing child, they can also affect his later behavior in marriage, thus creating a new round of marriage problems and another generation of disturbed parent-child relationships.[7]

Parental overambition (which Coleman identified as perfectionism) is a particularly difficult and disturbing problem. The case of Leroy in Chapter 18 illustrates some of the problems created in an upwardly mobile, perfectionist home.

The new family-interaction concept

Now the way of viewing the parent-child relationship has shifted again. More and more experts have come to believe that the parents are not altogether to blame. The child, they postulated, is not a passive victim of his environment but rather an active participant in his family group. Considerable evidence has been developed for the notion that, while the parents may affect the child, the child also affects the parents. Each family member

[6]Elizabeth B. Hurlock, *Child Development*, 4th ed., New York, McGraw-Hill, 1964, p. 656.

[7]James C. Coleman, ed., *Abnormal Psychology and Modern Life*, 3rd ed., Glenview, Ill., Scott, Foresman, 1964, p. 141.

TABLE 19-1
SUMMARY CHART OF FAULTY PARENT-CHILD RELATIONSHIPS

Undesirable condition	Typical personality development of child
Rejection	Feelings of insecurity and isolation. Attention-seeking, negativistic, hostile behavior. Unable to give and receive affection.
Overprotection—domination	Submission, inadequate lack of initiative, tendency to passive dependency in relations with others.
Overindulgence	Selfish, demanding, with inability to tolerate frustration. Rebellious to authority, excessive need of attention, lack of responsibility.
Perfectionism—unrealistic ambitions for child	Child internalizes parents' unrealistic standards. Inevitable failure leads to continual frustration, guilt, and self-devaluation.
Rigid, unrealistic moral standards	Extreme conscience development. Tendency to rigidity, severe conflicts, guilt, self-condemnation, and self-devaluation.
Faulty discipline	Overpermissiveness associated with insecurity, anti-social aggressiveness. Severe discipline typically leads to excessive condemnation of self for socially disapproved behavior, anxiety over aggressive behavior. Inconsistent discipline commonly results in lack of stable values for guiding behavior with tendency to inconsistency and vacillation in meeting problems.
Sibling rivalry	Direct or indirect hostility, insecurity, lack of self-confidence, regression.
Marital discord and broken homes	Anxiety, tension, insecurity, lack of secure home base, tendency to evaluate world as a dangerous and insecure place. Conflicting loyalties, lack of adequate models for proper ego development.
Faulty parental models	Internalization of unethical and socially undesirable value attitudes which frequently lead to difficulties with the law.
Contradictory demands ("double-bind")	Lack of integrated frame of references; confusion and self-devaluation.

The exact effects of faulty parent-child relationships on later behavior depend on many factors, including the age of the child, the constitutional and personality make-up of the child at the time, the duration and degree of the unhealthy relationship, his perception of the relationship, and the total family setting and life context, including the presence or absence of alleviating conditions and whether or not subsequent experiences tend to reinforce or correct early damage. There is no uniform pattern of pathogenic family relationship underlying the development of later psychopathology, but the conditions we have discussed often act as predisposing factors.

Source: *Abnormal Psychology and Modern Life,* Third Edition by James C. Coleman. Copyright © 1964 by Scott, Foresman and Company. Reprinted by permission of the publisher.

is, according to this whole-family concept, an important actor whose presence codetermines the total performance of the family group. Thus, while parents affect both the feelings and behavior of the child, the child also affects the feelings and behavior of his parents and his siblings in very significant ways.

Herbert Wimberger told of mothers who had dreamed of a cuddly infant but who had tense, nervous babies. These babies resisted the attention. The resulting resentment on the part of the mothers also affected the fathers and thus the entire family relationships were affected.[8]

In order to accept the concept that the child is in part responsible for the total family-relationships pattern, it is necessary to believe—and this has been shown by recent research—that the child himself has a temperament that affects his parents. Thus, "difficult" babies set up more stress patterns in the same parents than "easy" babies do.[9]

Child psychiatrists Stella Chess and Alexander Thomas and pediatrician Herbert Birch, in their report of an important study of behavior problems, validated the significant concept that behavior disturbance is a result of the interaction of the child's temperament with his family environment. They defined temperament as the behavioral style of the individual, his characteristic tempo, energy expenditure, focus, mood, and rhythmicity. Temperament, they said, refers to the "how" of behavior rather than to its "what" or "why."[10]

Chess, Thomas, and Birch believe that one specific temperamental pattern produces the greatest risk of behavior-problem development. This pattern is characterized by irregularity of biological functions, withdrawal responses to new stimuli, nonadaptability to change, frequent negative mood, and predominantly intense reactions. Mothers find that infants with irregular sleep and feeding patterns, slow acceptance of new foods, prolonged adjustment periods to new routines, and frequent loud periods of crying and laughter are hard to care for. Pediatricians frequently refer to them as "difficult" infants. The investigators found that the parents of these children were normal, but such infants require firm handling.[11]

[8]Herbert C. Wimberger, "Counseling in Parent-Child Problems," in Richard Klemer, ed., *Counseling in Marital and Sexual Problems: A Physician's Handbook*, Baltimore, Williams & Wilkins, 1965, p. 187.

[9]John E. Kysar, "Reactions of Professionals to Disturbed Children and Their Parents," *Archives of General Psychiatry*, **19** (1968).

[10]Stella Chess, Alexander Thomas, and Herbert G. Birch, "Behavior Problems Revisited: Findings of an Introspective Study," paper presented to the joint session on Child Development at the American Academy of Pediatrics and the Academy of Child Psychiatry, Chicago, October 24, 1965.

[11]Ibid., p. 5.

But what happens if the parents are not up to it? Then these parents become resentful. However, those parents who are up to it enjoy the vigor of the children.[12]

Does this mean that only difficult babies cause problems for their parents? No, indeed. While "easy" babies are a joy to their parents, pediatricians, and teachers, their very ease of adaptability may be the basis for later problem behavior. The child who first adapts easily to the standards and behavior expectations of his parents may have a difficult time when he moves to functional situations outside the home. In school, stress and malfunction may develop if the demands of the teachers or of the other children conflict sharply with the patterns he has learned at home. For instance, the child who has been urged to be creative and self-expressive at home may have a problem if his creativity or self-expression is not expected or desired by those he meets outside the home.

Chess, Thomas, and Birch described other temperament patterns of the child that affect the members of his family. One other such example was the "slow-to-warm-up" child. These children differ from the difficult infants in that their withdrawal from new situations is quiet rather than loud. For instance, on first being bathed, the child lies relatively still and fusses only mildly. With new foods, he turns his head away and lets the food dribble out of his mouth. With the stranger who greets him loudly, he clings to his mother. If given an opportunity to reexperience these new situations without pressure, such a child gradually comes to show quiet and positive interest in them. The key to whether he becomes a problem or a joy in his interaction with his parents and teachers is whether other people allow him to make an adaptation to the new situations at his own tempo, or insist on an immediate positive involvement.

Chess, Thomas, and Birch strongly rejected the concept that parents are completely to blame for all their children's problems. "The harm done by this preoccupation has been enormous."[13]

Consider this case:

CASE 67 MR. AND MRS. WHITE AND WENDY

Mr. and Mrs. White came to the family counselor because they were experiencing difficulties in controlling, disciplining, and obtaining the cooperation of their eight-year-old daughter, Wendy. Wendy's older brother behaved properly, according to the parents, though there were indications

[12]Ibid.
[13]Ibid., p. 10.

later that he cleverly fed his parents the answers which they expected. Her younger sister, aged five, was too young of course to understand the family's problems.

Wendy refused to wear the clothes laid out for her by her mother each morning; delayed her bedtime; had discipline problems at school; dropped from an A+ average to failing grades; and demanded attention through constant talking and even threatening to take an expensive article from a store.

Mr. and Mrs. White said their marital relationship was all right, insisting that their only problem was with Wendy. Yet clear indications were given that their sexual relationship was strongly inhibited. Both had come from unhappy homes, and as a result Mr. White was overdependent on his mother, while Mrs. White had not even spoken to her mother for over two years. They had great difficulty recognizing and dealing with their feelings. Their standards seemed to come from other people, and were not necessarily their own. Both feverishly engaged in time-consuming community interests, he with boys' hockey, and she with antipollution activities. They did not seem to know who they were, or indeed that they were unique persons with the inalienable right to their own values, views, and personal feelings.

How would you handle the obvious problem of the parents attempting to "scapegoat" the middle child? How would you approach this involved and complicated interrelationship?

Children not only know they do affect their parents' behaviors, but children have been taught methods for modifying their parents' behaviors. Joy Osofsky found that mothers do respond to their daughters' behavior which differs according to the situation.[14] Most children, however, do not know the principles on which such shaping of behavior operates. In 1974, Farnum Gray reported a research finding that young adolescent boys and girls could be taught both the principles and the techniques for modifying adults' behaviors. One girl reported that she had made an excellent homemaker of her mother by learning how to use those reinforcements that were important to her mother.[15] Parents, it seems, have taken both far too much blame and credit for the behavior of their children.

[14]Joy D. Osofsky, "The Shaping of Mother's Behavior by Children," *Journal of Marriage and the Family*, **32** (August, 1970), 400–405.
[15]Farnum Gray, "Little Brother Is Changing You," *Psychology Today*, **7** (March, 1974), 42–46. Also Eugene A. Ramp and Bill Hopkins, eds., *Behavior Analysis in Education*, Lawrence, Kans., University of Kansas, 1971.

PARENT-TO-CHILD COMMUNICATION

If, in fact, parent-child interaction is a two-way street, then the communication of ideas and attitudes becomes even more important. Although much communication is verbal, much of it is not verbal and is expressed through behavior and projected feelings. This is especially true in the case of the infant who has not yet learned to talk. But it is also true of the communication of unconscious wishes and desires by the parent in his relationship to the child.

One of the bases for good communication is listening to the meaning behind the words. Children often became experts at this, sometimes to the point where they can detect attitudes on the part of their parents that the parents themselves did not realize they had. If the attitude that the children "feel" is different from the attitude that the parent verbally expresses, only confusion and misunderstanding can result, for the inability of the parents to give clear direction will make the child uncertain about himself and the expectations that are set for him.

Most parents do not recognize that they are sending out confused messages. For example, the mother who tells her young child to go to school and at the same time holds him tightly, tells the child verbally that he should go while she simultaneously conveys to him by her actions that she does not want him to leave her. The unspoken message "stay with me" may be the one the child obeys, to the displeasure of his mother. In the same manner, a mother who unconsciously hates men can transmit the idea that it would be acceptable for her daughter to act out hostility toward her father, even though the mother puts on an outward appearance of perpetual sweetness toward her husband. This kind of confused message may also be readily apparent in the attitudes of a mother who eagerly says to her daughter, "You shouldn't do those naughty things with boys, but tell me more." Confused communication among family members is not always so obvious, however.

CASE 68 AGNES

"I don't know what I'm going to do with Agnes," the mother said to the counselor. "She won't go to school most of the time because she says she feels sick. I know she really should go to school, because I've had her to the doctor dozens of times, and he says he can't find anything the matter with the poor child. But I know how it is. I have headaches all the time, and sometimes I just absolutely can't get out of bed myself. And I remem-

ber when I was her age. I was just like her. I didn't have the strength to go to school some days.

"I don't think my husband understands about this, though. Sometimes he has to do all the housework after he gets home from the office. He seems to do it willingly, but I feel very badly about it.

"I certainly don't want a sickly child in the family. It's bad enough that I'm not able to do all that I should. The whole thing has made me so depressed that I can scarcely bear to live with myself sometimes. As a matter of fact, three weeks ago, I got so upset thinking about Agnes that I tried to take my own life. I just couldn't take it anymore. You must try to help us."

The counselor talked with Agnes's father. "My wife has always been sickly," the husband said. "My mother was that way, too. I can remember as a little boy taking hot soup up to Mother. She would pat me and call me her little doctor. Actually, it was one of the few times I can remember Mother smiling. Most of the time she yelled at me. I had an older brother who did all sorts of bad things and hollered back at her. Somehow she seemed to like that from him. But it was rare that I found a way to please her.

"I don't know what's the matter with Agnes. But it certainly worries her mother. She frets over the poor child all the time. A month ago I came into the room and found my wife taking sleeping pills. I grabbed them away from her just in time. I'm almost afraid to leave her alone now. I've asked Agnes a hundred times to help me do things for her mother, but every time I ask, Agnes complains about some pain she has, so in the end I wind up doing it.

"Sometimes Agnes says some very impertinent and nasty things to her mother. But we can't punish Agnes when she doesn't feel well. I'm hoping you can find some way to help her.

"Actually, Agnes has always been a difficult child. I guess we were spoiled because our son was born first, and he was so gentle and easygoing. But Agnes has been very demanding. As an infant she cried all the time. She nearly drove her poor mother out of her mind before she was a year old. My wife doesn't know how to cope with her. Really, I guess I should say that neither one of us knows how to cope with her now. I don't understand why Agnes doesn't want to be more like her brother. He's a good boy. He does well in school and never gives his mother any trouble at all.

"Agnes does very badly in school; that is, when she's there. Much of the time she tells us she doesn't feel well enough to go."

Agnes canceled two appointments in a row with the counselor. Each *time she didn't feel well enough to come. The third time her mother brought her, but Agnes sat in stony silence, giving the counselor one-word replies to questions. Toward the end of the hour, however, Agnes asked the counselor if he really believed she was sick. He replied that he was not a medical doctor but that he would certainly like to work with her and a medical doctor until they could find out what was wrong.*

At the next session, Agnes was considerably more voluble. "I don't think my father and mother really like each other," Agnes said. "To hear Mother tell it at the bridge club, she has the most wonderful man in the world, but if she really loved him she wouldn't impose on him the way she does.

"And he doesn't really like her, despite what he says. But he just can't seem to bring himself to tell her to get up off the bed and get her work done. He keeps trying to please her all the time. The more difficult she is to please, the harder he tries.

"I suppose you've heard that Mother tried to kill herself. That's a laugh. Father came in and found her stretched across the bed with an empty bottle of sleeping pills in her hand. She was mumbling about having taken them all. But they took her to the hospital and pumped out her stomach—she hadn't counted on that—and they found only a slight trace of the barbiturates. I guess she dumped the rest down the toilet. Do you think my father got angry when he found out that he had been tricked? Oh no, not him. He just said something about how much more terrible it was that she felt she had to deceive him.

"My mother doesn't love anybody, really. She'll gush all over you and tell you how sorry she is. I suppose she told you how sorry she was that I'm sick. Well, she isn't really. She doesn't care about much of anything except her precious son. She slobbers over him all the time. He can manipulate her into doing anything. She's always either giving in to him or backing him up in some fib he's telling my father."

Child-to-parent communication

In addition to inadequate communication from parent to child, there is often inadequate communication from child to parent. Perhaps it is even more important with children than with other adults to listen to their meaning instead of their words. Children need the security of someone who not only accepts their thoughts and feelings as expressed but who also can interpret what they would like to have said. Haim Ginott gives the following illustration:

Carol, age twelve, was tense and tearful. Her favorite cousin was going home after staying with her during the summer.

Carol (with tears in her eyes): Susie is going away. I'll be all alone again.

Mother: You'll find another friend.

Carol: I'll be so lonely.

Mother: You'll get over it.

Carol: Oh, mother! *(Sobs.)*

Mother: You are twelve years old and still such a crybaby.

Carol gave mother a deadly look and escaped to her room, closing the door behind her.

This episode should have had a happier ending. A child's feeling must be taken seriously, even though the situation itself is not very serious. In mother's eyes a summer separation may be too minor a crisis for tears, but her response need not have lacked sympathy. Mother might have said to herself, "Carol is distressed. I can help her best by showing that I understand what pains her." To her daughter she might have said any or all of the following: "It will be lonely without Susie." "You miss her already." "It is hard to be apart when you are so used to being together." "The house must seem kind of empty to you without Susie around." Such responses create intimacy between parent and child. When the child feels understood, his loneliness and hurt diminish, because they are understood, and his love for mother is deepened because she understands. Mother's sympathy serves as an emotional bandaid for the bruised ego.[16]

Strong feelings do not vanish because they are banished, but they do diminish in intensity when they are accepted with sympathy and understanding by a listener. Ginott illustrated how empathetic communication can alter relationships both between children and adults and between two adults by citing an excerpt from a parents' discussion group:

Leader: Suppose it is one of those mornings when everything seems to go wrong. The telephone rings, the baby cries, and before you know it, the toast is burnt. Your husband looks over the toaster and says: "My God! When will you learn to make toast?!" What is your reaction?

Mrs. A: I would throw the toast in his face!

Mrs. B: I would say, "Fix your own damn toast!"

Mrs. C: I would be so hurt I could only cry.

Leader: What would your husband's words make you feel toward him?

Parents: Anger, hate, resentment.

Leader: Would it be easy for you to fix another batch of toast?

Mrs. A: Only if I could put some poison in it!

Leader: And when he left for work, would it be easy to clean up the house?

Mrs. A: No, the whole day would be ruined.

Leader: Suppose that the situation is the same: the toast is burnt but your

[16]Haim Ginott, *Between Parent and Child*, New York, Macmillan, 1965, pp. 19–20.

husband, looking over the situation, says, "Gee, honey, it's a rough morning for you —the baby, the phone, and now the toast."

Mrs. A: I would drop dead if my husband said that to me!

Mrs. B: I would feel wonderful!

Mrs. C: I would feel so good I would hug and kiss him.

Leader: Why?—that baby is still crying and the toast is still burnt.

Parents: That wouldn't matter.

Leader: What would make the difference?

Mrs. B: You feel kind of grateful that he didn't criticize you, that he was with you, not against you.

Leader: And when your husband left for work, would it be difficult to clean up the house?

Mrs. C: No! I'd do it with a song.

Leader: Let me now tell you about a third kind of husband. He looks over the burnt toast and says to you calmly, "Let me show you honey, how to make toast."

Mrs. A: Oh, no. He is even worse than the first one. He makes you feel stupid.

Leader: Let's see how these three different approaches to the toast incident apply to our handling of children.

Mrs. A: I see what you're driving at. I always say to my child, "You are old enough to know this, you are old enough to know that." It must make him furious. It usually does.

Mrs. B: I always say to my son, "Let me show you, dear, how to do this or that."

Mrs. C: I'm so used to being criticized that it comes natural to me. I use exactly the same words my mother used against me when I was a child. And I hated her for it. I never did anything right, and she always made me do things over.

Leader: And you now find yourself using the same words with your daughter?

Mrs. C: Yes. I don't like it at all—I don't like myself when I do it.

Leader: You are looking for better ways of talking with your children.

Mrs. C: Yes, I sure am!

Leader: Let's see what we can learn from the burnt toast story. What is it that helped change the mean feelings to loving ones?

Mrs. B: The fact that somebody understood you.

Mrs. C: Without blaming you.

Mrs. A: And without telling you how to improve.[17]

SIBLING RELATIONSHIPS

When a discussion focuses on interaction between the children in a family, the first kind of relationship mentioned is sibling rivalry. Because it is often conspicuous and dramatic—indeed, in many modern families, it is the pre-

---

[17]Haim Ginott, *Group Psychotherapy with Children*, New York, McGraw-Hill, 1961, pp. 180–182.

dominant and controlling factor in the relationships among the children—sibling rivalry has received much professional attention.

Sibling rivalry results when a child feels replaced by another. But it may also result from the comparisons parents often make in front of the children. As Allison Davis and Robert Havighurst have suggested,

Whether a child is a first child (or not) . . . he will certainly have to come to grips with jealousy and rivalry. To make the situation worse, his parents . . . will urge him both to compete with his brothers and sisters in some ways, and not to compete with them in other ways.[18]

In early childhood, the result of a sibling rivalry frequently is clearly evident. Sometimes it takes the form of overt hostility on the part of the older child, as he all but pokes the baby's eyes out. In other cases, it manifests itself by a psychological retreat. The three-year-old may revert to wetting or soiling, infantile speech, or sucking on a bottle in an attempt to be a baby again, with the unconscious hope that the mother once more will lavish time and affection on him.

Some writers feel that some jealousy and rivalry are inevitable in American culture, since every child wants to be best loved by his parents. The first child usually wants it more than the others, since he was once the only child and knew what it was like to have all the attention. Davis and Havighurst, in studying two-child families, reported that most mothers thought that their first-borns were more jealous and selfish, no matter what type of training they had received or whether or not they were treated more indulgently than the second child.[19] They concluded that no type of training whatever, whether severe, moderate, or indulgent, was likely to eliminate the first child's sense of having been replaced by the second and having lost some of his parents' love. It is possible, of course, that the mother could control to some degree the development of sibling rivalry by overcompensating with her attention for the child who is experiencing severe jealousy. Most authorities recommend that a mother be constantly alert to minimize the effects of sibling competition.

Sibling rivalry is by no means the only problem of child interaction, as any harried young mother can testify. Children are subject to most of the same conflicts and hostilities as adults. But children's overt reactions to conflict situations are usually more direct and more honest than their

[18]Allison Davis and Robert J. Havighurst, *Father of the Man*, Boston, Houghton Mifflin, 1947, p. 120.
[19]Ibid., pp. 119–131.

elders' reactions. Sometimes, though, even a child is caught in a dilemma in which he cannot express his true feelings. Judith was a woman who had deep feelings of guilt and hostility because her mother had been unwilling to admit that Judith's retarded sister was abnormal and insisted that she go to school with Judith. Since Judith had been emotionally indoctrinated to be absolutely loyal to her retarded sister, she was tortured every day by the other students' taunts. She knew of no way to tell her mother what the children were saying, nor was she able to handle the emotional trauma that resulted from her own ambivalent feelings of embarrassment, shame, anger, and guilt. Soon she grew to hate her sister as the cause of her own emotional discomfort. This brought her into conflict with her conscience again. Later, long after her retarded sister had died, considerable psychotherapy was needed to help Judith.

Relationships among the children in a family are not always unhappy. Sibling rivalry notwithstanding, the advantages of having brothers and sisters are numerous. The first and primary advantage is that a sibling —especially an older sibling of the same sex—can serve as a role model. Some authorities believe that, in the long run, the positive significance of siblings in teaching social roles to their brothers and sisters far outweighs the negative aspects of sibling rivalry.[20] In some cases, older siblings are literally heroes or heroines to their younger brothers and sisters, and this hero worship often benefits both the older and the younger child.

But a close brother-sister relationship is not always beneficial either. Consider the following case:

CASE 69 DONISE AND DON

"Don and I were born on a farm," Donise begins. "It's good we were twins; we had no close neighbors. We had so much fun when we were younger; we did all sorts of things. I remember once we got lost while playing in the woods near our house. I started to cry but Don just put his arm around me and assured me that everything would be all right. He was so brave and he found our way out.

"When we were in junior high, we moved to the city. Don was smaller than the other boys his age and they made fun of him. They called him a shrimp, but I took up for him; I told Don he didn't need anybody else. He had me. But then Don started growing and soon he was as big as the other boys.

[20]Donald P. Irish, "Sibling Interactions: A Neglected Aspect of Family Life Research," *Social Forces,* **42** (March, 1964), 279–288.

"Don never had time for girls because he was always practicing so he could do his best for the team. He became a hero for the team. Everybody loved him. I worked especially hard at school so I could help Don with his studies. He was too busy with baseball to study hard so I helped him out. But Don never forgot me. He used to warn me about boys; you know how they are. They just want to see how much they can get out of a girl. I was lucky to have Don around to protect me.

"When we went away to the university, Don didn't have to spend so much time practicing baseball. Last spring, he started dating a cheerleader. He used to come over and let me help him with his studies, but now she helps him. When they went out, Don would invite me to go too. Now, she has told Don that she doesn't like having me around all the time. She wants Don to get me a date so we can all go out sometimes. She just doesn't want the three of us to be alone because she knows that Don prefers me to her. She's afraid that I'll show him that she's not as smart as I am.

"Besides, I don't know whether I want a date or not. I never dated anybody in high school and I don't think I missed out on anything. I always had Don. Well, now I'm almost afraid to go out with a boy. What would I do if he tried to attack me?

"Oh, I wish things were the way they used to be when it was just Don and me. We didn't want or need anybody else then."

Another advantage of having brothers and sisters is that the older siblings can serve as parent substitutes in the care and training of the other youngsters. Although they may not appreciate this role while they are involved in it, the older children receive considerable experience and grow toward adulthood faster as a result.

A third advantage is that siblings learn to share rights and privileges. Often they find it easier to accept life's greatest lesson, that some wishes cannot always be satisfied, because other people have needs, too. Still another advantage is that brothers and sisters in the same general age group can be playmates and lead each other to other playmates. Finally, siblings tend to reduce the egocentrism and oversensitivity that are often identified with the only child.

Sibling relationships affect not only the children involved but parent-child relationships as well. Moreover, relationships between the children can affect the relationship between the parents. It is not uncommon for one parent to take one child's side against his siblings and against the opposite-sex parent. This can be one of the most divisive forces in the family. Such a situation usually signals an imperative need for professional help in establishing new patterns of family interaction. To improve family living it is usually necessary to improve *all* the relationships among *all* the family members.

IMPROVING TOTAL FAMILY RELATIONSHIPS

The literature on parent-child relationships fills thousands of volumes, and every student who looks forward to being a parent would be well advised to take coursework in this infinitely complex field. It is difficult even to cover the basic essentials in any brief condensation.

Asked in 1965 to summarize the most frequent sources of parent-child conflicts and childhood emotional disturbances, Herbert Wimberger, Director of the Child Psychiatric Clinic at the University of Washington, suggested these:

> lack of emotional contact
> devaluating attitudes of the parents
> lack of defined limits[21]

Each of these problems has already been touched on. The effect of lack of emotional contact has been pointed out throughout the book; the case of Leroy earlier in Chapter 18 is a dramatic example of what devaluating attitudes can do to a child. Although the lack of limits has also been a frequently seen problem, perhaps it most of all warrants further discussion here. There is no more confused and controversial area of family difficulty in contemporary society than that of the parents' responsibility for, and methods of, providing guidance, direction, and discipline for the child.

Ever since the influence of parents on the development of the child became a popular field for critical examination in the early 1900s, parents, educators, and child-guidance specialists have been agonizing over what pattern of parental control is best. The pendulum has swung from strictness to permissiveness and appears to be swinging back again.

However, there are many who continue to argue that firm control inhibits the child's creativity, decreases normal self-assertiveness, and generates passivity and dependence. To some child-development experts in the mid-twentieth century, it appeared that more democracy and permissiveness

[21]Wimberger, op. cit., p. 186.

in family relationships was still the way to family improvement. Edward Dager summarized research studies that seemed to point to this: "Permissive (not extreme) and democratic parent-child interaction," he said, "appear to be associated with children who demonstrate self-confidence, initiative, independence, creativity, and cooperation. Restrictive or overprotective parent-child interaction is associated with children who are withdrawn, permissive, and dependent."[22]

On the other hand, Urie Bronfenbrenner concluded that the "democratic family which for so many years has been held up and aspired to as a model by professionals and enlightened laymen, tends to produce young people who do not take initiative, look to others for direction and decision and cannot be counted on to fulfill obligations."[23]

There is considerable hope that we are now moving into an era in parent-child understanding in which empirical research will be used as the basis for valid syntheses that can lead to improved family relationships. It may well be, for example, that, in parent-child interaction, *neither* permissiveness nor authoritarianism maximize child creativity and parental satisfaction. In her paper on the effects of parental control on child behavior, Diana Baumrind suggests another position, in which the parent is not authoritarian but authoritative. The authoritative parent differs from the authoritarian parent in that authoritativeness implies knowledge but does not encourage submissiveness.[24]

On the face of it, there would also seem to be many common-sense reasons for believing that the authoritative parent, in contrast to the demandingly authoritarian parent and the ultrapermissive parent, might provide more of the security and healthy opposition that allow a child to realize his maximum potential. After all, the child learns by imitation. Leadership is best learned by observing a leader, *not* by having to submit to a tyrant or by manipulating a nonopposer. In learning both to respect and to oppose the authority of the authoritative parent, the child can gain the self-confidence that will later let him be free to be self-directed in the face of group pressure. In the end, it is probably this child, conditioned to be neither reticently submissive nor uninhibitedly aggressive, who will

[22]Edward Z. Dager, "Socialization and Personality Development in the Child," in Harold T. Christensen, ed., *Handbook of Marriage and the Family*, Skokie, Ill., Rand McNally, 1964, p. 766.

[23]Urie Bronfenbrenner, "Some Familial Antecedents of Responsibility and Leadership in Adolescents," in L. Petrullo and B. Bass, eds., *Leadership and Interpersonal Behavior*, New York, Holt, Rinehart & Winston, 1961, p. 267.

[24]Diana Baumrind, "Effects of Authoritative Parental Control on Child Behavior," *Child Development*, **37** (December, 1966), 904–905.

provide his parents with emotional security and satisfaction and so improve family living.

Again, however, it should be remembered that good family relationships are a matter of *total* family interaction. Only in cases where *both* parents are satisfied with the method of control is there liable to be family harmony. Complete agreement on details is often difficult to achieve, even when all the family members concede the wisdom and appropriateness of a certain philosophical approach to child rearing. Again, as in every other facet of family relationships, improvement depends on the understanding and communication that exists—or can be created—between husband and wife.

20

WHAT MAKES A CRISIS?

All families face difficulties and crises. Why is it that some families survive, whereas others disintegrate? And why do some families actually grow stronger as a result of crisis? These questions have interested sociologists for many years. Few definitive generalizations have resulted from their studies, but a good many hypotheses have been suggested. There is general agreement that the ability of marriage partners or family members to meet the inevitable crises that will affect them depends on such factors as these: (1) the family's own definition of the trouble or whether they regard it as a crisis; (2) whether the problem came suddenly or slowly; (3) the preparation the family had made in advance for meeting just such emergencies; (4) the previous experience of the family in dealing with whatever the trouble is; (5) the number of supportive relatives, neighbors, and friends; (6) the social expectations of peers and customs; and (7) the family goals.

DEFINING A CRISIS

The definition of a crisis depends not only on the nature of the experience itself but also on the values and beliefs of the family members. What is defined as a crisis in some families is not even recognized as a problem in others.

The sudden loss of employment in a middle-class family might be defined as a total disaster, yet in some lower-class homes, where the breadwinner is laid off every few months, it might be just another period of belt-tightening. Discovering that one's husband has been unfaithful, finding out that one's daughter is pregnant out of wedlock, or learning that one's son has killed a man depends for its crisis effect on the cultural definition of the behavior involved, as well as on the particular circumstances surrounding the event.

In recent years, there has been considerable study of the "why" and "when" of family definitions of crises. For example, parents who define a child's mental illness as their fault are more adversely affected by it than parents who consider the illness independent of them.[1] Mothers with younger children tend to be able to accept mental retardation of an older child better, and this acceptance is encouraged by religious beliefs.[2]

[1]B. Farber, "Effects of a Severely Mentally Retarded Child on Family Integration," *Monographs of the Society for Research in Child Development*, **24** (1959), 13.
[2]G. H. Zuk, "The Religious Factor and the Role of Guilt in Parental Acceptance of the Retarded Child," *American Journal of Mental Deficiency*, **64** (July, 1959), 145.

The *actual* situation in which a family finds itself may be less important in determining the behavior of the family members than the *imagined* situation, as Hansen and Hill have pointed out.[3] To an individual, his perception of what is occurring constitutes the "real world." Although definitions influence the action one takes, the consequences do not always follow one's expectations, and unforeseen stress may result.

It is probable that the more successful families are the ones who can achieve the greater objectivity and thus greater reality in their definitions. Since cultural values vary so widely, it is also probable that there will not be universal standards in the foreseeable future by which an individual can measure the depth of real crises. But even if there were such objective measures, it is not very probable that any large number of people would use them. Conditioned values and personal anxieties would still operate to control behavior. In general, however, middle-class families, as Koos has shown, tend to have a greater sensitivity to crisis with a greater inclination to react (and sometimes overreact), than do lower- and upper-class families. Middle-class families recover more quickly and more often emerge with some positive benefit from their crises. Because of their less adequate preparation, lower-class families are seldom really strengthened by what they define as crises.[4]

It is not just social class that determines whether something is defined as a crisis. It may be the age, the sex, the situation, or the goals. Pregnancy may not be a crisis for your thirty-five-year-old sister who has been wanting a child, but could be for your thirty-five-year-old-neighbor who is unmarried and in the middle of planning a big job change to enhance her career. A broken leg might be disastrous for you in the middle of this semester but might be an attention-getter for a preteen boy who needed the attention.

SUDDEN CRISES VERSUS INSIDIOUS CRISES

Problems differ not only in their intensity and in their finality but also in the way in which they start. In some ways, sudden disasters are easier for the typical middle-class family to deal with. In fact, there is considerable

[3]Donald A. Hansen and Reuben Hill, "Families Under Stress," in Harold T. Christensen, ed., *Handbook of Marriage and the Family*, Skokie, Ill., Rand McNally, 1964, pp. 809–810.

[4]Earl L. Koos, "Class Differences in Family Reactions to Crisis," *Marriage and Family Living*, **12** (Summer, 1950), 78.

evidence both in research and observation that a sudden crisis can often be a unifying factor in family relations. Sometimes the husband and wife, having separated with apparently irreconcilable differences, are reunited by an accident that befalls their child. Working together to overcome some obstacle tends to lead to family unity in many cases.

Sudden disasters are not always unifying, of course. If all the basic emotional ties between the partners have been cut prior to the crisis, or if the disaster is so overwhelming that solution seems impossible and hope turns to despair, or if the partners were not very self-reliant to begin with, the family can be shattered by an unexpected catastrophe. Many families are literally torn to pieces or thrown into depression states from which they never recover by the death, unemployment, or illness of the breadwinner.

The varieties of sudden disaster that can strike a family are infinite. They range from such natural catastrophes as floods, tornadoes, and earthquakes to such man-caused problems as bankruptcy, automobile accidents, and social disgrace. Even if they may be unifying in the long run, the immediate impact of such disasters creates profound shock and temporary demoralization.

One often overlooked sudden family disaster is the rapid rise of one partner to fame or wealth. This may constitute a crisis quite as disruptive as economic loss or social disgrace. Every movie fan has read of actors who achieve stardom and then divorce their mates. Many people believe that, because actors are notoriously unconventional and temperamental, the fragility of their marriages is to be expected. But family dissolution occurs in other professions, too, when there is a swift change from poverty to riches or from obscurity to fame. No one is quite sure of the extent of this kind of family crisis in our affluent society, but it seems reasonable to speculate that a great many families have been at least partially disorganized by some of the same dynamics of upward mobility. One thing that contributes to this disorganization is the sudden dropping of old friends and relatives, leaving the upwardly mobile family with a feeling of insecurity and guilt in some cases. Consider the following case:

CASE 70 CHUCK AND STELLA

"Five years ago, before Chuck made all that money contracting, we were very happy," Stella told the counselor. "He was a good father and used to take a lot of interest in the children. Back then he was only a carpenter, but he worked hard and had some time off on Saturdays and Sundays. We'd all go out walking in the country and sometimes take a picnic with us.

"Now, all that seems like a dream. Somehow he was able to borrow enough money and get a little political help, and he landed a big contract to build low-income homes. He made a lot of money on the first job, but it was nothing to what he made on the second contract. Now I guess you'd say we're wealthy. Sure, I like the $300 dresses and all the jewelry, and I like having a car of my own and a summer place. And I like the things that money will buy the children. But I would give it all up to have Chuck back again the way he used to be.

"Now we hardly see him at all. He's always away on business. I don't even let myself wonder what kind of 'business' it is anymore. But I know it involves a lot of drinking and a lot of staying out all night. I think the drinking is the worst part about it. All those big-shot contractors get together and drink. They drink at lunch, and they drink before they have dinner. On a few occasions when he's come home recently, he's been high as a kite. I hate drinking. My father was an alcoholic, and I can remember how embarrassed I was. My father kept our family poor as church mice because he was forever drinking himself out of a job. And now I can see it happening to Chuck.

"I try to talk with him about it, but he doesn't pay any attention to me anymore. Oh yes, once in a while, if he gets drunk enough, he'll want to have sex. But ordinarily he doesn't even talk to me. It's just as if we lived in two different worlds now. He says, 'You have all the money you ever wanted, don't you?' He doesn't understand that I really don't want the money. I want him the way he was.

"He won't go out with any of our old friends now. He says they're stupid country bumpkins. It isn't as if he wasn't raised in the country himself. But now he wants to be with all those fancy people at the country club, and he doesn't ever want to play cribbage or go out on a family picnic anymore.

"The money hasn't made me happy, and I don't think it's made him happy, either. He thought he was doing me a big favor because he built me this enormous house. Actually, it's increased my work four times over. When I told him about it, he made me get a maid. But that isn't what I wanted. I haven't found a maid I can get along with. I think the problem is mostly with me. I never learned how to tell other people what to do. I'm much happier doing my own work. I think the people who come to work for me sense this, and they know they can take advantage of me. I don't like it, and I never will.

"I want him to stop drinking and to come back to me. I want to move back to a nice little cottage like we had when the children were young, when we were happy. I don't know why he won't do this. I try to be a good wife to him. I work hard in the house. Please tell him that he ought to try to act more like a husband and father should act."

The counselor saw Chuck after he had made and broken four appointments. He had obviously been drinking. "The trouble with Stella is she can't accept the good things," Chuck said. "She was just a little farm girl, and that's all she'll ever be. She's compulsive about working herself to death around the house. We've got all the money we'll ever need, and she's acting stupid. It isn't only that she's wearing herself out; it doesn't look good for me down at the country club. All the other women come down and play bridge, and some of them even make business contacts for their husbands in their social activities. Not Stella. She just hangs around the house. Well, believe me, I want something more out of life than that.

"I suppose she told you that I drink too much. I don't drink any more than the rest of the fellows I know. We have one or two at lunch and then after we finish work in the evening we always have a couple of rounds. Sometimes I do get a little high, but so what? The other fellows don't catch hell like I do. The real trouble is that Stella is afraid I'm going to turn into an alcoholic like her old man. She isn't really angry about the little bit of drinking I do; she's upset because it reminds her of all the problems she had when she was a kid. I get blamed for what her father did. If she could ever get over being anxious about it, she'd probably realize my drinking isn't so bad. Everybody has a social drink or two these days, so what's wrong with that? She'd be a lot better off if she'd do it, too.

"Since I've been down at the country club, I've found out there's a lot more to living, and there's a lot more to man-woman relationships than I ever knew with Stella. Sure, I've met other women. I've learned a lot from some of them. They don't nag me about the drinking. They just listen to me and try to understand me. I'm no worse than any other guy, but I'm no angel, either. When the cookies are passed, I have some. That's normal, isn't it?

"If Stella would go down there to the country club, maybe she'd learn something. Maybe if she was there, I wouldn't get to meet so many other women. But don't tell her I said that, because she might go and then she'd be there nagging me about drinking.

"I suppose she told you I wouldn't go out with her and our old friends anymore. Well, that's true, but not for the reason she thinks. It's just that we have nothing in common anymore. I don't like to do the things they want to do, and they can't afford to do the things that I like to do. I've told her a hundred times that I would go out with her and any new friends she wants to make, provided they've got the income to go *where I like to go and chip in for a round of drinks once in a while. How much more fair can I be than that?"*

The insidious problems

The slowly building crises that result from small degenerative changes are often more demoralizing and devastating to family relationships than sudden disasters. One of the worst of these is the disenchantment that seems to take place in many marriages. Peter Pineo analyzed the disenchantment process and postulated three indices of impending romantic crisis. The first of these, he said, was a drop in marital satisfaction. The second was a decline in such behaviors as confiding, kissing, and reciprocal settlement of disagreements. The third was a diminution of certain forms of marital interaction, such as sexual intercourse, mutual decision making, and talking. Pineo argued that disenchantment is an inevitable process, since the partners have maximum "fit" and maximum satisfaction at the beginning of marriage and thus have only one direction to go: down.[5]

Pineo's view is somewhat cynical, but the statistical data back him up, just as he says, *on the average.* Here again, though, this is actuarial data and has little to do with any particular individual's marriage. There are many marriages that continue to grow, and to grow richer as the years go by. Nonetheless, disenchantment does reach the crisis point for many people. This is how divorces happen. Yet, if we accept Pineo's proposition that marriage represents a high point from which the only direction is down, it might also be said that somewhere in the process there is a bottom from which the only direction is up. The idea that partners can be helped to find an earlier "bottoming out" for their conflicts is basic to marriage counseling.

Other insidious problems are alcoholism, mental and emotional illness, and certain physical conditions such as muscular dystrophy, cancer, heart condition, and hypertension. Some of these will be discussed at length later.

The aging problem

Of all the degenerative changes that affect the family, none is more insidious than the physical and emotional effects of the aging process. The physical effects of growing older (not necessarily growing *old,* just older)

[5]Peter C. Pineo, "Disenchantment in the Later Years of Marriage," *Marriage and Family Living,* **23** (February, 1961), 3–11.

are bad enough, but the emotional aspects are often devastating. The attractive young woman who has mirror-given self-confidence usually has enough ego strength to laugh and play with her husband and thus enhance their happy relationship. But when she begins to lose her physical beauty, she often begins to lose her self-confidence, too, and her interpersonal behavior then frequently reflects an anxious and serious quality that leads to unhappiness and conflict rather than harmony. Men are also victims of the psychological insults of aging, but they are not usually so anxious as women because the penalties for losing their figures are not ordinarily so severe.

There are other reasons why women have a more difficult time during the middle years. As they move into their late thirties, premenstrual tension often increases and a few years later some other physical and emotional changes preceding the menopause begin to take place. At this time, women are described as premenopausal and, sometimes, perhaps *because* of this labeling, develop many dispositional symptoms that create or exacerbate tensions among the family members. It is said, however, that many women do not suddenly develop such symptoms, but were like this in the years preceding menopause.

It is really the coincidence of a great many unhappy experiences that makes this period so difficult. As pointed out previously, it is just about this time that the children begin to leave home and the women begin to be dissatisfied with their diminished roles. This is the time of identity crisis when many women begin looking for something more than they have. For most middle-life women, the one helpful prescription is to busy themselves with new interests and activities. For some, this is a very satisfying solution. Others reject the activities that are open to them yet find themselves unqualified for the type of work they would like to do. This suggests that avoiding middle-life crisis for a woman probably involves two things: one is the motivation and the ambition to get out and do something once the children have left home; and the other is vocational preparation before marriage. The typical woman will spend at least twenty-five years of her life working outside the home. Yet it is surprising how many women come face-to-face with the middle-life role problem without having adequately anticipated it.

Usually the man's role-identity problem comes later in life. There comes a time in most men's lives when they have gotten the last promotion they will get. If it is not as high as the one they had set for themselves, this knowledge is disheartening. As suggested by the theory of cognitive dissonance (see the Appendix), they can alleviate some of their anxiety by changing either the belief or—if, in fact, there is nothing they can do to get the promotion they wanted—the goal. Some men do not get the feeling of "it's all over" until they are forced to retire from active employment. Here, too, anticipation and preparation are the only true preventives.

BEING PREPARED

Preparation involves some intelligence, because one has to be able to foresee what his problem most likely will be, but it is also closely associated with value conditioning. For example, on the island of Yap in the Philippine Sea, there is little preparation for the typhoons that regularly devastate the unprotected villages, in spite of the fact that the natives know from experience that the typhoons will be coming, if not this year then the next. D. M. Schneider has suggested that they fail to prepare for the typhoons because they believe that supernatural powers send the storms as punishment. Their best hope, they believe, lies in rituals and magic.[6]

Lest anyone think that cultural beliefs that preclude practical action are limited to uneducated island peoples, it should be noted that few modern American women really prepare for the role of homemaker, even though they may know from early childhood that this is basically what they want. And few men prepare for activities and attitudes after retirement.

In general, advanced preparation for anticipated crises has been more characteristic of middle-class family patterns than those of lower-social-level families in the past. Middle-class boys learned in their childhood homes that it was right for the father to buy insurance to protect his family. Girls learned that it was right to save pennies by careful home management. Lower-class family members, on the other hand, were often prevented by economic scarcity from protecting themselves against future problems. Moreover, they had less of the "socialized anxiety" that made such behaviors "right." In many lower-class homes, there was more inclination, because of deprivation, to use whatever was available today for today's needs and hope that something would turn up for tomorrow. Harold Hodges, Jr., after reviewing studies of class-related behavior, points out that living for the moment is not frowned on in a group where opportunities for "living it up" are rare.[7]

There are, of course, *individual* differences in defining preparation

[6]D. M. Schneider, "Typhoons on Yap," *Human Organization*, **16** (Summer, 1957), 10–15.

[7]Harold Hodges, Jr., *Social Stratification: Class in America*, Cambridge, Mass., Schenkman, 1964, pp. 195–220.

as a value, as well as social-class differences. Sometimes, as we have seen, two young people from the same family develop entirely different attitudes: One may gamble; the other may fear any form of risk. Although this may cause little inconvenience in their childhood family, it may be absolute disaster if they marry unlike mates. In such a marriage, one partner feels constantly inhibited and the other constantly anxious.

Adequate preparation for family living means more than buying insurance or learning home management. It also involves preparing psychologically to face the crisis of an empty house when the children are gone and the crisis of an empty heart when a loved one dies. No one is ever fully prepared for any crisis, but the more successful families are generally the more prepared.

Experience with problems

Experience can be the best and also the most costly part of preparation. Theoretically, little mistakes early in the marriage can prevent big ones later on. This probably happens more often than is recorded. Yet there are some "crisis prone" families that appear to be unable to learn from previous mistakes. Often these problem families have marriage partners with personality, motivational, and educational inadequacies that prevent them from solving their own problems.

College-educated people have a greater-than-average ability to succeed in family groups, both because of their larger incomes and because of their status-conferred self-confidence, but even among college graduates there are some people who seem to be chronically incapable of anticipating or solving their own practical and emotional problems. Many such individuals eventually seek psychiatric treatment. Most people and most families, however, profit from past errors and become better at avoiding crises as time goes by. In fact, some who have faced many early emergencies are more successful in the long run because of their early learning experiences.

THE IMPORTANCE OF SUPPORTIVE HELP

Families meet crises more successfully and recover from them more quickly when relatives, friends, and neighbors are available to support them. This is a common observation. It is also validated by research data. In his war-separation study, Reuben Hill found that the families who were slowest to adjust to the separation were often solitary families who had moved often and to great distances from their relatives.[8] Stating it more positively, he concluded that, "When the doors and kitchens of the neighbors are open to almost everyone, the long-term impact of stress may be resolved."[9]

Contemporary patterns of mobile and suburban living have many advantages, including new experience, greater self-reliance, and more independence from in-laws, relatives, and inquisitive neighbors. But there are disadvantages, too, and one of the greatest of these is the loss of comfort and support from people who really care in time of crisis.

FAMILY EXPECTATIONS, GOALS, AND BEHAVIOR IN CRISES

Families, like individuals, tend to behave the way they are expected to behave in the subcultural group in which they exist. Especially when under stress, families often take refuge in the rituals and customs that sustained their value system in the past, even if they gave little attention to those rituals and customs in noncrisis periods. This is especially true of religious ritual, but it is also true of community customs and social usage.

In those social groups in which it is appropriate for the widow to exhibit stalwart and stoic behavior at the funeral of her late husband, regardless of how she feels, the widow is likely to behave just that way. But in those subcultural groups where it is customary for the widow to express her grief animatedly, the performance of the stoic widow might be considered both curious and unfeeling.

In a family facing a crisis, the conditioned expectations of the partners are often heightened. Each partner becomes even more sensitive and more critical of the role behavior of the other. When under stress, family members can become devastatingly explicit in their accusations of how others have failed to meet their expectations.

Expectations have another way of affecting family problems, too. Parents who expect their adolescents to be difficult often have difficult adolescents. Parents who expect their child to have a religious "awakening" at puberty usually have a child who has a religious awakening at puberty. Families that have a self-expectation of pulling themselves out of crisis difficulties often do just that, and they will probably do it in just about the time that the social expectation says they should. For some, the expectation may require an extended period of grief and self-pity with a long, slow recovery

---

[8]Reuben Hill, *Families Under Stress*, New York, Harper & Row, 1949, pp. 123–124.
[9]Hansen and Hill, op. cit., p. 797.

period. In other families, the expectation may require an immediate effort on the part of all the members to face the situation realistically and set about restoring equilibrium. No one can really say which way is better. As with so many other things, a lot depends on what you're used to.

Family theorists and marriage counselors generally agree that the family that is well organized, has defined goals, and is steadily working toward them is far more likely to be successful than the family that has no purposeful direction.

The fact that many family members no longer have some of the goal satisfactions that families used to have may be, as we saw in Chapter 2, one important reason for today's high rate of marriage difficulty. Just producing enough to keep the family members alive was an important and satisfying achievement on the frontier, and being a "good provider" was a meaningful goal for a husband during the 1930s. These goals, however, derived from the necessities of living and did not have to be chosen in the same sense that family goals are chosen today.

In the present affluent society, short-range, pleasure-oriented goals are probably more easily attainable than at any time before. A new car, a color television set, or a European vacation can be procured by many individuals and families before these wishes have even attained the status of "fondest dreams." But it is the long-range, larger—yet less-specific—goals, carefully chosen and diligently sought after, that enlarge family unity and provide a steadfastness of purpose. Such goals as a "good family life," a "college education for the children," or even a "successful marriage" can give meaning to all the sacrifices that are involved in achieving them. It would be hard to overestimate the importance of family goals in maintaining family unity and stability.

Progression of behavior in crises

Most families exhibit a certain progression of behavior in adjusting to all crisis situations. In the beginning, the family is numbed by the blow. They continue to act at first as if the blow had not fallen; then, as the facts are assimilated, the family members tend to become disorganized and to show their resentments. Soon, conflicts develop and are converted into tensions that strain relations. Ultimately, however, the crisis bottoms out, and things begin to improve, with new routines being introduced that were arrived at either by chance or by thoughtful planning. Hope for the future continues the upward process of adjustment.[10]

[10]Ibid., pp. 809–810.

Although this progression usually occurs, it varies somewhat with the suddenness of the crisis, the family's preparation and experience, the help that friends, neighbors, and professionals can give, as well as what is expected from society and from the family itself.

The degree to which a person behaves with calm decisiveness in difficult situations, solves problems intelligently, seeks help from appropriate specialists when he needs it, and is adaptable enough to change himself and so adjust to the realities of the situation that confronts him also affects how a crisis is resolved. All of these behavior characteristics are crucial in effectively dealing with the difficulties in marriage and in family living that inevitably arise. It is probable that a family will be successful to the degree and extent to which its members possess these characteristics.

SPECIFIC CRISIS SITUATIONS

If the situation that is a crisis to one family is not a crisis to another family, then it is difficult to select specific events as crises to discuss. We have not presented marriage as a crisis in this book and yet the marriage of a widowed father may be a crisis to his children. A promotion may turn out to be a crisis if the family does not want to move or if the promotion demands more than the person promoted can give. However, crises may be categorized as to change in family number, socioeconomic status, role, or morale.

A family eventually either increases or decreases by birth, deaths, a relative coming to live with the family, divorce or desertion, or by the children leaving home. Each one of these can be a welcome change or a crisis, according to who is involved and what happens in the family as a result.

A family crisis may result from a change in its socioeconomic status or a failure to change. Poverty is said to be a perpetual crisis. A loss of a job or a promotion may be a crisis, although promotions are generally viewed as a bonus. Both may affect social status. Either loss of property or an inheritance may create a crisis.

Although roles would appear not to be critical, they may be, as when a woman gets a raise so that she makes more money than her husband. A man who becomes incapacitated and a child who is belligerent both are in different roles from those that society expects, and may place strains on their families which result in a crisis. The role of new fatherhood is a crisis for some men. New motherhood can be a crisis for some women, too.

Demoralization of one or more family members may result from any of the above situations which are perceived as crises. It can also be the result of the birth of a handicapped child or alcoholism or infidelity. But what may be a crisis for some is a solution for others.

Any sudden event that changes a family's normal behavior is defined as a crisis. The extent of disorganization and the long-term effects determine how serious it is. If the long-term effects are favorable, then the change is good; if disastrous, obviously the change is not welcome.[11]

Certain events that can, and generally do, make family relationships and the personal growth of family members more difficult will be presented below, with discussions of how different families react to them.

DEATH

If you were thirty years old and your spouse died, nearly everyone would consider the situation a crisis, yet if you were eighty or even seventy and your spouse died it might be a crisis to you, but others would not see it as nearly as big a crisis as that of the thirty-year-old.

Death differs from every other crisis. Its finality leaves no hope of change except in those who are still alive. But herein lies the point of this discussion. What people do after a death can no longer be influenced by the presence of the dead person. Past influences are still operating, maybe even legally, but the decisions of the living are completely their own responsibility.[12]

As mentioned earlier, there is a normatively influenced progression of behavior after any crisis, including death, although the person most closely associated with the one who died does not operate with these in mind. After a death, in the beginning there is disbelief on the part of close survivors. There is even a searching to see if the death is a dream. The numbness that occurs may allow one to proceed with the details of a funeral. Even after the death has been accepted, the family members continue to talk about what the person would have preferred or hoped to do. All of this is a transition from nonacceptance to reality. Then as all the realities connected with the death continue to force themselves upon the survivors, some people begin to experience feelings of resentment, guilt, loneliness, despair, fear, or resignation. Those who were closely attached to the one who died may have any one or all of these feelings. Strange as it may seem, a wife may even resent the fact that her husband died and left

---

[11]Paul H. Glasser and Lois N. Glasser, eds., *Families in Crisis*, New York, Harper & Row, 1970, p. 6.

[12]Ernest Morgan, ed., *A Manual of Death Education and Simple Burial*, Burnsville, N.C., The Celo Press, 1973.

her in such trouble. A son may feel guilt over having been so belligerent to his father just prior to a sudden death. A person can feel guilt merely over continuing to live. A widower may feel despair when he attempts to take care of a house and several children. (See Case 24, Henry.)

If the family has been disorganized, a death may or may not reorganize them. It is doubtful that a family will become closer after a death if there has been real reason for dissension and separateness between the family members prior to the death. If the dead person was the only tie the family had, then disorganization will probably continue at an even faster rate. If the person was the cause of the disorganization there is more hope for reorganization. Some guilt may interfere with reorganization at first, due to the relief the family feels about the death.

Those families with strong ties and problem-solving abilities and the resources to continue will rebuild after a death. Even these families, however, will go through periods of disbelief, grief, guilt, and loneliness.

People seem to have a need to express grief. If there is enormous grief and it is not expressed, the tension will show in other ways. Such dissonance cannot be contained. According to dissonance theory, a person will either change his belief or change his behavior. In the case of a person who withholds grief, the behavior does change, but it comes out in another form. If a person chooses not to believe the reality of the death, it could be that he has chosen to change reality, rather than his behavior, in order to rid himself of the dissonance. A true nonacceptance of reality is worse than a wish that the fact were not true.

A person is more affected by the death of a significant person if he is going through some critical period or growth-change period in his life. A boy in his very early teens is usually far more affected by a father's death than his sixteen-year-old or eight-year-old brothers are. A wife in a personal growth-change period, for example, at around thirty, is more affected if her husband dies than a woman who is in a relatively calm period.

A woman seems to be able to manage being widowed better than a man can. One of the reasons appears to be the man's inability to cope with child rearing, home management, and a job simultaneously. Part of the problem may be his lack of conditioning to expect to be able to do so, coupled with a lack of cultural reinforcement to do all three. Many times, however, a widowed man receives more actual help than a widowed woman, who receives more sympathy than help. Table 9-1 shows that the number of widowed women exceeds the number of widowed men in every age category. As age progresses, the ratio of widowed women to widowed men increases many times over. The mere knowledege of this fact places a higher expectation on the woman to cope with the possibility of death. Women, however, may also have been conditioned to take dual and triple roles more than men have.

The period following death, like other crisis periods, must be dealt with. Sympathetic outsiders should treat survivors as persons who are recuperating from an illness—giving pure physical help at first, sympathy, empathy, support, and eventually encouraging self-help and later reinforcing independence. Knowing that time helps sorrow may be more solace for the one helping than for the survivor, however.

Read the following case:

CASE 71 MARTHA AND ANDREW

"If I had only fixed those brakes last week when I started to, Tom would be alive today." Andrew Brown kept saying this as he grieved over his son's death. His wife, Martha, made no comment. In fact she didn't even cry. She just stared into space when she wasn't compulsively busy with food and chairs, as sympathetic callers arrived.

Martha commented several times in this manner, "Tom planned to go to the coast this weekend. The coast is beautiful this time of year. We usually go every summer and stay a couple of weeks. I hear the fishing is not as good as it has been."

Three weeks later Martha told her friend that Tom had planned to go to the coast the next weekend, and never mentioned him again.

DIVORCE

If divorce were perceived as a reorganization of a family rather than a breakdown of a family, would we react to it differently? If divorce is ever a solution, then is it always a problem? If divorce is a solution to some family members and a problem to others, then was the marriage, too, both a solution and a problem?

Divorce was once unacceptable because of the great need for marriage as an institution to serve the function of socialization of family members. But going back even further, the pressures that cause divorce today were taken care of in the extended family. One woman did not have constant responsibility for child care; one spouse did not have exclusivity over the other; one man was not expected to be the sole provider.

Marriage came after the family; it did not precede it in history. Marriage came about as a societal means of designating responsibilities for certain activities. When a society begins to offer alternative means of meeting these needs, then marriage—lifetime or otherwise—is no longer an absolute need. Today, adults can care for themselves without a marriage partner and children can be cared for in a one-parent home. Certain roles entail certain responsibilities, but they do not require a specific sex to carry them out. This is why divorce is now more acceptable than it used to be. Even though divorce is more acceptable and may be a solution, the *change* that occurs in every divorce is a crisis to some extent.

The divorce rate is rising—not so much because people are not able to get along so much as because people are not willing to tolerate the same frustrations once resignedly accepted in a family. Divorce is also easier to obtain. The new so-called no-fault divorce seems to have encouraged a greater willingness to try divorce (although the old legal separation was, in effect, a prelude to no-fault divorce).

Table 9-1 shows that there are a million more divorced woman than divorced men; rational thinking should make you wonder how this can be so. There are two speculations. The people counted in the married category include both those in first marriages and in remarriages; therefore some of the divorced men have remarried and are included in the married category. The other speculation is that when the divorced men died, their ex-wives began to call themselves widows.

The same adjustment process occurs in divorce as in other crises—disbelief, resentment and guilt, disorganization, conflict, and then a reorganization. Still, the person going through a divorce is not relieved by a knowledge of this process. How well the person manages depends upon his definition of divorce, how strongly he feels himself to be a victim, how well he can manage his resources, and the opportunities for return to society as an unmarried person.

ALCOHOLISM AND DRUG ADDICTION

Some drug intake is necessary for certain people to function normally. When these drugs are prescribed by an authority, then the individual and society accept their intake. When drugs are taken by individuals on their own—such as pain reducers or spirit builders—they may or may not be acceptable, according to the codes of a given subculture. It is when drug intake hampers normal functioning, and thereby relationships, that drugs are cited as a problem. Likewise, alcohol intake is widely accepted socially except when it becomes excessive.

Views on the causes of excessive use have varied. The excessive use of alcohol was once thought to be sinful and the treatment was repentance. Then it was thought to be the result of an illness and the treatment was either medical help or counseling. More recently it has been thought that alcoholism may be a conditioned behavior in some people and must be treated by behavior modification. For the widespread addictive drug intake that has occurred in the last decade, treatments have been a combination of medicine, counseling, and behavior modification. (Counseling is noted separately from behavior modification because counseling here is defined as use of techniques other than behavior modification.)

Alcoholism and drug abuse are easy to hide in their early stages. The person involved and his family may choose to hide alcoholism or addiction because of cultural nonacceptance. The lesser cultural acceptance of alcoholism and drug addiction as compared with other physical disabilities is probably due to the belief that they are symptomatic of other stresses that individuals cannot handle. If a person is conditioned to believe that he should be able to work out his own problems, then turning to drugs to alleviate stress gives that person a feeling of weakness. Furthermore, if his reference group believes the same thing, then his self-concept is lowered even more.

The first acquaintance with alcohol or drugs usually takes place in a warm, socially acceptable situation and does not come from a searching for relief from stress. Since alcohol is so much more readily available and is legal to possess and since it is believed to be nonaddictive for most people, the use of alcohol is far greater among all age groups than is the use of other drugs.[13]

CASE 72 DAVE AND JUDY

"Judy and I had a good marriage up until two years ago. When we were first married I was in school and she was working to put me through. We didn't have much money then but we were happy and close. And we did things together. After graduation I was lucky enough to land this great job as an executive in a well-known firm. We paid off my educational bills and really got started on building a good life. Since I was making a pretty big salary I had Judy quit working—thinking that she'd get involved in the country club that we'd joined. I really enjoy the club myself. I play a great deal of

---

[13]Jules Saltman, *The New Alcoholics: Teenagers*, Public Affairs Pamphlet No. 499, New York, Public Affairs Commission, 1973.

golf and have plenty of friends. We get together quite a bit to talk, play cards, and have a few drinks. At first Judy fit right in with the group. She liked the get-togethers and dances and the drinking. Boy, did she like the drinking! Halfway through the night she'd be all juiced up and the belle of the ball. It really got to be quite embarrassing. That went on for about a year and now it's worse. All she does now is sit at home drinking and complaining. She never goes out to the club anymore. I guess I should stay home with her some but I just can't. We don't enjoy the same things anymore and I can't communicate with her. She's certainly not the girl I married. I've got a good life now and I want someone to enjoy it with me. Judy and I have either got to get things worked out or all I know to do is get a divorce."

Next the counselor spoke with Judy.

"Dave doesn't love me anymore. He never sits down and talks with me. He just goes down to his silly old club and sees his buddies. I suppose he told you that I drink too much. But really, I don't drink any more than he does. Sure I went to the club for a while. But I never really fit in with the crowd. I only went for Dave, in the first place. Everyone there is so smart and sophisticated. Now that Dave's so successful he feels more at home with them than he does with me. We were so happy when we were first married. I dropped out of school to put Dave through after only one semester. I didn't mind then but if I'd known he would change like this I would never have done it. At the club he'd act as if I weren't even there. So I quit going. At first I tried to join in with everyone, but we had nothing in common. Every time I went I ended up alone with a drink in my hand— my only companion. Finally I got fed up with the whole bit. Now I stay at home and do what I want and Dave does what he wants. It's just as though we've become strangers. I just don't know what's gone wrong with us."

THE HANDICAPPED FAMILY MEMBER

The definition of a family crisis involving a handicapped member probably varies more than the definition of other crises. In fact, the presence of handicapped family members may never be defined as a crisis. Certain congenital defects that do not severely restrict the person's activities probably would not even be defined as a handicap and certainly not as a cause for crisis unless the parents had an extremely high desire for perfection in body structure or had a specific, high goal for the child that this particular variation would hamper. Again, the definition and the effect depends on the person.

The self-concept of the individual labeled as handicapped is the determining factor in his relationships with others. His self-concept is determined by his own view of himself, in light of how others view him. Since self-direction and skills are highly prized in this culture, the more a handicapped person can do for himself and the more profitable skills he has, the better concept others have of him and consequently the better concept he has of himself. But when others, out of their own guilt for being glad they have no handicap, give in to him, they are encouraging him to regard his handicap as a deterrent. At the same time, they are making life more difficult for themselves.

It makes a difference in the effect on the family and the individual whether the handicap is from birth or something that happened after the person had lived a normal life for some length of time. It also makes a difference how important the recently handicapped person's former role in the family was. One of the problems with one person's taking on too much of the responsibility for the family is that a sudden loss of his services hampers both his own later adjustment and the family's ability to manage.

When an adult becomes severely handicapped and realizes that he may never work again, he personally goes through the process already described of disbelief, disorganization, and resentfulness before he can reorganize. If family members know that he *must* be allowed to disbelieve, to disorganize, and to show resentful feelings, then they can aid him in the process of recovery.

Events can be crisis producing and still not ruin a person or a family. The evidence seems to be increasing that those people who have the personal and material resources to plan for and deal with *change* are the ones who also have the most satisfactory family life.

ADDITIONAL READINGS

1 THE EMPATHETIC APPROACH

GOODE, WILLIAM J., ELIZABETH HOPKINS, AND HELEN MCCLURE, *Social System and Family Patterns: A Propositional Inventory*, Indianapolis, Bobbs-Merrill, 1971.

KLEMER, RICHARD H., AND REBECCA M. SMITH, *Teaching About Family Relationships*, Minneapolis, Burgess Publishing Co., 1975.

MEHRABIAN, A., AND N. EPSTEIN, "A Measure of Emotional Empathy," *Journal of Personality*, **40** (November, 1972), 525–543.

RATHS, LOUIS E., MERRILL HARMIN, AND SIDNEY B. SIMON, *Values and Teaching*, Columbus, Ohio, Merrill, 1966.

ROKEACH, MILTON, *Beliefs, Attitudes, and Values*, San Francisco, Jossey-Bass, 1968.

STOTLAND, EZRA, "Exploratory Investigations of Empathy," in Leonard Berkowitz, ed., *Advances in Experimental Social Psychology*, vol. 4, New York, Academic, 1969, pp. 271–314.

"Value Clarification," *Forum*, New York, The J. C. Penny Co., Inc. (Spring/Summer, 1972), entire issue.

WEINSTEIN, EUGENE A., "The Development of Interpersonal Competence," in David A. Goslin, ed., *Handbook of Socialization Theory and Research*, Skokie, Ill., Rand McNally, 1969, pp. 753–775.

2 WHAT'S HAPPENING TO MARRIAGE AND THE FAMILY?

"The American Family: Future Uncertain," *Time*, December 28, 1970, 34–39.

BERNARD, JESSIE, *The Future of Marriage*, New York, World Publishing, 1972.

CARR, GWEN B., ED., *Marriage and Family in a Decade of Change*, Reading, Mass., Addison-Wesley, 1972.

CONSTANTINE, LARRY, AND JOAN CONSTANTINE, "Where Is Marriage Going?" *The Futurist*, **4** (April, 1970), 44–46.

The Family, A Collection of Monthly Letters, Montreal, Royal Bank of Canada, 1973.

FARSON, RICHARD E., ET AL., *The Future of the Family*, New York, Family Service Association of America, 1969.

GOODE, WILLIAM J., ED., *The Contemporary American Family*, Chicago, Quadrangle Books, 1971.

ISHWARAN, KARIGOUDAR, ED., *The Canadian Family: A Book of Readings*, Toronto, Holt, Rinehart & Winston, 1971.

LEDERER, WILLIAM J., AND DON D. JACKSON, *The Mirages of Marriage*, New York, Norton, 1968.

SHERWIN, ROBERT VOIT, "The Law and Sexual Relationships," *The Journal of Social Issues*, **22** (April, 1966), 109–122.

SKOLNICK, ARLENE S., AND JEROME H. SKOLNICK, EDS., *Family in Transition*, Boston, Little, Brown, 1971.

ZIMMERMAN, CARLE C., "The Future of the Family in America," *Journal of Marriage and the Family*, **34** (May, 1972), 323–333.

3 EXPECTATIONS IN MARRIAGE

BIRDWHISTELL, RAY L., "The Idealized Model of the American Family," *Social Casework*, **51** (April, 1970), 195–198.

CROSBY, JOHN F., *Illusion and Disillusion: The Self in Love and Marriage*, Belmont, Calif., Wadsworth, 1973.

DREIKURS, RUDOLF, "Equality: The Life-Style of Tomorrow," *The Futurist*, **32** (August, 1972), 153–156.

DUNN, MARIE S., *Marriage Role Expectations, An Inventory*, Saluda, N.C., Family Life Publications, Inc., 1974.

FOGARTY, MICHAEL P., RHONA RAPOPORT, AND ROBERT N. RAPOPORT, *Sex, Career, and Family*, New York, Sage Publications, 1971.

LEDERER, WILLIAM J., AND DON D. JACKSON, *The Mirages of Marriage*, New York, Norton, 1968.

MACE, DAVID, *Getting Ready for Marriage*, Nashville, Tenn., Abingdon, 1972.

MADDOCKS, MELVIN, "Brave New Marriage," *Atlantic*, **230** (September, 1972), 66–69.

OTTO, HERBERT A., "Man-Woman Relationships in the Society of the Future," *The Futurist*, **33** (April, 1973), 55–61.

SHERESKY, NORMAN, AND MARYA MANNES, *Uncoupling: The Art of Coming Apart*, New York, Viking, 1972

4 THE IMPORTANCE OF PERSONALITY IN RELATIONSHIPS

COTTRELL, LEONARD S., "Interpersonal Interaction and the Development of the Self," in David A. Goslin, ed., *Handbook of Socialization Theory and Research*, Skokie, Ill., Rand McNally, 1969, pp. 543–570.

HALL, CALVIN S., AND GARDNER LINDSEY, *Theories of Personality*, 2nd ed., New York, Wiley, 1970.

JAMES, MURIEL, AND DOROTHY JONGEWARD, *Born to Win*, Reading, Mass., Addison-Wesley, 1972.

MCCANDLESS, BOYD, "Childhood Socialization," in David A. Goslin, ed., *Handbook of Socialization Theory and Research*, Skokie, Ill., Rand McNally, 1969, pp. 791–819.

ROGERS, CARL R., *On Becoming a Person*, Boston, Houghton Mifflin, 1961.

SATIR, VIRGINIA, *Peoplemaking*, Palo Alto, Calif., Science and Behavior Books, 1972.

5 RELATABILITY: THE BASIS OF LOVE

COUTES, ROBERT L., *Love and Intimacy: A Psychological Approach*, Danville, Calif., Consensus Publishers, 1973.

CROSBY, JOHN F., *Illusion and Disillusion: The Self in Love and Marriage*, Belmont, Calif., Wadsworth, 1973.

KEPHART, WILLIAM M., "Some Correlates of Romantic Love," *Journal of Marriage and the Family*, **29** (August, 1967).

MAY, ROLLO, *Love and Will*, New York, Norton, 1969.

MILLER, HOWARD L., AND PAUL S. SIEGEL, *Loving: A Psychological Approach*, New York, Wiley, 1972.

MOUSTAKAS, CLARK, *Individuality and Encounter*, Cambridge, Mass., Howard A. Doyle, 1968.

ZETTERBERG, HANS L., "The Secret Ranking," *Journal of Marriage and the Family*, **28** (May, 1966), 134–142.

6 THE DEVELOPMENT OF A LOVE RELATIONSHIP

CROSBY, JOHN F., *Illusion and Disillusion: The Self in Love and Marriage*, Belmont, Calif., Wadsworth, 1973.

DRAKEFORD, JOHN W., *This Insanity Called Love*, Cleveland, Ohio, World Publishing, 1970.

MURSTEIN, BERNARD I., "Self-Ideal–Self-Discrepancy," *Journal of Consulting and Clinical Psychology*, **27** (1971), 47–52.

MURSTEIN, BERNARD I., "Stimulus-Value-Role: A Theory of Marital Choice," *Journal of Marriage and the Family*, **31** (November, 1969), 772–775.

MURSTEIN, BERNARD I., ED., *Theories of Attraction and Love*, New York, Springer, 1972.

7 SOCIAL FACTORS IN MATE SELECTION

BESANCENEY, PAUL H., *Interfaith Marriages: Who and Why*, New Haven, Conn., College and University Press Services, 1970.

FELDMAN, SAUL D., AND GERALD W. THIELBAR, *Life Styles: Diversity in American Society*, Boston, Little, Brown, 1972.

GORDON, ALBERT I., *Intermarriage*, Boston, Beacon, 1964.

LARSSON, CLOTYE M., ED., *Marriage Across the Color Line*, New York, Lancer Books, 1965.

PETRONI, FRANK A., "Teen-Age Interracial Dating," *Transaction*, **8** (September, 1971), 54–59.

REISS, IRA L., *The Family System in America*, New York, Holt, Rinehart & Winston, 1971.

SCHULTZ, DAVID A., *The Changing Family: Its Function and Future*, Englewood Cliffs, N.J., Prentice-Hall, 1972.

STUART, IRVING R., AND LAWRENCE E. ABBOTT, *Interracial Marriage: Expectations and Realities*, New York, Grossman, 1973.

WASHINGTON, JOSEPH R., JR., *Marriage in Black and White*, Boston, Beacon, 1970.

8 PSYCHOLOGICAL FACTORS IN MATE SELECTION

ALBRECHT, RUTH E., AND E. WILBUR BOCK, EDS., *Encounter: Love, Marriage and Family*, Boston, Holbrook Press, 1972.

HODGE, MARSHALL BRYANT, *Your Fear of Love*, Garden City, N.Y., Doubleday, 1967.

MILLER, HOWARD, AND PAUL S. SIEGEL, *Loving: A Psychological Approach*, New York, Wiley, 1972.

MURSTEIN, BERNARD I., ED., *Theories of Attraction and Love*, New York, Springer, 1972.

PERUTZ, KATHRIN, *Marriage Is Hell*, New York, Morrow, 1972.

SCHULZ, DAVID A., *The Changing Family: Its Function and Future*, Englewood Cliffs, N.J., Prentice-Hall, 1972.

SIMONS, JOSEPH, AND JEANNE REIDY, *The Risk of Loving*, New York, Seabury, 1968.

TYRELL, DONALD J., *When Love is Lost*, Waco, Tex., Word Books, 1972.

9 MALE-FEMALE RELATIONSHIPS AMONG THE SINGLES

BERGER, MIRIAM E., "Trial Marriage: Harnessing the Trend Constructively," *The Family Coordinator*, **20** (January, 1971), 38–43.

DOUGLAS, WILLIAM, *The One-Parent Family*, Nashville, Tenn., The Methodist Publishing House, 1971.

HUNT, MORTON, *The World of the Formerly Married*, New York, McGraw-Hill, 1966.

KIRKENDALL, LESTER, AND ROBERT W. WHITEHURST, *The New Sexual Revolution*, New York, Donald W. Brown, 1971.

KLEIN, CAROLE, *The Single Parent Experience*, New York, Walker, 1973.

LYMAN, HOWARD W., *Single Again*, New York, McKay, 1971.

LYNESS, JUDITH L., MILTON E. LIPETZ, AND KEITH E. DAVIS, "Living Together: An Alternative to Marriage," *Journal of Marriage and the Family*, **34** (May, 1972), 305–311.

MACE, DAVID, *Abortion: The Agonizing Decision*, Nashville, Tenn., Abingdon, 1972.

MORAN, ROSALYN, "The Singles in the Seventies," in Joann S. Delora and Jack R. Delora, eds., *Intimate Life Styles: Marriage and Its Alternatives*, Pacific Palisades, Calif., Goodyear, 1972, pp. 338–344.

NELSON, FREDERIC, *Bachelors Are People, Too*, Washington, D.C., Public Affairs, 1964.

PANNOR, FRED M., AND BYRON EVANS, *The Unmarried Father*, New York, Springer, 1971.

PARKER, TONY, *In No Man's Land*, New York, Harper & Row, 1972.

SHERWIN, ROBERT VOIT, "The Law and Sexual Relationships," *The Journal of Social Issues*, **22** (April, 1966), 109–122.

THORMAN, GEORGE, "Living Together Unmarried," *The Humanist*, **34** (March/April, 1974), 15–17.

WINICK, CHARLES, "The Desexualized Society," *The Humanist*, **29** (November/December, 1969).

10 RELATIONSHIPS IN VARYING FAMILY LIFE-STYLES

BERNARD, JESSE, *The Future of Marriage*, New York, World Publishing, 1972.

CASLER, LAWRENCE, "Permissive Matrimony: Proposals for the Future," *The Humanist*, **34** (March/April, 1974), 4–9.

FRANCOEUR, ROBERT T., *Eve's New Rib: Twenty Faces of Sex, Marriage and the Family*, New York, Harcourt Brace Jovanovich, 1972.

GORDON, MICHAEL, *The Nuclear Family in Crisis: The Search for an Alternative*, New York, Harper & Row, 1972.

HART, HAROLD H., *Marriage: For and Against*, New York, Hart, 1972.

KANTER, ROSABETH MOSS, *Communes: Creating and Managing the Collective Life*, New York, Harper & Row, 1973.

LIBBY, ROGER W., AND ROBERT N. WHITEHURST, *Renovating Marriage: Toward New Sexual Life Styles*, Danville, Calif., Consensus Publishers, 1973.

O'NEILL, NENA, AND GEORGE O'NEILL, *Open Marriage*, New York, Evans, 1972.

OTTO, HERBERT A., ED., *The Family in Search of a Future*, Englewood Cliffs, N.J., Prentice-Hall, 1970.

ROGERS, CARL R., *Becoming Partners: Marriage and Its Alternatives*, New York, Delacorte Press, 1972.

ROY, RUSTUM, AND DELLA ROY, "Is Monogamy Outdated?" *The Humanist*, **30** (March/April, 1970), 19–26.

SCHULTERBRANDT, JOY G., AND EDWIN J. NICHOLS, "Ethical and Ideological Problems for Communal Living: A Caveat," *The Family Coordinator*, **21,** (October, 1972), 429–434.

SUSSMAN, MARVIN B., ED., *Non-Traditional Family Forms in the 1970's*, Minneapolis, National Council on Family Relations, 1973.

11 INTERPERSONAL RELATIONSHIPS IN MARRIAGE

BACH, GEORGE R., AND PETER WYDEN, *The Intimate Enemy*, New York, Morrow, 1969.

COX, FRANK D., *Youth, Marriage, and the Seductive Society*, 2nd ed., Dubuque, Iowa, Brown, 1974.

CROSBY, JOHN F., *Illusion and Disillusion: The Self in Love and Marriage*, Belmont, Calif., Wadsworth, 1973.

GLIDEWELL, JOHN C., *Choice Points: Essays on the Emotional Problems of Living with People*, Cambridge, Mass., M.I.T. Press, 1970.

GREY, ALAN L., ED., *Man, Woman, and Marriage: Small Group Process in the Family*, New York, Atherton, 1970.

RENNE, KAREN S., "Correlates of Dissatisfaction in Marriage," *Journal of Marriage and the Family*, **32** (February, 1970), 54–67.

ROLLINS, BOYD C., AND HAROLD FELDMAN, "Marital Satisfaction over the Family Life Cycle," *Journal of Marriage and the Family*, **32** (February, 1970), 20–28.

SATIR, VIRGINIA, *Peoplemaking*, Palo Alto, Calif., Science and Behavior Books, 1972.

TURNER, RALPH H., *Family Interaction*, New York, Wiley, 1970.

12 IMPEDIMENTS TO MARITAL ADJUSTMENT

BIRD, JOSEPH, AND LOIS BIRD, *Marriage Is for Grownups*, Garden City, N.Y., Doubleday, 1971.

BULLOCK, RUTH C., ROSE SIEGEL, MYRNA WEISSMAN, AND E. S. PAYKEL, "The Weeping Wife: Marital Relations of Depressed Women," *Journal of Marriage and the Family*, **34** (August, 1972), 488–495.

CHARNEY, ISRAEL, *Marital Love and Hate*, New York, Macmillan, 1972.

FULLERTON, GAIL PUTNEY, *Survival in Marriage: Introduction to Family Interactions, Conflicts, and Alternatives*, New York, Holt, Rinehart & Winston, 1972.

KNOX, DAVID, *A Behavioral Approach to Marriage Happiness Counseling*, Champaign, Ill., Research Press Co., 1972.

NEWMAN, MILDRED, AND BERNARD BERKOWITZ WITH JEAN OWEN, *How to Be Your Own Best Friend*, New York, Random House, 1971.

SCANZONI, JOHN, *Sexual Bargaining: Power Politics in the American Family*, Englewood Cliffs, N.J., Prentice-Hall, 1972.

SPREY, JETSE, "The Family as a System in Conflict," *Journal of Marriage and the Family*, **31** (November, 1969), 699–706.

13 COMMUNICATION AND INTIMACY

BACH, GEORGE R., AND RONALD M. DENTS, *Pairing: How to Achieve Genuine Intimacy*, New York, Avon Books, 1970.

BACH, GEORGE R., AND PETER WYDEN, *The Intimate Enemy*, New York, Morrow, 1967.

BERNARD, JESSIE, *The Sex Game*, Englewood Cliffs, N.J., Prentice-Hall, 1968.

BIRD, JOSEPH, AND LOIS BIRD, *Marriage Is for Grownups: A Mature Approach to Problems in Marriage*, Garden City, N.Y., Doubleday, 1971.

CLINEBELL, HOWARD J., AND CHARLOTTE H. CLINEBELL, *The Intimate Marriage*, New York, Harper & Row, 1970.

JAMES, MURIEL, AND DOROTHY JONGEWARD, *Born to Win: Transactional Analysis with Gestalt Experiments*, Reading, Mass. Addison-Wesley, 1973.

MILLER, SHEROD, ELAM W. NUNNALLY, AND DANIEL B. WOCKMAN WITH RONALD BROY-MAN, *The Minnesota Couples Communication Program Couples Handbook*, Minneapolis, published by the MCCP, 1972.

MILLER, SHEROD, ELAM W. NUNNALLY, AND DANIEL B. WOCKMAN WITH RONALD BROY-

MAN, *The Minnesota Couples Communication Program Instructors Manual*, Minneapolis, published by the MCCP, 1972.

O'NEILL, NENA, AND GEORGE O'NEILL, *Open Marriage*, New York, Evans, 1972.

OTTO, HERBERT A., *More Joy in Your Marriage*, New York, Hawthorn, 1969.

SALZ, VICTOR, *Between Husband and Wife*, Paramus, N.J., Paulist Press, 1972.

SATIR, VIRGINIA, *Peoplemaking*, Palo Alto, Calif., Science and Behavior Books, 1972.

SMITH, GERALD W., *Me and You and Us*, New York, Peter H. Wyden, 1971.

WEINER, MELVIN L., *Personality: The Human Potential*, Elmsford, N.Y., Pergamon, 1973.

14 MALE AND FEMALE SEXUAL CONDITIONING

ARMOUR, RICHARD, *My Life with Women*, New York, McGraw-Hill, 1968.

BARDWICK, JUDITH, *Psychology of Women*, New York, Harper & Row, 1971.

BEDNARIK, KARL, *The Male in Crisis*, New York, Knopf, 1970.

BELLIVEAU, FRED, AND LIN RICHTER, *Understanding Human Sexual Inadequacy*, New York, Bantam, 1970.

BENSON, LEONARD, *Fatherhood: A Sociological Perspective*, New York, Random House, 1968.

BERGER, DAVID G., AND MORTON G. WENGER, "The Ideology of Virginity," *Journal of Marriage and the Family*, **35** (November, 1973), 666–676.

BRENTON, MYRON, *The American Male*, Greenwich, Conn., Fawcett Publications, 1967.

CARNS, DONALD W., "Talking About Sex: Notes on First Coitus and the Double Sexual Standard," *Journal of Marriage and the Family*, **35** (November, 1973), 677–688.

KOGAN, BENJAMIN, *Human Sexual Expression*, New York, Harcourt Brace Jovanovich, 1973.

MONEY, JOHN, AND ONKE A. EHRHARDT, *Man and Woman Boy and Girl*, Baltimore, The Johns Hopkins Press, 1972.

PENGELLEY, ERIC T., *Sex and Human Life*, Reading, Mass., Addison-Wesley, 1974.

SEAMAN, BARBARA, *Free and Female*, New York, Coward-McCann, 1972.

15 SEXUAL RELATIONSHIPS IN MARRIAGE

BERNARD, JESSIE, *The Sex Game*, Englewood Cliffs, N.J., Prentice-Hall, 1968.

BIRD, JOSEPH, AND LOIS BIRD, *Marriage Is for Grownups: A Mature Approach to Problems in Marriage*, Garden City, N.Y., Doubleday, 1971.

KOGAN, BENJAMIN, *Human Sexual Expression*, New York, Harcourt Brace Jovanovich, 1973.

MACE, DAVID R., *Sexual Difficulties in Marriage*, Philadelphia, Fortress, 1972.

PENGELLEY, ERIC T., *Sex and Human Life*, Reading, Mass., Addison-Wesley, 1974.

ROBERTIELLO, RICHARD C., "The Clitoral Versus Vaginal Orgasm Controversy and Some of Its Ramifications," *Journal of Sex Research*, **6** (November, 1970), 307–311.

VINCENT, CLARK, *Sexual and Marital Health*, New York, McGraw-Hill, 1973.

16 EXTRAMARITAL RELATIONSHIPS

BARTELL, GILBERT D., *Group Sex: A Scientist's Eyewitness Report on the American Way of Swinging*, New York, Peter H. Wyden, 1971.

BERNARD, JESSIE, *The Future of Marriage*, New York, Bantam, 1973.

DELORA, JOANN S., AND JACK R. DELORA, EDS., *Intimate Life Styles*, Pacific Palisades, Calif, Goodyear, 1972.

HUNT, MORTON, *The Affair*, New York, New American Library, 1969.

MAZUR, RONALD, *The New Intimacy: Open-Ended Marriage and Alternate Life Styles*, Boston, Beacon, 1973.

NEUBECK, GERHARD, ED., *Extra-Marital Relations*, Englewood Cliffs, N.J., Prentice-Hall, 1969.

THORP, RODERICK, AND ROBERT BLAKE, *Wives: An Investigation*, New York, Evans, 1971.

17 MONEY: WHO MAKES IT AND WHO SPENDS IT

BEBBINGTON, A. C., "The Function of Stress in the Establishment of the Dual-Career Family," *Journal of Marriage and the Family*, **35** (August, 1973), 530–537.

BLOOD, ROBERT O., "Division of Labor in Two-Income Families," in George Roleder, ed., *Marriage Means Encounter*, Dubuque, Iowa, Brown, 1973.

COX, FRANK D., "Economic Entrapment: The Modern Slavery System," in Frank D. Cox, *Youth, Marriage, and the Seductive Society*, 2nd ed., Dubuque, Iowa, Brown, 1973.

ORDEN, SUSAN, AND NORMAN BRADBURN, "Working Wives and Marriage Happiness," *American Journal of Sociology*, 74 (January, 1969), 392–407.

RIDLEY, CARL A., "Exploring the Impact of Work Satisfaction and Involvement on Marital Interaction When Both Partners Are Employed," *Journal of Marriage and the Family*, **35** (May, 1973), 229–238.

TROELSTRUP, ARCH W., *The Consumer in American Society: Personal and Family Finance*, 4th ed., New York, McGraw-Hill, 1970.

18 INTERGENERATIONAL RELATIONSHIPS IN ADULTHOOD

BISCHOF, LEDFORD J., *Adult Psychology*, New York, Harper & Row, 1969.

DAVIS, KINGSLEY, "The Sociology of Parent-Youth Conflict," in Jacqueline P. Wiseman, ed., *People as Partners*, San Francisco, Canfield Press, 1971.

EDWARDS, JOHN N., AND MARY BALL BRANBURGER, "Exchange and Parent-Youth Conflict," *Journal of Marriage and the Family*, **35** (February, 1973), 101–107.

FRIED, BARBARA, *The Middle-Age Crisis*, New York, Harper & Row, 1967.

HILL, REUBEN, AND NELSON FOOTE, *Family Development in Three Generations*, Cambridge, Mass., Schenkman, 1970.

KALESH, RICHARD A., AND ANN I. JOHNSON, "Value Similarities and Differences in Three Generations of Women," *Journal of Marriage and the Family*, **34** (February, 1972), 49–54.

KOLLER, MARVIN R., *Families: A Multigenerational Approach*, New York, McGraw-Hill, 1974.

LIDZ, THEODORE, *The Person: His Development Throughout the Life Cycle*, New York, Basic Books, 1968.

19 AFTER THE CHILDREN COME

CHRISTENSEN, HAROLD T., "Children in the Family: Relationship of Number and Spacing to Marital Success," *Journal of Marriage and the Family*, **30** (May, 1968), 283–289.

CUTRIGHT, PHILLIPS, "Timing the First Birth: Does It Matter?" *Journal of Marriage and the Family*, **35** (November, 1973), 585–596.

FIGLEY, CHARLES R., "Child Density and the Marital Relationship," *Journal of Marriage and the Family*, **35** (May, 1973), 272–282.

HILL, REUBEN, AND JOAN ALDOUS, "Socialization for Marriage and Parenthood," in David A. Goslin, ed., *Handbook of Socialization Theory and Research*, Skokie, Ill., Rand McNally, 1969, pp. 885–950.

ROSSI, ALICE, "Transition to Parenthood," *Journal of Marriage and the Family*, **30** (February, 1968), 26–39.

RYDER, ROBERT G., "Longitudinal Data Relating Marriage Satisfaction and Having a Child," *Journal of Marriage and the Family*, **35** (November, 1973), 604–606.

20 WHAT MAKES A CRISIS?

ALVAREZ, WALTER C., "Death with Dignity," *The Humanist*, **31** (1971), 12–14.

BOHANNAN, PAUL, *Divorce and After*, Garden City, N.Y., Doubleday, 1970.

CLARK, JUNE S., WILLIAM C. CAPEL, BERNARD M. GOLDSMITH, AND GORDON T. STEWART, "Marriage and Methadone: Spouse Behavior Patterns in Heroin Addicts Maintained on Methadone," *Journal of Marriage and the Family*, **34** (August, 1972), 496–502.

COGSWELL, BETTY E, AND MARVIN B. SUSSMAN, "Changing Family Forms and Marriage Forms: Complications for Human Service Systems," *The Family Coordinator*, **21** (October, 1972), 505–516.

FOSTER, HENRY, JR., "Reforming a Divorce Law," in Gwen B. Carr, ed., *Marriage and Family in a Decade of Change*, Reading, Mass., Addison-Wesley, 1972.

GLASSER, PAUL H., AND LOIS N. GLASSER, eds., *Families in Crisis*, New York, Harper & Row, 1970.

GOUGH, AIDON R., "Divorce Without Squalor: California Shows How," in Gwen B. Carr, ed., *Marriage and Family in a Decade of Change*, Reading, Mass., Addison-Wesley, 1972.

IRWIN, THEODORE, *How to Cope with Crisis*, Public Affairs Pamphlet No. 464, New York, Public Affairs Commission, 1971.

JACKSON, JOAN K., "Alcoholism and the Family," in Jacqueline P. Wiseman, *People as Partners*, San Francisco, Canfield Press, 1971.

KUBLER-ROSS, ELIZABETH, *On Death and Dying*, New York, Macmillan, 1969.

LOVE, HAROLD, *Parental Attitudes Toward Exceptional Children*, Springfield, Ill., C. C Thomas, 1970.

MONAHAN, THOMAS P., "National Divorce Legislation: The Problem and Some Suggestions," *The Family Coordinator*, **22** (July, 1973), 353–358.

MORGAN, ERNEST, *A Manual of Death Education and Simple Burial*, Burnsville, N.C., The Celo Press, 1973.

OGG, ELIZABETH, *When a Family Faces Stress*, Public Affairs Pamphlet No. 341, New York, Public Affairs Commission, 1969.

ROBBINS, NORMAN, "Have We Fault in No-Fault Divorce?" *The Family Coordinator*, **22** (July, 1973), 359–362.

ROGERS, JOHN G., "How to Make a Good Divorce," *Parade Magazine*, July, 1973, 18.

SALTMAN, JULES, *The New Alcoholics: Teenagers*, Public Affairs Pamphlet No. 499, New York, Public Affairs Commission, 1973.

SALTMAN, JULES, *What We Can Do About Drug Abuse*, Public Affairs Pamphlet No. 390, New York, Public Affairs Commission, 1969.

SCHULZ, DAVID, A., AND ROBERT A. WILSON, "Some Traditional Family Variables and Their Correlations with Drug Use Among High School Students," *Journal of Marriage and the Family*, **35** (November, 1973), 638–631.

SOMERVILLE, ROSE, "Death Education as Part of Family Life Education: Using Imaginative Literature for Insights into Family Crises," *The Family Coordinator*, **20** (July, 1971), 209–224.

UPDIKE, JOHN, *Of the Farm*, New York, Knopf, 1966.

VOGEL, EZRA F., AND NORMAN W. BELL, "The Emotionally Disturbed Child as the Family Scapegoat," in Norman W. Bell and Ezra F. Vogel, eds., *A Modern Introduction to the Family*, 2nd ed., New York, Free Press, 1968.

APPENDIX

GENERALIZATIONS ABOUT HUMAN BEHAVIOR FROM A BEHAVIORISTIC POINT OF VIEW[1]

1. When a new behavior is consistently reinforced, then that behavior is more quickly learned.
2. When a learned behavior continues to be consistently reinforced, then the reinforcement loses its value and the behavior tends to be reduced.
3. When a learned behavior is intermittently reinforced, then it tends to continue and becomes a part of a repertoire of responses.
4. For something to be reinforcing to a particular person, the person must have a need for the reinforcer. (People have different needs at different levels and in a different order at different times.)
5. When a stimulus is aversive or when a supposed reinforcement is aversive to the person, then he tends to move away from the aversive stimulus, reinforcer, object, person, or punishment. When a stimulus is both aversive and positive with equal strength, the person becomes immobile. His behavior states, "I don't know what to do."
6. When two behaviors have equal opportunity to be executed, that behavior learned first in life tends to be the behavior that is expressed.
7. When a person is under stress, the most likely behavior to be exhibited is that which was learned earlier in life or that behavior which was most well conditioned (learned).
8. When a behavior is no longer reinforced, that behavior tends to be reduced or even extinguished.
9. When a person is punished for a behavior, that behavior tends to be exhibited less, even though the desire to carry it out may not be extinguished.
10. Either positive or negative reinforcement may be used to condition a behavior. When positive reinforcement (receiving of a wanted reinforcement) is used, the relationship between the behavior and the reinforcement is more easily recognized. When negative reinforcement (the withdrawal of a painful stimulus or not imposing punishment) is used to condition or control a behavior, the relationship between the negative reinforcement and the behavior is not as readily recognizable.
11. When a change in behavior is desired, old reinforced behavior must no longer be reinforced and only the new behavior reinforced. Since so many things are

[1]Albert Bandura, *Social Learning and Personality Development*, New York, Holt, Rinehart & Winston, 1963.

Albert Bandura, *Principles of Behavior Modification*, New York, Holt, Rinehart & Winston, 1969.

Calvin S. Hall and Gardner Lindsey, *Theories of Personality*, 2nd ed., New York, Wiley, 1970.

B. F. Skinner, *Beyond Freedom and Dignity*, New York, Knopf, 1971.

B. F. Skinner, *Science and Human Behavior*, New York, Free Press, 1953.

reinforcing and are not easily distinguishable by either the person changing his behavior or the person facilitating the change, it is difficult to be certain what is reinforcing for which behavior.

12. When a person is in a stimulus situation similar to, but not exactly like, a former situation, his responses will be similar. This is known as stimulus generalization and response generalization.

13. When the stimulus is general, the response will be a generalized response. To get a more discriminant response, the stimulus must begin to be noticeably individual or different from the general stimuli. To condition a specific (discriminant) response to a specific (discriminant) stimulus, the reinforcement must be appropriate and must be constant at first, then continuously intermittent as long as the response is desired.

14. Different people need different levels and types of reinforcements at different times, and therefore their responses are not always predictable unless the particular reinforcement and need level is known.

15. Different people have differing levels or thresholds of anxiety, which comes from both the inherent physical makeup of each person and the learning process he has experienced; therefore each person will react in different ways to the same situation.

GENERALIZATIONS ABOUT HUMAN BEHAVIOR FROM A PERCEPTUAL AND SELF THEORY POINT OF VIEW[2]

1. When a person acts, his main goal is to protect, actualize, and enhance his self-concept.

2. A person develops a concept of himself from the reactions of others to his actions; therefore, when another person judges his actions, that judgment acts to alter or reinforce his self-concept.

3. If a person gains a negative self-concept early in life, he tends to select those judgments from the environment that contrive to reinforce his early belief. (This is also explained by the cognitive dissonance concept that a person attempts to keep former beliefs and present situations in consonance, or if they are dissonant, he changes one or the other. He will tend to change the one easiest to change, so that the newest input is more likely to be rejected than the reinforced belief of the past.)

[2]Calvin S. Hall and Gardner Lindsey, *Theories of Personality,* 2nd ed., New York, Wiley, 1970.

Carl R. Rogers, *Client-Centered Therapy: Its Current Practice, Implications, and Theory,* Boston, Houghton Mifflin, 1951.

Carl R. Rogers, "A Theory of Therapy, Personality, and Interpersonal Relationships, as Developed in the Client-Centered Framework," in S. Koch, ed., *Psychology: A Study of Science,* vol. 3, New York, McGraw-Hill, 1959, pp. 184–256.

Carl R. Rogers, *On Becoming a Person,* Boston, Houghton Mifflin, 1961.

4. When a person has a great discrepancy between his self-concept and his ideal self-concept, he is not at ease with himself and will show tendencies toward irritability or irrationality.
5. When a person is not recognized as a worthwhile individual or when he is not recognized at all, he develops a poor self-concept and cannot act rationally when treated as a worthwhile individual.
6. If a person perceives a situation as real, then he will behave as if it were real.
7. If a person changes his perception about a situation, the situation has essentially changed without any physical movement or change on the part of any other person.
8. Perception is highly individualistic and is determined by the totality of a person's former experiences; therefore no two people perceive the same experience alike.
9. People from similar cultural backgrounds will tend to perceive things more similarly than people from differing cultural backgrounds.
10. When a person is around different people, he acts differently, because he perceives himself in different roles with different people.
11. Psychological stress is as real as physiological stress and each can affect the same body process. When a person perceives a threat to the body (or self), the body reacts as if the threat were actually happening.

GENERALIZATIONS ABOUT HUMAN BEHAVIOR FROM A COGNITIVE DISSONANCE POINT OF VIEW[3]

1. When a person's beliefs about a situation are the same as the situation, then there is consonance within himself and no action is precipitated on his part.
2. When a person's beliefs about a situation are different from the situation, there is cognitive dissonance, and he will tend to move to gain consonance through changing either the situation or his belief about the situation.
3. In order to cause a person to act, it is believed that a state of cognitive dissonance must be set up, either by changing the situation or his belief about it.
4. When a discrepancy occurs between a past belief and a presented possibility, then the person will likely move to change the past belief or reject the newly presented possibility.

[3]Elliot Aronson, "The Theory of Cognitive Dissonance: A Current Perspective," in Leonard Berkowitz, ed., *Advances in Experimental Psychology*, vol. 4, New York, Academic, 1969.

J. A. Arrowood, L. Wood, and L. Ross, "Dissonance, Self Perception of Others: A Study in Cognitive Dissonance," *Journal of Experimental Social Psychology*, **6** (July, 1970), 304–316.

Leon Festinger, *Conflict, Decision, and Dissonance*, Stanford, Calif., Stanford University Press, 1964.

Leon Festinger, *A Theory of Cognitive Dissonance*, Stanford, Calif., Stanford University Press, 1957.

5. What at one time was a consonant state (no-problems state) may become a dissonant state (the need for diversity versus boredom) and action may be precipitated.

GENERALIZATIONS ABOUT HUMAN BEHAVIOR FROM A TRANSACTIONAL ANALYSIS POINT OF VIEW[4]

1. When a transaction between two people is positively productive, then they are responding from complementary ego states. (The three ego states are: child, adult, and parent.)
2. When a person acts from the adult-ego state (rational), a complementary response is from the adult-ego state of the other person.
3. When a person acts from the parent-ego state (accusing or nurturing), a complementary response is from the child-ego state (submissive or joyful) of the other, and vice versa. (A parent-to-parent ego state response is also complementary.)
4. When two people are in conflict, then each is responding from an ego state that differs from the one expected by the other.
5. When a person acts from the adult-ego state, a crossed or conflict transaction occurs when the response of the other is from either the parent- or child-ego state, and vice versa.
6. When a person is reinforced for certain behavior as a child, he tends to play that part throughout life, as if it were a script.
7. When a person has many diverse stimuli directed toward him, he tends to categorize or structure his environment in order to deal with them.
8. The type and amount of responses (strokes) a person needs are determined early in life, through experiences, and he seeks this type and amount in later life. (If the type learned is negative stroking in large amounts, the person tends to look for this pattern throughout life.)

[4] Eric Berne, *Transactional Analysis in Psychotherapy*, New York, Grove, 1961.
Muriel James and Dorothy Jongeward, *Born to Win: Transactional Analysis with Gestalt Experiments*, Reading, Mass., Addison-Wesley, 1971.

INDEX

Rollins, Boyd C., 11, 126, 243, 366
Ross, Edward A., 202
Roth, Julius, 135

Saltman, Jules, 400
Samelson, Nancy, 181
Sanua, Victor, 144
Schlesinger, Arthur, Jr., 300
Schmitt, Robert, 115
Schneider, D. M., 391
Schulman, Marion, 150, 181
Schulz, David, A., 62
Scott, John Finley, 132, 133, 161
Sears, Robert, 260
Self-actualization
  in marriage, 185–190
Self-concept, 55, 56. *See also* Self-
    esteem; Self-image
  and the handicapped person, 402
  and role perception, 56
Self-confidence and aging, 390
Self-esteem, 69, 172. *See also* Self-con-
    cept; Self-image
  as self-confidence, 93–95, 108
Self-fulfilling prophecy, 177, 178, 300
Self-image, 62–65. *See also* Self-concept;
    Self-esteem
  acceptance of, 63
  congruence between ideal and real, 64
  family influence on, 63, 64
  and perception of others, 64
  perceptions of, 63
  perceptions of others' perceptions, 62,
    63, 64
  and physical structure, 64, 156
Sennett, Richard, 184
Sex-role
  undifferentiated, 96
Sexual adjustment, 282–295
  and communication, 283–285
  and frequency of coitus, 282, 291–
    295
  and orgasm, 282
Sexual conditioning, 256–280
  for female, 272–280
  for male, 258–272

sex-role identification, 264, 274, 275
  and social class, 261–263, 268, 269
Sexual relationships
  disillusionment in, 285, 286
  effect of social changes on, 173–178
  emotional security in, 289
  fears in, 288, 289
  incompatibility in, 288–291
  in marriage, 282–295
  without marriage, 170–180, 178
  resentments in, 288, 289
Sheldon, William H., 59
Sherwin, Robert V., 171, 293, 304
Shostrom, Everett L., 232
Sibling relationships, 376–380
  rivalry in, 376–378
Singles, 166–181
  and abortions, 171
  and age, 167, 169, 170, 171
  with children, 178, 179
  and contraceptives, 171
  cultural attitudes about, 167–170
  divorced, 166–181
  and illegitimate births, 171, 172
  men, 166–181
  never married, 166–181
  and pregnancy, 171, 172
  and the right not to marry, 180, 181
  and sexual relationships, 170–180
  statistics about, 166, 167
  and suicide, 181
  widowed, 166–181
  women, 159, 166–181
Smarden, Laurence, 12
Smith, William, 12
Social class, 132–140, 161
  and child-rearing practices, 133–135
  and crises, 385
  and interfaith marriage, 125
  and marital success, 133, 143–145
  in mate selection, 132–140, 161
  and racial intermarriage, 116
  and sex, 134
  toward spending money, 134
Social factors, 112–145
  in mate selection, 112–145
  sociocultural, 112

75 76 9 8 7 6 5 4 3 2 1